Reframing 9/11

REFRAMING 9/11

Film, Popular Culture and the "War on Terror"

Edited by Jeff Birkenstein, Anna Froula and Karen Randell

continuum

Continuum International Publishing Group
80 Maiden Lane, Suite 704, New York NY 10038
The Tower Building, 11 York Road, London SE1 7NX

www.continuumbooks.com

© 2010 by Jeff Birkenstein, Anna Froula, and Karen Randell

First published 2010
Reprinted 2011

Library of Congress Cataloging-in-Publication Data
Reframing 9/11 : film, popular culture and the "war on terror" / edited by Jeff Birkenstein,
Anna Froula and Karen Randell.
    p. cm.
Includes bibliographical references and index.
ISBN-13: 978-1-4411-1132-6 (hardcover : alk. paper)
ISBN-10: 1-4411-1132-8 (hardcover : alk. paper)
ISBN-13: 978-1-4411-1905-6 (pbk. : alk. paper)
ISBN-10: 1-4411-1905-1 (pbk. : alk. paper) 1. Terrorism in motion pictures. 2. Psychic
trauma in motion pictures. 3. September 11 Terrorist Attacks, 2001–Influence. 4. War on
Terrorism, 2001—Influence. 5. Popular culture–Political aspects–United States–History–
20th century. 6. Motion pictures–Political aspects–United States. 7. Terrorism and mass
media–United States. 8. September 11 Terrorist Attacks, 2001, in mass media. 9. War on
Terrorism, 2001– , in mass media. I. Birkenstein, Jeff. II. Froula, Anna. III. Randell, Karen.
IV. Title: Reframing Spec.

PN1995.9.T46R44 2010
791.43'6552--dc22

2009037173

ISBN: HB: 978-1-4411-1132-6
      PB: 978-1-4411-1905-6

Typeset by Pindar NZ, Auckland, New Zealand
Printed and bound in the United States of America

Contents

SECTION III PROPHETIC NARRATIVES

Anna—for my family
Karen—for the Americans who have enhanced my life;
especially Jason and Jessie Rae
Jeff—also, for my family

Acknowledgments

Well, if you are reading this, then you already know the cliché: we couldn't have completed this book without an axis of sublime support for which we are grateful. We also couldn't have wished for a better international collaboration. It has been immensely enjoyable since its inception at the 2006 American Studies Association Conference, Oakland, CA: thank you to Jonathan Vincent for helping to organize that panel with Anna. Somehow we have figured out how to communicate, even though Jeff lives on the West Coast of the US, Anna on the East Coast, and Karen in the south of England. We have met and discussed this project in London, Southampton, and Dublin and near the beaches of North Carolina: we look forward to planning the next one.

We would like to thank David Barker at Continuum for supporting this project and to Katie Gallof and Kim Pillay for their good counsel and enduring patience.

Jeff Birkenstein: I would like special thanks to go to the following: my proofreaders and so much more: Diana Michaels (hi Mom!) and Ashley Elaine Reis; and, at the eleventh hour, my cousin Su(si)e Felshin. I am grateful to Amber Graves and Karen Jaskar for help with the bibliography. John Cawelti, Professor Emeritus and teacher extraordinaire, taught me in his "Pop Genres" course at the University of Kentucky that any genre was ripe for critical inquiry. As friend and mentor, I deeply appreciate David Price, and all our bull sessions (many of which were serious) at the Fish Tale Brewpub in Olympia, WA. Thank you to my beautiful friends and colleagues in the English department at Saint Martin's University who supported the class David and I team taught: "Mining 9/11: Narratives from the Aftermath." And, of course, the students in that class; together, we tried to make sense of this jumbled American story. Thank you to my father, Robert Birkenstein, who has never stopped sending me newspaper clippings in the mail, even though I moved away from Southern California 13 years ago. Thank you to all the rest of my family for all your love and support, wherever and whenever you may be . . .

Anna Froula: I would like to thank John Cawelti, Armando Prats, Gregory Waller, and Susan Bordo who opened the world of popular culture to me as a field of endless critical possibilities and nurtured my initial intellectual queries into this area when I was a graduate student at the University of Kentucky; I remain grateful for their mentorship. Dana D. Nelson also offered fantastic feedback on the San Domingo revolution portion of my chapter.

At East Carolina University, Will Banks, Michelle Eble, Rick Taylor, Jim Holte, Kirk St. Amant, Joyce Middleton, Randall and Christie Martoccia, Gera Miles, and Marc Petersen are among the wonderful faculty who have patiently engaged my interests in war and zombie culture. The students in my spring 2008 "Post-9/11 Film and American Culture" class offered excellent inspiration and conversation. My summer 2009 students supplied numerous insights about horror and London in *28 Days Later . . .* I particularly appreciate the colleagues and friends at ECU who helped me revise and edit portions of this book: my beloved "Femidemics" (Marame Gueye, Su-Ching Huang, Amanda Ann Klein, Anne Mallory, and Marianne Montgomery), my copyeditor extraordinaire, Brent Henze, and my technical advisor, Donna Kain.

My Froula, Leftwich, and Morris families are constant with their love and support as well as in their enthusiasm about my projects. Mom and Dad, thank you for the zombie comics, and please keep them coming. And finally and most of all, thanks go to my husband, Sean, for bringing delicious meals to my office during the last push, taking an incisive pencil to my prose, and everything else.

Karen Randell: I would like to acknowledge the Faculty of Media, Arts and Society at Southampton Solent University for its research support: in particular Professor Rod Pilling (Dean) and Paul Marchbank MA (Head of School of Media). And to Darren Green and Rosemary Waldock for getting to me to the right conferences, right hotels, and on the right planes: you two are my unsung heroes.

Many thanks to my friends and colleagues in the Film and Television Program at Southampton Solent University for their continued encouragement, constructive feedback, and good humor: Mark Aldridge, Jackie Furby, Claire Hines, Darren Kerr, Donna Peberdy, Tony Steyger, and Mark de Valk; you all make the work look easy. Thanks also to all my students of "Visualizing War" (at SSU and at The University of Otago, Dunedin, NZ) whose insightful thoughts and enthusiasm have kept me inspired and motivated. Finally, special thanks to my family—always love, always loud, and always on my side.

Foreword

If it sounded like the plot to a Hollywood movie, it's because that is precisely what it was.

In October 2001, a little more than a month after the World Trade Center was leveled and the Pentagon attacked in a coordinated assault that itself seemed choreographed by a Hollywood director, the Bush Administration mulled a Justice Department proposal to send the military to a suburb of Buffalo called Lackawanna, to arrest six members of what was thought to be a sleeper cell in league with al-Qaeda.[1] The image of US troops cordoning off neighborhoods and armored tanks rolling through the streets of a quiet American town comes directly from the 1998 Hollywood blockbuster, *The Siege*, starring Denzel Washington and Bruce Willis. The movie, written by *New Yorker* scribe Lawrence Wright, whose non-fiction account of the events leading up to 9/11, *The Looming Tower*, became a bestseller, conjures up a New York City made so paranoid by a series of terrorist attacks that the government must declare martial law and send in the military to police the petrified residents.

Of course, the homegrown terrorist plot in Buffalo turned out to be a bit more banal than what one finds in the average Hollywood thriller. The Arab-American "terrorists" who became known as the Lackawanna Six were ultimately revealed to be a crude and clumsy parody of the villainous geniuses imagined by the movies. The men were hardly zealots seeking martyrdom; indeed, you could hardly call them *men*.[2] According to journalist Dina Temple-Raston, who wrote a book about the Lackawanna Six, these were kids in their twenties looking for a thrill. Their flirtation with jihadism was, in Temple-Raston's words, akin to "a teenager's decision to steal a car: he knew he shouldn't, but a youthful rush made him do it anyway."

In the spring of 2001, the boys from Lackawanna traveled to an al-Qaeda training camp in Afghanistan where they watched jihadist propaganda videos—al-Qaeda's version of the Hollywood blockbuster—went through a few obstacle courses, and learned how to talk tough about Israel and the United States. But by all accounts they were frightened and appalled by the ideology of violence propagated by the camp's leaders and desperate to return to the US as soon as possible. Some of them even feigned injuries so as to be allowed to leave early. Once back in the US, they immediately put the camp behind them and moved on with their lives.

Even the Bush Administration admitted that the six were not plotting any kind of attack against the US when they were arrested. In fact, it was precisely the lack of evidence of an impending attack that prompted Justice Department lawyers John Yoo and Robert Delahunty to draft a memo explicitly authorizing the president to suspend both the Constitution and the Posse Comitatus Act of 1878, which expressly forbids the American military to act in a law enforcement capacity, in order to allow for greater leeway in arresting and detaining the men indefinitely and without probable cause.

In the end, the Bush Administration decided to comply with Posse Comitatus and instead to rely on the FBI—created precisely for such a purpose—to investigate and eventually arrest the six Lackawanna residents. Yet it is not so much the facts of the case against the Lackawanna Six that concerns the authors of the present volume. Almost no one associated with the affair, including President Bush himself, believed that it was necessary to enlist the military to apprehend a group of kids. What concerns us is the very real possibility that the Justice Department lawyers who devised the absurdly theatrical, utterly unnecessary, and thoroughly unconstitutional idea to send American troops into the suburbs of Buffalo—lawyers who, by the way, had absolutely no national security or military credentials—may have come up with their harebrained scheme from watching a movie.

It is not so farfetched a notion. After all, the most common refrain voiced by both witnesses to the attacks of 9/11 and the media who covered them (not to mention the hundreds of millions who watched the attacks unfold on television) was that the entire harrowing affair seemed "like a movie." The constant repetition of this phrase on television, on the radio, and in print cannot simply be attributed to what psychologists call "cinematic vision"—the tendency for eyewitnesses of a disaster to distance themselves from the horror of reality by viewing events as though through the lens of a camera. The fact is that the events of 9/11 were truly *like a movie*: the hijacked airplanes, the crumbling skyscrapers, the crush of people on the ground suddenly shrouded by a cloud of ash and rubble. It all seemed as though it were plucked from a Hollywood script—and a fairly fantastical one at that. The great American filmmaker Robert Altman went so far as to blame Hollywood for the attacks. "The movies set the pattern, and these people have copied the movies," Altman told the Associated Press. "Nobody would have thought to commit an atrocity like that unless they'd seen it in a movie."[3]

If the attacks of 9/11 seemed so much "like a movie," then it is perhaps not so surprising that the response to 9/11 also took on a distinctly theatrical flair. The machine gun-toting cops guarding the streets. The mawkish displays of patriotism. The glamorizing of torture (itself a product of the movies, where torture is always used to extract just the right kind of information at just the right time). All of this is to say that it was cinema, and popular culture in general, that, more than anything else, helped cast the disturbing events of 9/11, and the even more disturbing events that followed, into an easily accessible, easily digestible *story*, one in which everyone had a role to play, as either hero or villain, good or evil, "with us" or "against us."

Nearly a decade later, that simple story of us versus them has grown muddled. Wiretapping. Waterboarding. Constitutional violations. The narrative that Americans constructed to help make sense of 9/11 no longer seems as straightforward and uncomplicated as it so often does in the movies.

Still, the desperate need to wrap the chaos and confusion of these past few years into a simple narrative persists. And just as popular culture helped shape our reaction to the events of 9/11—for better or worse—so too does it now inform our collective memory of those events. Indeed, as the essays in this volume reveal, it is within popular culture that we may discover not only the meaning and context of what happened on that fateful September morning, but perhaps more importantly, how those events have permanently altered our national mythology.

Reza Aslan
Los Angeles, California

Notes

1   See Mark Mazzetti and David Johnston, "Bush Weighed Using Military in Arrests," *New York Times*, July 25, 2009, A01.

2   Dina Temple-Raston, "Enemy Within? Not Quite," *Washington Post*, September 9, 2007, B01. Temple-Raston's book on the Lackawanna Six is *The Jihad Next Door: The Lackawanna Six and Rough Justice in an Age of Terror* (New York: Public Affairs, 2007).

3   "Altman Says Hollywood 'Created Atmosphere' for September 11," *The Guardian*, October 18, 2001, http://www.guardian.co.uk/film/2001/oct/18/news2 (accessed October 2, 2009).

Introduction

JEFF BIRKENSTEIN, ANNA FROULA, AND KAREN RANDELL

> To speak of history's horrors, or historical trauma, is to recognize
> events as wounds.
>
> —Adam Lowenstein, *Shocking Representations: Historical Trauma,*
> *National Cinema, and the Modern Horror Film*

> Without a story, we are, as many of us were after September 11,
> intensely vulnerable to those people who are ready to take advantage of
> the chaos for their own ends. As soon as we have a narrative that offers
> a perspective on the shocking events, we become reoriented, and the
> world begins to make sense again.
>
> —Naomi Klein, *The Shock Doctrine: The Rise of Disaster Capitalism*

On May 8, 2009, three young writers, all of whom were on the cutting edge of reporting during the George W. Bush administration, appeared on *Real Time with Bill Maher*: Reza Aslan, Matt Taibbi, and Naomi Klein. In a lively debate, they discussed such disparate matters as corporate tax evasion and the question of prosecuting the architects of the American torture program (or "enhanced interrogation techniques"). *Rolling Stone* journalist Taibbi asked if the US could be taken seriously in its long-standing defense of human rights around the globe if such prosecution were absent. He also addressed the question, commonly avoided in the "torture debate," as to whether or not the US government should punish other rogue countries for torturing Americans (military or civilian). Klein pointed out that the pervasive labelling and embodiment of the US as a "Christian Nation" results in a "Christian Army," fighting in the name of a US Christian Empire. As illustration, she related Lt. Gen. William Boykin's post-9/11 story of meeting a Muslim warlord in Somalia: "I knew that my God was bigger than his. I knew that my God was a real God, and his was an idol."[1] Did such actions under the Bush administration, Klein wondered, not usher in precisely the perverse New Crusade that Aslan explores in his new book?[2]

We believe that this is exactly the type of serious conversation that should have been happening in the body politic in the aftermath of 9/11. Yet we find it simultaneously encouraging and dismaying that, more than nine years after the terrorist attacks, these important issues are instead being debated in a popular culture medium—a pay-cable television talk show. This situation is unsettling because, in our view, these questions have not been adequately treated by the leaders charged with considering them. Yet, as scholars committed to the notion that popular culture provides an important space for lively, relevant, and essential debate of such matters, we are excited by this evidence of the undeniable significance of popular culture: it has become a creative space in which nuanced participatory debates take place among public citizens rather than with (and between) our elected representatives in Washington, DC.

This volume endeavours to highlight the popular cultural spaces in which the salient (and often uncomfortable) issues raised in the aftermath of 9/11 are discussed in myriad creative ways. In particular, this book focuses on those popular culture responses that have engaged with the notion of the "War on Terror": the negotiation of trauma, the machinations of George W. Bush's administration, the wars in Afghanistan and Iraq, our understanding of collective memory, and the dawn of a new era under President Barack Obama.

On January 20, 2009, the new president, whose campaign had been based on promises of change, inherited a traumatized national economy, intensifying housing and banking crises, increasing costs for energy, food, healthcare, and transportation, and two ongoing wars. Central to the changes of the new era has been a linguistic shift from the phrase "War on Terror" to "overseas contingency operation."[3] This rhetorical turn highlights the ways in which the post-9/11 discourse continues to be reframed even as it remains a focal point of American consciousness: a site demanding ongoing excavation, a site that marks *before* and *after* "everything" changed. In ways both real and intangible, the entire sequence of events of that pivotal day continues to resonate in an endlessly proliferating aftermath of meanings that have changed and continue to change; 9/11 is the site of this volume's investigation, both temporally and metaphorically.

Presenting a collection of analyses by an international body of scholars examining America's recent history, this book focuses on popular culture as a profound discursive site of anxiety and discussion about 9/11. The volume demystifies the day's events in order to contextualize them in an historically grounded series of narratives that recognizes the complex relations of a globalized world. Indeed, the closest official attempt at such an inquiry—the "9/11 Commission"—produced more questions than it answered and, even more troubling, left many legitimate questions unexamined. The cohesive post-9/11 political and mainstream media rhetoric supporting the war in Iraq and the "Global War on Terror" continues to fragment as the public comes to believe that failures and deceit were (and are) rampant. A strong undercurrent persists that demands silence and unquestioning fealty in the name of fear and patriotism (as the 2008 Republican National Convention's handling of protesters and journalists illustrates). Susan Faludi argues that, not surprisingly, the official rhetoric employed the national mythology of the American captivity narrative, a story personified in the captivity and release of Pfc. Jessica Lynch in 2003, which Stacy Takacs documents in this volume.[4] Indeed, we believe that the official 9/11 response impeded the creation and use of a constructive post-traumatic language, one that is still needed both to historicize and to cope with the traumas of this national and international event. This collection, then, reclaims and rearticulates a discourse of response that focuses on the visual and the poetic in order to encourage a critical analysis that will help move us toward closure and recuperation, even as it acknowledges our painful coexistence with loss, horror, and incomprehension.

Such a discourse is apparent in 11 international short films compiled by Alejandro González Iñárritu into the film *11'09"01—September 11* (2002), released in several countries on the first anniversary of 9/11. Ken Loach's segment shows Chilean artist Vladimir Vega addressing those grieving the tragedy in an 11-minute documentary. Loach and Vega recount via epistolary narration and archival footage another Tuesday, September 11: the 1973 US-supported overthrow of Salvador Allende's Chilean government. A still-grieving Vega revisits his memories of the violent coup and its horrific aftermath, a history that demands reconsideration of the United States' appropriation of "9/11" as a singular, commodified incident, an event that insists on dividing ways of experiencing the globalized world into a binary of pre- and post- terms and that eschews historical analysis and national self-critique.

Thus, a direct faultline within American foreign policy runs through the two September 11 events that have culminated in US-supported torture, the suppression of human rights, and the disappearance and the deaths of thousands. Loach and Vega cinematically juxtapose the US and the Chilean victimization by crosscutting coverage of George W. Bush's post-9/11 rhetoric onto images and voice-over descriptions of Chile's 9/11. The film contains segments of Bush's September 20, 2001, speech in which he solemnly proclaims, "On September eleventh, enemies of freedom committed an act of war against our country, and night fell on a different world—a world where freedom itself is under attack." By following this speech with 1973 footage of fighter jets launching rockets into La Moneda, Allende's presidential palace, Vega and Loach attempt to reclaim "9/11" within its twentieth-century historical context, a context in which the apparently CIA-authorized torture of Allende's allies prefigures the United States' post-9/11 system of torture and interrogation camps under the Bush Administration's "Coalition of the Willing." As "War on Terror" interrogator Tony Lagouranis puts it, "Those [9/11] attacks ... made us want to respond in kind. Suddenly, their defeat was not enough. Standard military operations using high-tech weaponry and the utter obliteration of the enemy via cruise missiles and five-thousand pound bombs was not enough ... This kind of dominance requires evil."[5] Vega's short film implicitly argues for the instability of and subsequent need for reframing "9/11" as a named event, as *the* event, as a mythic yet history-altering event, and as an event that would lead to other horrors in other places under the authority of some of the same influential architects who forever altered Chile in 1973, ironically the year of the ribbon-cutting ceremony celebrating the completion of the World Trade Center in New York City. "We will remember you," assures Vega in the end of his sympathetic remarks and remembrances of trauma. "I hope you will remember us."

This volume and its essays do not start or stop at the historic events of September 11, 2001 alone. Individually and collectively, the essays speak to the popular culture responses of that day, its aftermath, and the events leading to it. The 9/11 attacks, catastrophic as they were on the day that they happened, represent a pure distillation of so many of the conflicts that this world faces, among them: West vs. (Middle) East, capitalism vs. the vast class of exploited and underprivileged, and religious fundamentalism vs. irreligious humanism. As a locus of historical and cultural scrutiny, this flashpoint insists that we examine the wreckage of that day, its endlessly competing narratives, and its echoes of the past and its conflicting meanings in the present. Clearly, this is a task too large for any one volume, and we do not pretend to universality or completeness. We acknowledge and build upon earlier work produced in other volumes on 9/11 and popular culture, including *Rethinking Global Security: Media, Popular Culture, and the "War on Terror"* (eds Andrew Martin and Patrice Petro, Rutgers University Press, 2006), *Film and Television after 9/11* (ed. Wheeler Winston Dixon, Southern Illinois University Press, 2004), and *The Selling of 9/11: How a National Tragedy Became a Commodity* (ed. Dana Heller, Palgrave, 2005). As we approach the ten-year anniversary of the event, we offer a reevaluation of its cultural salience. The day has been usurped by the post-9/11 discourse of trauma, uncertainty, and revenge. The disjointed collective popular culture response to 9/11 is the *post*-9/11 story. As John Cawelti's afterword discusses, within twenty-first century culture, virtually everything lies within the domain of popular culture, and no political statement, no image, no voice lies beyond the potential boundaries of media consumption.

Section I, (Re)Creating Language, begins with David Altheide's essay "Fear, Terrorism, and Popular Culture," which provides context for the West's relationship with a news media that has become increasingly invested in entertainment via "infotainment" and in which, for many audience members, the distinction between "news" and "real TV" becomes trivial. Altheide argues that, by aiming to please audiences and key political leaders, news media and especially major TV networks (with some exceptions) embraced the emotional sweep of the 9/11 attacks and enabled the making of war. Notwithstanding the long relationship in the United States between fear and crime, the role of the mass media in promoting fear has become more pronounced since the United States "discovered" international terrorism on September 11, 2001.

In "The Aesthetics of Destruction: Contemporary US Cinema and TV Culture," Mathias Nilges discusses the cultural convergence of our fascination with representations of large-scale destruction and the loss of the strong, white male action hero in film since the 1990s. The collective US imagination, he argues, is most easily influenced by annihilation fantasies in an era of threatening complexity, anxiety, and, above all, loss. In "9/11, British Muslims, and Popular Literary Fiction," Sara Upstone argues that, in the wake of the American "War on Terror," British culture not only consumed American attitudes, but also—through both governmental cooperation and a perceived cultural proximity—saw these attitudes become incorporated into mainstream British popular opinion. The events of 9/11 and their offshoots in Britain, most notably the July 7, 2005, Tube bombings, have meant that the British literary imagination has been profoundly affected by American fears of Islamic fundamentalism. In particular, the events of 9/11 stimulated literary engagement with British Muslim identity and its relationship to both alternative media representation and a more deeply rooted stereotyping of this identity.

In "*Left Behind* in America: The Army of One at the End of History," Jonathan Vincent reads the vastly popular *Left Behind* book series and identifies some of the ways that evangelical fiction embodies tenets of post-9/11 popular culture by providing a means for thinking about the relationship between conservative ideology and American foreign policy. Evangelical culture has long held a significant place in American religious consciousness. While not exactly a dominant cultural force, it nonetheless organizes a significant portion of the American population and its ideological orientation toward the world, both locally and globally. These books, Vincent argues, have galvanized a new subculture of "rapture" or "second-coming" enthusiasts. Their more worrisome appeal is a new way of registering a messianic global outlook as well as their casual revitalization of the militaristic ideologies of the "crusade" or "clash" of irreconcilable civilizations.

In "Manhood, Mourning, and the American Romance," John Mead reads William Langewiesche's three-part *Atlantic Monthly* series on the excavation of the World Trade Center site as mythologizing an "urgent all-American creation," symbolizing the reopening of the frontier and the reinvestment in our Manifest Destiny. Langewiesche, Mead argues, weaves together American frontier mythology, Tom Peters-esque 1990s entrepreneurial manifestos, contemporary pop psychology, and consumerism into imperialist propaganda. Mead contrasts this series with Bruce Springsteen's 9/11 album, *The Rising*, revealing something about the iconic singer's body of work that few critics have noted—the impotence of his protagonists. The songs on *The Rising*, Mead suggests, offer competing narratives of manhood and mourning in post-9/11 America.

In "An Early Broadside: The Far Right Raids *Master and Commander: The Far Side of the World*," Jeff Birkenstein analyzes the curious responses to the 2003 mainstream film that many critics lauded. Though almost everyone seemed to like the film, the opinions about its cultural message differed vastly. Its value for conservative political and religious commentators, and for some mainstream political (and not film) critics who appeal to small yet passionate constituencies, lay in the seeming single-mindedness and ultimate success of an outnumbered crew fighting for God and country. These commentators saw the film as a desirable narrative with which to support George W. Bush's "War on Terror." Imprinted upon a pop cultural artifact, this protracted Internet battle was one of the early post-9/11 sociocultural battles regarding the "War on Terror" and how it should be fought.

In the final chapter of this section, Corey Creekmur analyzes the soundscape of terror. In "The Sound of the 'War on Terror,'" Creekmur suggests that terrorism— insofar as we might agree on a definition—produces its own dreadful soundscape: the "real" sounds of violence, combat, fear, and pain, the eardrum-shattering blasts of improvised explosive devices, and the deafening roar of the US military's "shock and awe." Sound, Creekmur argues, is an often ignored object of scrutiny in a mass media in which the image takes priority.

Section II, "Visions of War and Terror," opens with David Annandale's essay "Avatars of Destruction: Cheerleading and Deconstructing the 'War on Terror' in Video Games." He argues that video games, thanks to their pervasive violence and narratives of war, generally support the entrenchment of military culture. However, some games question the policies of America's post-9/11 military ventures, as well as their underlying premises. Responses to the "War on Terror" range from games developed in cooperation with the armed forces (e.g., *Full Spectrum Warrior*), to their ideological soul mates (*Tom Clancy's Ghost Recon: Advanced Warfighter*), to the games that either problematize the binary oppositions of the "War on Terror" (*Halo 2* and *Gears of War*) or are in outright revolt against it (*Raze's Hell* and *Crackdown*). The conflicting positions of these games reveal a struggle to define an American identity torn between the competing fantasies of post-9/11 victimhood, of identification with the underdog, and of military triumphalism. In "The *Land of the Dead* and the Home of the Brave: Romero's Vision of a Post-9/11 America," Terence McSweeney argues that, despite the American film industry's reluctance to explicitly represent the events of 9/11 in cinema, the event and its turbulent political aftermath are frequent allegories in horror films, such as *Land of The Dead* (2005), the fourth entry in Romero's influential zombie franchise. *Land of the Dead* is a stereotypical addition to the horror genre with the prerequisite violence and gore. Yet, to focus primarily on these elements is to deny the film's cultural relevance, intelligence, and wit, as well as its scathing, thinly veiled attack on the Bush administration and its prosecution of the "War on Terror."

Alex Evans discusses the numerous incarnations of the comic hero, Superman, in his essay "Superman *Is* the Faultline: Fissures in the Monomythic Man of Steel." Evans argues that the image of Superman has often shifted political positions. In 1942, Superman supports the war that he decried three years earlier as emanating from the capitalist arms trade; in the 1990s, the union-busting hero saves the arms trade from "terrorist" activities. At the same time, his arch-nemesis, Lex Luthor, is reinvented as a Machiavellian capitalist. After George W. Bush's presidency, Luthor becomes President, producing redolently subversive parallels with reality. While some assume that the myth of Superman will heal America and repair the damage of the earth-shattering disaster—including the fissures and splinters of ideology—we find instead that the superhero is himself a "faultline" from which competing narratives struggle for ideological dominance of the Superman myth. The discussion of the comic book hero continues with Justine Toh's essay "The Tools and Toys of (the) War (on Terror): Consumer Desire, Military Fetish, and Regime Change in *Batman Begins*." Here she argues that Christopher Nolan's *Batman Begins* (2005) is not only a post-9/11 origin story of the dark knight of Gotham City but a complex allegory for the conduct of America's "War on Terror." Batman is a freedom fighter who develops his skills at a terrorist training camp, indicating the inextricability of "Western civilization" from its so-called dark others. The film also highlights the collusion of the military-industrial-entertainment complex that develops military gear in tandem with consumer products. Wayne's world of privilege provides Batman with access to high-tech equipment, which he pretends to squander as a thrill-seeking playboy. Does Batman ultimately solve Gotham's problems or merely recreate the conditions for their reproduction?

In "'It Was Like a Movie': The Impossibility of Representation in Oliver Stone's *World Trade Center*," Karen Randell argues that the *mise-en-scène*'s evocation of the blockbuster disaster film provides a means by which the "incomprehensible" can be understood, for, as Thomas Elsaesser has asked, how can we "represent the unrepresentable" that is trauma?[6] *World Trade Center* addresses this issue by nostalgically referencing the well-trodden path of a familiar genre. Trauma here is located within the family and the everyday. Randell asks whether the everyman embodiments of Port Authority Policemen John (Nicolas Cage) and Will (Michael Peña) dilute the wider political issues of the 9/11 event as these two men become the locus for both mourning and hope—both within and outside the film. The final essay in this section, "The Contemporary Politics of the Western Form: Bush, *Saving Jessica Lynch*, and *Deadwood*," explores the role of Western discourse and Western imagery in the construction and legitimation of a remilitarized US foreign policy post-9/11. Examining two recent manifestations of the Western on TV, the made-for-TV movie *Saving Jessica Lynch* (NBC, 2003) and the HBO series *Deadwood* (2004–06), Stacy Takacs argues that the first text illustrates the role of Western motifs in the Bush administration's depiction of the War in Iraq as a defensive struggle to protect "civilization" against the forces of "savagery." The second calls this construction into question by presenting a world in which "civilization" and "savagery" are inextricably intertwined and moral clarity is impossible. Such an anti-heroic depiction of the American West constitutes a counter-narrative that not only challenges the righteousness of a militarized foreign policy but also offers an alternative conception of national identity and power, predicated on an ethic of social obligation and responsibility for the future.

Section III, "Prophetic Narratives," opens with an essay by David H. Price: "Governing Fear in the Iron Cage of Rationalism: Terry Gilliam's *Brazil* through the 9/11 Looking Glass." Price argues that the world depicted in Terry Gilliam's *Brazil* (1985) foresaw the ways that the Bush administration used the "War on Terror" to foster a climate of fear that is transforming American attitudes toward torture, civil liberties, and dissent. Gilliam's film is set in an intentionally vague location and time, marked with technologies anachronistically combining futuristic and outdated contraptions of questionable reliability. In Gilliam's world and Bush's America, the government uses fear and threats of terrorist attacks to herd the public, and a climate fostering secrecy allows the government to conduct surveillance on members of society to cover up its actions. America's engagement in the "War on Terror" increases the relevance of *Brazil*'s dark vision of the dangers of an anti-democratic state capitalizing on the fears of the populace and engaging in wanton acts of torture in the name of security and freedom. In "Cultural Anxiety, Moral Clarity, and Willful Amnesia: Filming Philip K. Dick After 9/11," Lance Rubin engages with similar issues in his discussion of Dick's fiction and its adaptation into films in the early twenty-first century. His case studies suggest that Dick's prescient stories have anticipated the culture of the "War on Terror." The narratives adopt dimensions of allegory and participate in metonymical and metaphorical meanings. Dick's stories engage America's post-9/11 apprehension, particularly regarding the manipulation of memory, a tremulous, erratic sense of individual and collective identity, and ever-increasing government surveillance.

In the final essay of this section, "Prolepsis and the 'War on Terror': Zombie Pathology and the Culture of Fear in *28 Days Later . . .*," Anna Froula analyzes Danny Boyle's 2002 film, one of the first post-9/11 horror movies. *28 Days Later . . .* imagines an England decimated by a synthetic biological contagion known as the "rage virus" that causes zombie-like behavior. Zombies, Froula argues, have long been allegories for global trauma. In its exploration of social rage, the movie dramatizes the imperialist worldview and the material realities that inform the Bush Doctrine of preemptive war and the conditions of the Iraq invasion and occupation. In particular, Boyle allegorizes the endless incarceration of enemy bodies from legal due process, the ramifications of torture, and the folly of governments that respond too late to threats and trauma. While concerned with various forms of violence in the world that bloodily embody social injustice, the film's zombie allegory operates as a proleptic mirror of the ways in which the Bush administration has conceived of and spoken about terror, terrorists, and terrorism throughout its tenure.

As the gut-level response of many eyewitnesses to the destruction of the World Trade Center suggests, the arresting spectacle of the transformation of commercial planes into explosive missiles was "something out of the movies." And even as Hollywood was reluctant to explicitly represent the terrorist attacks and their aftermath, a reluctance shorter in duration but similar to the lack of explicit engagement with the Vietnam War between 1968 and 1978, cinematic allegories entered the post-9/11 discourse, along with music, television, and written texts. The following chapters offer several critical analyses of films and consider a broad range of popular culture forms. Together, the essays in this volume seek to encourage new and original approaches for understanding the issues both within and beyond the official and quasi-official political rhetoric of the events of the "War on Terror" and issues of "national security." Because there has been no conclusive recovery from the trauma of the event—indeed, because there cannot be—this volume speaks to the continuing need to grapple with the still-incomprehensible.

Notes

1 "US Is 'Battling Satan' Says General," *BBC News*, Friday, October 17, 2003, http://news.bbc.co.uk/2/hi/americas/3199212.stm (accessed July 15, 2009).

2 See Reza Aslan, *How to Win a Cosmic War: God, Globalization, and the End of the War on Terror* (New York: Random House, 2009).

3 Scott Wilson and Al Kamen, "'Global War on Terror' Is Given New Name," *Washington Post*, March 25, 2009, A04, http://www.washingtonpost.com/wp-dyn/content/article/2009/03/24/AR2009032402818.html (accessed April 4, 2009).

4 See Susan Faludi, *The Terror Dream: Fear and Fantasy in Post-9/11 America* (New York: Metropolitan Books, 2007).

5 Tony Lagouranis and Allen Mikaelian, *Fear Up Harsh: An Army Interrogator's Dark Journey through Iraq* (New York: NAL, 2007), 247.

6 Thomas Elsaesser, "Postmodernism as Mourning Work," *Screen* 42 no. 2 Summer (2001), 195.

SECTION I

(Re)Creating Language

CHAPTER 1

Fear, Terrorism, and Popular Culture

DAVID L. ALTHEIDE

We learn about the world and how the world is run through the mass media and popular culture. Indeed, the state of a citizenry's worldview can be gleaned by its dominant news sources. This is becoming more apparent with foreign policy and international affairs.[1] Mass media information provides a context of meanings and images that prepare audiences for political decisions about specific actions, including war. This chapter draws on qualitative document analysis[2] to illustrate how news reports and popular culture depictions about the "War on Terror" (WOT) were grounded in a discourse of fear, as well as familiar cultural images that proclaimed the moral and social superiority of the United States. Moreover, the "crisis" of the 9/11 attacks was artfully constructed through news accounts as the "world has changed" and that future survival would depend on giving up many basic civil liberties, particularly "privacy." These messages were folded into the previous crime-related discourse of fear, which may be defined as the pervasive communication, symbolic awareness, and expectation that danger and risk are central features of everyday life.

News media and popular culture depictions of the US reaction to terror attacks reflect a culture and collective identities steeped in marketing, popular culture, consumerism, and fear. The military-media complex managed press releases and cultivated news sources to produce terrorism scenarios that were reflected in national agendas and everyday life. The attacks on the United States on September 11, 2001, were defined in the news media and popular culture as an assault on American culture, if not civilization itself.[3] These definitions were aligned with a broad context and a preexisting discourse of fear, which is discussed below, along with symbolic images of "Arabs" as the "Other," or marginalized outsiders who are threats to personal and national security.[4]

Fun with Terrorism and Fear

War and conflict are the stuff of superheroes and run-of-the-mill politicians. Popular culture's engagement of audiences' emotions and aspirations to be extraordinary, "in the know," and relevant—in the face of bureaucratic everyday routines—promotes identification with narratives and tales of tragedy, overcoming adversity, and rising to defeat enemies. It is ironic—and very important—that during the Iraq War one of the most important sources of news for younger people was *The Daily Show* with Jon Stewart, a comedic parody on the news of the day, mixed with truly informative insights from selected authors, who would discuss their more reflective take on issues of the day, including foreign policy, imperialism, and faux concern with fear.

Fear is the foundation for much of the dominant narrative of the last 50 years.[5] Notwithstanding the long relationship in the United States between fear and crime, the role of the mass media in promoting fear has become more pronounced since the United States "discovered" international terrorism on September 11, 2001. The dominant "story" since the attacks of 9/11 was the "WOT." The American news media, and especially network TV news organizations, chose not to present important contextual and background information about the Middle East, and especially Iraq, because it was not consistent with other news themes, nor was it as entertaining. Threats to invade other countries—the "axis of evil"—that included Iraq, were part of an effort to "defend" the United States from future attacks. This broad story included US retaliation, the hunt for al-Qaeda leaders (e.g., Osama bin Laden), and plans to attack countries and "outlaw regimes" that supported or harbored terrorists. Implementing these programs involved invading Afghanistan and expanding the US military presence throughout the world. Other adjustments were made in foreign policy, military budgets, domestic surveillance, and attacks on civil liberties.[6]

Fear and terrorism became broad symbols that encompassed consumption and international intervention.[7] Previous analysis of numerous news reports pertaining to terrorism shows that citizens' concerns about victims of 9/11 attacks were joined by politicians and advertisers, who marketed and framed fear and dread of terrorism as part of a national identity that was commensurate with personal caring and community.[8] The meaning of terrorism expanded from a tactic to also mean an idea, a lifestyle, and ultimately, a condition of the world. News reports contributed to this broad definition of terrorism as a condition. A key source for this news theme was the Project for the New American Century (PNAC).

Terrorism and the Project for the New American Century

Key policymakers had long considered invading Iraq.[9] Planned for nearly ten years, bringing about a "regime change" in Iraq was part of a complex plan for the United States to become the hegemon, including withdrawing from—if not negating—certain treaties (e.g., nuclear test ban) and becoming more independent of the United Nations.[10] The most detailed coverage of the history of the PNAC and its role in shaping US foreign policy was David Armstrong's 2002 essay in *Harper's*:

> The plan is for the United States to rule the world. The overt theme is unilateralism, but it is ultimately a story of domination. It calls for the United States to maintain its overwhelming military superiority and prevent new rivals from rising up to challenge

it on the world stage. It calls for dominion over friends and enemies alike. It says not that the United States must be more powerful, or most powerful, but that it must be absolutely powerful.[11]

The US invasion of Iraq was justified, in the main, by claims that Saddam Hussein possessed "weapons of mass destruction" (WMD), was in league with the terrorists who attacked the US, and that he was likely to place these weapons at the disposal of other terrorists.[12] It took less than a year for the world to learn that none of these assertions were true, and indeed, there was strong evidence that members of the Bush administration were quite aware that such WMDs did not exist.[13]

Vice President Dick Cheney knew for two decades that Iraq was a prime target. He knew this because he was part of a group that drew up a blueprint for US world domination: PNAC.[14] On the fifth anniversary of the 9/11 attacks, Vice President Cheney made it very clear that the Iraq War did not hinge mainly on the existence of WMDs. Cheney stated on *Meet the Press*:

> The world is much better off . . . It was the right thing to do, and if we had to do it over again, we'd do exactly the same thing . . . The people obviously are frustrated because of the difficulty, because of the cost and the casualties . . . You cannot look at Iraq in isolation. You have to look at it within the context of the broader global war on terror . . . . Any retreat by the United States would indicate to the terrorists that the "US has lost its will" in the war against terrorism and would damage US credibility.[15]

Given such emphasis, it is perhaps no surprise that six years after the invasion of Iraq one-third of the American people still believed that Saddam Hussein was involved.[16] Well into 2009, conservative politicians, including Dick Cheney when he was out of office, would chide newly elected President Obama for not keeping us safe.

The Iraq War was informed by PNAC efforts and the resulting propaganda campaign to convince the American people that attacking Iraq was tantamount to attacking "terrorists" and others who threatened the United States.[17] Many members of the PNAC joined the Bush administration and became credible claims-makers, who constructed the frames for shaping subsequent news reports. Among the members who signed many of the proclamations laying the foundation for a new American empire[18] were former and current governmental officials, including: Elliot Abrams, William Bennett, Jeb Bush, Dick Cheney, Steve Forbes, Donald Kagan, Norman Podhoretz, Dan Quayle, Donald Rumsfeld, and Paul Wolfowitz.

The PNAC emphasized changing American foreign policy to become a hegemon and police its international interests as a new kind of benevolent American empire.[19] This would include expanding the military, withdrawing from major treaties, as well as engaging in preemptive strikes against those who would threaten US interests. These messages were carried by the mass media for months leading up to the invasion of Iraq.[20] Indeed, with the exception of a few critical reports about the rush to war and the role of the PNAC by National Public Radio (NPR) and the Public Broadcasting Service's *Frontline*, there were virtually no analytical pieces about the rush to war.[21] The support by the mainstream media was consistent with the way that the "Arab CNN"—Al Jazeera—would be characterized several years later:

> ... Arab journalists said Al Jazeera's seeming willingness to toe the Saudi line was proof that there still were no truly independent media outlets in the region. "The Arab media today still play much the same role as the pre-Islamic tribal poets, whose role was to praise the tribe, not tell the truth," said Sulaiman al-Hattlan, a Dubai-based media analyst and the former editor in chief of *Forbes Arabia*.[22]

In 1992, the United States was well on its way to justifying an attack on Iraq when Dick Cheney and others, who would occupy positions in the Bush administration eight years later, drafted the Defense Planning Guidance document. Making a pitch for a threatened military budget in 1992, Colin Powell told the House Armed Services Committee that the United States

> required "sufficient power" to "deter any challenger from ever dreaming of challenging us on the world stage." To emphasize the point, he cast the United States in the role of street thug. "I want to be the bully on the block," he said, implanting in the mind of potential opponents that "there is no future in trying to challenge the armed forces of the United States."[23]

The upshot was that the goal was "to prevent the reemergence of a new rival."[24] When the plan was leaked to the press, it went through several changes, with new drafts suggesting that the US would act in concert with allies, when possible. The First Gulf War came and went, President George Bush was not reelected, and many of the co-authors and supporters of the plan left office for think tanks, businesses, and various publications. The plan, with revisions, was promoted repeatedly during the next decade, even though some members were out of office for as much as eight years, and was in full swing one month before the infamous 9/11 attacks. Ultimately, the plan was oriented to freeing the US from several alliances and treaties that limited military and weapons planning and testing, including the 1972 anti-ballistic missile treaty, and several nuclear nonproliferation treaties.[25] Other global and environmental agreements were also avoided or broken, including those designed to protect the environment and limit pollution (e.g., the United Nations' Kyoto Protocol, ratified or signed by 209 countries).

As news sources, cabinet members, presidential advisors, journalists, and publishers, the PNAC played a major role in leading the US to war with Iraq. Political decision-makers quickly adjusted propaganda passages, prepared as part of the PNAC, to emphasize domestic support for the new US role in leading the world. Most of the Gulf War coverage originated from the White House and the federal government.[26] Network news shows were quite consistent with guests who supported the war. An analysis by Fairness & Accuracy in Reporting (FAIR) of network news interviewees one week before and one week after Secretary of State Colin Powell addressed the United Nations about Iraq's alleged possession of WMDs found that two-thirds of the guests were from the United States with 75 percent of these being current or former government or military officials. Only one—Senator Kennedy—expressed skepticism or opposition to the impending war with Iraq.[27]

As noted previously, the PNAC received very little news media coverage prior to the invasion of Iraq, even though it was part of the "public record" in government documents and had been briefly mentioned in several newspaper and radio reports in the late 1990s.[28] Only a few newspaper articles dealt with PNAC six months before the United States attacked Iraq on March 20, 2003. No reports appeared on the major TV networks' regular evening newscasts during this time, although *Nightline* did examine the "conspiracy claims" and interview William Kristol on March 5, 2003. Reporter Ted Koppel dismissed the conspiratorial charges by several foreign newspapers. He framed it in terms of what could be called "it depends on how you look at it":

> They did what former government officials and politicians frequently do when they're out of power; they began formulating a strategy, in this case, a foreign policy strategy, that might bring influence to bear on the Administration then in power, headed by President Clinton.[29]

This report was broadcast just a few days prior to a congressional vote authorizing that war. Thus, there was a clear sense of urgency to intervene in Iraq. After all, the US had already fought the First Gulf War with Hussein, and that effort was fueled by a massive propaganda campaign headed by the US Public Relations firm, Hill and Knowlton, which promoted the lie that Saddam's troops had killed babies in Kuwait.[30]

The major news agencies in the United States, and particularly the TV networks, limited their coverage of the role the PNAC played in shaping the Iraq War (as noted, with the exception of NPR and *Frontline* reports). News organizations explicitly and implicitly editorialize through their use of news sources for certain issues.[31] These propaganda efforts occurred as the various PNAC members served as routine news sources, primarily in TV network news accounts oriented to infotainment. The major news media presented virtually no strong disclaimers to this scenario, partly because the military worked very closely with them, even to the point of letting reporters become "embedded" with the troops. The grateful news organizations became even closer to military sources.

Terrorism, Consumerism, and National Identity

Analysis of news reports and advertisements suggests that popular culture and mass media depictions of fear, patriotism, consumption, and victimization contributed to the emergence of a "national identity" and collective action that was fostered by elite decision-makers' propaganda.[32] Terrorism became a perspective, an orientation, and a discourse for "our time," the "way things are today," and "how the world has changed." The subsequent campaign to integrate fear into everyday life routines was consequential for public life, domestic policy, and foreign affairs.[33] The tragic loss of lives and property fueled patriotic slogans, thousands of commercial advertisements, public contributions of more than $2 billion, major domestic and foreign policy changes, and the largest increase in the military budget in 35 years. Stores sold out of flags, businesses linked advertising to patriotic slogans (e.g., General Motors' "Keep America Rolling"), baseball fans sang "God Bless America" instead of "Take Me Out to the Ball Game," and children helped raise money for starving Afghani children.

Domestic life became oriented to celebrating/commemorating past terrorist acts, waiting for and anticipating the next terrorist act and taking steps to prevent it. Everyday life and language reflected terrorism (and terrorist) disclaimers (e.g., "since 9/11 . . .," ". . . how the world has changed," ". . . in our time," etc.). International order and conduct were consistent with the domestic definition of a "terrorism world," as well as an expansive claim that the "new world" was governed by evil terrorists rather than political gamesmanship. Good and evil turned on terrorism. International borders, treaties and even US constitutional rights were mere symbols that could detract from the single largest threat to civilization and "good." Such evil was to be feared and constantly attacked. To be against terrorism and all that it entailed was a mark of legitimacy and membership that would be demonstrated in various ways. Using similar symbols and expressing opposition to terrorism promoted communalism by putting the good of the citizenry over any group or individual.[34] The celebration of terrorism would carry over into President Obama's first hundred days in office as he pledged that the war in Afghanistan is a war "we must win."

Audience familiarity with terrorism traded on decades of news and popular culture depictions of crime myths about the "crime problem," crime victims, and the drug war.[35] The emphasis of the coverage of 9/11 was on the commonality of the victims rather than the cause or the rationale for the attacks. The popular refrain was that all Americans were victimized by the attacks, and like the "potential victims" of crime featured in a decade of news reports about the crime problem, all citizens should support efforts to attack the source of fear.[36] The news media were pressured to toe the line. With network and local nightly newscasts draped in flag colors, lapel flags, and patriotic slogans reporting events "primarily through the viewpoint of the United States" (e.g., "us" and "we"), news organizations presented content and form that was interpreted by the publisher of *Harper's* as sending: ". . . signals to the viewers to some extent that the media are acting as an arm of the government, as opposed to an independent, objective purveyor of information, which is what we're supposed to be."[37] Dan Rather, CBS anchorman, acknowledged the pressure to comply with propaganda and that many of the tough questions were not being asked. Rather told a British journalist:

It is an obscene comparison . . . but you know there was a time in South Africa that people would put flaming tyres around people's necks if they dissented. And in some ways the fear is that you will be necklaced here, you will have a flaming tyre of lack of patriotism put around your neck," he said. "Now it is that fear that keeps journalists from asking the toughest of the tough questions . . ."[38]

Anyone who suggested that the "cause" of the attacks was more complex and that the

United States had angered many political groups by previous actions (e.g., support for Israel) was denounced. Talk-show host Bill Maher, who argued that the terrorists were not really cowards, was among those pilloried and lost his job; Clear Channel, a radio consortium, put out a blacklist of 150 songs with critical themes (e.g., Simon and Garfunkel's "Bridge over Troubled Water") that should not be played.[39] The Dixie Chicks, an outspoken country-rock group which criticized President Bush, were blackballed from country music radio stations and award presentations.

The "younger generation" was implored to meet the new challenge; this was, after all, their war, and the mass media carried youthful testimonies of newfound loyalty and awakening that would have made a tent-meeting evangelist proud. Identity and commensuration were presented to audiences through various messages in the established mass media. Notwithstanding the tsunami-like swell of comedy shows and critical and reflective Internet blogs about the failed military efforts and the absurd propaganda claims by Fox news and other religious followers of the Bush administration, the established mass media lent support to an emerging national identity that was commensurate with moral character and a discourse of salvation or "seeing the light" to guide our way through the new terrorism world. For example, *Newsweek* magazine published statements by young people, one "confessing" her naiveté about the "real world," and another by a former university student who criticized "antimilitary culture" with a call to arms:

> Before the attack, all I could think of was how to write a good rap . . . *I am not eager to say this*, but we do not live in an ideal world . . . I've come to accept the idea of a focused war on terrorists as the best way to ensure our country's safety.[40] (Note the disclaimer; my emphasis).

Advertising and the market economy joined with giving and "selfless" assistance to others. Americans gave millions to charities to help the victims of 9/11. Indeed, businesses and corporate America offered rebates and contributions to charities from individual purchases. The slumping US economy was in a recession prior to 9/11 and it plummeted thereafter.

The US advertising industry sprang into action.[41] For example, the Ad Council (Advertising Research Foundation) noted in an online communication that "it was originally founded as the War Advertising Council during World War II in the aftermath of the bombings of Pearl Harbor." Following an "all advertising industry meeting," a strategy was adopted on September 18, 2001 to "inform, involve and inspire Americans to participate in activities that will help win the war on terrorism."[42]

The politics of fear was central to commensuration practices in forging a national identity. This was accomplished symbolically by expanding the tragic events into an interpretive scheme that connected attacks with renewal, revenge, and deference to leaders who would attack the enemy and save us from other attacks. The communal reaction was informed by drawing on national experiences of fear, consumption, and the role of national leadership in molding a response that would also constitute and justify future actions and relationships between nations, state control, and citizens.

Terrorism and Social Control

The discourse of fear was joined with the politics of fear that enabled decision-makers to couch control efforts as being in the best interests of citizens in order to protect them.[43] *The Daily Show* and others (e.g., *The Colbert Report*—the parody on hard-talking right-wing commentators) played with and sarcastically resisted dominant mass media images and themes about risk and safety. These control efforts included fundamental violations of international law, custom, and the Geneva accords: "torture" programs and policies, operation of secret prisons, denial of habeas corpus to detainees—which can be applied to all who threaten national security[44]—kidnapping and illegal international transport, and domestic and international surveillance of telephone and computer communication. Only a handful of American news media carried reports about German and Italian arrest warrants for CIA agents who kidnapped German and Italian citizens, respectively, and shipped them to other countries to be tortured and questioned because they were thought to be terrorists.[45]

The seriousness of the German and Italian charges, along with widespread revulsion throughout the European Community, can be illustrated by the Bush administration's efforts to have Congress pass legislation that would grant immunity to key officials—including President Bush—and CIA agents who carried out their superior's orders. According to one report:

> Congress has eased the worries of CIA interrogators and senior administration officials by granting them immunity from US criminal prosecutions for all but "grave" abuses of terrorism detainees . . . "The obstacles to these prosecutions are not legal, they're political," said William Schabas, director of the Irish Center for Human Rights at the National University of Ireland in Galway.[46]

US news audiences, who learned about the most grotesque abuses at the Abu Ghraib prison, were also told that things were not that bad, that we were "at war," and this should be forgotten. But, opined conservative talk-show host Rush Limbaugh, the treatment of Iraqi prisoners wasn't really that bad after all. In response to a caller on his May 4, 2004, show, he commented that the guards just had a "need to blow some steam off," adding that really nothing more was done than what Madonna or Britney Spears would do on stage and that "the torturers are . . . Women! The babes! The babes are meting out the torture."[47] Five years later, newly elected President Obama would fight the release of more photos of these egregious abuses in order to protect American personnel. He stressed that the Abu Ghraib prison abuses were due to the excesses of a few people and not part of systemic effort sanctioned by higher officials.

During the critical eight-month period between the 9/11 attacks and the US invasion of Iraq, the American news media essentially repeated administration claims about terrorism and Iraq's impending nuclear capacity:[48]

> Rarely has television functioned so poorly in an era of crisis, generating more heat than light; more sound, fury, and spectacle than understanding; and more blatantly

grotesque partisanship for the Bush administration than genuinely democratic debate over what options the country and the world faced in the confrontation with terrorism.[49]

Civil liberties and decency were dimmed by the mass mediated shadow of terrorism. Attorney General Ashcroft made it clear that anyone concerned with the civil rights of the suspicious was also suspect. Ashcroft told members of Senate committees that critics "aid terrorists" and undermine national unity: "They give ammunition to America's enemies, and pause to America's friends."[50] This message resonated even with those attending university events. *Sacramento Bee* president and publisher, Janis Besler Heaphy, was booed off the stage during a commencement address at California State University, Sacramento, after she suggested that the national response to terrorism could erode press freedoms and individual liberties. A professor in the audience remarked: "For the first time in my life, I can see how something like the Japanese internment camps could happen in our country."[51]

The drug war and ongoing concerns with crime contributed to the expansion of fear with terrorism. Messages demonizing Osama bin Laden, his Taliban supporters, and "Islamic extremists" linked these suspects with the destructive clout of illegal drugs, especially drug lords. News reports and advertisements joined drug use with terrorism and helped shift "drugs" from criminal activity to unpatriotic action. A $10 million ad campaign promoted the message from President Bush: "if you quit drugs, you join the fight against terror in America."

Conclusion

Terrorism discourse is part of a general context involving the discourse of fear, which was mainly associated with crime, as well as nearly two decades of negative reporting and imagery about the Middle East and Iraq in particular. The politics of fear emerged from this discourse, but so did the resistant *Daily Show* and *The Colbert Report*, serious comedies with an international audience, especially young people. Other examples of resistance include *Countdown with Keith Olbermann*, and very importantly, the emergence of dozens of "alternative media" sites and blogs (e.g., *The Onion*).

Still, fear dominated the symbolic landscape. Citizens became accustomed to "safety rhetoric" by police officials, which often required them to permit police searches, condone "overaggressive" police action, as well as join in a myriad of crime-prevention efforts, many of which involved human (as well as electronic) surveillance of workplaces, neighborhoods, stores, and even our bodies, in the form of expansive drug screening. The discourse of fear promotes the politics of fear and numerous surveillance practices and rationales to keep us safe.[52] By the mid 1990s, many high-school students had "peed in a bottle" as a condition of participating in athletics, applying for a job, and, in some cases, applying for student loans and scholarships. Several legal challenges to this scrutiny were turned down, as the courts (with a few exceptions) began to uphold the cliché that was echoed by local TV newscasters and others: "why worry if you have nothing to hide?" In short, many US citizens had been socialized into the garrison state, no longer being offended by surveillance and, indeed, many chose to use the rapidly expanding—and inexpensive—technology to monitor their own children, including testing them for drugs.

Rituals of control were embodied in physical screening and inspection of travelers, including demands that they publicly sacrifice personal items in line with the "terror threat." The 9/11 attacks and the coalescing of the discourse of fear with terrorism meant that more of our lives would be subject to closer scrutiny, particularly air travel. A new federal organization was invented, the Department of Homeland Security, and with its multi-million dollar budget was a requirement to establish an army of federal airport security personnel, the Transportation Security Administration (TSA). Notwithstanding numerous "experiments," which continue to demonstrate that conscientious "smugglers" can bring an array of weapons and explosives on board,[53] the discourse of terrorism continued to promote the claim that such screening was keeping us all safe and that it should continue because, after all, the world changed after 9/11.

Notes

1   William C. Adams, *Television Coverage of International Affairs* (Norwood, NJ: Ablex Publishing Corp., 1981); David Campbell, *Writing Security: United States Foreign Policy and the Politics of Identity* (Minneapolis: University of Minnesota Press, 1998); Stephen Hess, *International News & Foreign Correspondents* (Washington, DC: Brookings Institution, 1996); Douglas Kellner, *From 9/11 to Terror War: The Dangers of the Bush Legacy* (Lanham, MD: Rowman & Littlefield, 2003); Philo C. Washburn, *The Social Construction of International News: We're Talking about Them, They're Talking about Us* (Westport, CT: Praeger, 2002).

2   David L. Altheide, *Terrorism and the Politics of Fear* (Lanham, MD: Alta Mira Press, 2006).

3   David L. Altheide, "Consuming Terrorism," *Symbolic Interaction* 27 (2004): 289–308.

4   William C. Adams, *Television Coverage of the Middle East* (Norwood, NJ: Ablex Publishing Corp., 1981); David L. Altheide, "Iran vs. US TV News! The Hostage Story out of Context," in *Television Coverage of the Middle East*, edited by William C. Adams (Norwood, NJ: Ablex Publishing Corp., 1981): 128–58; David L. Altheide, "Three-in-one News: Network Coverage of Iran," *Journalism Quarterly* Fall (1982): 482–6.

5   David L. Altheide, *Creating Fear: News and the Construction of Crisis* (Hawthorne, NY: Aldine de Gruyter, 2002); Frank Furedi, *Culture of Fear: Risk-Taking and the Morality of Low Expectation* (London: Cassell, 1997); Barry Glassner, *The Culture of Fear: Why Americans are Afraid of the Wrong Things* (New York: Basic Books, 1999).

6   Chalmers Johnson, *The Sorrows of Empire: Militarism, Secrecy, and the End of the Republic* (New York: Metropolitan Books, 2000); Kellner, *From 9/11 to Terror War*.

7   Douglas Kellner, "Media Propaganda and Spectacle in the War in Iraq: A Critique of US Broadcasting Networks," *Cultural Studies/Critical Methodologies* 4 (2004): 329–38.

8   Altheide, "Consuming Terrorism."

9   David Armstrong, "Dick Cheney's Song of America: Drafting a Plan for Global Dominance," *Harper's*, October, 2002, 76–83.

10   Elaine Sciolino and Alison Mitchell, "Calls for New Push into Iraq Gain Power in Washington," *New York Times*, December 3, 2001, 9.

11   Armstrong, "Dick Cheney's Song," 76.

12   Chalmers Johnson, *Blowback: The Costs and Consequences of American Empire* (New York: Metropolitan Books, 2000).

13   Elizabeth de la Vega, *The United States v. George W. Bush et al.* (New York: Seven Stories Press, 2006); Douglas Jehl and David Johnston, "Rule Change Lets C.I.A. Freely Send Suspects Abroad to Jails," *New York Times*, March 6, 2005, http://www. nytimes.com/2005/03/06/politics/06intel.html?ex=1110776400&en=e36cc36fc5ef2f8 1&ei=5070 (accessed October 2, 2009).

14   David L. Altheide and Jennifer N. Grimes, "War Programming: The Propaganda Project and the Iraq War," *The Sociological Quarterly* 46 (2005): 617–43.

15   Catherine Dodge, "Cheney Defends Iraq War, Says World Safer Today," *Bloomberg*, September 10, 2006, http://www.bloomberg.com/apps/news?pid=20601170&sid=aM uFuSmq5znA&refer=special_report (accessed October 2, 2009).

16   Frank Davies, "Many Americans Believe There Was a Link Between Iraq, Sept. 11," *San Jose Mercury News*, September 11, 2007.

17   Armstrong, "Dick Cheney's Song."

18   Andrew Bacevich, *American Empire: The Realities and Consequences of US Diplomacy* (Cambridge, MA: Harvard University Press, 2002); Robert Kagan, *Of Paradise and Power: America and Europe in the New World Order* (New York: Knopf, 2003); Robert Kagan and William Kristol, *Present Dangers: Crisis and Opportunity in American Foreign and Defense Policy* (San Francisco: Encounter Books, 2000).

19   Bacevich, *American Empire*; Benjamin R. Barber, *Fear's Empire: War, Terrorism, and Democracy* (New York: W.W. Norton & Co., 2003); Johnson, *Sorrows of Empire*; Robert D. Kaplan, "Supremacy by Stealth: Ten Rules for Managing the World," *The Atlantic Monthly*, July/August 2003, 66–90; Michael Mann, *Incoherent Empire* (London: Verso, 2003).

20   Altheide, *Terrorism and the Politics of Fear*; Kellner, *From 9/11 to Terror War*; Kellner, "Media Propaganda."

21   Altheide and Grimes, "War Programming."

22   Robert F. Worth, "Al Jazeera No Longer Nips at Saudis," *New York Times*, January 4, 2008, A1.

23   Armstrong, "Dick Cheney's Song," 78.

24   Ibid.

25   George Perkovich, "Bush's Nuclear Revolution: A Regime Change in Nonproliferation," *Foreign Affairs* March/April 2003, http://www.foreignaffairs.org /20030301facomment10334/george-perkovich/bush-s-nuclear-revolution-a-regime-change-in-nonproliferation.html (accessed October 2, 2009).

26   Stuart Allan and Barbie Zelizer, *Reporting War: Journalism in Wartime* (London: Routledge, 2004); W. Lance Bennett, *News: The Politics of Illusion* (New York: Pearson/ Longman, 2005); Kellner, "Media Propaganda."

27   Fairness and Accuracy in Reporting [FAIR], "In Iraq Crisis, Networks Are Megaphones for Official Views," *FAIR*, March 18, 2003, http://www.fair.org/index.php?page=3158 (accessed October 2, 2009).

28   Altheide and Grimes, "War Programming."

29   ABC News, "The Plan," *Nightline*, March 5, 2003.

30   John Stauber and Sheldon Rampton, *Toxic Sludge Is Good for You: Lies, Damn Lies, and the Public Relations Industry* (Monroe, ME: Common Courage Press, 1995).

31   Justin Baer and William J. Chambliss, "Generating Fear: The Politics of Crime Reporting," *Crime, Law and Social Change* 27 (1997): 87–107; Frankie Y. Bailey and Donna C. Hale, *Popular Culture, Crime, and Justice* (Belmont, CA: Wadsworth Pub. Co., 1998); Steven Chermak, *Victims in the News: Crime and the American News Media* (Boulder, CO: Westview Press, 1995); Edward J. Epstein, *News from Nowhere* (New York: Random House, 1973); Richard V. Ericson *et al.*, *Representing Order: Crime, Law and Justice in the News Media* (Toronto: University of Toronto Press, 1991); Richard V. Ericson *et al.*, *Visualizing Deviance: A Study of News Organization* (Toronto: University of Toronto Press, 1987); Glasgow University Media Group, *Bad News* (London: Routledge & Kegan Paul, 1976); Greg Philo and Glasgow University Media Group,

Really Bad News (London: Writers and Readers, 1982); Ray Surette, *Media, Crime and Criminal Justice: Images and Realities* (Belmont, CA: West/Wadsworth, 1998); Wallace Westfeldt and Tom Wicker, *Indictment: The News Media and the Criminal Justice System* (Nashville: First Amendment Center, 1998).

32   Altheide, "Consuming Terrorism."

33   Kellner, *From 9/11 to Terrorism.*

34   Karen A. Cerulo, "Individualism Pro Tem: Reconsidering US Social Relations," in *Culture in Mind: Toward a Sociology of Culture and Cognition*, edited by Karen A. Cerulo (New York: Routledge, 2002), 135–71.

35   Victor E. Kappeler *et al.*, *The Mythology of Crime and Criminal Justice* (Prospect Heights, IL: Waveland Press, 1999).

36   David Garland, *The Culture of Control: Crime and Social Order in Contemporary Society* (Chicago: University of Chicago Press, 2001).

37   Jim Rutenberg and Bill Carter, "Draping Newscasts with the Flag," *New York Times*, September 20, 2001, C8.

38   Matthew Engel, "War on Afghanistan: American Media Cowed by Patriotic Fever, Says Network News Veteran," *The Guardian*, May 17, 2002, 4.

39   Kellner, *From 9/11 to Terror War*, 68.

40   Rachel Newman, "The Day the World Changed, I Did, Too," *Newsweek*, October 1, 2001, 9.

41   Robert Jackall and Janice M. Hirota, *Image Makers: Advertising, Public Relations, and the Ethos of Advocacy* (Chicago: University of Chicago Press, 2000).

42   Advertising Research Foundation, "The ARF Supports Ad Council Coalition against Terrorism," *Informed*, December 2001, http:// www.arfsite.org/Webpages/informed/vol14-np6/page (accessed June 20, 2002).

43   Altheide, *Terrorism and the Politics of Fear.*

44   Sheryl Gay Stolberg, "President Signs New Rules to Prosecute Terror Suspects," *New York Times*, October 17, 2006, 20, http://query.nytimes.com/gst/fullpage.html?res=990DE1D71E30F93BA25753C1A9609C8B63&sec=&spon=&&scp=2&sq=Stolberg%20President%20signs%20new%20rules%20to&st=cse (accessed October 2, 2009).

45   Tracy Wilkinson, "Court Widens Net for 22 CIA Agents to EU; Italian Prosecutors Seek to Try the Operatives in the 2003 Abduction of an Imam on a Milan street. The Warrants Expand the Hunt to 25 Nations," *Los Angeles Times*, December 24, 2005: A3; Hugh Williamson, "Germany Pressed to Arrest CIA Team." *Financial Times*, September 22, 2006, 11.

46   Greg Gordon and Marisa Taylor, "US Interrogators May Not Be in the Clear Yet; Bill on Abuses Won't Stop Prosecutions in Other Countries, Experts Warn." *Sacramento Bee*, September 30, 2006, A16, http://web.lexis-nexis.com.ezproxy1.lib.asu.edu/universe/document?_m=d80652d20e771dc3cce2b25851fdad6f&_docnum=1&wchp=dGLbVzb-zSkVA&_md5=29a184922fe7c2c6ef498c271153e0c3.

47   Mediamatters.org., "Limbaugh on Torture of Iraqis: US Guards Were 'Having a Good Time,' 'Blow[ing] Some Steam Off,'" May 5, 2004, http://mediamatters.org/research/200405050003 (accessed October 2, 2009).

48   John R. MacArthur, "The Lies We Bought: The Unchallenged 'Evidence' for War," *Common Dreams*, May 1, 2003, http://www.commondreams.org/views03/0605-02.htm (accessed November 23, 2009).

49   Kellner, *From 9/11 to Terror War.*

50   "Ashcroft," *Star Tribune*, December 9, 2001, 30A.

51   Timothy Eagan, "In Sacramento, a Publisher's Questions Draw the Wrath of the Crowd," *New York Times*, December 21, 2001, Late Edition (East Coast), B1.

52   Torin Monahan, *Surveillance and Security: Technological Politics and Power in Everyday Life* (New York: Routledge, 2006).

53   Cheryl Phillips *et al.*, "Airport-Security System in US Riddled with Failures," *Seattle Times*, July 11, 2004, http://seattletimes.nwsource.com/html/localnews/2001976972_tsa11.html (accessed October 2 2009).

CHAPTER 2

The Aesthetics of Destruction: Contemporary US Cinema and TV Culture

MATHIAS NILGES

We have always been fascinated by cultural depictions of destruction. Destruction contains what William Butler Yeats famously calls a "terrible beauty."[1] Destruction is not just terrifying, but the spectacle of destruction, its overwhelming power and potential for radical change, has a distinct aesthetic, sublime appeal. Cultural representations of the large-scale destruction of cities, regions, nations, or our entire civilized world have a longstanding history in American cultural production, as we have seen in *The Towering Inferno* (Irwin Allen, 1974) or *The Day After* (Nicholas Meyer, 1983). However, especially in the context of the "War on Terror," we cannot simply understand the beauty contained in cultural representations of destruction throughout the last two decades as connected to the sublime appeal of the spectacular. Instead, we need to complicate the analysis of this specific kind of beauty by thinking of representations of destruction as narrative form, as a specific manifestation of culture's attempt to narrativize the relationship between our existence and the external world. In other words, the form of representations of destruction is contingent upon a specific historical context we need to examine to arrive at a detailed understanding of the forces that influence cultural form. The first step in such an analysis is to suggest that representations of destruction grow in number and popularity especially in times of (national) political, moral, and psychological uncertainty. Thus, we must analyze the beauty of such representations in relation to the specific fears, anxieties, and desires a historical period produces—psychological reactions that directly affect cultural form and our understanding of beauty. During the last two decades, we have witnessed another surge in the popularity of representations of destruction, specifically of (post) apocalyptic representations that depict large-scale destructions of civilization. What can we learn about the sociopolitical function of such representations when we locate them firmly within the historical context of the last few decades, specifically in the context of the "War on Terror"? Moreover, what can we learn about the psychological condition of our times by looking at the ways in which culture represents the dominant emotions that people feel about the historical situation they inhabit?

We can understand representations of destruction throughout the twentieth century as a popular way of working through or at least highlighting psychological contradictions produced by moments of severe crisis. During the Cold War, the fear of nuclear warfare or Communist invasion that dominated US society translated not surprisingly into various narratives of global destruction or hostile takeovers. Within the sociopolitical climate of the post-9/11 US, we see a renaissance of such narratives. The alien-invasion genre that functioned during the Cold War as a thinly-veiled vehicle for the fear of Communism reappears in the context of the contemporary fear of terrorism, just as the "body-snatcher" genre returns as a means of narrativizing the fear of an unseen ideological enemy: Communist, terrorist, or otherwise. Yet merely discussing representations of destruction and invasion as the result of a pervasive fear of the threat of terrorism neither allows for a rigorous analysis of the function of this cultural form, nor for a precise understanding of the kind of beauty it contains.

Looking at the beauty of destruction in a post-9/11 climate may seem counter-intuitive to arriving at an understanding of the contemporary relationship between cultural form and the psychological and sociopolitical constitution of the US. Yet, as we shall see, examining the beauty contained in representations of destruction helps get us beyond a mere analysis of dominant fears and enter into an analysis of how these fears are being resolved ideologically, sociopolitically and, ultimately, culturally. It is precisely this understanding of contemporary representations of destruction that I would like to propose here: in the aftermath of 9/11 and in the context of the "War on Terror," destruction functions culturally and primarily as a solution to the problems posed by a complex and anxiety-inducing present. The beauty contained in contemporary representations of destruction is thus less an immediate aspect of the sublime spectacle that is destruction itself but rather constitutes a result of the effect of destruction. Unlike Cold War-era representations of destruction that mediated a dominant fear of annihilation, contemporary representations of destruction are beautiful because destruction is in fact an antidote to a world that produces the fears we seek to escape.

How does this make sense, especially in the aftermath of 9/11 and during the "War on Terror," where the desire to prevent further destruction has caused a large-scale sociopolitical shift? To understand the relationship between destruction and beauty in contemporary cultural production, we need to understand the source of the fears and anxieties that define the contemporary moment, as well as the intricacies of the historical context that produces them. First, however, let us pause to consider some examples of the relationship between destruction and beauty. Contrary to what one would expect in the aftermath of 9/11, films such as *The Day After Tomorrow* (Roland Emmerich, 2004) and *I Am Legend* (Francis Lawrence, 2007) do not represent the destruction of New York City primarily as terrifying. Yes, the movies depict the large-scale devastation of the metropolis and of clearly recognizable icons of US civilization as a clearly disastrous event. What is more striking than the terrible beauty of the disaster itself, however, is the beautiful representation of life after the destruction. Destruction is not just beautiful as a spectacle, but it is retroactively endowed with beauty, since destruction makes possible a form of post-apocalyptic

Figure 1: Big game hunting in Manhattan

existence that is frequently portrayed as more enjoyable than our present. In *I Am Legend* this finds expression in the replacement of the chronological succession of events by a narrative that primarily focuses on the effects of destruction and only subsequently introduces the events that brought about the new situation. The film introduces the main character Robert Neville (Will Smith) by showing him hunting and picking corn in the romantic, pastoral setting of a post-destruction Manhattan. Wildlife has returned along with the pleasures and freedom of the simple life, sunsets are breathtaking, and the destroyed city is beautiful in its tranquility. Were it not for the carnivorous mutants that roam Manhattan's streets at night and the utter lack of social contact, Neville's life, it seems, would be perfect. Simply put, the destruction of civilization in itself is not necessarily terrifying. On the contrary, destruction creates beauty, and the horror of the film must develop by introducing a threat in the form of monstrous mutants and the theme of social isolation. Why, however, would life after the apocalypse frequently appear at least partially beautiful and enjoyable in contemporary cultural production?

The present in *The Day After Tomorrow* appears paralyzed by ecological and social problems (most notably homelessness and transnational migration). Luckily, the northern part of the globe is devastated by a new ice age, which brings about a revolution in consciousness that illustrates the necessity to rethink the dramatic global rift between the North and the South and the politics of ecology in the context of capitalism. Again, destruction is retroactively endowed with beauty, since destruction positively transforms the world and finds answers to the problems that plague our present existence and seem unsolvable. It only takes an ice age for the homeless African-American man and his dog to be allowed into the New York Public Library where a doorman previously did not grant them access. Similarly, the survivors of the catastrophe, including politicians, rediscover the value of collectivity and humanism only in the aftermath of the tragedy. Even the vice president (Kenneth Welsh), a thinly disguised Dick Cheney, can be humbled and educated by global destruction. During the era of the Cold War, the destruction of civilization was a problem (to put it mildly) and threatened to destroy the world we love. Contemporary representations of destruction, however, frequently portray the devastation of civilization as the antidote to a present we tend to dislike, a present that is in itself unstable, chaotic and threatening and which we cannot seem to change. Destruction is, therefore, not beautiful in itself but becomes associated with the beauty it can bring about, the beauty of an existence that is often represented as more enjoyable since simpler—if not more sublime—than our chaotic present. If this is true, what is it about the present we do not enjoy?

The Terror of a New World

In Astra Taylor's recent pseudobiographical documentary *Žižek!* (2005), cultural critic and philosopher Slavoj Žižek remarks that it seems strange that we seem to lack the ability to imagine smaller systemic changes that could improve US society while we are easily able to imagine scenarios of complete global devastation and destruction.[2] Though it does not offer an explanation for the phenomenon, Žižek's remark contains a suggestion that serves as a valuable basis for an inquiry into the psychic life of contemporary representations of destruction. As exemplified by *I Am Legend* and *The Day After Tomorrow*, destruction frequently functions as a way out of a present that has become threateningly complex in ways that make it virtually impossible to account for all the forces that determine individual and collective life.

Especially in the aftermath of the attacks of 9/11, the inability to rely upon traditional definitions of order, safety, and protection has become ever more apparent. The desire to respond to the fear of terrorism by returning to a state of national isolation clearly conflicts with the organization of the world market from which the US cannot withdraw. One of the main sources of post-9/11 paranoia results precisely from this new structure of the US in the context of a global economy. We are not only scared of new attacks, more importantly, we are frightened by the realization that we cannot realistically prevent attacks without risking, for example, the breakdown of the economy as an effect of re-erecting strict regulations and protective mechanisms that would contradict the logic of global trade. In times of globalization, the idea of a strong, protective nation state and a protected national market must be abandoned. Contrary to popular sensationalist claims, this means that 9/11 did not "make everything new." Rather, 9/11 dramatically amplified previously existing negative perceptions of the radical socioeconomic change the US (and the entire globe) underwent throughout the last few decades, changes that just as dramatically impacted the sociopolitical constitution of the US.

As the dominant socioeconomic system of the first half of the twentieth century began to face a crisis, the US and global capitalism itself resolved this crisis by reinventing its structural logic. Nations moved away from the protected, centralized, and standardized structures commonly described as "Fordist" (in reference to the ideal of Henry Ford's assembly line) and toward a deregulated, globalized, decentralized structure economists describe as "post-Fordist." This development began in the early 1960s, yet a dominant post-Fordist social and economic structure did not truly emerge until the late 1980s and early 1990s, by which time free market capitalism and technoculture began to constitute a globally pervasive force. Traditional power structures began to be deregulated along with economies and structures of trade, and moral and identity structures began to be replaced with the ideology of diversity and multiculturalism. Difference, pluralism, change, and productive chaos took the place of repetition, standardization, stability, and centralized order as the logic of a new world order economists frequently describe as "free-market anarchy."[3]

These developments, however, as cultural production illustrates, have not always exactly been cause for celebration. The emergence of the US as a globalized, post-Fordist nation in the late 80s and early 90s also created the widespread need for new forms of subjectivity. In this new socioeconomic situation, we must leave behind traditional models of identity and formulate "life-narratives" that allow us to navigate our way through a globalized planet. Yet, while the idea of leaving behind traditional forms of identity was frequently represented as pleasurable and desirable during the 60s, 70s, and early 80s, contemporary cultural production often represents giving up ideas such as home in favor of the idea of being a "global citizen" negatively.[4] A simple explanation for this difference may be that during the 60s and 70s superseding traditional "life-narratives" still seemed to contain the possibility of future liberation. Today, however, we *must* abandon tradition in favor of the new, at which point this mandatory, functional abandonment is less associated with liberation than with loss and instability. As a consequence, cultural production begins to be characterized by representations of the struggle with a large-scale transition into a world that is widely perceived as chaotic, complex, confusing, and threatening. The effects of 9/11 can be considered in this context. The fear of lack of control and stability represented in contemporary cultural production is not new and cannot simply be explained in reference to the "War on Terror." Instead, such cultural narratives indicate a more complex problem, namely the way in which the "War on Terror" is linked to a psychological struggle created by a radical socioeconomic shift that predates 9/11.

The connection between the "War on Terror" and what amounts to a widespread negative reaction to the socioeconomic transformation of the past few decades is a multi-faceted problem. At this point, contemporary cultural production is substantially shaped by the logical similarity between the form of subjectivity ideally suited for global capitalism and that of the terrorist. The global subject and the terrorist inhabit a post-national network society in which centralized order is replaced by the viral logic of technoculture. We can detect examples of this logical connection in the current popularity of disaster films that feature global viruses or zombies, an allegorical structure that is in *28 Weeks Later* (Juan Carlos Fresnadillo, 2007) especially clearly connected to the "War on Terror." In a present that is determined by a widespread rejection of the new deregulated forms of subjectivity the globalized world demands, hunting down the terrorist becomes an exercise in hunting down our own dark doubling. Consequently, the "War on Terror" has to be understood as at least partially motivated by the fight against the chaos and complexity of our own post-Fordist world. The "War on Terror" is in part an existential struggle marked by the displacement of the fight against the things we reject about our own identity but would like to repress. In other words, we have to fight the dark underbelly of our radically changed present (identity) "over there," outside of us, so we don't have to fight it "at home."

It is for this reason that fights against terrorism portrayed in contemporary culture must—as a general rule—be lost, as opposed to the time when globalization was not yet dominant (or at least the time before 9/11 shocked us into the realization that we can no longer avoid the new, dominant global socioeconomic structure). Characters like TV drama *24*'s (2001–present) Jack Bauer (Kiefer Sutherland) therefore synecdochically stand in for the general feeling of the absence of paternally protective structures and become a testament to the association of the present with the loss of traditional forms of stability and protection. Bauer fights the terrorist threat, yet at the end of each episode and each season there is no doubt that terrorism will re-appear and that Bauer will remain unable to truly protect the nation from a threat the way the Schwarzeneggers, Stallones and Willises of the 1980s still could.

The apparent trauma from the inability to formulate stable traditional life narratives, hence, becomes nowhere as obvious as in the general crisis of the figure of the white male action hero, who, especially in the aftermath of 9/11, is portrayed as increasingly unable to avert threats to family, community, and nation.[5] Consequently, both Jack Bauer and John McClane (Bruce Willis) in the latest installment in the *Die Hard* series, *Live Free or Die Hard* (2007), appear as solutions to terrorism that are remarkably atavistic and, especially significantly in the case of John McClane, impotent. Unlike previous versions, the contemporary John McClane of *Live Free or Die Hard* is entirely out of touch with the world. Individually, he is not merely unable to fight the attack on the US economy by cyberterrorists, but in fact requires the help of a young hacker to understand the problem. McClane's previous agency as defender is thus reduced to that of a comical sidekick whose exaggerated physical "solutions" to cyberproblems appear humorously out of place and, in their nostalgic nature, clearly underscore the death of the white male action hero as the anthropomorphized narrative of protection in the present world.

Similarly, we see a revival of narratives that fearfully reject radical reformulations of the idea of a human society and of what it means to be human. Whereas films such as *Blade Runner* (1982) famously argue for a progressive politics that abandons traditional understandings of humanity in order to arrive at a more tolerant and pluralistic idea of community, films like *I Am Legend* express a distinct fear of this loss of traditional definitions of subjectivity in a new, scary world. This fear becomes apparent in a scene in which Dr. Neville clearly and intentionally misinterprets the actions of a male mutant who exposes himself to lethal sunlight in a desperate attempt to reach his female partner whom Neville has trapped. In order to stabilize his own subjectivity, Neville is compelled to read this behavior not as group mentality and emotional attachment indicating the emergence of a new society that would make traditional humanity a "legend," but instead as the complete loss of reason and, therefore, of humanity. The subjectivity of the mutant consequently fuses the fear of a threatening world (terrorism and globalization) with the fear of a new, dominant form of subjectivity that corresponds to a new global situation. Neville responds to this problem by holding on to a traditional, clearly outdated definition of subjectivity and idealizing a return to a controllable, simplified past.

From Dread to Anxiety—The End of the Future

Cultural representations of large-scale destruction, however, do not merely function as mediations of problems of the present. Possibly just as (if not more) interesting for social and cultural critics are instances in which the logic of destruction is mobilized to restore future possibilities that appear to be lacking in the present. The crucial questions to ask here are: what is it that disrupts our imagination of the future and how is this impasse culturally resolved? In his latest book, *The Culture of the New Capitalism*, Richard Sennett examines reactions to the new life narratives that correspond to our present: we seem to associate the present with alienation and anxiety and develop a nostalgic attachment to the past that progressive movements of the 60s and 70s sought to supersede. Compared to our existence in the new capitalism, prior life narratives and forms of labor suddenly appear increasingly positive in their stability. They are at least characterized by the development of stable skills, the existence of a regulated workday, career, and social services provided by a strong state and a protective nation. However, as Sennett is quick to point out, this desire is not altogether logical, since instability, as noted by Marx, has always been essential to the capitalist mode of production (productive contradictions).[6] Still, he claims this nostalgic and reactionary response to the new capitalism has become widespread and is motivated by a logic of the "lesser evil." Even though Henry Ford, the personification of a centrally regulated socioeconomic structure, was dramatically unequal to his employees regarding wealth and power, at least he was closer to them in sociological terms, "just as the general on the battlefield was connected to his troops."[7] Thus there existed, at least on some level, a connection to what Sennett calls a "paternalistic" figure.[8] For Sennett the decision comes down to choosing between a social situation that induces "dread" and one that induces "anxiety": "anxiety attaches to what might happen; dread attaches to what one knows will happen. Anxiety arises in ill-defined conditions, dread where pain or ill-fortune is well defined. Failure in the old pyramid was grounded in dread; failure in the new institution is shaped by anxiety."[9] It is within such a perception of our present existence that cultural representations of destruction no longer merely signify as scary narratives of tragic events that disrupt a safe and happy existence.

Instead, such narratives represent destruction, if not positively, then at least as a means of destroying an anxiety-inducing present and returning to a dread-inducing past. In the "good old days" of Cold War culture, unlike times of globalization and terrorism, we at least knew who or what was threatening our existence. Destruction in contemporary culture is simplification, and simplification is represented as a good thing. Destruction, therefore, is associated with beauty because it allows us to return to those past structures that the US has superseded as a result of its recent, large-scale transformation, structures we appear to be unwilling to abandon, and, as suggested by contemporary cultural production, to which we form nostalgic attachments. Psychologically and ideologically, we seem to lag behind the forward progress of a rapidly changing new world. The imagined destruction of this new world reverses a progress we often do not approve of and promises safety via the return to a simpler and more controllable past. We can thus propose this partial explanation for Žižek's challenge: we become unable to imagine a better future because we locate the solution to present problems in a return to a nostalgically idealized version of the past. This return is made possible by large-scale destruction. Consequently, contemporary representations of the future frequently do not represent the future per se but rather a future return to the past.

The appeal of contemporary destruction films is that post-destruction societies present simplified versions of life that stand opposed to the complexity of our present. US literary and cultural critic Fredric Jameson describes this contemporary problem as a problem of "cognitive mapping."[10] In order to answer the question of who we are and in order to understand our existence in relation to the world that surrounds us we draw cognitive maps. A present that is complex and unrepresentable to the degree that it becomes impossible to draw such a map of our existence produces feelings of unease and anxiety that, in turn, give rise to desires for simplification, for the return to an idealized time when it was supposedly easier to articulate our existence in relation to the world that surrounded us. However, such desires are clearly problematic, since this past we tend to romanticize is clearly a simulacrum.[11] While this objection is certainly valid, the study of such illogical desires remains crucial. However simulated the version of the past that is represented as a post-destruction ideal may be, it can provide us with a rather accurate index of the forces that simulate it. Put differently, cultural representations of future solutions to present problems that regressively seek answers in a return to an idealized past can provide us with valuable insights into the psychological constitution of the present.

The Terror of the Absent Father

The regressive desires that underlie these narratives do not merely bring about the positive return to the desired stability and simplicity of social arrangements corresponding to previous moments in history. The beauty of destruction that masks the nostalgia and desire for simplification and regression emerging out of the present also obscures another concrete sociopolitical effect that is closely connected to the work of contemporary culture: the inevitable resurrection of those power structures that correspond to the "good old days." The most noticeable example of such an atavistic power structure that begins to resurface in cultural production is that of paternalism. In a global socioeconomic situation that is founded on decidedly anti-paternalistic structures (diversity, difference, deregulation, the abolition of restricting forms of bureaucracy, production, and national protectionism that stands in conflict with the nature of global trade and production, in short, free-market anarchism), paternalism becomes part of those structures that paradoxically begin to be perceived positively. Whereas progressive movements of the 60s and 70s fought paternalism (in its various manifestations as hegemonic production, gender norms, nationalism, moral and identity structures that resulted in exclusion and domination), the loss of paternalistic structures in the present, especially after 9/11, is increasingly understood not as liberating but as frightening. We also have lost other traditional structures of protection and stability that are connected to the logic of fathering, as well as universal structures upon which we could ground stable life narratives. The loss of paternalism does not equate to the absence of repression and oppressive order, but to the lack of stability and protection. One of the most frequent narratives within cultural representations of the desire to return to prior moments in history and/or reject the present state of the world is the narrative of the absent, troubled, or impotent father (be this the father of the family, the father of/as the nation, or father as God/heavenly father). Consequently, the return to paternalism and the restoration of the strong father becomes positively associated with the rejection of an unpleasant present.

It is not difficult to find other examples of contemporary representations of anxiety and loss that channel this psychological condition through the narrative of the lost or weak father. The TV dramas *Lost* (2004–present) and *Invasion* (2005–06) allegorize the general feeling of loss of traditional subjectivity and forms of stability and order in a post-Fordist world, especially in the context of the "War on Terror." This narrative is humorously exaggerated in the rather unfit father in *Family Guy* (1999–present) and the hypermasculine, hyperpatriotic, governmental-agent father in *American Dad* (2005–present), who illustrates the regressive ideological connection between patriotism, national protection, and paternalistic logic in the context of the "War on Terror." However, whereas shows such as *Lost*, *American Dad*, or *The Sopranos* caricature or criticize regressive paternalistic desires, shows such as *Jericho* (2006–present) represent the return to traditional gender conventions in an increasingly uncritical manner.

The return to the nuclear family and to traditional conceptions of masculinity becomes part of the enjoyable outcome of the destruction of the present that allows for return to a better time. In fact, we can note a general regressive trend in contemporary culture that re-legitimizes traditional gender roles and norms. As critics such as Susan Faludi note, hypermasculinity in cultural representation is a rather traditional response to moments of national instability that are regressively equated to threats to masculinity.[12] Hence, concepts such as order and control are gendered and frequently produce a "crisis of masculinity" once threatened. Yet, it is not sufficient to suggest that we have entered another period that is determined by a crisis of masculinity. In order to understand the complexities of contemporary cultural production, it is necessary to examine the context that produces the crisis of masculinity as a symptom and to which narratives of hypermasculinity and paternalistic order are a solution. As suggested above, we must locate the present surge in such cultural narratives in the context of the socioeconomic shift that became dominant during the late 1980s and early 1990s and which is ideologically connected to and dramatically amplified by the "War on Terror."

Examining cultural representation in this context illustrates that the transition into a new socioeconomic structure is—from the moment this structure begins to become dominant—represented as a threat to masculinity. Examples of this emerging cultural narrative that rose to dominance alongside the post-Fordist economy include shows such as *Who's the Boss?* (1984–92), the story of a former professional athlete turned single father and professional housekeeper. *Who's the Boss?* displays the association of a newly emerging era defined by the struggle for masculinity and the threat of "feminization." The beginning dominance of white collar labor and the increasing obsolescence of the white, male, physically laboring body in the context of emerging technoculture begin to be represented as a new socioeconomic structure that has a feminizing effect. Hence, existence in the new world creates anxieties that produce regressive desiring structures, which in turn revive the investment in definitions of labor and masculinity that remain tied to the physically laboring body. Such nostalgic desires that stand opposed to present subjectivity have come to define the cultural representation of the last two decades. Films such as *Fight Club* (1999) and *American Psycho* (2000) overtly represent the present, immaterial economy as feminized, producing forms of anxiety and alienation that only the return of (male) physicality, the father, and patriarchy can solve. Aware of the prevalence of this regressive cultural narrative in times of the "War on Terror," shows such as *Lost* satirize male angst in the form of characters such as John Locke (Terry O'Quinn) whom the island allows to develop from a paraplegic into a strong hunter with an ultimate sense of purpose. Shows such as *Jericho* and *Invasion*, however, allow for the celebration of traditional masculinity and the re-centering of the male laboring body as a result of the post-apocalyptic return to the good old times. As exemplified by the reality show *Survivor* (2000–present), this return is frequently associated with an idealized return to nature as the locus of stable identity and the necessity of developing skills that suggest more control over one's existence and survival than existence in our hypertechnologized world tends to offer. It is in relation to this regressive gender-political trend that we can explain the current fascination with reality shows such as *The Deadliest Catch* (2005-present), *Man vs. Wild* (2005–present), *Survivorman* (2004–present), and *Dirty Jobs* (2003–present).

The wish to return to a world in which we are safe from the chaotic threat of global terrorism as well as the complexities of post-Fordist subjectivity, however, creates a problem for the contemporary imaginary, since such an existence is far from readily available. It is at this point that destruction emerges as the beautiful answer in its ability to bring about the desired radical simplification and regression. Destruction is beautiful because it makes it possible, as the character Anna (Alice Braga) puts it toward the end of *I Am Legend*, to once again "hear the word of God" because the world has become quiet. Amid the contemporary "War on Terror" that amplifies the anxieties of a post-Fordist world, the answer to the present becomes destruction that promises solutions provided by the *deus ex terra silentia*. Yet these solutions to the defining psychological struggle of our age present at the same time one of the most pressing sociopolitical problems. Especially in the context of the "War on Terror," culture takes on an increasingly vital role in the process of working through this psychological struggle, and, especially in the aftermath of 9/11, we consequently must be aware of the great responsibility that comes with our participation in the proliferation, contestation, and the enjoyment of spectacularly destructive cultural engagements with our current psychological condition.

Notes

1   See W.B. Yeats, "Easter, 1916," http://www.online-literature.com/yeats/779/ (accessed October 4, 2009).

2   Fredric Jameson first presents a version of this argument in *The Seeds of Time* (New York: Columbia University Press, 1994).

3   For an in-depth analysis of the shift from Fordism to post-Fordism and its sociopolitical consequences see Michael Aglietta, *A Theory of Capitalist Regulation* (New York: Verso, 2000).

4   For a detailed discussion of this perception of the present see Zygmunt Bauman, *Liquid Times: Living in an Age of Uncertainty* (Cambridge: Polity, 2007).

5   Especially significant here is the delayed release of Andrew Davis's 2002 film *Collateral Damage*. Initially scheduled for release in October 2001, the film was not merely too poignant and timely, but its plot that revolves around a firefighter played by Arnold Schwarzenegger who brings the terrorists who killed his family to justice appears, as argued above, too obviously archaic in its ideology.

6   Richard Sennett, *The Culture of the New Capitalism* (New Haven & London: Yale University Press, 2006), 7–16.

7   Ibid., 55.

8   Ibid.

9   Ibid., 53.

10 Fredric Jameson, *Postmodernism or, The Cultural Logic of Late Capitalism* (Durham, NC: Duke University Press, 1991), 51–4.

11 The concepts "simulacrum" and "simulation" are borrowed from Jean Baudrillard, *Simulacra and Simulation* (Ann Arbor: University of Michigan Press, 1995).

12 See Susan Faludi's *Stiffed: The Betrayal of the Modern Man* (London: Chatton & Windus, 1999) and *The Terror Dream* (New York: Metropolitan Books, 2007).

CHAPTER 3

9/11, British Muslims, and Popular Literary Fiction

SARA UPSTONE

Terrorist policies may also be implemented, fear and compliance may be sought or achieved, through the construction of a collective enemy, through discursively dis-placing threat to one or more distant Others, through scare stories and fear-mongering. [...] Through success-fully perpetuating "imaginative geographies" of Their Terrorist/Arab/ Muslim space and Their uncivilized, subhuman barbarism. Through successfully folding distance into monstrous Difference. Through successfully insisting that They are a pervasive military threat to Our Civilization, to the security of Our way of life [...] Through suc-cessfully implanting a just-below-the-surface sense of fear by way of redundant representations strewn across the paths of everyday life.[1]

As the above epigraph suggests, terror comes in a plethora of disguises: the waves resonating out from a terrorist attack produce a ripple of fear which extends long after the initial event. Even when direct experience has dulled and faded, fear continues. In the wake of terror, the need to imagine a terrorist subject—to put a face to the threat—is essential for both a sense of personal security and for driving and justifying reactions to the initial event. An identification of the "next terrorist" becomes essential. What Pred calls "imaginary geographies" are the means by which the "next terrorist" can be located. This subject outside of the "safe" space of the quotidian is not merely a subject of an imagined geography, however, but also an "imagined body" and an "imagined culture": identified, it seems, not just through where he/she is located but through his/her appearance and way of life. Not only places, but physical appearances, movements, life practices, indicate the "next ter-rorist" in the midst of safety. What results is an "imagined identity": the "other" in "our" midst who must be identified, scrutinized, and—ultimately—either rejected or reformed. In their representations of the British Muslim subject, contemporary novels such as Zadie Smith's *White Teeth* and Hanif Kureishi's *The Black Album* reinforce this "imagined other," even before the events of 9/11. In this context, more recent representation of terror in Ian McEwan's *Saturday*, Monica Ali's *Brick Lane*, or Nadeem Aslam's *Maps for Lost Lovers* must be viewed not only within the context of post-9/11 relations but also as part of a broader imagining of the Muslim subject as threatening "other." These texts draw attention to the powerful function of popular literary fiction in creating imagined identities: a function that has been both overlooked and underestimated in contrast to other modes of representation.

In reporting terrorism, the media offers a physical representation of the subject, which allows the public to imagine the threat against its own "safe" space with an unparalleled detail in direct opposition to the ambiguity often surrounding the terrorist's actual identity. It is only a small step from identifying the perpetrators of a terrorist act to transferring the detailed picture assembled from media representation into a "wanted" poster of the "next terrorist." Gradually, subjects who fit this imagined identity become, even when the threat of terrorism has faded, associated with this imagined identity: no longer the "next terrorist," perhaps, but nevertheless tarred with a residual "otherness."

In this sense, 9/11 and its aftermath provided a watershed moment for representations of British Muslims, which transformed the representation of ethnic groups, resonating far beyond initial events. American media attention on 9/11 and its aftermath created an "imagined identity" of the "other" which was Muslim, defined not simply as dangerous but in terms of a number of associated behaviors.[2] British culture consumed American attitudes, creating quickly a discourse not simply of the "other" but the "other within."[3] Inflammatory publications such as Melanie Phillips' *Londonistan* and the Institute for the Study of Islam and Christianity's *Islam in Britain: The British Muslim Community in February 2005* presented a dangerous post-9/11 world where British Muslims threatened the cohesion of British society. Yet many media commentators have pointed to the ways in which reaction to 9/11 must be seen within the context of Said's theory of Orientalism (1978): the fear of the Muslim, they suggest, is an extension of the "othering" of the Muslim subject throughout history.[4]

Although there are equally well noted limitations to Said's theory; nevertheless, his focus on the Orient as imagined threat continues to be relevant in contemporary contexts. In *Covering Islam* (1981), Said himself draws attention to how Western media repeats Orientalist stereotypes in constructing the "threatening Arab" and the "Muslim fundamentalist." Ziauddin Sardar argues that "Orientalism is very much alive in contemporary cultural practice [...] reworked [...] from one historical epoch to another."[5] New terms—anti-Arab racism and Islamophobia—have emerged.[6] Yet Orientalism continues to be a useful framework, particularly in a British context where the majority of Muslims are not Middle Eastern, but South Asian. Their Muslim identity has seen them subject to the same representation as those from the Middle East, making the use of Orientalism to describe the treatment of this group most appropriate, representing as it does the specific focus on the Muslim "other" but at the same time the identification with the "East," which must be seen as an integral part of the contemporary stereotyping of Muslims.

There has been little discussion of how popular literature informs such imagined identities. Knowledge and writing is central to Orientalist attitudes[7] but Said

focuses largely on nineteenth-century literary representation, and popular literature has received only limited comments in works inspired by Said's theories.[8] In
particular, attention can be drawn to popular literary fiction: those texts straddling
the worlds of mass literary consumption and serious literary critical debate. Such
texts are particularly important because of their rather contradictory positioning.
Selling hundreds of thousands of copies, these texts have the potential to contribute
significantly to how ordinary consumers construct imagined identities. Yet, as prize-
winners and university reading, access to serious literary critical debate also allows
these texts to impact upon wider cultural practice. Popular literary fiction representing the British Muslim has been profoundly influenced by American post-9/11
attitudes to the potential threat of Islamic fundamentalism and the consequential
"imagined identity" of the Muslim. Yet examining literary fiction both before and
after 9/11 calls attention to how awareness of the "othering" of Islam, and British
Muslims more specifically, must also be situated within a wider understanding of
what must be termed Orientalist attitudes. In this sense, literary representation
echoes analysis of media discourse which has stressed that, contrary to the idea
that 9/11 represented a "watershed moment," what in fact post-9/11 representation
offered was only an escalation of and support to existing stereotypes of Muslim
communities.[9]

Pre-9/11 Literary Fiction

A pre-9/11 imagined British Muslim identity, often with negative connotations,
clearly exists in popular literary fiction. The visions of Islamic fundamentalism
offered by Hanif Kureishi's *The Black Album* and Zadie Smith's *White Teeth*, for
example, represent Islam as the most dangerous and current threat to British
democracy. *The Black Album* is contextualized by acts of violence in London, as a
"bomb had exploded on the main concourse of Victoria Station."[10] Based on real
events, the bombing can be placed as a reference to the IRA terror campaign. Yet,
significantly, the IRA is not mentioned in the text. Instead, the bombing campaign
comes to stand for a more general threat of violence, which, by the end of the novel,
is no longer in the hands of the IRA but Riaz and his gang, as the novel culminates
with a fatal firebombing. Islam comes to be represented as the unknown threat, the
dangerous "other" in the midst of "civilization," in a strategy which can be seen to
precede recent media reporting and government action in which the ambiguous
nature of the threat "allowed the actors to name the terrorist enemy as and when
it became necessary."[11] Although the real threat at this time is Irish nationalism,
Kureishi's ambiguity encourages the reader—in the context of the central Muslim
characters—to give their own, Islamic, face to the perpetrators:

> What did they feel? Confusion and anger, because somewhere outside lurked armies
> of resentment. But which faction was it? Which underground group? Which war,
> cause or grievance was being demonstrated? The world was full of seething causes
> which required vengeance—that at least was known.[12]

Equally, in Zadie Smith's *White Teeth*, devout Islam is represented as a violent threat. As with *The Black Album*, one of the central protagonists, named Millat, has turned towards radical Islam. At the end of the novel, Millat is involved in a shooting that results in the injury of another of the central characters.

In both *The Black Album* and *White Teeth*, however, representation of strong Islamic belief reflects not events in the Middle East but rather an internal literary dialogue about the role of literature originating in the reception of Rushdie's *The Satanic Verses*. Whilst debates over the book's alleged offensiveness are too numerous to recount, the reaction to protests against the book indicate the re-making of Orientalist stereotypes,[13] frequently casting Muslim protesters as "irrational, fanatical, and violent."[14] Both *The Black Album* and *White Teeth* make explicit reference to "The Satanic Verses Affair" without giving the objections of the Muslim community any serious consideration: in *The Black Album* the book is simply "insulting,"[15] whilst in *White Teeth* Millat protests despite the fact that he "knew nothing about the writer, nothing about the book."[16] The Muslim reaction is cast as purely ignorant and uninformed, whilst we are offered a defense of literature as social force, dividing Islam from the West. This is exemplified in Shahid's debate on literature with his Muslim "brothers." Shahid's defense of books is that they "make us think."[17] Riaz's reply—"What is there to think?"[18]—represents Islam as closed-minded. An equally strong satirical tone furthermore presents the Muslim position as ludicrous. In *The Black Album* the fact that the sign which motivates the young men to act is a "holy eggplant"[19] makes the men appear absurd. In the same way, the fact that the group Millat goes on to join is entitled KEVIN pronounces that it should not be taken seriously.

In the wake of debates surrounding free speech and liberal freedom, Orientalism metamorphoses here into a discourse of postmodern fluidity. Opposing alleged Muslim rigidity is both Orientalist and postmodern, as the Orientalist trope of freedom becomes postmodern hybridity and movement, the celebration of the shifting signifier, and the rejection of the grand narrative of religion. Riaz's "single-mindedness" to Shahid makes him "pitiful"[20] so that, whilst Kureishi has some sympathy with the men and the value of religious faith, his ultimate belief in the hybrid, free-floating identity of postmodern discourse prevents an ultimate engagement with those who hold belief in universal truths and values.[21] In the same way, Muslim radicals are at the center of the denial of the twin pillars of freedom and rationality for Smith: Islam turns Millat not only against arts but also against science, represented in the "FutureMouse" experiment. Although FutureMouse is presented ambiguously, nevertheless it is significant that it is KEVIN who are at the center of protests against it:

> There is a man who presumes to change, adjust, modify what has been decreed. He will take an animal—an animal that Allah has created—and presume to change that creation. To create a new animal that has no name but is simply an abomination.[22]

Archie's celebration of the mouse's escape on the novel's final pages is metaphoric for the celebration of hybridity, of freedom, of movement: the same postmodern qualities Kureishi, too, valorizes. Once again, therefore, in rejection of the mouse, Muslims are represented as against these values: they are again "othered" against postmodernity but also against the Western Orientalist values it echoes.

Post-9/11

In the wake of these representations, post-9/11 content is less a reaction to a "watershed" moment and more a continuation of pre-existing Orientalism. 9/11 transformed these stereotypes, but it did not bring them into being; rather, it acted as the catalyst for a more vociferous engagement with Muslim identity, with resulting reciprocal increase in the strength of the "imaginary identity" of Islam.

Perhaps the first novel to engage specifically with 9/11 in this context is Monica Ali's *Brick Lane*. In some senses, this novel *does* offer a counter-discourse to post-9/11 Orientalism. Keen to point out the distance most Muslims feel from perpetrators of terrorism, the central Muslim character Chanu proclaims "The world has gone mad"[23] as he watches media coverage of the plane crashes. Yet even a novel, which, on one level is counter-discourse, may promote Orientalist stereotypes. In *Brick Lane* the Muslim world is seen only through letters written to the central protagonist Nanzeen by her sister Hasina, a world defined by suffering, exploitation, and backwardness.[24] Against this, the end of the novel, in which we are told "This is England [...] You can do whatever you like," repeats Kureishi's dichotomous opposition between Western freedom and Muslim constraint. More concerned with internal hypocrisy than white attitudes, the narrative sides with the white press by drawing attention to the community's failure to engage with its own problems: "There were no gangs at all. The white press had made them up to give Bangladeshis a bad name [...] Not so long ago, Karim had used the word freely."[25]

These small echoes of media representation point to a wider tendency that is less generous. Whilst *Brick Lane* stresses post-9/11 radical sentiment as a passing reaction, by the end of the novel a new generation emerges who "wouldn't go for Jihad in some faraway place. There's enough to do here."[26] In contrast, both Nadeem Aslam's *Maps for Lost Lovers* and Ian McEwan's *Saturday* present more pervasive social divides, which are more terrifying and thus more tuned into the discourse of fear offered in media representations. Such writings can be considered within the definition of what Cindi Katz refers to as "banal terrorism": the everyday imaginings of the threat of a dangerous other, which leads to distinctions between "them" and "us."[27] In both *Saturday* and *Maps* terror comes into the heart of everyday life, and terrorism is woven into the very fabric of ordinary existence. In the former, McEwan presents a novel in which the home of the central protagonist is invaded; in the latter, an honor killing and its consequences disrupt the mundane lives of a British Muslim community. Akin to post-9/11 fears, the "other" is offered as a fixed and permanent presence with the potential to slip unnoticed into the heart of "civilization."

McEwan's *Saturday* does not explicitly explore British Muslim identity. It is essentially a parable, however, in which the concept of "banal terrorism" is central. Set on the day of the anti-Iraq War demonstrations in 2003, it parallels a personal attack on the life of a London neurosurgeon, Henry Perowne, with debates surrounding entering into a post-9/11 war with Iraq to produce a "high-handed attempt to pair global and local terror [...] barbarism or invasion."[28] When Perowne's home is invaded by a mysterious figure known only as "Baxter," his earlier ambiguity regarding war is replaced with a resolution that offers a comment on government intervention in the Middle East. Invading Perowne's family home, Baxter is the "banal terrorist." As Lee Siegel, the only reviewer to pick up on this direct parallel, notes: "there is the car accident, which echoes the sudden upheaval of 9/11, and which brings into Henry's life Baxter, a disenfranchised person, who is a kind of echo of the hatred and anger of the disenfranchised, militant, impoverished Third World."[29] In other words, Baxter is the terrorist made "domestic"—the personalized version of the Muslim threat. Baxter may not literally be identified as a Muslim (he is undescribed and his ethnic identity is not commented upon), but within the setting of McEwan's book and its focus on the Gulf War this is the natural role he takes in the parable, just as in the 1980s he would have been most likely associated by the reader with the IRA.

McEwan's rendering of the terrorist as a domestic threat is the most subtle example of popular literary fiction placing terror at the center of normal, everyday life. It unites *Saturday*, nevertheless, with a novel such as *Maps*, which reinforces these oppositions on a more direct scale. Here, strong Muslim belief is represented by the central female character of Kaukab, a devout Muslim. Her views are seen as uncompromising, harsh, and filled with vitriolic and bigoted hatred: she declares "England is a dirty country, an unsacred country full of people with disgusting habits and practices."[30] The alternative, the novel suggests, is not a more nuanced possibility *within* Islam that reflects its diversity,[31] but rather a Westernized, liberal, secular ideology, such as that adopted by her husband Shamas and their children. The fact that these latter individuals are involved in adultery and visually explicit art does nothing to prevent them being presented as positive models against Kaukab's belief system. This again mirrors the circumstances in Kureishi's and Smith's novels, in which "traitors to their faith" and "unpalatable personifications of Western technocracy" both "escape disaster unharmed."[32]

On one level, such juxtaposition is driven by a post-9/11 sensibility. What *Maps* offers is a community, it seems, willing to kill for its faith—however misguided. The association of Muslims most prominently with irrational and unjustifiable violence is a post-9/11 remaking of the barbaric Oriental into an even more dramatic and menacing form. In the same way, some elements of the novel are particularly related to a post-Rushdie Orientalism: the association in *Maps* of Islam with strict values, against Western freedom of expression, is reinforced by Shamas' love of literature, his past in Pakistan as a Communist organizer of poetry readings by exiled poets, and his own experience—echoing Rushdie—of being the author of a "destroyed" literary work.

Much of the representation in *Maps*, however, is not explicitly post-9/11 or post-Rushdie. Although these events lead to specific reference to issues of terror or censorship, they do not account for the more generalized characterization of Muslim characters. These, rather, offer the strongest evidence for a continuance of earlier prejudices against Islam in classic Orientalist fashion. Kaukab is literally dehumanized by her daughter, who describes her as "the most dangerous animal she'll ever have to confront."[33] As she starves her baby son by refusing to breast feed him during daylight hours of Ramadan, Kaukab has—echoing a figure such as Lady Macbeth—seemingly denied an implied "normal" biological programming and become more animal than human.[34] Thus as the colonist would justify colonization on the basis of the inferior native, proven through racial science and theories of polygenesis, so figures such as Kaukab provide the continued subject matter for such dubious racial hierarchies.

What ultimately affirms the novel's Orientalism, however, is how the central events are reinforced by a layering of incidences, which together build an overwhelming picture of Islam as barbaric. The honor killing in *Maps* is contextualized by additional incidences. In one, a holy man conducts an exorcism, which results in a young girl's death. This scene, unrelated to the personal relationships of the novel, is recounted in great detail, the girl forced to stand on a red hot metal tray, her arms and legs broken with a cricket bat.[35] In another incident, again not plot-related, the religious community's brutality is added to with a representation of their sexual depravity as a Muslim cleric is reported for sexually assaulting young children.[36] Here, the old stereotype of the Oriental as sexual predator resurfaces.[37] The community suggests that the failed exorcism does not disprove the existence of Ginns, furthering itself an additional stereotype of magic, witchcraft, and supernatural irrationality.[38]

Such problematic representations *are* challenged by some popular and literary works. Nadine Gordimer's *The Pickup*, written shortly before 9/11 but in the wake of increased concerns about Islamic fundamentalism, for example, represents Islam as a faith engaged in debate and modernization, rather than consumed by the protection of tradition.[39] Equally, more humorous and ironic engagements with Orientalism can also be found, for example, in Randa Abdel-Fattah's children's novel *Does My Head Look Big in This?* that charts a young Muslim woman's decision to wear the hijab:

> School from Year Seven to Year Ten was Hidaya—The Guidance—Islamic College. Where they indoctrinate students and teach them how to form Muslim ghettos, where they train al-Qaeda for school camp and sing overseas national anthems. Not![40]

In these terms, the most powerful comparison to be made is between those texts I have focused on here—written by British writers—and those which address Muslim life in Britain from an alternative perspective: those writers who come from outside Britain and write not of British Muslims but Muslims in Britain. Against the motifs of violence and social alienation presented in relation to the British Muslim, the Muslim in Britain is often represented as a figure conversely of peace. Most notable in this regard in works written in English is the writing of Sudanese writer Leila Aboulela, whose first novel *The Translator* presents an acceptance of Islam as a positive and nonthreatening force that "draws Western emptiness into a rooted Islamic-African core"[41] and whose second novel *Minaret* presents religious faith not as the source of confusion but rather as respite from it. In this latter, post-9/11 novel, the central male character, deeply interested in Islam, is distinguished from the concept of terrorism: his involvement in the mosque and desire to study Islamic Studies do not make him a potential terrorist. Nor do those around him, such as his mother, approve of this possible development:

> Once or twice he did sound fanatical, nagging me and Lamya to wear the hijab, making a fuss because I smoked—but he kept his limits, he was never extreme [. . .] At times I worried that he was spending too much time at the mosque. Maybe, I thought, a terrorist group would mess up his mind and recruit him but thankfully he's not interested in politics, so that's a relief.[42]

As a whole, therefore, the Muslim community is not excusing of violence, as Ali's characters sometimes are, but are rather presented as conscientious and socially responsible: concerned about the dangers of radicalism but firmly distinguishing this from devout faith. What these novels offer, therefore, is a much more sharply nuanced and complex sense of Muslim identity: not simply secular versus terrorist but with the possibility of a devout – yet tolerant, modern, rational, and peaceful – religious practice. Rather than repeating the media stereotype of "ordinary" being equated with the irreligious,[43] as Kureishi, Smith, Ali and Aslam can be seen to do, here there is a natural, and unthreatening, profound faith.

Conclusion

On the whole, whilst literary fiction may aim to complicate and contextualize post-9/11 stereotypes of the British Muslim, its overall representation must be seen as a depressingly static reflection of, rather than challenge to, these stereotypes. Rather than a counter-discourse, what British Muslim authors seem to indicate most noticeably is a model of what Nevzat Soguk refers to as the "Orientalized Oriental":

> S/he announces her/himself to be "post-Oriental" or "postcolonial," yet is a practicing member of the "Orientalising" praxis in its daily operations in the interdisciplinary realms of art, aesthetics, folklore, media, education, and so on. S/he is the non-Western subject who makes her/himself largely in the image of the West, its experiences, designs, and its expectations. In spite of endless assurances to her/himself to the contrary, for her/him the "West" is always more intelligible and fulfilling, and thus more attractive than the East.[44]

To identify Islam in this Orientalist fashion is not just prejudiced; it is not just offensive. It is also dangerous. As Michael Watts has argued, Islam's rejections of the West "are not the product of superstition and ignorance" but of a "radically hybrid project."[45] To not acknowledge this is thus to underestimate any opposition that might exist: to truly come to terms with al-Qaeda one must accept a postmodern identity, with "no fixed abode,"[46] driven by new media technologies[47] and capable of being re-made anew as its existence is more virtual than physical. With the US offering an equally imagined American reality,[48] to continue to imagine Islam in such limited colonial terms underestimates its power as a discourse "at once universalist, multicultural, and internationalist"[49] against Westernization, perhaps, but not against modernization.[50] Yet—more crucially—it also prevents the necessary dialogue between those with different political or religious perspectives, which is vital for a more peaceful future. British Muslims are more complex than British popular literary fiction on the whole suggests, and without such acknowledgment there seems little hope of meaningful cultural exchange.

Notes

1 Allan Pred, "Situated Ignorance and State Terrorism," in *Violent Geographies: Fear, Terror, and Political Violence*, eds Derek Gregory and Allan Pred (New York: Routledge, 2007), 364.

2 Derek Gregory and Allen Pred, "Introduction," *Violent Geographies: Fear, Terror, and Political Violence* (New York: Routledge, 2007), 1–6.

3 See Tahir Abbas, "British South Asian Muslims: Before and After September 11," in *Muslims in Britain: Communities Under Pressure*, ed. Tahir Abbas (London: Zed, 2005), 4; Chris Allen, "From Race to Religion: the New Face of Discrimination," in *Muslims in Britain: Communities Under Pressure*, ed. Tahir Abbas (London: Zed, 2005), 51; Elizabeth Poole, *Reporting Islam* (London: I.B. Tauris, 2002), 13.

4 Poole, *Reporting Islam*, 2, 16.

5 Ziauddin Sardar, *Orientalism* (Buckingham: Open University Press. 1999), 107.

6 Steven Salaita, "Beyond Orientalism and Islamophobia: 9/11, Anti-Arab Racism, and the Mythos of National Pride," in *The New Centennial Review* 6.2 (2006), 245–65.

7 Malcolm D. Brown, "Orientalism and Resistance to Orientalism: Muslim Identities in Contemporary Western Europe," in *Practicing Identities: Power and Resistance*, eds Sasha Roseneil and Julie Seymour (Basingstoke: Palgrave Macmillan, 1999), 182.

8 Sardar, *Orientalism*.

9 Poole, *Reporting Islam*, 2.

10 Hanif Kureishi, *The Black Album* (London: Faber, 1995), 101.

11 Poole, *Reporting Islam*, 3.

12 Kureishi, *The Black Album*, 103.

13 Ahsan and A.R. Kidwai, eds, *Sacrilege Versus Civility: Muslim Perspectives on The Satanic Verses Affair*. Revised expanded edn (Leicester: The Islamic Foundation, 1993), 26.

14 Humayun Ansari, *The Infidel Within: Muslims in Britain since 1800* (London: Hurst and Company, 2004), 9.

15 Kureishi, *The Black Album*, 68.

16 Zadie Smith, *White Teeth* (London: Hamish Hamilton, 2000), 202.

17 Kureishi, *The Black Album*, 184.

18 Ibid.

19 Ibid., 170.

20 Ibid., 173–4.

21 Hanif Kureishi, "The Road Exactly," in Introduction to "My Son the Fanatic" screenplay, *The Word and the Bomb* (London: Faber, 2005).

22 Smith, *White Teeth*, 407.

23 Monica Ali, *Brick Lane* (London: Doubleday, 2003), 303.

24 Yasmin Hussain, *Writing Diaspora: South Asian Women, Culture and Ethnicity* (Hampshire: Ashgate Institute for the Study of Islam and Christianity, 2005), 93.

25 Ali, *Brick Lane*, 323, 339.

26 Ali, *Brick Lane*, 407.

27 Cindi Katz, "Banal Terrorism: Spatial Fetishism and Everyday Insecurity," in Gregory and Pred, *Violent Geographies*, 349–61.

28 Dennis Lim, "The Life of Brain," *The Village Voice*, March 15, 2005, paragraph 5, http://www.villagevoice.com/books/0511,bklim,62101,10.html (accessed March 30, 2007).

29 Lee Siegel, "The Imagination of Disaster," *Nation*, April 11, 2005, http://www.thenation.com/docprint.mhtml?i=20050411&s=siegel article (accessed March 30, 2007).

30 Nadeem Aslam, *Maps for Lost Lovers* (London: Faber 2004), 267.

31 Fred Halliday, "West Encountering Islam: Islamophobia Reconsidered," in *Islam Encountering Globalization*, ed. Ali Mohammadi (London: Routledge Curzon, 2002), 16.

32 Helga Ramsey-Kurz, "Humouring the terrorists or the terrorised? Militant Muslims in Salman Rushdie, Zadie Smith, and Hanif Kureishi," in *Cheeky Fictions: Laughter and the Postcolonial*, eds Susanne Reichl and Mark Stein (Amsterdam: Rodopi, 2005), 84.

33 Aslam, *Maps for Lost Lovers*, 111.

34 Ibid., 140–1.

35 Ibid., 186.

36 Ibid., 234–5.

37 Ansari, *The Infidel Within*, 74.

38 Aslam, *Maps for Lost Lovers*, 245.

39 Nadine Gordimer, *The Pickup* (London: Bloombsbury, 2001).

40 Randa Abdel-Fattah, *Does My Head Look Big in This?* (London: Scholastic. 2006), 12.

41 Geoffrey Nash, "Re-siting Religion and Creating Feminised Space in the Fiction of Ahdaf Soueif and Leila Aboulela," *Wasafiri* 35 (2002): 31.

42 Leila Aboulela, *Islamophobia: a Challenge for Us All* (London: Runnymede Trust, 2005), 264.

43 Poole. *Reporting Islam*, 9.

44 Nevzat Soguk, "Reflections on the 'Orientalised Orientals,'" *Alternatives* 18 (1993): 363.

45 Gregory and Pred, "Introduction," *Violent Geographies*, 3.

46 Michael Watts, "Revolutionary Islam: A Geography of Modern Terror," in Gregory and Pred, *Violent Geographies*, 188.

47 Bassam Tibi, *Islam: Between Culture and Politics*. Second edn (Basingstoke: Palgrave Macmillan, 2005), 248.

48 Mitchell Gray and Elvin Wyly, "The Terror City Hypothesis," in Gregory and Pred, *Violent Geographies*, 332.

49 Watts, "Revolutionary Islam," 197.

50 Samuel P. Huntington, *The Clash of Civilizations and the Remaking of World Order* (New York: Simon and Schuster, 1996), 110.

CHAPTER 4

Left Behind in America: The Army of One at the End of History

JONATHAN VINCENT

At the close of the twentieth century, American evangelical authors Tim LaHaye and Jerry Jenkins began writing a series of bestsellers that has become, by some accounts, the most profitable in American history. The ubiquity of the *Left Behind* books at century's end was only exacerbated by the events of September 11 and the ensuing "War on Terror," which produced a 60 percent increase in sales.[1] Throughout 2001, for instance, while Americans were watching the desecration of downtown Manhattan by "evil" conspirators, *Left Behind* enthusiasts treated themselves to the event's cosmic analog in *The Desecration*, the ninth volume and year's number-one bestseller, which portrays the destruction of Jerusalem by the Antichrist.[2] By 2005, one in eight Americans had read at least one of the 12 books, with collective sales exceeding 65 million copies. Taking as its opening theme the immanent rapture of "true-Christian" Americans into heaven, the saga develops an adventure involving the subsequent rise of the Antichrist, the seven-year period of "Tribulation," the final Battle of Armageddon, and the triumphal "Glorious Appearing" of Christ on Earth. Through this medium, LaHaye and Jenkins stage an apocalyptic drama that links the fantastical visions of John of Patmos's Revelation and Old Testament prophesies with the horrifying catastrophes that parade nightly across our television sets (if not our actual lives).[3] Collaborating in devastating scenes of global violence, natural disaster, and contagious epidemics, *Left Behind* simultaneously stimulates a range of profound anxieties while stabilizing them within its own narrative framework.

To many, End Times speculation conjures images of stargazers scrutinizing the skies for signs of angels and trumpeting messiahs. It recalls sandwich-board fanatics at football games and political rallies. But to a significant segment of the American populace, apocalyptic rhetoric is just good sense. Today, roughly one-third of Americans claim to be "born-again" evangelicals.[4] As many as half of Americans believe that the events described in Revelation are the authentic, infallible forecast of the world's demise.[5] Many of these believe that we are bearing witness to these events now. The incontrovertible fact that we wake to find ourselves *still here* only momentarily delays the "pestilence" of AIDS, "one world" globalization, and continuing warfare in Israel, which prove the world is steering inevitably down its divinely preordained course.

The renewed popularity of apocalyptic discourse—a long tradition in the US—has led to a corresponding interest in academic and journalistic circles for, among other things, its preoccupation with "network culture" and the anti-Semitism and homophobia of the "LaHaye empire."[6] Rather than take issue with any of these, this chapter meditates first on a worrisome ideological braiding occurring between the US military and influential sectors of the contemporary evangelical community. Second, I more directly consider *Left Behind*'s interpretive filter and the way it shares a structural intimacy with ideological orientations in the post-Cold War milieu. As Amy Johnson Frykholm rightly suggests, premillennial dispensationalism—or "prophesy belief"—"must be understood as a fluid part of the broader culture, not as the realm of isolated believers."[7] As such, it discloses a political rationality that is at work in the distorted cultural logic of the American present, a logic suffused with an apocalyptic imaginary that has gained traction concurrent with the spread of US imperialism—be it old-school military occupation or the economic "neo-imperial" variant.

The Double Articulation of American Militarization

My argument orbits a view of the *Left Behind* books as complicit with two seemingly contradictory features of the "new militarism," an American dispensation toward violence and national identity recast in the wake of the Vietnam War and implemented during the so-called "Global War on Terror."[8] The first concerns the triumph of geopolitical "realism" extolled by neoconservative disciples of a more interventionist, expansionist foreign policy, a political viewpoint that promulgates its initiatives through a mixture of biblical and classical values.[9] Invoking the "cartoon" discourses of an "Evil Empire" and "Axis of Evil"—what Jan Nederveen Pieterse calls "narcissistic and Manichean provincialism elevated to globalism" —neoconservatives of recent administrations have actively sought a conceptual framework that would corral support for their chauvinistic global initiatives.[10]

The ascendance of "muscular Christianity" has been the response to that need. As an ideological legacy of the New Christian Right that gained traction during the late 1970s and 1980s, muscular Christianity revived the means to overcome cultural isolationism partly by equating pro-biblical and pro-military values.[11] While Billy Graham's receipt of the Sylvanus Thayer award at West Point, Jerry Falwell's use of the "Moral Majority" newsletter to support Reagan's nuclear buildup, proxy wars, and "Star Wars," and the LaHaye family's fund-raising for the Nicaraguan contras are emblematic examples, the more startling advent has been the increasingly symbiotic language of military and religious sectors. Today, for instance, civilian congregations increasingly use martial language—"Kingdom Warriors," "Force Ministries," "Campus Crusade"—just as military personnel voice prayers for "deliverance," speak of "having faith in the mission," and, in General Boykin's infamous rechristening of the US military, construe themselves as soldiers in the "army of god."[12] Though the idea of a locked-and-loaded, camo-clad Christ may make many uneasy, it is a resonant reality in the minds of many believers that problematically links sanctified visions of the local with the dream of substantiating its "dominion" on a wider global scale.

The revival of metaphysical rhetoric to describe the dirty business of making war takes place in the political sphere as well. While in office, President George W. Bush repeatedly summoned an idiom of crusades and struggles between good and evil and even implied that the invasion of Iraq was at divine bequest. While pundits and some religious commentators have grown leery of a national "theology of war," Bush was not alone.[13] Conservative columnist George Will has asked today's soldiers to serve as moral "exemplars" to a morally emaciated domestic sphere.[14] Viewing a parade of soldiers preparing to embark for Iraq, neoconservative military historian and occasional Bush speechwriter Victor Davis Hanson similarly described the bellicose pageantry as "transcendence at work."[15] Such proclamations recall an exceptionalist, militarist past that viewed righteousness and martial practices as two sides of the same coin. As the neoconservative Project for the New American Century's "Statement of Principles" attests, however, "military strength and moral clarity" are inseparable political virtues.[16]

The rhetorical echo chamber enjoining the military barracks and contemporary megachurches, however, is only the first feature of the new militarism. In stark contrast to the myth-laden language of divine calling has been a corresponding withering of the civic sensibility that has traditionally accompanied military duty. While the language of liberal democracy and international humanism—rights, freedom, self-determination—is omnipresent in the current political climate, the appeal within recruitment circles increasingly focuses on the individual as a privatized agent of war. In the apocalyptic present, the soldier emerges as a self-contained "Army of One": the consumer of a private adventure, a self-regulating and compartmentalized repository of inner mettle and "extreme" experience. In the fallout from the Cold War, the new agent of war has emerged as a "purpose-driven" operative in the mystical, deterritorialized drama that has opened at the alleged "end of history."

The shrinkage of the political subject of war is a legacy of the Bush administration's disarticulation of the military from democratic and public sources of social meaning. In the push to privatize virtually every sector of the home front, it is understandable that the military has been among the principal targets. Substituting the language of adventure and gain-through-risk for traditional appeals to duty and honor, the military is reinventing its members as entrepreneurial strategists in a cost-benefit calculus of personal "becoming"—the army of one, now "army strong," being "all you can be." As brokers of a personal "journey"—"It's not just a job, it's an adventure"—the new war worker finds her- or himself redefined along market lines, outsourced from rationales connected to citizenship for benefits indexed on a more individualized scale. Though the "surrogate soldiers and private mercenaries" of companies like Blackwater, Vinnell Corporation, and Military Professional Resources, Inc. make around five times the money for the same work, the army continues to enlist new recruits with lures of future professional marketability in "specialist" services or the more bluntly fiscal incentive of enlistment bonuses.[17] One should "aim high," the recruit learns, in an effort to "get an edge on life."

The shift from political to private appeals in the national bolstering of the soldier's profession is a symptom of the broader neoliberal restructuring of public life. As "calculating creatures whose moral autonomy is measured by their capacity for 'self-care,'" claims Wendy Brown, the "model neoliberal citizen is one who strategizes for her- or himself among various social, political, and economic options, not one who strives with others to alter or organize these options."[18] Eroding foundations of the citizen-soldier tradition, the military is promoting more mercenary forms of consciousness, ones devoted to individual acquisition and the supreme authority of the state. The intense quarantining of the self from communal registers of meaning—frequently expressed as atomization—is the signal feature of a larger diminishment of democratic energy within American political life.

Recent essayists have described the encroachment of these rationales into the Christian marketplace as well, predominantly through the *Left Behind* books. Andrew Strombeck, in his piece "Invest in Jesus," has shown the way that a seemingly contradictory "commitment to neoliberal values" permeates the *Left Behind* books.[19] Its consumerist protagonists, for instance, "use every technological advantage available including sport-utility vehicles, satellite cell phones, and solar-powered wireless laptops" to shore up as much of the mobility and security that neoliberal subjectivities crave.[20] Peter Yoonsuk Paik has also described the "consumerist lifestyle" that the novels celebrate as a corollary to the neo-imperialist fantasies they enact. For Paik, the core of that neo-imperialism involves a "quilting-point" scenario in which Christian Americans deploy "religious fantasies" to justify inhabiting other countries like Afghanistan and Iraq supposedly fallen victim to "irrational fanatics" and religious fantasy.[21]

What these authors have rightly discerned is the uniquely American strain of individualism standing behind much of the current reconciliation of Christian values to the explicitly non-Christian valuation of the marketplace. But it is individualism with a theological twist. As much as an ethos of professionalism and profit thrives in neoliberal Christian culture, so do intensified calls for discipline, sacrifice, and self-subordination. Consider, for instance, the self-denying lesson inherent in much recent activity among extreme evangelical sects. Increasing in popularity are militarized Christian academies like Bethel Boot Camp that privilege "military discipline" because "it teaches conformity to authority, structure and submission," or Back to Basics Military Academy in which a 13-year-old boy was killed during one of its "leadership" sessions.[22] Also on the rise are retreats and camps like "Kids on Fire Summer Camp" depicted in the recent documentary *Jesus Camp* (Heidi Ewing and Rachel Grady, 2006). Here children can engage in proto-martyrdom drills, camouflaged and face-painted marching rituals enlivened by the playing of baroque Christian anthems.[23] "I want to see them [her Christian students] as radically laying down their lives for the gospel," declares Pastor Becky Fischer, "as they [Muslim radicals] are in Palestine and Pakistan and all those different places." Even if most of the camps are less extreme, many of them often conflate the cultivation of survival skills and the pseudo-guerilla navigation of woodland obstacle courses with a revitalizing adherence to "leadership training." Love Demonstrated Ministries Christian Boot Camp in San Antonio, Texas, runs endurance drills so fiercely as to have been recently fined for dragging a 15-year-old girl behind a van with a rope when she was unable to keep up with the physical regimen.[24] Others like Elijah Generation International, moreover, claim to "train special forces" for the "army of God" at their "spiritual boot camp." The advertisement on their website denotes images of M16-toting soldiers as having been "chosen" to "answer the call."[25] Force Ministries is another organization professedly "equipping military and law enforcement personnel for Christ-centered duty." Their homepage pictures a menacing US soldier beneath a Bible verse that reads: "From the days of John the Baptist until now, the kingdom of heaven has been forcefully advancing, and forceful men lay hold of it."[26] December 2007's posting presents "A Letter from an American Soldier in Iraq" declaring that "God has placed too many very strong Christians in one area for there not to be some sort of spiritual awakening to take place. This camp is God's and there will be a great difference in the Kingdom by the end of this trip."[27] For a religion purporting a theology of grace which "saves" individuals, the lingering allure of blood sacrifice—the return of modernity's repressed—seems a kind of squaring of the balance, the settling of a cosmic transaction.

Left Behind's Cultural Work: An Interpretive Formula for the Apocalyptic Present

Nowhere is this double-articulation—the straining between the mytho-historical and the private-subjective—more visible than in apocalyptic fiction. To contend with just one example of this yoked belief structure, *Left Behind* opens with one of the main characters, a star newspaper reporter named Cameron "Buck" Williams, speculating on a grave episode to which he has recently borne witness. He has been in Haifa, Israel covering a story for his newspaper, *Global Weekly*. Responding to a sudden windfall in Israel's economy, the nation is attacked by a barrage of airplanes from the north, a modern adaptation of a prophesy in Revelation. With a rhetorical flourish that bafflingly substitutes left-collectivists into the history of right-collectivists, the attackers, we learn, are genocidal *Russians*—historically, fascism's most ardent adversaries—armed for a total "holocaust" of the Israelis.[28] Their vast technological superiority outnumbers what the authors portray as an enfeebled Israeli military—perhaps, the text implies, in need of more support from American weapons manufacturers. Buck recalls standing helpless as an enormous fleet of Russian MiGs descended from above.

As the planes enter Israeli airspace, however, they destroy *themselves* in what the authors call "a firestorm, along with rain and hail and an earthquake, that consumed the entire effort."[29] Though wreckage went crashing into Haifa, Jerusalem, Tel Aviv, Jericho, even Bethlehem, leveling ancient walls and tearing up huge sections of the city, not a soul is scratched. Considering the bizarre scene, Buck recollects, "he became a believer in God that day."[30] As it turns out, he muses, the hand of God had interfered to smite the invaders and to protect his people exactly as predicted in

Scripture. In a perverse twist on Cold War nationalism—since Israel and the US, for LaHaye, constitute a culturally homogenous "people," and since Jews are essentially proto-Christians—the authors muddy historical memory and cultural affiliation by veering Cold War tensions into the Middle East and by recodifying Israel as essentially an extension of American territory.

Thus begins the *Left Behind* series by translating modern (non)events into cosmic terms. Buck consequently joins the Tribulation Force, a newly Christianized militia of highly specialized technocratic warriors. Though the members have themselves only recently converted, the failure of others to confirm their newly acquired disposition toward the cosmos is warrant enough for their violent destruction. As a computer-savvy, evangelical *avant garde*, its members are called upon to dispense God's wrathful vengeance upon unbelievers as part of a secret network of mercenaries in an apocalyptic crusade that is occurring . . . well, when?: In biblical history? The future? The eschatological present? The ambiguity of *Left Behind*'s time and place disfigures any real temporal footholds. As a consequence, the narrative sets up a disorienting arrangement of phenomena that registers the unfamiliar in a way that feels partially familiar but that slides unevenly into a contorted labyrinth of political-historical leaps, twists, and inversions. Though the soldiers resemble the iconic bourgeois Americans of the J.Crew catalog, their small but fluid and widely dispersed network of vigilante operatives is more akin to a terrorist cell than an imperial army. The cultural reversal is further confused by depicting contemporary American Christians in the anachronistic roles of early church martyrs—those who endured torture, deprivation, imprisonment, and death at the will of a Roman imperium—rather than as agents of current imperial globalism. The books' interpretive screen possesses a kind of synchronic, transhistoric lens that obscures local causation and, instead, refracts diffuse events from different points in time into one symbolic constellation. The war the characters are fighting is at once the continuation of an ancient war (crusade), the unfolding of a military episode in the present (escalations of actual wars in the Middle East), and the forecast for a future war with an evil global state (apocalypse).

The principle obstacle for the protagonists, for instance, is Nicolae Carpathia—the antichrist director of the Global Network, a "pacifist" United Nations-like organization now relocated to Iraq and intent on the ostensibly sinister project of universal nuclear disarmament. For Lahaye and Jenkins, any international effort to seek world peace is perceived as deliberately duping Americans by divesting them of their one defense against transnational evil. In another astonishing reversal, American Christian readers learn about their own domination by a massive transnational corporate state, one which collapses the historical memory of Imperial Rome and the Cold War Soviet Union into a rethreaded narrative of international human rights organizations and centers of US concentration in the "Global War on Terror." Americans are recast as an embattled minority of fringe survivalists, not liberal-capitalist agents at the economic and structural epicenter of exploitative international relations. Such contorted representation may have much to do with the fact that, in the biblical apocalypse story, the United States is conspicuously absent. Conversely, such nonrepresentation might also have everything to do with the fact that, in reality, the United States is deeply represented in the actual space of the Middle East with enough military bases to ensure its presence until, well, time immemorial. Thus, as Lee Quinby has argued, "though the apocalyptic narrative is a story with a beginning, and a middle, and an earthly setting, it is a narrative that seeks to be nonnarrative, to get beyond the strictures of time and space."[31] With characteristic circularity, it imports the "reality" of its narrative onto the real of the present in order to substantiate the "reality" of the narrative by making it real in the present.

The "cosmifying" disruption of time and space is not the only disorientation the books enact, however. Though the United States is not represented in biblical forecasts for the end of time, it is ironically the Bible itself that provides evangelical readers with the mythological anchor to come to terms with modern American political realities. Rather than demand that scriptures answer to historical gaps, "Dispensationalists," as Susan Harding memorably puts it, "submit history to the Bible and find history wanting." "The rise of the West, the development of capitalism, and the expansion of American hegemony," she claims, "are not central stories in world history [to dispensational believers]. History instead is centered in the Middle East and narrated as a relentless road toward fulfillment of biblical prophesies in which re-emergent biblical empires plunge into war."[32] Events like 9/11 and US occupations in the Middle East, then, represent only the current installment of that syndicated theological thriller waged in theaters beyond the jurisdiction of modern political observation. Contemporary commentators who try to give nuance and texture to the political, historical, and economic tensions that loom behind episodes of terrorism and war are held in suspicion for what are deemed to be a filmy set of historical eyes, a cracked and corroded interpretive lens that—like that first smug skeptic to die in any Hollywood horror film—fails to grasp the broader spiritual forces at work.

In addition to erasing an episodic historical narrative, to put it another way, apocalypse posits the prime activity of the real as an interpretive negotiation that individuals enact in opposition to the political narratives of modernity. It is a kind of splitting and compression that saddles the self with the metaphysical task of deciphering the present as the substantiation of a biblical riddle, of comprehending it as merely one stage in a continuum that day by day grows nearer and nearer to its eventual violent resolution. As Lee Quinby explains, "the apocalyptic self stands on a threshold positioned between imminent end and an uncertainty about the exact moment and means of that end."[33] The political reality of the present, consequentially, is always only an outgrowth of the much larger story unfolding off-screen. War in such an elliptical world is not the unfortunate outgrowth of relational global political regimes in asymmetrical transition but the inevitable symptom of sin's primacy, the original disease infecting a corroded world rightfully spinning toward its necessary conclusion.

To return to the scene of the Russian plane assault, as Buck processes what must have been an absurdly amazing experience, his response is instantly to register its effect only on himself—exclusively in the form of a conversion from cosmic indifference to sudden, personally transforming belief in God. Though the unfathomable scene of assault must have incomparable consequences for the world community, the books focus mostly on how cataclysm compels characters to alter their personal interiors. In episode after episode, the centripetal focus of these international dramas is always . . . oneself, the state of one's soul-preparedness (for the characters as well as the audience). Large global incidents, devastating and horrifying, simply happen. At one point, a plague eliminates one-third of the earth's population. But conveyed as merely the backdrop to the self-ministrations of a handful of Christian survivalists, the real question in the face of community disasters is "What does this say about me?" Foreclosing channels of empathy, it asks only "is my interior state adequate?"

The answer, of course, is that the characters (and readers) need a self-renovation through conversion to Christianity, helmed by a militarized Christ who has master-minded whatever scenes of atrocity and destruction have recently passed. Through a constant ritual of disavowal, the characters undergo a purifying internal gymnastics in which they exorcize the naturalized, rationalist proclivities of their modern liberal subjectivities to better discern the masked cosmic significance they obscure. Airplane pilot Rayford Steele, for instance, constantly berates his "old self" for its former inability to comprehend the spectral biblical reality behind modern political events. Chloe Steele, his daughter, learns to overcome her "secular" education at Stanford to concentrate on her evolving inner faith and capacity for meting out retributive guerilla violence. It is this oscillation between the macro-historical (a perspective in which ancient texts from the past about events in the future have everything to do with the present) and the micro-private (in which the present is always about the individual's interior) that is, I am suggesting, the narrative's cultural work.

The New Christian Nationalism

The argument that I have been advancing is that this variant of the apocalyptic imaginary emerges in the dementia of a paranoid political present where the seem-ingly contradictory logics of neoliberal selfhood and neoconservative political belief have joined. While these often competing currents have long circulated in American life—the monastic entrepreneurial self and the mystical interpretation of national history—the ideological echo chamber opened by the collapse of the Soviet Union has done much to sanction this odd ideological cohabitation. The unchallenged ascendance of liberal democracy and globalization of market capitalism in the decades since 1989 have been greatly enabled by the slacking of that once tautly strung dialectic, by the loss of that antagonism that left Americans untethered from their self-constituting Other. American national identity—particularly the version advanced by neoconservatives—is a structure of feeling often given stabil-ity by constitutional distinctions of exclusive and intractable differences between those outside the territory of the United States and those within it. As Peter Gowan observes, the US had primacy in the Cold War only *"in the form of the Cold War."*[34] To properly maintain its hegemony, the US needs the kind of existential gridlock that the political tensions of the mid-to-late twentieth century helped to solidify.

It is into the post-Cold War vacuum—spatial, rhetorical, historical—that the narrative of apocalypse and its "abstract geography" begins to take shape and gain legitimacy.[35] As prophesy theorist and American historian Paul Boyer has claimed, prophesy belief "mediates antinomies," or contradictory political logics, "as a middle way between theological and practical realities."[36] Entering such a political void, apocalyptic Christian nationalism can function as a zone of indeterminacy reconciling the seemingly dissident strains of neoliberal and neoconservative belief—individualism and transhistorical belonging, spiritualism and materialism, profit and sacrifice. In this way, apocalypse's "anarchist sublime," its overwhelming capacity to both fascinate and repulse, forms a porous middle point between the self and geopolitical history that permits an imperialist nationalism to flourish, even within the domain of a liberal-democratic society.[37] If neoconservativism erases the political by substituting a mythic cartography to chart out the present, neoliberal rationalities institute a similar distortion by saddling isolated individuals with the burden of interpreting that present. In the miasma that follows, states, communities, and collectives that work to institute social change are blocked out in exchange for a narrative universe where history is cosmic and the cosmic only has bearing for those who can correctly decipher it.

To this end, the *Left Behind* series fuses Christian individualism with versions of a nationalist militarism by generating a narrative "logic" that gives coherence to the present, while actively evading today's more relational political textures. Now since the ideological desires of these narratives are unstable and provide ample opportunity for counter-readings, they contain the contradictory seeds of their own unraveling (particularly the linking of "values" to a market rationale that knows none). Nonetheless, their enthusiastic erasure of contextual, material, and human solutions to political problems supports a larger cultural reality outside their apocalyptic story world.[38] The paranoid void that opens where the army of one meets the end of history accommodates political deliriums that make sense of ideas like preemption as good defense, "security" as the preeminent role of the state, "clashes" of civilizations, "forward-leaning" military procedures, permanent states of emergency, and the inevitable omnipresence of fear. In such a universe, the transhistorical and transnational conflicts that shape our world are always, finally, allegorical myths about our endangered national selves that necessarily leave behind others.

Notes

1   Robert Dreyfus, "Reverend Doomsday," *Rolling Stone*, January 8, 2004, http://www. rollingstone.com/politics/story/5939999/reverend_doomsday/ (accessed December 14, 2007). See also Bible Discernment Ministries' review of the series at http://www. rapidnet.com/~jbeard/bdm/BookReviews/left.htm (accessed July 15, 2009). According to this website, "more than 65 million copies have been sold (over 75 million counting the graphic novels and children's versions), generating more than 650 million dollars in sales since first published in 1995."

2   Nancy Gibbs, "Apocalypse Now," *Time.com*, July 1, 2002, http://www.time.com/time/ covers/1101020701/story.html (accessed July 15, 2009).

3   John of Patmos is believed to be the author of the final book of the Christian Bible from which most of the speculation about the "end of times" gets its rhetoric and imagery.

4   Paul Boyer, "When US Foreign Policy Meets Biblical Prophesy," *Alternet*, February 20, 2003, www.alternet.org/story/15221 (accessed July 14, 2006). In addition, Boyer's *When Time Shall Be No More: Prophesy Belief in Modern American Culture* (Cambridge: Harvard University Press, 1992) provides a breakdown of Gallup poll statistics in terms of believers over decades, 2–15. See also Michelle Goldberg, *Kingdom Coming: The Rise of Christian Nationalism* (New York: Norton, 2006), 8–10; and Timothy Weber, "On the Road to Armageddon" *Beliefnet*, June 20, 2006, www.beliefnet.com/story/151/story_15165.html (accessed June 15, 2006).

5   Boyer, *When Time Shall Be No More*, 2.

6   See Amy Johnson Frykholm, *Rapture Culture: Left Behind in Evangelical America* (New York: Oxford University Press, 2004); and Glenn Shuck, *Marks of the Beast: The Left Behind and the Struggle for Evangelical Identity* (New York: NYU Press, 2004).

7   Frykholm, *Rapture Culture*, 4.

8   Andrew Bacevich, *The New American Militarism: How Americans are Seduced by War* (New York: Oxford University Press, 2005). See also Chalmers Johnson, *The Sorrows of Empire: Militarism, Secrecy, and the End of the Republic* (New York: Metropolitan Books, 2004), which delineates between "Imperialisms, Old and New" in Chapter 1. See also David Harvey, *The New Imperialism* (New York: Oxford University Press, 2003).

9   For an extensive definition of "conservative realism" consider the summary provided by Samuel Huntington, himself a professed "conservative realist," in *The Soldier and the State: The Theory and Politics of Civil-Military Relations* (Cambridge: Harvard University Press, 1981), 79.

10 Jan Nederveen Pieterse, "Scenarios of Power," in *The War on Terrorism and the American "Empire" after the Cold War*, eds Alejandro Colas and Richard Saull (New York: Routledge Press, 2006), 185.

11 "Muscular Christianity" is attributed to a movement in Victorian American culture that sought to invigorate a neurasthenic, enfeebled version of manhood by welding Christianity into Theodore Roosevelt's cult of the "strenuous life" and a new privileging of might, struggle, and survival. It has been resuscitated by recent historians and critics to describe the militancy of the New Christian Right. See Heather Hendershot, *Shaking the World for Jesus: Media and Conservative Evangelical Culture* (Chicago: University of Chicago Press, 2004), 226. See also Clifford Putney, *Muscular Christianity: Manhood and Sports in Protestant America, 1880–1920* (Cambridge: Harvard University Press, 2001). For a description of the militarization of Christianity in the late nineteenth century, see T.J. Jackson Lears, *No Place of Grace: Antimodernism and the Transformation of American Culture, 1880–1920* (Chicago: University of Chicago Press, 1994), 109. For an analysis of the New Christian Right's increased militarization and politicization, see also Sara Diamond, *Roads to Dominion: Right Wing Movements and Political Power in the United States* (New York: Guilford Press, 1995), 228–56.

12 Richard T. Cooper, "General Casts War in Religious Terms," *LA Times.com*, October 16, 2003, http://articles.latimes.com/2003/oct/16/nation/na-general16 (accessed July 15, 2009).

13 Jim Wallis, "Contesting a Theology of War Confessing Christ in a World of Violence," *Catholic New Times*, December 5, 2004, http://findarticles.com/p/articles/mi_m0MKY/is_19_28/ai_n8698007 (accessed June 15, 2006). Wallis is a Christian who has organized against the Bush Administration's conflation of religious and military languages.

14 Bacevich, *The New Militarism*, 23.

15 Ibid., 24, 122–46.

16 Project for the New American Century, "Statement of Principles," June 3, 1997, http://www.newamericancentury.org/statementofprinciples.htm (accessed June 11, 2007).

17 Johnson, *Sorrows of Empire*, 140. There is also an excellent unpacking of military privatization in Robert Greenwald's documentary, *Iraq for Sale: The War Profiteers* (Culver City, CA: Brave New Films, 2006).

18   Wendy Brown, *Edgework: Critical Essays on Knowledge and Politics* (Princeton: Princeton University Press, 2005), 42–3.

19   Andrew Strombeck, "Invest in Jesus: Neoliberalism and the *Left Behind* Novels," *Cultural Critique* 64 (2006): 165.

20   Ibid.

21   Peter Yoonsuk Paik, "Smart Bombs, Serial Killing, and the Rapture," *Postmodern Culture* 14, no. 1 (2003): 1, 4, 7.

22   Dadelus, "A fatal triumph of privatization and faith based initiatives," *Blah3.com*, http://www.blah3.com/article.php?story=20060816100036444 (accessed June 11, 2008).

23   Bethel Academy, http://www.bethelacademy.org/discipline.html (accessed June 11, 2008).

24   Jeorge Zarazua, "Pastor Accused of Dragging Girl behind His Van," *ReligionNewsblog*, August 11, 2007, http://www.religionnewsblog.com/18991/charles-flowers (accessed March 10, 2008).

25   Elijah Generation International, http://www.spiritualbootcamp.org/ (accessed June 11, 2008).

26   Matthew 11:12 (NIV).

27   Force Ministries, http://www.forceministries.com/ (accessed June 11, 2008).

28   Tim LaHaye and Jerry B. Jenkins, *Left Behind: A Novel of the Earth's Last Days* (Wheaton: Tyndale House, 1995), 12.

29   Ibid., 14.

30   Ibid., 14.

31   Lee Quinby, *Anti-Apocalypse: Exercises in Genealogical Criticism* (Minneapolis: University of Minnesota Press, 1994), xiv.

32   Susan Harding, *The Book of Jerry Falwell: Fundamentalist Language and Politics* (Princeton: Princeton University Press, 2000), 237–8.

33   Quinby, *Anti-Apocalypse*, xxi.

34   Peter Gowan, "The Bush Turn and the Drive for Primacy," in *The War on Terrorism and the American 'Empire' after the Cold War*, eds Alejandro Colas and Richard Saull (New York: Routledge Press, 2006), 143.

35   Neil Smith, "Afterword," in *War, Citizenship, Territory*, eds Deborah Cowen and Emily Gilbert (New York: Routledge, 2008), 390–1. Smith elaborates this term in his explanation of the "ontological insecurity" produced by the current "insecurity state."

36   Boyer, *When Time Shall Be No More*, 296.

37   Timothy Brennan, *Wars of Position: The Cultural Politics of Left and Right* (New York: Columbia University Press, 2006), 145–59. He characterizes the "anarchist sublime" as the moment when the Left abandoned any project of taking hold of the state, a political turn resulting in a political vacuum in which the New Christian Right has risen to power.

38   The German theorist Ernst Bloch, for instance, has seen millenialist thinking as potentially revolutionary. In addition, Strombeck views depictions of disaster as a potential "means for an imaginary identification with neoliberalism's Other, the refugee" (185).

CHAPTER 5

9/11, Manhood, Mourning, and the American Romance

JOHN MEAD

"I'm here to create the new imperial empire
I'm going to do whatever circumstances require"
—Bob Dylan, "Honest with Me", from *Love and Theft*,
released September 11, 2001

After the horrifying attacks on United States targets on September 11, 2001, many pundits hoped for an "end to the age of irony"[1] and a commitment to a more meaningful culture; journalists saw "a post-9/11 America searching for its best qualities, not its worst."[2] Many asked if making art was relevant, or even possible, after such an event. As Mark Slouka points out in the September 2002 issue of *Harper's*, this sentiment not only jumps the gun but overlooks the sad reality that the desire to create art survived every day of the genocidal Twentieth Century[3] (one might ironically, but not entirely inappropriately, read the first statement of post-September 11 America as Bob Dylan's grimly smirking *Love and Theft*, released the very morning of the attacks, containing the wry aside "some things are too terrible to be true").[4]

Slouka's point is to question how the belief in American exceptionalism (along, thankfully, with irony) managed to survive an event that hinted at a world beyond the edges of this continent. Many simply looked for evidence of continued American greatness. The *Atlantic Monthly's* three-part series by freelance writer and former war correspondent William Langewiesche on the excavation of the World Trade Center site mythologizes what came to be called "Ground Zero"[5] as an "urgent all-American creation," symbolizing the reopening of the frontier and the collective reinvestment in our Manifest Destiny. The *Atlantic* trades on Langewiesche's war correspondent past to underline the parallels between the World Trade Center excavation and the great battles of the past: their writer was "the only journalist to be 'embedded'[6]—to use the Pentagon term for reporters who live and travel with the units they cover—in the World Trade Center operation." Langewiesche is no Ambrose Bierce; he is not at the site to coldly consider the hubris and folly of man's adventures. The article is celebratory, even upbeat, seeking out every image of the American Spirit he can paint.

Langewiesche, thankfully, refuses to entertain any cant about a "loss of innocence," but what he sees instead is "a shift from an era of complacency preceding the attack to a period of creative turbulence just afterward."[7] What we're offered is a sort of boldly definitive American experience for the dawning of a frightening new world. What we actually get is a series of well-drawn and entertaining clichés culled from the lexicon of American tough-guy iconography and adventure yarns: frontier and war stories, thrillers and westerns, where determined men, undeterred by the foolish rules of civilization, rise to the occasion to become heroes—men whose "success in the midst of chaos" becomes for Langewiesche the most significant part of the story of "these monolithic buildings that in the final stretch of the twentieth century had stood so visibly for the totalitarian ideals of planning and control."

Here Langewiesche cleverly recasts the buildings, not as phallic symbols of global capitalism, but as outworn remnants of Soviet-style authoritarianism, as though the bombers were some sort of Howard Rourkes wiping collectivism from the face of the planet. He can now continue with glee and without implicating the American economy. This characterization of the function of the buildings seems an odd slip until we realize that this scene of chaos is exactly what Langewiesche values—the manly world of danger and decision-making far from the reach of hearth and home. The site is now "a tabula rasa for the United States. Among the ruins now, a large and unscripted experiment in American life had gotten under way."[8] Langewiesche is reading the experience into the template of the American Romance in terms Leslie Fiedler laid out in *Love and Death in the American Novel*[9]—the true American is the man in the wilderness, far from the sinister corruption of the civilized world. The site provides a peculiarly American experience, completely unlike "other countries," where "clear answers would have been sought before action was taken," and "a tightly scripted response would have been imposed." Here, in America, "for whatever reasons, probably cultural, probably profound," all "the learned committees were excluded," and common men "in heavy machines simply rolled in and took on the unknown."[10]

And for whatever reason, "probably cultural, probably profound," Langewiesche avoids probing for the causes. Much of the series reads like a script for an unmade John Ford film, filled with ordinary men rising to extraordinariness, setting their jaws and walking into danger while the women who love them remain resolutely at home and off-screen.[11] Langewiesche weaves tales of spectacular deaths and sensational escapes into the grim but sweeping and ambitious epic of the excavation of the pulverized buildings, a combination of mass gravesite, urban disaster area, potential time bomb, and Dante's Inferno, in which men discover the kind of meaning and clarity usually reserved for the battlefield. The writing is vivid and frequently cinematic, like when a group of engineers and "tough construction guys" walk onto the site for the first time:

> . . . the skeletal walls and smoking hills of rubble where the towers had been, the boxy shell of the Marriott hotel, the heavy steel spears protruding from neighboring

buildings, the collapsed north pedestrian bridge, the massive external column sections thrown every which way across the streets, and everywhere the fires ... The ground was littered with hundreds of shoes, presumably from victims, but characteristically for this unusually imploded killing zone, not a single corpse lay in sight.[12]

The site of disaster and carnage is transformed by the cleanup into a landscape "courageous and creative, an authentic piece of American ground," which Langewiesche never sees as anything more than this hallowed space of can-do attitude and pluck.[13] He doesn't see American Ground as a space that is contested, mythologized, blood-soaked, and unfinished, but as a wilderness, cursed by the sin of the Old World—the politics of the terrorist attacks virtually never enter the story—and ready to be claimed by the fortitude of simple men. Langewiesche's title itself evokes the classic of American literary criticism, Henry Nash Smith's *Virgin Land*, and reinscribes the irony of the title: American Ground was not virgin when the pilgrims arrived (putting aside the rapidly dying indigenous population, ravaged by European viruses, the Mayflower was beaten here by a cargo ship of African slaves), nor was it innocent when successfully attacked for the first time since the War of 1812.

Though the series is a piece of journalistic nonfiction, what Langewiesche is doing here is writing the Great American Novel; the piece was intended to be published as a full-length book after all three pieces ran in the magazine.[14] The articles are brimming with colorful characters, hairsbreadth escapes, and Deeper Meanings:

> The truth was that people relished the experience ... it served for many of them as an unexpected liberation—a national tragedy, of course, but one that was contained, unambiguous, and surprisingly energizing. Was this not war, after all?[15]

Well, no—it was the cleanup of a disaster site, a massive and dangerous engineering and demolition chore. But Langewiesche reads all the glory of war into the process. "The urgency of the job," he says, "swept away ordinary responsibilities and the everyday dullness of family life, and made nonsense of office paperwork and tedious professional routines." This was Democracy at work, a Horatio Alger story in the making: "hierarchies broke down" as "[a]ction and invention were required on every level, often with no need or possibility of asking permission." As a "vital new culture" emerged, "even the lowliest laborers and firemen were given power," and some of the men "who gained the greatest influence were people without previous rank who discovered balance and ability within themselves, and who in turn were discovered by others."[16]

Despite these claims, Langewiesche doesn't tell many stories of "lowly" men "without previous rank." Often his romantic vision of individual character-building in the face of irrelevant hierarchy is reminiscent not of American frontier myth but of early 1990s entrepreneurial manifestos by authors like Tom Peters—books carried in day-bags, along with Sun Tzu's *The Art of War*, by mid-level corporate office workers through the dot-com boom. Most of his heroes are highly-trained and well-educated engineers, specialists, and business owners—many long-time employees of the Port Authority of New York and New Jersey, an enormous organization "exempted from ordinary governmental constraints"[17]—men used to making decisions and giving orders. If one questions the premise that Langewiesche is writing a Great American Novel and not simply solid, straightforward journalism, they might look at his digressions into secondary cast members. When the writer introduces the "affable, boyish-looking" David Griffin, the site's "token southerner," we're given a detailed and gratuitous portrait of his father, a figure at best peripheral to the action. David Senior, "D.H.," is the po' boy made good, a "ninth-grade dropout" who scratched and bootstrapped his way to being worth "about a quarter billion dollars ... or more" through pluck and hard work: Thomas Sutpen or Jay Gatsby without the tragedy or megalomania—the classic American success story. In the next scene, his son, a "rich and busy man" in his own right, packs up his Suburban and drives to New York—he can't *stand by*—his wife and children loyally accompanying him. When he gets to New York, he slips onto the site, as lucky and plucky as his father, and "six months go by"; the qualities of the father are passed on to the son, and American Life goes forward.

More fascinating than the "burly," massive men who run them are the heavy machines used in the cleanup. Langewiesche is so enamored of them that he gives a full account of their actions in Part One and another in Part Three, "The Dance of the Dinosaurs"—in some ways the most macho installment—which includes a long, rapturous description of the "stars of the show." The "big diesel excavators" were "marvels of hydraulics and steel" that "in the hands of their operators became living things, the insatiable king dinosaurs in a world of ruin." The excavators "picked the ruins apart one piece at a time," lifting broken pieces of "the heaviest [steel] ever used in a building"; the job was tough, but the machines "were just tough enough to take it on." This is "a fight," and the operators are soldiers: "At the start of a shift they didn't just climb aboard and sit down but seemed, rather, to strap on the equipment much as good pilots strap on their wings." These Mike Mulligans inside their MaryAnnes are "said to be the best in the business, and this was easy to believe." They are "artists of motion—fluid, expressive, and intuitively at one with their machines":

> The operators might drive to work like ordinary commuters, frustrated by traffic, by parking regulations, by lines at Starbucks for insipid coffee; but after they settled into their machines, they could put all that aside, and go rumbling off into the faraway land of ruin; and if they came to terrain too wild to cross, often they could build their way through; and when they came to the field of battle, typically among other grapplers straining there, they could reach their own arms out twenty feet, clamp their own steel claws around multi-ton splinters, and with fire and smoke erupting, while shuddering and rocking forward onto the toes of their tracks, they could wrestle those splinters clear . . . Now they had been given a high purpose, and been told roughly what Sam Melisi had been told: just go and see what you can do. It was a liberation, because they knew they could do a lot. They were resourceful. They were like pioneers.[18]

It is difficult at this point in the narrative to hope for actual analysis, but in the third installment Langewiesche looks away from the machines and goes meta, extending his metaphor and distancing himself from the cries of the firemen ("my son is in there!"). Like the struggle of the machines, the clannishness he witnesses among the firemen and police—a microcosm of the struggles of tribes all over the world—is a "dance of the dinosaurs." Though this analogy doesn't bode well for any further championing of the lowly worker, it promises a more incisive view than he's previously offered, as though he is now ready to begin dissecting the adventure he's shared. "Bring our brothers home!"[19] one man shouts, perhaps anticipating the antiwar cries that are sure to be heard when George W. Bush sends troops to finish his father's war, Langewiesche might be inferring.

Instead he lets the metacritical moment pass and begins to slide back into the voice with which he's been successful prior to this point. The police and firemen, previously the antagonists of the piece (until a brief mention toward the end when he passes quickly over a number of violent beatings and fistfights between the two "tribes"), fade from the spotlight, and the work goes on:

> And so the recovery proceeded, not as a united or a heroic exercise but as a set of accommodations worked out among self-centered groups sharing a pragmatic understanding that this was an important job, and that it was primarily a physical one. The only solution was to attack the ruins.[20]

If this is not a "heroic exercise," Langewiesche casts his characters heroically anyway. If this were a movie, his cast would include all the actors from *Reservoir Dogs* or better, perhaps, *The Sopranos*. They are beleaguered, tough-talking, set-jawed, grimly humorous, strong-willed men who speak in tough Americanese peppered with contemporary pop psychology ("closure") and the language of the supermarket ("Excavation, remains, recovery, removal—repeat").

Women are almost completely excluded from the series; the most substantial appearance of females in the first installment is as corpses, and even here the conventions of their gender unsuit them for the site:

> Generally, the bodies that endured best were those of firemen, because they were wrapped in equipment and heavy clothing, whereas the most devastated were those of women, whose stockings and blouses offered poor protection during the collapses and after death.[21]

The only other significant appearance by a woman early in the series features the homespun wisdom of one of the heroes' wives, a schoolmarm in Langewiesche's pioneer drama. Part Two is more sensational, so while men experience harrowing, heroic escapes, a woman is used to symbolize the terror and helplessness of the victims. There's a depressing sense by this point that Langewiesche is not just writing a novel, but a screenplay. The writer is able to piece together a scene inside the cabin of American Flight 11 from the cellphone call a passenger is supposedly able to place, climaxing in her horrified epiphany when she glances out a window to realize that the plane is screaming low over Broadway toward the financial district:

Seconds before 8:46 and the impact she looked through a window to give a position report, and to her surprise saw the city flashing by. She said, "I see water and buildings!" She may have been the first person to understand the hijackers' intentions. She said, "Oh, my God! Oh, my God!"[22]

In Part Three women reappear with a vengeance, emerging from the shadows to throw themselves hysterically across caskets and shriek wildly at the cooler-headed men who try to appease them. When the firemen's widows appear, Langewiesche has an appropriate object on which to hang the uncomfortable emotions of the situation. The scene of the widows' meeting in Part Three resembles nothing so much as the scene of the bank panic in *It's a Wonderful Life*, where George Bailey calms the angry townsfolk. But in this script there is no Lionel Barrymore ("sentimental hogwash!") or Akim Tamiroff—the shade of villainy that Langewiesche begins to suggest for Giuliani early on is dispelled here, as he becomes the voice of reason. Late in the story another breed of woman appears to upset the workings of the Inner World—a consulting psychologist:

> She had a slow, soothing way of talking, which had the immediate effect of irritating him. He told me about it the next day, exaggerating the intervals between her words.
> He said, "She says, 'Close . . . your . . . eyes.'
> "So I close my eyes. Okay, now what?
> "She says, 'Imagine . . . a . . . safe . . . place.'
> "I think, safe place? What's that? At least she could have said 'Imagine a steak house.' I mean, where've you been, lady? . . ."[23]

This is the story of these men's new lives—the trappings of civilization are no more appropriate to them than they are to Huck Finn; the street smarts of these warriors trump the book-learning of the women and the bureaucrats every time. As the operation winds down, Langewiesche observes the sagging spirits of the "Inner World" as they realize that they will soon be "returning to a workplace of fluorescent-lit cubicles and networked computers—an environment that, paradoxically, was all too much like that of the World Trade Center before the collapse." Langewiesche's frontier tale has no frontier; there's nowhere to go from the war zone except back to the office. These are pioneers without a New World, no territories to light out for. They describe themselves as having "gone to the moon."[24]

But there is a new world here, a world in which the myths of American empire have been challenged by a brutal intrusion as surely as Rome's imperial myths were exploded by the Visigoths. Instead of advancing to this frontier, Langewiesche is content to turn us back to the myths that lie torched, scavenged, and buried in the Fresh Kills landfill. Langewiesche's final scenes return to the John Ford iconography; the heroes are dutifully dismissed to take their places in a world they can no longer inhabit, while the forces of civilization close in.

> Safety restrictions were increasing by the day. Ken Holden was philosophical about it, and as his father might have years before, he played a little word game—something

like metaphor-cramming. He said, "When the smoke clears, the nitpickers come out of the closet." And it was true: the regulators had arrived in force. Those from the federal safety agency called OSHA were most in evidence . . . [25]

Langewiesche can't resist metaphor-cramming himself: like father, like son. His hero dispenses wisdom that is at once profound and awkward, in streetwise but—to the educated journalist—slightly ridiculous language. What is more striking about the passage is the odd construction he uses to describe OSHA; does Langewiesche, or his editors, really assume that *Atlantic* readers don't know what the agency is, or is this a ploy to defamiliarize it? One of his tough-guy heroes, on seeing the blinking lights of the agency's safety helmets, says "Look! The Martians have landed . . ." Another man remarks "The safer things get, the greater the restrictions." He is, Langewiesche notes, "a realist." Safety, regulations, rules—do-gooder nonsense from the world of civilization, the world of women, the world back behind the frontier. Langewiesche and his heroes want the thrill of the war-zone back; he wants to see good ol' boys from North Carolina knocking down buildings while standing on top of them—the way men do things:

> Regulation was simply not possible at the start, and even after it began to creep in, its real purpose was to exist officially on the books, playing a rearguard position while the project surged ahead and continued to allow personal responsibility and individual choice to prevail.[26]

This is one of the points where Langewiesche's language most baldly confuses adventure-yarn hyperbole with politically coded think-tank doubletalk, reinscribing not just pioneer virtue but punitive Reagan-era attacks on social institutions. Ironically, the final villain to emerge is the West Coast civil engineering corporation Bechtel, looking for a piece of the action before the trough is empty—the appearance of these Reagan cronies and profiteers in the final chapter is weirdly appropriate (and a final act of heroism on the part of protagonist Ken Holden is to surreptitiously and "at great risk" undermine their efforts until they retreat—at least one of Langewiesche's heroes makes it from the frontier to the rough-and-tumble world of urban politics).

But Langewiesche isn't John Ford—whatever one may say about Ford's conflicted and troubling movies, he recognized the dangerous side of his heroes. In his arguably greatest film, *The Searchers* (1956), Ethan Edwards, portrayed by John Wayne, is a more violent and destabilizing presence on the frontier than the Comanche war chief Scar. Once he's conquered his own rage long enough to fulfill his quest in the movie, he can no longer enter his family's home and, however poignant this scene is, the audience understands its tragic necessity. But when Langewiesche's heroes go home, they're for the most part simply better placed for future careers:

> After dinner the conversation drifted to the meaning of it all, and the subject of history came up. He said he hadn't cared about it before, but cared about it now. He said he sometimes worried about an apocalyptic future. The conversation might then have become too lofty for either of our tastes, were it not for the children at the

table ... who were bored by all the vague talk ... [so he] forgot about history, and simply got on with living.[27]

And that is what Langewiesche wants us to do here—forget about history. Be comforted instead by familiar images of tough guys displaying the can-do American spirit; "loftier" thoughts should be put aside—we wouldn't want to alarm the children with analysis, certainly not at a point when the cradle of civilization is once more contested by any number of apocalypse-minded factions. Langewiesche ends instead bemusedly watching the huge salvaged pieces of the WTC support columns loaded into a Turkish freighter by a "filthy" crew who are "obviously indifferent to the meaning of this load" (though he doesn't seem to actually ask any of them). The pieces are then shipped all over the world, a fitting and ironic end for the pillars of world trade, while the author muses on the White Man's Burden and the passing of the frontier. What he is watching is probably much closer to the passing of empire (and the final stage of removal of unexamined evidence from a crime scene), but his insistence on romanticizing the site of the carnage that signaled it and his reliance on the clichés of the American adventure story are a haze in front of his eyes, and ours, and prevent him from seeing it, a haze as thick as the poison cloud that filled lower Manhattan when the Towers fell. What Langewiesche is doing in his way is presenting the same paradigm by which constitutional law is always set aside in the prospect of war and conquest: men of action need freedom to make tough decisions; they can't be held back by weak-kneed committee-think.

Langewiesche wasn't the only writer looking for ways to make sense of what happened on 9/11 and of the American iconography that seemed threatened by it. In further pursuit of the need to fend off the horror of a world spiraling out of control, many Americans hoped for words of comfort from their icons. They got them. Bruce Springsteen released *The Rising* with a massive publicity campaign at the end of July 2002; he did not release this album as an artist or musician so much as a Rock & Roll Legend and American Hero. In the Reagan era, Springsteen had become the sort of icon of American manliness that even Langewiesche might admire, and as an icon he responded to 9/11 by producing an iconic album with his similarly iconic E Street Band, their first collection of original material since before Reagan left office.

The album seems to be Springsteen's own version, perhaps, of rushing to Ground Zero. In an anecdote reported in every major story about the album, Springsteen was in his car a few days after 9/11 "when a fan rode by": The man rolled down his window, shouted, "We need you!" and drove on. It was the kind of moment, Mr. Springsteen said, that made his career worthwhile.[28]

Springsteen takes his role seriously, and early in the album he offers a prayer to the rescuers who died when the buildings fell:

> May your strength give us strength
> May your faith give us faith
> May your hope give us hope
> May your love give us love.

But this is the last such glimmer of comfort and strength; the songs are mostly desperate calls to the unanswering dead. Though intended as a direct response to the attacks, they draw on Springsteen's standard songwriting imagery (two of the better songs were written before 9/11) and so underline more than ever the hopelessness and impotent defiance in his previous anthems of determination and hope, casting some light on the bleakness of the rest of his work and its true place in the American canon. His albums document the collapse of the American working and middle classes. They extend from the guy who catches his big break in "Rosalita" in 1972 as the Vietnam War winds to a belated end and Richard Nixon's efforts to rig an election begin to unravel, to the fireman who is vaporized in "The Rising," as Americans find a reason to forget about the latest stolen election and to begin a new not-so-Cold War. Consciously or unconsciously, Springsteen has been the voice of a Lost Generation that doesn't quite realize it's lost; he signals the shell shock of his characters in lines like the one in "Prove It All Night" that echoes the end of Hemingway's *The Sun Also Rises*: that "if dreams came true, wouldn't that be nice."

Criticisms of *The Rising* (notably a review in *The Village Voice*) that take Springsteen to task for his political vagueness and reliance on the spectacle of populist heroism[29] suggest a sinister relationship to American politics and culture, but don't go far enough in puzzling out what is problematic in Springsteen's iconography. His work is typically read, in the words of Mikal Gilmore, as "the refusal to accept life's meanest fates or painful limitations." But, on *Nebraska*, *Darkness on the Edge of Town* and *The River*, the albums that earned him this reputation, the refusals are empty and impotent, however powerfully stated. Life's meanest fates are exactly what Springsteen's characters accept. The guy who believes in "The Promised Land" is the same guy who watches his girlfriend's empty eyes in "Racing in the Street" and who leaves his life behind in "Darkness on the Edge of Town," "Stolen Car," and "Hungry Heart," ending up desperate in "Atlantic City" or alone and dangerous in "State Trooper," "Johnny 99" and "Born in the USA." Springsteen's post-*Born to Run* anthems like "Badlands" and "Prove It All Night" were always haunted by the ghost of Tom Joad—the ghost of resistance to murderously overwhelming odds but a ghost nevertheless. From *Born to Run* on, Springsteen fights off a despair that is always at his throat.

It's never been more clear than in the new songs he presented after 9/11 that the resistance to despair that his characters grasp at—so American, so uplifting—is so out of reach:

> It's a fairytale so tragic, there's no prince to break the spell
> I don't believe in magic but for you I will.

In song after song, Springsteen's characters look up to the sky or cry out to their loved ones, but an answer is never forthcoming. Springsteen's vision of death, in fact, though steeped in Catholic imagery, is bleak and terrifying. In the two songs written from the perspective of the dying, the world beyond is an empty lie or a searing blast, and it's these two songs that bring the album to its bleak climax, "My City of Ruins."

In "Paradise," Springsteen's narrator is a woman and a suicide bomber, and her only hope beyond her final act (which is left uncontextualized, depoliticized) is to see her child again. But her death isn't what she expects; though she finally "break[s] above the waves" and feels "the sun upon my face," her hopes are dashed:

> I search for you on the other side
> Where the river runs clean and wide
> Up to my heart the waters rise
> I sink 'neath the water cool and clear
> Drifting down, I disappear
> I see you on the other side
> I search for the peace in your eyes
> But they're as empty as paradise.

In the song preceding this one, the title track, the fireman who's "lost track of how far I've gone . . . how high I've climbed" finally realizes that he is watching his own death come at him, and the world burn away, in images that are hair-raising:

> There's spirits above and behind me
> Faces gone black, eyes burnin' bright
> May their precious blood bind me
> Lord, as I stand before your fiery light.

The narrator's shock and surprise are in Springsteen's voice, and the song ends not with a triumphant entrance to paradise but a yearning "dream of life," grim and conflicted:

> Sky of blackness and sorrow
> Sky of love, sky of tears
> Sky of glory and sadness
> Sky of mercy, sky of fear
> Sky of memory and shadow
> Your burnin' wind fills my arms tonight
> Sky of longing and emptiness
> Sky of fullness, sky of blessed life.

The album ends with "My City of Ruins," a song that Springsteen wrote about the decaying Jersey shore and performed almost a year before September 2001. The song returns thematically to the *Nebraska* album and uses a slight variation of the chord progression to that album's "Atlantic City." When we see "My City of Ruins" as a rewrite/continuation of that song, the call to "rise up" is emptied of anything but bitter and impotent irony. Springsteen doesn't use "these hands" (the repeated evocation at the end of the song and the album) to rebuild the ruins; he uses them to pray for strength and faith, leaving his fate in hands beyond. Springsteen leaves no more hope than Harriet Beecher Stowe did in *Uncle Tom's Cabin*—"the victory":

freedom, equality, dignity, salvation—lies in the next world. In this world, only more blood, more injustice, more struggle. For the characters in Springsteen's songs, 9/11 was a denouement, a finishing touch on the destruction the Nixon-Reagan-Bush-Clinton era was able to wreak on American citizens, and predictably, Springsteen's attempt to rush to the scene ends in agonized, empty gestures and empty hands.

Filmmaker T.S. Bennett reminds us in *What a Way to Go* (2007) that we are "captives to stories,"[30] and it seems to be the insistence on clinging to familiar stories that has brought us to this pass. Late in *The Shape of Things to Come* pop culture critic Greil Marcus draws a parallel between Steve Darnall and Alex Ross' 1997 *US—Uncle Sam* and John Grisham's most "radical" novels of the same time, *The Runaway Jury* and *The Partner*. In Grisham's books, Marcus says, the United States is "an interlocking directorate of corruption that links public institutions, the law, corporations, and crime until none is distinguishable from the other . . . There are no national fairy tales of innocence and good intentions, no comforting bedtime stories like the Declaration of Independence or the Gettysburg Address."[31] 9/11 made such a naked picture of the United States almost blasphemous, until it finally began to become clear—again—that Grisham's picture is, if incomplete, essentially correct. But the will to shatter—or to finally realize—the fantasy of democracy by destroying the hideous reality now seems like the wildest fairy tale imaginable. The story of America—of the world—after September 11, 2001, needs to be a story of change; the very terms by which American Ground is to be understood must be radically re-visioned. But for many in the field of American cultural production—as with the march of commerce, as with the maneuverings of politics—it's business as usual.

Notes

1   Roger Rosenblatt, "The Age of Irony Comes to an End," *Time.com*, http://www.time.com/time/covers/1101010924/esroger.html (accessed October 12, 2009).

2   Ben Schwartz, "'It Seems Like Exactly the Wrong Film to Make,'" *Salon.com*, October 15, 2002, http://dir.salon.com/story/ent/movies/int/2002/10/15/avary/index.html (accessed October 12, 2009).

3   Mark Slouka, "A Year Later: Notes of America's Intimations of Mortality," *Harper's*, September 2002, 35–43.

4   Though no one to my knowledge hung the "prophet" sign on Dylan after the attacks, it's a little chilling to go back to hear some of the images emerge in the dark, poisoned landscape through which his songs twist.

5   The name is a bit off-putting but perhaps emblematic of the storytelling methods common in the United States that are under discussion here; prior to 9/11, the name had most often been assigned to the spots on which (more accurately, above which) atomic bombs were detonated at Hiroshima and Nagasaki.

6   The term would soon become common—and notorious—as the Pentagon for a time took complete control of news coming out of Iraq, allowing only "embedded" journalists to come anywhere near US military operations.

7   William Langewiesche, "American Ground: Unbuilding the World Trade Center, Part One: The Inner World," *The Atlantic Monthly* 290.1 July/August 2002, 52.

8   Ibid., 48. This has so far proven to be untrue, since the site is now meant to simply hold a taller building.

9   In fairness to Fiedler, if not Langewiesche, the reporter doesn't completely follow the template the critic laid out for the American Romances of the nineteenth century.

There is no Queequeeg here, no Jim, no Chingotchgook. Langewiesche's cast is almost all white.

10   Langewiesche, 50.

11   This may be unfair to Ford, who sometimes had strong women characters in his films, though they were often as monolithic as the men.

12   William Langewiesche, "American Ground: Unbuilding the World Trade Center, Part Two: The Rush to Recover," *The Atlantic Monthly* 290.2 *The Atlantic Monthly*, September 2002, 55.

13   William Langewiesche, "American Ground: Unbuilding the World Trade Center, Part Three: The Dance of the Dinosaurs," *The Atlantic Monthly* 290.3 October 2002, 98.

14   Langewiesche may have been overzealous in his pursuit of a good story; he has been accused of simply inventing details, and both he and the *Atlantic* have admitted to lax, or nonexistent, fact-checking on the story in some instances. See the WTC Living History Project Group's account of the controversy.

15   Langewiesche, "American Ground . . . Part One," 48.

16   Ibid.

17   Ibid., 55.

18   Langewiesche, "American Ground . . . Part Three," 115.

19   Ibid., 95.

20   Ibid., 106.

21   Langewiesche, "American Ground . . . Part Two," 76.

22   Ibid., 50.

23   Langewiesche, "American Ground . . . Part Three," 119.

24   Ibid., 125.

25   Ibid., 124.

26   Ibid., 118.

27   Ibid., 126.

28   Jon Pareles, "His Kind of Heroes, His Kind of Songs," *New York Times*, July 14, 2009, section 2, page 1.

29   And rightly so; Springsteen's tepid support of John Kerry in 2004, appearing at a few rallies to sing an acoustic version of "No Surrender," was too little, too late—to say the least—in making overt the political implications of his songs.

30   *What a Way to Go: Living at the End of Empire*, DVD, directed by Timothy S. Bennett (Hancock, VT: Vision Quest Pictures, 2007).

31   Greil Marcus, *Shape of Things to Come: New Sculptures* (New York: Rizzoli, 2009): 260.

CHAPTER 6

An Early Broadside: The Far Right Raids *Master and Commander: The Far Side of the World*

JEFF BIRKENSTEIN

"Of course, there must be subtleties. Just make sure you make them obvious."

—Billy Wilder

"We in Hollywood have to get on with doing our creative work . . . The country needs what we create."

—Jack Valenti, September 27, 2001

"Historic Truths"

—Sign, not meant to be ironic, above a doorway on the second floor of the War Remnants Museum, Ho Chi Minh City

The War Department Wants to Know: Is Hollywood With Us or Against Us?

On June 16, 2003, President George W. Bush lamented ongoing efforts to "reinterpret" his reasons for invading Iraq: "Now there are some who would like to rewrite history—revisionist historians is what I like to call them."[1] Bush had seen his own father use the Persian Gulf War with mixed results to, in part, try to end the "Vietnam Syndrome." A simulacrum of the "real" war of his youth, the senior Bush knew that the historic view of his war would depend as much on the message as the results, for, as Melani McAlister argues, "The Gulf War was simultaneously a major military action and a staged media event . . . the United States and its allies responded with military actions that were also consciously staged with the media in mind."[2] Twelve years later, George W. Bush was desperate to prevent Iraq from becoming his own "Vietnam," so he employed Old West bluster to help frame the argument, including: "Bring 'em on!" and "Wanted: Dead or Alive." As Stacy Takacs points out in this volume, the simple "good vs. bad" in the Westerns of Bush's youth is a particularly apt metaphor for how he styled both his public image and his attempt to craft the national narrative. In *The End of Victory Culture*, a pre-9/11 book, Tom Engelhardt asks, "whether a national story [as in such Westerns] will . . . be sustainable for a superpower in a world of transnational media entities intent on their own styles of global storytelling."[3] The younger Bush had also seen message control largely work with Republican patriarch Ronald Reagan, a Hollywood cowboy who finally found his ideal acting role as president. Post-9/11, Bush and his supporters believed that America required a narrative right out of the "Old West," and they were going to do what it took to supply it.

In the Internet Age's first major American military engagement, the visual image (and its absence) continues to play a central strategic and propagandistic role. We are familiar with the myriad post-9/11 propaganda fronts: we have "Fair and Balanced," "Mission Accomplished," "embedded" journalists, yellow ribbons, and the invention of "swiftboating." This list could be very long indeed. But as of the summer of 2009, no Hollywood blockbuster speaking overtly to our post-9/11 condition has come to the fore. True, we have had a number of related Hollywood dramas, but they have been box office failures. The general lack of financial success of such films (e.g. *Syriana*, 2005; *In the Valley of Elah*, 2006; *Lions for Lambs*, 2007; *Redacted*, 2007; *Rendition*, 2007)[4] is perhaps a sign that America rejects such allegedly anti-jingoistic films, though maybe such dramas hit too close to the truth to be enjoyed as entertainment. As the Bush administration wound down, more documentaries arrived (such as Errol Morris's *Standard Operating Procedure*, 2008 and Alex Gibney's *Taxi to the Dark Side*, 2007), but despite excellent reviews they, too, did not much affect the national narrative. Perhaps the only post-9/11-related film to make a substantial amount of money *and* become a cultural force was Michael Moore's *Fahrenheit 9/11*, a film that does not wear well with time.[5]

Nevertheless, cultural warriors on all sides recognize the power of a popular Hollywood film. Thus, one of the first post-9/11 battles over a major Hollywood production and its connection to the "War on Terror" was the curious case of film criticism that erupted in 2003 when the film *Master and Commander: The Far Side of the World* arrived in theaters.[6] A film widely lauded for its intense early-nineteenth-century naval warfare verisimilitude, it was produced before but released after America's invasion of Iraq. Roundly praised, many critics also noted its potential relevance to post-9/11 events. For instance, A.O. Scott writes that "[i]t is tempting to read some contemporary geopolitical relevance into this film."[7] For most reviewers, this temptation proved too strong to resist.

In this chapter, I will examine a small but important front in the post-9/11 American culture war: the attempted far right usurpation of *Commander* as an early propagandistic shot across the bow in support of President Bush's Iraq adventure. For example, Melinda Ledman at *Hollywoodjesus.com* argues: "*Master and Commander* finally provides some new food for thought, rejecting the bleeding heart treatment of war and exploring several other aspects which can offer valuable lessons in our daily grind."[8] If "[m]odern Western history essentially begins," as Michel de Certeau argues, "with differentiation between the *present* and the *past*,"[9] 9/11 is certainly such a site, endlessly recycled and re-visioned by political design; it is the latest Pearl Harbor or JFK assassination. *Commander* was enlisted in this war because it fit the meme of how the far right wanted the US to conduct itself in the post-9/11 era. Conservative commentators crafted a meta-narrative of the film that created of it an idealized example of how to fight and win President Bush's "War on Terror," a war he "declared" in a speech to a Joint Session of Congress on September 20, 2001.

However, I argue that the film, carefully examined, actually undermines the goals of the "War on Terror." *Commander* (a kind of Western on the high seas) does not celebrate an endless war between clashing civilizations, but repudiates it. Far right critics who embraced the film misunderstood it, both on its own terms and as it relates to our post-9/11 condition. They highlighted the film's sense of the ideal, unquestioned leader; nostalgia for a supposedly simpler time of men and paternalism uncluttered by female influence; and the concept of perpetual war as the ideal state of society. Instead, *Commander* is a nuanced and questioning narrative that challenges the very notion of war that its far right supporters celebrate.

Commandeering the Celluloid

Thought by most on the right to be a "superb and proudly conservative film,"[10] *Commander*, starring Russell Crowe as the beloved Captain "Lucky" Jack Aubrey, was embraced as the exact expression of how the US should comport itself during this troubled time: an unequivocal expression of martial might and victory which, according to *National Review* writer Ross Douthat, "celebrated patriotism, military valor, and masculine solidarity."[11] The reviews and commentary from the right supporting *Commander* originated from across this socio-political spectrum. For instance, omnipresent conservative critic Charles Krauthammer, not normally in the business of film reviews per se, nevertheless takes a stab at *Commander*. Krauthammer's column appears not in the established *film* section, but on the *op/ed* pages of newspapers. Because of his ubiquitous presence in the American popular media (in syndication, on Fox News), Krauthammer's review represents the tip of a wide-ranging conservative spear, most of which falls largely under the radar.

Krauthammer understands that a film's perceived success is tied to its box office receipts. And while he acknowledges that "[i]t is perhaps odd to worry about a film's box office," he wants to do his part to make the film a success, because he believes so much in the film's supposed message. Here, the article's "money shot":

> Perhaps it will be helped in the United States by its timing. We are at war, and this is a film not just about the conduct of war but about virtue in war. Its depiction of the more ancient notions of duty, honor, patriotism and devotion is reminiscent of what we glimpsed during the live coverage of the dash to Baghdad back in April but is now slipping from memory.
>
> The film was apparently planned a decade ago, long before Sept. 11, long before Afghanistan, long before Iraq. But it arrives at a time of war. And combat on the high seas—ships under unified command meeting in duelistic engagement in open

waters—represents a distilled essence of warfare that, in the hands of a morally serious man such as Weir, is deeply clarifying.[12]

Krauthammer is, in November 2003, already afraid the US is failing to win the "War on Terror" and looks to *Commander* as a model of the "distilled essence of warfare" not readily visible, but fervently yearned for, in his and Bush's "War on Terror."

Knowing Krauthammer is an ardent and public supporter of Bush's policies (at least at one time; many of Bush's supporters are, curiously, not as vocal anymore), it is easy to see why the surface of the film would seduce him and his colleagues. John Collee, quoted in Peter Thompson's review of the film, said about his *Commander* screenplay (co-written with director Peter Weir) that it "is selling people about a philosophy of life . . . selling an idea about how life should be led."[13] But *Commander* is more nuanced then those on the right acknowledge. Thomas Foster argues that neoconservative "post-9/11 nationalist discourses and policies pose a basic challenge to the left intellectual tradition of ideology critique."[14] This is in part because a substantial chunk of this narrative depends not on objectivity per se (or an attempt at it) but paeans to a visceral, jingoistic, often irrational sense of belonging to a US that is both superior to all other nations and infallible.

Most reviews (on the right *and* the left) point out that *Commander* is taken piecemeal from several Patrick O'Brian novels. The film takes place almost entirely at sea and on the Galapagos Islands. On the surface, both environments are austere and orderly, though one is overcrowded and the other deserted (even the ocean is a kind of desert). The drama begins in 1805: "Napoleon is master of Europe / Only the British fleet stands before him / Oceans are now battlefields." Jack and the men of the *HMS Surprise* are fighting to the death, and their full concentration and ability to work together on the task at hand will in part determine their survival. Luck plays a part, too, of course, so it is a good thing they are commanded by Lucky Jack. Their mission: "Intercept French Privateer ACHERON en route to Pacific / INTENT ON CARRYING THE WAR INTO THOSE WATERS / . . . Sink, Burn or take her as a Prize." For the next two hours, we see in exacting detail the *cri de coeur* that is the orgasm of battle and the postcoital recovery of wounded bodies and ships. The warfare, even at its most heated, remains a team sport, as methodical and controlled as possible amidst the blood and guts. Discipline, unquestioned fealty, rank, and an eighteenth-century understanding of gentlemen's honor (among the English "gentlemen" anyway; the French don't live up to their end of the bargain) are mostly maintained throughout the savagery of combat. There is a certain time-honored nobility to the warfare, a pre-World War I sensibility about the splendor of the bloodlust. This proves to be a powerful attraction to Krauthammer and others who lament that the "War on Terror" does not offer enemies meeting on a field with agreed-upon terms. Another powerful aphrodisiac for the right is the virtual lack of dissent onboard. The necessity of the war against Napoleon is never questioned; the Royal navy believes it is England's last, best hope against a Bonaparte invasion. Unlike our current wars (especially Iraq), action against Napoleon is accepted absolutely by almost all members of Jack's ship. The one exception is Jack's friend, the surgeon and naturalist Stephen Maturin, who acts as the film's conscience, the ship's Doubting Thomas.

In *The New American Militarism*, Andrew J. Bacevich illuminates the modus operandi behind the right's embrace of *Commander*: "through war, [the neoconservatives believe,] the United States might yet save the world, and in doing so might also save itself. In America's future loomed the prospect of one, two, many Iraqs, and the future at long last appeared bright."[15] This belief nestles easily, if superficially, into the film's worldview of perpetual war between England and Bonaparte's France. Presciently, the film's antagonist differs from the book, which saw Jack fighting a superior *American* warship. After 9/11, and on the heels of juvenile reactions to perceived slights—like renaming French fries "Freedom Fries" and using the supposed epithet "cheese-eating surrender monkeys" liberally—France was widely shunned in the US. This change from book to film and the film's timing were downright serendipitous for its conservative promoters. Krauthammer cannot resist celebrating this change, which "allows US audiences the particular satisfaction of seeing Anglo-Saxon cannonballs puncturing the Tricolor."[16] Touché.

But the Frenchness of Jack's opponent is merely the *pièce de résistance* for Krauthammer and others. Of prime import is the belief in the protagonists' attributes, including their seeming single-mindedness, righteous claims to purity, and their apparent success fighting for God and country far from home (in the film: Captain Jack and the crew of the *Surprise*; in the "War on Terror": Bush, Cheney, Rumsfeld, Rice, and their unquestioning supporters). If, as Chris Hedges sardonically argues, war is a force that gives us meaning,[17] then that meaning must at all times and from a variety of social, political, and cultural angles be bolstered by those who, for whatever reason, have a vested interest in seeing war continue.

Lucky Jack vs. Former-President Bush

Jeffrey Overstreet (of *Christianitytoday.com*) writes in his review of the film that "[t]here are few subjects more relevant than that of a leader's responsibilities in wartime."[18] Critics on the right, perhaps uncomfortable with Bush's inadequacies, posit Lucky Jack to be an ideal master and commander. Ken Masugi, who once worked for Clarence Thomas and is a Senior Fellow at The Claremont Institute, writes that Jack's "men trust him like a god—he can preach, exhort, condemn them to death. The ship is his kingdom. And he drives his men to superhuman achievements, against their own doubts. He has mastery of all science, religion, and politics."[19] Public Jack is beyond question, beyond reproach, yet loved by his entire crew. He is also a benevolent dictator, and this, too, is understood to be the natural order of things by his crew. One can see why unquestioned leadership would be attractive to some; it appears to simplify things. Because of Bush's half-joking, we know he is not completely unsympathetic to such a form of leadership: "If [the US] were a dictatorship, it'd be a heck of a lot easier, just so long as I'm the dictator."[20] At every turn, a disconnect lies between the film's idealized commander and the Bush his supporters wish he could be.

Two key rallying scenes in *Commander* stand in stark contrast to Bush's triumphalism, even if appeals to patriotism and fear of the Other are similar. First, the crew practices their broadside firing time:

> Lads! That's not good enough. We need to fire two broadsides to her one. You wanna see a guillotine in Piccadilly?—No! [roars the crew]—You wanna call that raggedy-ass Napoleon your king?—No! [the crew]—You want your children to sing the "La Marseillaise"?—No! [the crew].

Second, and reminiscent of Bush's impromptu rallying cry atop World Trade Center rubble, Jack speaks to his men with the French ship, the *Acheron* (named after the river in Hades which can only be navigated once), bearing down on them:

> I know you're as anxious as I am to get into close action. But we must bring 'em right up beside us before we spring this trap. That will test our nerve. And discipline will count just as much as courage . . . England is under threat of invasion. And though we be on the far side of the world, this ship is our home. This ship is England.

When Bush grabbed a bullhorn and spoke at Ground Zero, it was arguably one of the last times he had the sympathy and/or support of an overwhelming majority of Americans. Bush and his handlers understood it was crucial to their many policies to extend the "absolute presentness"—how art critics describe the act of viewing a "singular visual event"[21]—of the 9/11 moment indefinitely in order to ensure the maintaining of an enemy around which Americans could rally.

But a British ship of war during the Napoleonic wars is far different from the ship of state Bush turned over to Obama in January 2009. While Jack is about to see his men killed before him, Bush not only banned the photographic distribution of flag-covered coffins, but long eschewed attending funerals of dead American soldiers. The *Surprise* may be a microcosm for England—and for our critics on the right, a proxy for America—but on it civil liberties do not exist, an irony Krauthammer and others overlook. The *Surprise* is not a democracy but a dictatorship; indeed, some seamen are probably impressed men and not even volunteers. Further, all the men aboard seek prize money, a lure so compelling that men will kill, die, and send others to their death for it. Just before they board the *Acheron* in the film's climax, Jack yells "For England, for home, and for the prize!" His emphasis is squarely on "the prize!"

Today, American soldiers are not allowed to secure such bounty (see the Persian Gulf war film, *Three Kings*, 1999[22]), but instead must protect higher paid civilian contractors who secure modern forms of bounty: government and industrial contracts. Ultimately, Jack operates within a system that the contemporary US, hopefully, could or would never tolerate: absolute rule. In the eighties, Ronald Reagan invoked the superhuman warrior Rambo when "making real threats against Middle East hostage takers."[23] Post-9/11, Lucky Jack became a surrogate for a weak president who presided over a divided nation.

Masculine Solidarity

Steve Sailer writes in *The American Conservative*:

> Crowe is putting on weight as he ages, making him even more of a man's man star. Here, he plays the kind of leader that men wish to serve under—fair and amiable in peace, but as cunning as Odysseus in battle . . . you only get to be an enduring star if you primarily appeal to your own sex.[24]

Commander was commonly seen by the conservative commentariat as a "man's movie." Jay Levitz of *Christianspotlight.com* calls the film an "ideal experience for young men on their way to manhood."[25] Holly McClure argues in *Crosswalk.com* that it is "for mature audiences, but I think teenagers (especially boys) will enjoy watching a story about men (and young men) who united, overcame odds and achieved victory."[26] There are almost no women in the film and, superficially anyway, few, if any, troubling issues of sexuality.

The desire to reduce or negate the importance of sexuality and sexual power—and women's roles—in war conforms to long-established masculinist narratives. Contemporaneously, "in the immediate aftermath of 9/11, dominant representations of the US self-as-nation were constructed through particular discourses in ways that resonated with the prior masculinization of US identity."[27] *Commander*, then, was used by its far right supporters to counteract the increasing "feminization of Western culture,"[28] a culture where, in the US anyway, women are increasingly integrated into the military. This integration includes the heightened normalization of both women in combat and women dying in combat. Though hardly equal, women occupy a space in the US military today scarcely imagined even a few decades ago. This is a troubling development for many on the right and another reason why they embraced *Commander* as an example of how the "War on Terror" *should* be fought.

Regarding sexuality and power in war, the film has a kind of "Don't Ask, Don't Tell" quality, one that reviewers on the right either ignored or never saw. It is hard to know because such references were roundly missed in the mainstream, too. For example, Scott, writing in the *New York Times*, references Churchill, and his claim that the British navy owes its success to "rum, sodomy, and the lash." Scott smugly notes that *Commander* "settles for two out of three."[29] In his inimitable way, Christopher Hitchens weighs in:

> Patrick O'Brian was also very stern, as he had to be, about the facts of life aboard ship. There is buggery at sea and rampant heterosexual carnality on land. None of that in this PG-13 version, which has one glance exchanged between Aubrey and a dusky maiden, and not so much as a sight gag about the vulnerable presence of preteen midshipmen among the scrotum-like swinging hammocks.[30]

This is a skewed reading of the film. The film, in fact, harbors strong suggestions of child rape, prostitution, and sadomasochistic male warrior rituals (the lash, among other things).

The male body and its conquest (through war, power, and/or sex) is a key narrative in the film. Though a significant difference between *Commander* and a classic Western is that a ship of war is a community, the Western ethos of a lone man (or outcast renegades) fighting the civilizing, and feminizing, effects of community persists. Steve Neale explains that "the western['s] conventions . . . function precisely to privilege, examine, and celebrate the body of the male."[31] Chris Holmlund writes that ". . . many film theorists now stare at the bodies of male stars. Today's hot male box office bodies may not always be as 'powerful and omnipotent' as Neale claims the young Eastwood's was, but they are still white, and still heterosexual."[32] Russell Crowe is certainly a performer begging to be stared at, but he is a new kind of Clint Eastwood, portly and vulnerable.

Sensing this weakness in the film's protagonist, the reviews from the right express a certain thankfulness that no substantive female roles exist,[33] like the love interest plaguing Gregory Peck in a similarly-themed film, *Captain Horatio Hornblower* (1951).[34] The Brothers Judd explain: "Rather than introducing a Hollywood romance . . . Weir tosses out source material that might broaden the movie's appeal."[35] The brief, normative heterosexual scene most referenced (and the one Hitchens mentions above) occurs when the *Surprise* reprovisions. Brown-skinned women, their ethnic status unclear, seem to be offered as prostitutes by the Portuguese administrator. The women are dressed in European-style clothing, parasols spinning seductively, while their apparent counterparts—male and native with long black hair, body paint, and loincloths—canoe them about. Prize money from vanquished ships is not the only benefit of imperial conquest; indigenous bodies are also part of the plunder.

Though Jack orders the ship to depart, he continues staring. In the background we hear (difficult to hear fully without the subtitles): "Put that woman down, Slade! This is a ship of His Majesty's Navy, not a floating bordello. Get yourself back aboard." Jack is himself chastened by this remonstration. Fortunately, no one has noticed his transgression and he escapes without any loss of gentlemanly stature.

In this provocative shot, Jack is shown left of center. On the right is the base of the mast, thick and erect, covered with blood-vessel-like lines. And as long as he cannot tear his eyes from the siren's gaze of the woman and her hypnotic, phallic parasol, Jack's masculinity, based on unwavering commitment to the war machine, is at risk. Sex and romance can never be seen to interfere with the male commander in charge and at war. That the mast in this scene is a hyper-erect phallus is further substantiated by Jack's later emasculation of the *Acheron* (by toppling the mainmast, on which everything depends).

Also celebrated in many far-right reviews is the bond shared by Jack and Maturin, a friendship supposedly at its most basic, devoid of complexity or subterfuge, utterly male. But these reviews rarely understand the relationship's power struggle. Maturin is the film's voice of science and reason beneath Jack's visceral lust for battle. At every turn—after Jack is "forced" to cut loose some rigging thereby drowning one of his own sailors, after Jack is "forced" to mete out a savage lashing, and after Jack is "forced" to renege on his promise to Maturin that there will be ample time to explore the pre-Darwin Galapagos Islands—it is Maturin who must submit. Jack explains:

Figure 2: Lucky Jack gazes down on local women

"Subject to the requirements of the service. I cannot in all conscience delay for the sake of an iguana or giant peccary. Fascinating, no doubt, but of no immediate application." Maturin storms out, coitus interruptus. David Di Certo of *Catholic News Service* sides with Jack: "friendship versus duty and the role of hierarchy in staving off anarchy."[36] Irony wins the day, however, because it is through Maturin's research on insect disguise that Jack learns how to fool the *Acheron*. True, Jack's stay-the-course mentality and dictatorial captain's powers silence Maturin, yet Jack cannot win without him.

Weir also repeatedly undermines the apparent chaste camaraderie aboard ship. True to life, there are young boys aboard. Though buggering is an old activity at sea, *Commander* does not show it directly. In one of several scenes among the crew, talk turns to the *Acheron*:

SEAMAN 1: She's a right phantom she is. The way she come up again, *right behind us like that* [italics added]. Out of nowhere, and *right behind us*. Like that first time out of the fog with our shot bouncin' off her.

SEAMAN 2: Captain's not called Lucky Jack for no reason.

SEAMAN 1: Phantom or no, she's a privateer and Lucky Jack'll have her.

This conversation incorporates complicated issues of hetero- and homosexual power relationships in a community comprised solely of one gender and with a clear hierarchy. The discussion concerns a man (their Captain) versus an elusive female enemy (the ships are all female; defending the *Surprise* in another scene Jack says, "She's not old. She's in her prime!"[37]). The men are disgusted that she has twice surprised the *Surprise*. And when they do couple with the *Acheron*, their (fire)power bounces off the *Acheron*, their shot unable to penetrate the more modern, thicker-hulled ship. But they believe in their captain, as well as their role in the seduction, eventual rape, and conquest: whatever the costs, they will help Jack have her and will celebrate the *Acheron*'s submission.

After this exchange, a young boy, who appears to have the first hint of a moustache—or, is that dirt?—asks if the *Acheron* is a pirate. No, a third seaman, balding and beefy, says, "Oh, no, if they were we could hang them when we catch 'em."[38] He grabs the boy's neckerchief and pulls it upward, forcing the boy's head back, eyes upward, waiting. The seaman's hand lingers on the boy's chest for a moment too long, leaving little doubt about who is in charge and what will happen later. Through military ritual, life aboard ship may pretend to be normalized ("This ship is England"), but it can never re-create civilian life. Yet, many critics on the right see this womanless world as an ideal space where Lucky Jack (and his faithful crew), acting as what Richard Goldstein calls a "neo-macho man," can play war in a gender-sanitized, post-9/11 world: "As women rose, so did male anxiety, and in this edgy climate a new archetype appeared in pop culture: the sexual avenger. His rage often focused on personal betrayal, but implicit in his tirades was a sense of the world turned upside down."[39] These are not relationships that the right wishes to acknowledge.

Conclusion: Perpetual War

The film's conclusion serves also as an exclamation mark for my argument, because it is, well, not conclusive. *Commander* problematizes the very same concept of success in Bush's wars that Krauthammer and others believe the film prognosticates, or at least which they view as an ideal. While critics on the right roundly see a "mission accomplished," the film deconstructs the convenient idea that war can be won decisively, and/or by deliberate design. When Bush and his supporters set out to convince the American people that Iraq required an invasion, they believed a 9/11 connection was crucial.[40] Though they told the American people this was a new era—where the old rules didn't apply—they never seemed to quite trust their own claim. Because the post-9/11 era does not exist in a vacuum, the Bush administration had to override the American belief that, ironically explained here by Ronald Reagan: "[t]he defense policy of the United States is based on a simple premise: the United States does not start fights."[41] Bush knew also, from Korea to Kosovo, that America no longer declares war according to the precepts set out in the Constitution. Bush's Iraq War continues this tradition of avoiding responsibility, thus furthering what Michael Ignatieff argues was the "decay of institutional checks and balances on the warmaking power of the executive."[42]

Figure 3: "This ship is England."

Despite everything he stands for, Jack cannot win with brute force; he must employ guile. The *Surprise* is older and less technologically advanced than the *Acheron*, its hull weaker, its cannons inferior (an officer boldly declares their losses an unfair match and thus without dishonor). The *Surprise*, then, must live up to its name. This Jack and his crew do by disguising themselves as a slow, clumsy whaler, thus bringing the overconfident *Acheron* in close before springing a trap. With the front wheels taken off the cannons so that they angle upwards, the *Surprise* has only one broadside with which to disable the French ship by toppling its mainmast. After the mainmast falls, Jack rams the *Surprise* into the *Acheron* and boards it; the battle is bloodily fought and soon won.[43] In a ritual exchange of phallic power, the doctor hands Jack the dead French Captain's sword. Victory!

Or . . .?

Immediately after the battle, the British dead are mourned and buried at sea; life resumes its monotony, repairs underway. Jack will return to the Galapagos for provisions and "to give the doctor a few days to find his bird," an act of science continually delayed by duty to war. But, alas, this is not to be. When Jack and Maturin retire to the captain's quarters to literally make sweet music together, they engage in something akin to post-coital talk of the just-concluded sex act that is battle. Consequently, they realize that the French Captain is not dead, but disguised himself as the doctor; he is no doubt now plotting his escape on the captured *Acheron*. Just as the ship seems to return to a desired normalcy—reminiscent of Bush's post-9/11 call for Americans to return to their routines and shopping—the drums of war are again sounded. Victory proves both illusory and elusive. Though the audience still has Lucky Jack on their side—just as the American people were lucky to have Bush on theirs, his supporters remind us—the film ends inconclusively, the ship beating to quarters. Not a single writer in question acknowledges this.

During World War II, Paul Virilio reminds us, American "cinema production was watched closely by the military high command."[44] Although perhaps in a very different form, this remains the case post-World War II, for the Pentagon often cooperates on films with which, one can assume, it largely approves (*The Green Berets*, 1968; *Top Gun*, 1986; and, more recently, *Pearl Harbor*, 2001[45]). But overt propaganda now also falls to the many think tanks and columnists on both sides of the current American socio-political civil war. Despite all the advancements in technology, Virilio argues, "[w]ar can never break free from the magical spectacle because its very *purpose* is to produce that spectacle: to fell the enemy is not so much to capture as to 'captivate' him, to instill the fear of death before he actually dies."[46] Shock and awe. From D.W. Griffith's *The Birth of a Nation* (1915) and Leni Riefenstahl's *Triumph of the Will* (1935)[47] to today's commercials for the military and National Guard (often shown before a film begins at the theatre), the purpose of producing complicit spectacles is little changed.

In *Gladiator* (2000), another film starring Russell Crowe, we meet the post-modern, and pre-9/11, former-general-turned-slave Maximus. After he has single-handedly killed a band of gladiators, he demands of the crowd, "Are you not entertained?" before throwing his sword down and spitting in disgust.[48] Maximus is at once a postmodern skeptic even as his film—and his life—depends on the very spectacle its protagonist mocks. The (neo-)(religio-)conservative narrative (no term is all-encompassing, of course) enveloping *Commander* is not about life and death (because the propagandists' lives are not on the line), but something more important: it is about untold political and spiritual power and military-industrial profit, predicated on an endless and just war. And if Lucky Jack can help America effect such a war, then this is what the right will try to make him do, sound argument or not.

Notes

1   George W. Bush, "Bush Raps 'Revisionist Historians' on Iraq," *CNN.com*, June 16, 2003, http://www.cnn.com/2003/ALLPOLITICS/06/16/bush.iraq/ (accessed October 13, 2009).

2   Melani McAlister, *Epic Encounters: Culture, Media, and US Interests in the Middle East, 1945–2000* (Berkeley, CA: University of California Press, 2001), 239.

3   Tom Engelhardt, *The End of Victory Culture: Cold War America and the Disillusioning of a Generation* (New York: Harper Collins, 1995), 301.

4   *Syriana* (Stephen Gaghan, 2005); *In the Valley of Elah* (Paul Haggis, 2007); *Lions for Lambs* (Robert Redford, 2007); *Redacted* (Brian De Palma, 2007); *Rendition* (Gavin Hood, 2007).

5   *Standard Operating Procedure* (Errol Morris, 2008); *Taxi to the Dark Side* (Alex Gibney, 2007); *Fahrenheit 9/11* (Michael Moore, 2004).

6   *Master and Commander: The Far Side of the World* (Peter Weir, 2003).

7   A.O. Scott, "Master of the Sea (and the French)," *New York Times*, November 14, 2003.

8   Melinda Ledman, "Review of *Master and Commander: The Far Side of the World*," *Hollywoodjesus.com*, November 7, 2003, http://www.hollywoodjesus.com/master_commander.htm (accessed October 13, 2009).

9   Michel de Certeau, *The Certeau Reader*, ed. Graham Ward (New York: Blackwell, 2000), 24.

10 The Brothers Judd, "Review of *Master and Commander: The Far Side of the World*," *Brothersjudd.com*, April 24, 2004, http://brothersjudd.com/index.cfm/fuseaction/reviews.moviedetail/movie_id/83/Master%20and%20Commander:%20The%20Far%20Side%20of%20the%20World.htm (accessed October 13, 2009).

11 Ross Douthat, "So, You Want to Win the Culture Wars? It Would Help to Engage in a Little Culture," *Theamericanscene.com*, December 13, 2004, http://theamericanscene.com/pubs/nr121304.html (accessed October 13, 2009).

12 Charles Krauthammer, "*Master and Commander*: Success on the High Seas," *Jewish World Review.com*, November 14, 2003, http://www.jewishworldreview.com/cols/krauthammer111403.asp (accessed October 13, 2009).

13 Peter Thompson, "Review of *Master and Commander: The Far Side of the World*," *Ninemsn.com*, http://sunday.ninemsn.com.au/sunday/film_reviews/article_1458.asp?s=1 [Link broken].

14 Thomas Foster, "Cynical Nationalism," in *The Selling of 9/11: How a National Tragedy Became a Commodity*, edited by Dana Heller (New York: Palgrave Macmillan, 2005), 254.

15 Andrew Bacevich, *The New American Militarism: How Americans Are Seduced by War* (New York: Oxford University Press, 2005), 96.

16 Krauthammer, "*Master and Commander*."

17 Chris Hedges, *War Is a Force That Gives Us Meaning* (New York: Anchor, 2003).

18 Jeffrey Overstreet, "Review of *Master and Commander: The Far Side of the World*," *Christianitytoday.com*, http://www.christianitytoday.com/movies/reviews/2003/masterandcommander.html?start=2 (accessed October 13, 2009).

19 Ken Masugi, "Review of *Master and Commander: The Far Side of the World*," *The Claremont Institute*, December 5, 2003, http://www.claremont.org/publications/pubid.314/pub_detail.asp (accessed October 13, 2009).

20 George W. Bush, "Transition of Power: President-Elect Bush Meets with Congressional Leaders on Capitol Hill," *CNN.com*, December 18, 2000, http://transcripts.cnn.com/TRANSCRIPTS/0012/18/nd.01.html (accessed October 13, 2009).

21 Øyvind Vågnes, "'Chosen to be Witness': The Exceptionalism of 9/11," in *The Selling of 9/11: How a National Tragedy Became a Commodity*," ed. Dana Heller (New York: Palgrave Macmillan, 2005), 57.

22 *Three Kings* (David O. Russell, 1999).

23 Stephen Prince, *Visions of Empire: Political Imagery in Contemporary American Film* (New York: Praeger, 1992), 64.

24 Steve Sailer, "Review of *Master and Commander: The Far Side of the World*," *The American Conservative* (December 1, 2003): 24–5.

25 Jay Levitz, "Review of *Master and Commander: The Far Side of the World*," *Christian Spotlight on Entertainment*, http://christiananswers.net/spotlight/movies/2003/masterandcommander.html?zoom_highlight=master+and+commander (accessed October 13, 2009).

26 Holly McClure, "Review of *Master and Commander: The Far Side of the World*," *Crosswalk.com*, November 14, 2003, http://www.crosswalk.com/movies/1231139/ (accessed October 13, 2009).

27 Laura J. Shepherd, "Constructions of Gender in the Bush Administration Discourse on the Attacks of Afghanistan Post-9/11," *International Feminist Journal of Politics* 8.1 (March 2006): 21.

28 J. Ann Tickner, "Feminist Perspectives on 9/11," *International Studies Perspectives* 3 (2002): 334.

29   Scott, "Master of the Sea."

30   Christopher Hitchens, "Empire Falls: How *Master and Commander* Gets Patrick O'Brian Wrong," *Slate.com*, November 14, 2008, http://www.slate.com/id/2091249/ (accessed October 13, 2009).

31   Chris Holmlund, *Impossible Bodies: Femininity and Masculinity at the Movies* (London: Routledge, 2002), 143.

32   Ibid.

33   In one scene Jack is writing to his "dearest beloved Sophie." The small part we can read is not about their relationship, but about his quest: "Another day in our chase . . ."

34   *Captain Horatio Hornblower* (Raoul Walsh, 1951).

35   Brothers Judd, "Review of *Master and Commander*."

36   David Di Certo, "Review of *Master and Commander: The Far Side of the World*," *ChristinityToday.com*, http://www.christianitytoday.com/movies/reviews/2003/masterandcommander.html?start=3 (accessed October 13, 2009).

37   Ibid.

38   Ibid.

39   Richard Goldstein, "Neo-Macho Man: Pop Culture and Post-9/11 Politics," *Nation* (March 24, 2003): 16.

40   Michael R. Gordon and Jim Rutenberg, "Bush Links Al Qaeda in Iraq to 9/11; Critics Reject Connection," *New York Times*, July 13, 2007, http://www.nytimes.com/2007/07/13/world/africa/13iht-qaeda.1.6641919.html (accessed October 13, 2009).

41   Prince, *Visions of Empire*, 50.

42   Michael Ignatieff, *Virtual War: Kosovo and Beyond* (New York: Metropolitan, 2000), 181.

43   I deliberately did not use the phrase "boards her" though that would have been the vernacular of the day, with all of the male-domination/female-subjugation steadily in tow. In fact, such language is not just from history, but is used today.

44   Paul Virilio, *War and Cinema: The Logistics of Perception*, trans. Patrick Camiller (London: Verso, 1989), 9.

45   *The Green Berets* (Ray Kellogg & John Wayne, 1968); *Top Gun* (Tony Scott, 1986); *Pearl Harbor* (Michael Bay, 2001).

46   Virilio, *War and Cinema*, 5.

47   *The Birth of a Nation* (D.W. Griffith, 1915); *Triumph of the Will* (Leni Riefenstahl, 1935).

48   *Gladiator* (Ridley Scott, 2000).

CHAPTER 7

The Sound of the "War on Terror"

COREY K. CREEKMUR

Question (in Arabic from an Iraqi journalist): General Kimmitt, the sound of American helicopters, which fly so low to the ground, is terrifying young children, especially at night. Why do you insist on flying so low and scaring the Iraqi people?

Brigadier General Mark Kimmitt: What we would tell the children of Iraq is that the noise they hear is the sound of freedom.

—Coalition Provisional Authority press briefing, Baghdad Convention Center (February 25, 2004)

After a while, everything started to sound like a bomb. A door slamming in the house sounded like a bomb. A car backfiring sounded like a bomb. Sometimes it felt like the sounds of bombs and the call to prayer were the only sounds the country could produce, its own strange national anthem.

—Dexter Filkins, *The Forever War*

Many media critics have emphasized that, in tandem with its most brutal manifestations, the "War on Terror" is also a "war of images," a battle over representation, as much a fight for hearts and minds as a geopolitical struggle over land, oil, or idealistic goals such as freedom and security. Jane Gaines insists that "we are engaged in two image wars . . . the *imaged conflict*, a conflict in which one historical moment might have been understood as 'images of war'" and ". . . *the other war*, the one over the imaged war . . . the war about how we view—*how we see what we see as well as what we make of the images that we see and what they make of us*."[1] Similarly, Susan Buck-Morss claims, "the global violence initiated by September 11 has had an impact generally on perception and expression—on seeing and speaking . . . the very tools of our trade—language and image—are being appropriated as weapons by all sides." As she reiterates, "Language—the tool of thought, and image—the tool of cognitive perception, are being appropriated today by discourses of power in a very particular way, one that negates their usefulness for *critical* practices of art."[2]

I can only affirm the call for sustained critical attention to the visual spectacles of terrorism (and counterterrorism) and the terminological wars waged over them. Such claims, while widespread among media critics, still demand emphasis in the midst of persistent blurring of appearance and reality in the service of what can only be imagined as a war without end, because an enemy as elusive as "terror" promises to remain unconquered.

However, for those concerned with contemporary *aural* as well as *visual* culture, the almost exclusive attention critics have paid to *images* (or language) in the "War on Terror" threatens to return to a once common neglect of the role of *sound* (including voice) in the production and reception of mass media, including its pervasive yet non-linguistic or non-musical forms, broadly categorized across media as "sound effects." For instance, in a "post-9/11" chapter written for the updated edition of her insightful study of US media and the Middle East, Melani McAlister analyzes five photographs taken since September 11, 2001, "to argue that the images participated in the process of meaning-making that, from the ashes of 9/11, forged the imperial reach of the Iraq War."[3] Yet even if such images seem to "speak" to us, they do so in literal silence once they have been isolated from their original sonic contexts: the overwhelming roar, screams, cries, and sirens that were fully part of the horrific perceptual experience of 9/11 are often removed from representations of the event, typically viewed in "respectful silence" or with appropriately muted music (in implicit recognition of the power of sound in relation to disturbing images). Similarly, critical discussions of the rise of surveillance technologies have often emphasized the ubiquity of cameras but not of equally pervasive microphones. To take up one of McAlister's iconic examples, we have been appalled by the images of abused Iraqi prisoners in Abu Ghraib. Yet, we have remained deaf to the sounds (including voices of prisoners) of that hellish place, even as (many critics noted) audiences were eager to consume the performed screams of popular "torture-porn" films like *Saw* (James Wan, 2004) and *Hostel* (Eli Roth, 2005), both widely understood as displacements of the witnessing of actual torture.

In order to extend critical accounts of the representation of the "War on Terror" in popular culture, this chapter catalogs and considers some of the increasingly familiar, rapidly conventionalized *sounds* of the "War on Terror." The examples collected here are not meant to be distinctive but rather typical and representative uses of sound across a range of recent films and television programs. Rather than being a realm for invention, the "sound of the War on Terror" found in popular media already draws upon a repetitive, limited repertoire. Before proceeding to identify some of its dominant tropes, a few qualifications and enforced limitations seem necessary. In addition to my desire to question the spurious notion of a "War on Terror" in the first place, I will make the perhaps obvious point that terrorism (insofar as we might agree on a definition of that contested term) produces its own dreadful soundscape: these are the "real" sounds of violence, combat, fear, and pain, the eardrum-shattering blasts of improvised explosive devices (IEDs) and the deafening roar of the US military's "shock and awe" attacks. This soundscape includes pre-packaged sound bytes (from authoritatively technical acronyms to notoriously obfuscating phrases such as "collateral damage") that attempt to reduce the full volume (in both senses) of actual terrorism and responses to it.

While my focus will be the constructed and manipulated sounds of mass media texts, the "actual" sounds of war and violence, of course, haunt these representations, and rare accounts of the wars in Iraq and Afghanistan are attentive to these sounds. For instance, journalist Dexter Filkins' vivid account is notable in part because he frequently describes the sound of modern war, often heard rather than seen:

> The night sky echoed with pops and pings, the invisible sounds of frantic action. Most were being made by the AC-130 gunships, whose propellers were putting out a reassuring hum. But over the droning came stranger sounds: the plane's Gatling gun let out long, deep burps at volumes that were symphonic. Its 105 mm cannon made a popping sound, the same as you would hear from a machine that served tennis balls. A pop! Followed by a boom! Pop-boom. And then there was the insect buzz of the ScanEagle, the pilotless airplane that hovered above us and beamed images back to base. It was as if we were witnessing the violent struggles of an entire ecosystem, a clash of airborne nocturnal beasts we could not see.[4]

Artists and technicians regularly attempt to reproduce these sounds within popular narratives and hyper-realistic battle-centered films, like *Rules of Engagement* (William Friedkin, 2000), *Black Hawk Down* (Ridley Scott, 2001), and *The Kingdom* (Peter Berg, 2007). Similarly, television series, such as *Over There* (2005) and *The Unit* (2006–09), are significantly reinforced by the dense sound design of loud explosions rendered alongside the audibly precise details of automatic weapons firing (with the ping of ejected bullet casings hitting the ground, a favorite of contemporary sound designers).

As part of the audio mix of recent films, launched rockets and helicopters also traverse the sonic space of the auditorium (or properly equipped living room), and tortured or wounded characters howl in amplified and echoed pain. Post-production studios, clearly responding to the market, now include in their sound effects libraries (along with conventional "explosions and fire bursts" or "machine guns and shot guns") pre-packaged collections of general "terrorism sound effects." These archived and marketed sounds, while intended to simulate the noise of actual war and terrorism, must be understood as entirely constructed and fully mediated. Whatever their cumulative "realistic" effects, such sounds are assembled through the layering of musical tracks, scripted screams, and crafted Foley effects, and they are enhanced and reproduced in pristine Dolby and engulfing surround sound. Almost immediately conventionalized through generic repetition, the sound of the "War on Terror" is indeed most effective insofar as it remains *unheard* by critics and audiences as anything but realistic sound reproduction, even when these same spectators have become adept at questioning and resisting the formulaic images that this unquestioned soundtrack persistently accompanies.

I will thus set aside the actual sounds of terrorism—experienced by far fewer people than the sound effects simulating them—and for reasons of space will also neglect the increasingly complex soundtracks of the large number of relevant documentaries (not to mention far more popular video games) engaged with the "War on Terror." I will only briefly note relevant film scores, increasingly themselves a standardized blend of somber elegiac strings, military drumbeats (as well as the now persistent Japanese *taiko* drums underlying action films), and pseudo-Oriental or sometimes even authentic Middle Eastern music. This genre is typically dominated by the signifying presence of conventional Arab instruments like the *oud* (lute) or *nay* (single reed pipe) that override regional or less familiar variations. *Rendition* (Gavin Hood, 2007), for instance, relies on a soundtrack that consistently marks its regular transitions between the United States and the Middle East through the arrival or departure of Middle Eastern musical instruments and styles. At one point, though, the sound of the Middle East briefly invades Washington, DC, when an American wife (Reese Witherspoon) enters an office with a visibly pregnant belly containing the unborn child of her imprisoned and tortured Egyptian husband, as if the multiracial fetus demands a brief sign of its father's cultural heritage on the film's soundtrack.

The broad, but, in fact, often unstable, distinction I am drawing between the authentic sound of terrorism and the fabricated sound of the "War on Terror" is effectively captured by the opening of Jonathan Raban's darkly comic novel *Surveillance* (2006). Set in the near-future United States, the first paragraph evokes what is now recognized as a familiar trope in the soundscape of terrorism, the "deafening roar" of a blast that brings together equally terrifying sound and silence:

> After the explosion, the driver of the overturned school bus stood beside the wreck-age, his clothes in shreds. He was cupping his hands to his ears, as if to spare himself the noise of sirens, car alarms, bullhorns, whistles, and tumbling masonry. When he brought his hands away and held them in front of his face, both palms were dripping blood. His mouth opened wide in a scream that was lost in the surrounding din.[5]

Just one page later, we discover that this horrifying scene, juxtaposing overwhelm-ing noise and traumatic silence, actually concludes a performance that is staged and recorded by the Department of Homeland Security as part of a government program to both prepare for and generate continual public fear of terrorist attacks. As Raban suggests, large and small dramatizations of terrorism are now regularly staged throughout American popular culture, with the borders between reality and fantasy increasingly blurred. Moreover, such formal deceptions—presenting events as frightening reality before revealing their status as performances—have become commonplace in the mass media texts of the "War on Terror," exploiting the fear at the heart of terrorism itself. The sudden violence of terrorism may not be antici-pated or visible, unlike encounters with a uniformed enemy army. Despite frequent recourse to visual stereotypes of Arabs and Muslims, the terrorist or "insurgent" cannot be visibly distinguished from the citizen or "native." For example, the second season of the Showtime television series *Sleeper Cell* (2005–06) begins with what has become a familiar establishing image and sound in recent American popular culture: a mosque and the *adhaan* (or *azaan*), the call to prayer by a *muezzin*, now almost always heard through the amplified distortion of a tinny loudspeaker rather than from an unmediated voice. However, as the camera tracks back, revealing the image of the mosque to be a photograph on a wall, the soundtrack reveals itself to be apparently non-diegetic once we find ourselves in the prison cell of the drama's principal villain, charismatic terrorist leader Faris Al-Farik (dangerous in part because of his ability to "pass" as either an American Jew or Christian). Momentarily, at least, the danger, no longer easily isolated in what is still identified as "the Muslim world" or "Middle East," has again been safely contained, both to a secure cell and presumably to the interior of a terrorist's mind. The mosque is just a photograph of a distant location, although, perhaps in retrospect, the obscure source of the *adhaan* is troubling precisely because it retains a disturbing freedom to circulate beyond this otherwise controlled space.

Found on the soundtrack of virtually all films invoking Islam or the Middle East, the *adhaan* is now more frequently heard in American cinema and television than the ostensibly more familiar Christian bells or perhaps the Jewish *shofar*. Its function, nonetheless, is rarely to provide a simple geographical or cultural cue, as images of the Eiffel Tower and the sound of an accordion might obviously announce a narrative's shift of location to Paris. The *adhaan*, and the simultaneous, massed prayer it solicits, are not just deployed to identify a location or to signal exotic cultural differences. Rather, it is employed as a sound of dread, establishing narrative tension through an emphatic aural announcement of the narrative threat unfolding before us. In fact, this now persistent use of a single sound to summarize Islam and to conflate Muslim prayer with political violence recovers the historical bias of early Christians against the "highly significant and intolerable symbol" of the *adhaan*, as Norman Daniel summarized decades ago in his classic study *Islam and the West*.[6]

Unlike the Christian Lord's Prayer—shared in an intimately cross-cut vocal duet between a doomed passenger and an air traffic controller in the made-for-TV docudrama *Flight 93* (Peter Markle, 2006)—Muslim prayer in "War on Terror" media signals unthinking, indoctrinated repetition rather than the spiritual power of sacred ritual and is thus often heard in the voice of an undifferentiated crowd. In short, in popular American media, Muslim prayer has become the sound of Islamic fundamentalism rather than a common cultural practice; it anticipates political violence while masquerading as religious ritual, narratively functioning as the sonic prelude to the danger that soon follows. *Syriana* (Stephen Gaghan, 2005) is actually invoked *as a film* – prior to the beginning of any narrative content—by an Arabic prayer that perhaps ironically accompanies the movie's paratextual corporate logos. *United 93* (Paul Greengrass, 2006) more conventionally begins with a prayer by the hijackers on the morning of September 11. The film then proceeds without soliciting our suspense (for we all know what will happen) but still relying upon almost unbearable dread. *United 93*, of course, ends with the terrorists' and their victims' oblivion (depicted through silence and a white screen), returning to the void from which the opening prayer issued. Invoked in such cases to begin a recent American film or television program, Muslim prayer asks audiences to brace themselves for the terror sure to follow.

As with *Syriana*, however, such voices often exceed the diegetic world of characters, moving about freely on the soundtrack to intensify an almost literally floating, unmoored anxiety. Such voices are key contemporary manifestations of what Michel Chion famously identified as the *acousmetre*, the voice of an invisible or visually withheld body that, Chion says, "brings disequilibrium and tension." As Chion also noted, the *acousmetre* maintains specific cultural prohibitions: "This interdiction against looking, which transforms the Master, God, or Spirit into an acousmatic voice, permeates a great number of religious traditions, most notably Islam and Judaism."[7] In the "War on Terror," the keening, wailing voice, often only approaching an identifiable "foreign" language, stands for the eternally unknowable Middle East. *The War Within* (Joseph Castelo, 2005), a low-budget portrait of a Muslim terrorist, concludes with a suicide bombing in Grand Central Station that shifts from an unexpected (though now standard) silence when we are braced for a jarring explosion at the moment of detonation to the rising chatter of news media reporting on the attack across the landscape of the city. The soundtrack then finally gives way to non-diegetic male and female voices—"Middle Eastern" although freed of the signification of any specific language—suggesting ongoing threats as well as lamentations. The film concludes with the bomber's young son praying, which depicts the continuation of both faith and violence, now typically conjoined, in successive generations.

I am not engaging here in the fraught debate over the accurate representation of Islam as a violent or peaceful religion, often centered on the interpretation of the term and concept of *jihad*. Instead, from the perspective of a media critic, I wish to emphasize the way in which the reduction of Islam to a very limited set of sounds, and the easy conflation of those with terrorism, is also a travesty of the complex role sound, language, and the voice (in poetry and song as well as explicitly religious genres like prayer or sermons) play in a range of Arab and Muslim cultures. Islam's soundscape is misrepresented not only through the simplification of the production of sound and language, but perhaps even more importantly, through scant attention to actual practices of audition in Muslim culture. A number of cultural and linguistic anthropologists have recently examined the complex intersections of language, technology (particularly the audio cassette), religion, and, especially, audition in contemporary Muslim cultures.[8] Hafia Zangana has also examined a set of sounds that, like images of the dead and wounded, have largely been withheld from American audiences. As she notes, the war in Iraq destroyed the Iraqi music industry years ago, and since April 2003 "as many as seventy-five well-known [Iraqi] singers have been killed," while most music shops have long been destroyed or shut down.[9] Nevertheless, the war has generated a genre of anonymously recorded and quietly distributed resistance songs (*aghani al muqawama*) which obviously have not had the wide commercial distribution of such jingoistic American country songs as Toby Keith's "Courtesy of the Red, White and Blue (The Angry American)" (2002) or Clint Black's "I Raq and Roll" (2003).[10] Such examples should be considered part of a broad, diverse soundscape of the "War on Terror" but are excluded from the limited examples that popular media continue to present as the easily opposed sounds of the "clash of civilizations."

If the now-common conflation of the terrorist with the Muslim Arab has been facilitated through the reduction of terrorism to virtually a single sound (the *adhaan*), the actual languages of the Middle East have suffered similar fates. Notably, recent films have largely abandoned the once-common use of comic or melo-dramatically evil Arabs speaking exclusively in hissing, broadly accented English. Greater sociopolitical realism has motivated the increased use of Arabic (or other Middle Eastern languages and dialects), with *jihad*, at least assumed to be an Arabic word American audiences no longer need translated.[11] However, this increased realism ironically allows the "foreignness" of foreign languages to be sustained, especially through the careful *absence* of translation through subtitles or dialogue. Legal scholar Steven W. Bender has persuasively argued that the "War on Terror" has had significant consequences for American Latinas/os as well as Arab Americans, Arabs, and Muslims in the United States. These consequences are achieved in part through increasingly intolerant "English-only" legislation, aimed not at improving crosscultural communication or assimilation but driven by a desire to disallow "foreign" languages in the public sphere, with particular focus on the fear of conspiracies crafted "openly" in foreign languages most Americans cannot understand.[12]

In recent films that include Arabic, Farsi, Urdu or other "Middle Eastern" languages, the authenticity that their use brings is typically offset by the language's reduction to sound rather than communication, to a signifier of mystery and danger rather than simply untranslated information. Again, the subtitling of such languages is often strategically withheld, as in *United 93* or *Syriana*, which selectively provide subtitles for only some of the non-English dialogue heard throughout the films. Tension intensifies when Americans (on screen or in the audience) simply cannot understand what is being said. In the opening sequence of *Home of the Brave* (Irwin Winkler, 2006) in Iraq (the film otherwise concentrates on returning veterans in Washington state), the first words heard in the film are an Iraqi woman's unsubtitled speech to an American medic (played by Samuel L. Jackson) treating her wounded daughter. Exasperatingly interfering with his work, her speech is presented as annoying gibberish. Her lack of English merely distracts an American trying to do his job rather than demonstrates the failure of crosscultural communication in the Iraq War. Even the DVD's close-captioning offers only "[Woman speaking Arabic]" for hearing-impaired viewers.

While rightly condemned by critics such as Jack Shaheen and Tim Jon Semmerling for its outrageous demonization of Yemeni men, women, and even children, the pre-9/11 *Rules of Engagement* nevertheless unusually reveals the function of sound in distinguishing "us" from "them."[13] In order to prove that the "innocent," if noisy, crowd slaughtered by American soldiers outside the US embassy was in fact a terrorist mob, the Army lawyer (Tommy Lee Jones) has mysterious Arabic cassette tapes found in his investigation translated in court. The translations prove that the rabble-rousing rhetoric within this previously ignored evidence is indeed to be feared, confirming the guilt of even little Arab girls. But even before the Arabic cassettes are translated, their inaccessibility to the character and audience (who presumably cannot read their labels, the text of which is also found in graffiti) ensures their danger.

In the first episode of David Mamet's television series *The Unit* about a covert American counterterrorism squad, Arabic must not only be translated, but fully captured and processed on screen like all of the data filling the high-tech monitors in the dark command centers of *24*'s Counter Terrorist Unit or, what in *The Unit* is called "the cave." This nickname ironically suggests Osama bin Laden's infamous Tora Bora hideout, a supposedly primitive location that also managed to produce video and audio "messages to the world." Arguably, one of the West's distinct failures in the "War on Terror" has been its obsessive attention to Osama bin Laden's face rather than to his voice, in many ways a greater source of inspiration to his followers.

Finally, in the Spike TV miniseries *The Kill Point* (2007), about a group of Iraq War veterans holding hostages after a botched bank robbery, the police technician monitoring communications with the bank under siege receives a message from the most traumatized of the vets. "I don't know what he's saying ... it sounds like gibberish," he says before the narrative's single well-adjusted vet, a female African American SWAT team leader, pinpoints the disturbing sound, ominously announcing it as "Arabic." In such American films and television programs, Arabic retrieves the notorious characterization it received in Eleanor Shouby's once influential 1951 essay, "The Influence of the Arabic Language on the Psychology of the Arabs," which, in Edward Said's damning summary, argued "that Arabic as a language is a dangerous ideology," because the Arab's language, unlike the European's, is made "equivalent to mind, society, history, and nature."[14]

Thus reduced, spoken Arabic or other foreign languages are presented as chatter or babble, the mindless noise of indoctrinated mobs rather than the medium of individual expression. Rather than distinct phrases or dialogue, which typically remains the privilege of English speakers only, foreignness is registered in chants, cries, screams, and wails (especially exoticized ululation). The two American soldiers in *Rules of Engagement*, who call for the attack on the crowd of men, women, and children outside the US embassy in Yemen, cannot hear one another except via their walkie-talkies even though they are only a few feet apart and their lines are made audible to us in the sound mix. "Waste the motherfuckers!" Samuel L. Jackson's infamous line from the film, which is questioned but finally justified in his military trial, is twice distinctly isolated from the loud gunfire and screaming crowd that surrounds it. In the "War on Terror," single American voices—often of course the distinctive voices of movie stars—cut through the din that is the collective voice of the terrorist "other."

As noted earlier, "War on Terror" films are typically filled with the cacophony of explosions, gunfire, shouted orders, and screams of pain. *Black Hawk Down* and *The Kingdom* are exemplary cases of the full arsenal of the modern soundtrack with the sounds of battle coming at the audience in the modern auditorium from all directions. Still, most of these films also employ moments of silence in unsettling contrast to overwhelming sound. This sonic juxtaposition is a familiar technique updated from horror films or, more appropriately, a contemporary manifestation of the "silent enemy" of many classic war films or Westerns in which the silence of a Japanese or Indian attack is presented as more terrifying than war whoops. At times these moments of silence figure as the sonic acknowledgment of the unrepresentability of traumatic events. Again, the ending of *United 93* is understood to be too horrible to witness *or hear*, and so the plane's crash is rendered by a white screen and *silence* rather than through the unbearable images and terrible noise that we understand to be the film's actual but withheld referents. I have already noted the similarly (though fictional) silent and unseen explosion in Grand Central Station at the end of *The War Within*. Likewise, the suicide bombing that is depicted twice in *Rendition*, while fully visualized, is also muted on the soundtrack to replicate the main character's shock. The now famous assassination by a missile located miles above the earth at the end of *Syriana* is spatially distanced from us at the moment of impact by its representation on high-tech screens, on which cold efficiency is reinforced by the sudden silence surrounding the event. As part of the montage construction of *Redacted* (Brian De Palma, 2007), a shocking and grisly IED explosion is immediately repeated though its capture and transmission on a terrorist website with its original sound reduced and overlaid with a Muslim chant. We now understand the killing to have been an event staged for a camera and given a "new" soundtrack at least as troubling as its more realistic, "original" sounds.[15] As a now common trope, the dramatic shift in volume accompanying moments of extreme violence seeks to (like terrorism itself) suddenly, shockingly upset common expectations. Preparing ourselves for loud explosions, we are momentarily shocked by their absence until the comfort of realistic sound returns.

What I wish to suggest through this accumulation of typical examples is that the sound of the "War on Terror," despite the technical sophistication of the contemporary soundtrack, is as limited and conventional as the visual stereotypes that this small repertoire of sounds accompanies. We are hearing what might be identified, in homage to Edward Said, as aural Orientalism, the sound of cultural difference mediated through questionable forms of expertise and ideological control. The prayer of the irrational Middle Eastern terrorist is thus countered by the rational speech of the Western humanist or the decisive commands of the strong leader. The undifferentiated chanting of the faceless crowd in a foreign tongue is countered by the sonically isolated and humanly individuated voice of the English-speaking American movie star. Finally, terrifying silence—the exact aural representation of the unspeakable—is employed for moments of traumatic violence but typically is then relieved by the return of reassuring music or recognizable voices.

Could the "War on Terror" sound otherwise? Careful audition of films from around the world would suggest so. Yet, rather than point to the evident rewards of carefully listening to art films such as Palestinian filmmaker Elia Suleiman's celebrated (and slyly quiet) works, I will conclude by citing the often boldly playful sound of recent Egyptian comedies, such as *The Night Baghdad Fell* (Muhammad Amin, 2006), which takes on the "War on Terror" with savage wit rather than grim righteousness (and, unlike most of the American films discussed here, was a box office hit). In the earlier hit film *Terrorism and Kebab* (Sharif Arafa, 1992), the hero (superstar Adil Imam), a meek everyman attempting to negotiate the labyrinth of Cairo's bureaucracy, is mistaken for a terrorist, and the police insist that he, like all proper terrorists, must have "demands." Lacking a better idea, he requests lunch, a suggestion that turns his "hostages" (a mix of government workers and the beleaguered public they serve) into exactly the sort of chanting mob that American films have taught us to fear. The now familiar, vengeful soul of the militant *jihadist* is replaced by the empty stomach of the average citizen, whose praise of Allah mutates easily into a demand for decent food and service rather than Islamic revolution. As a good parody can, the film's playful mobilization of the trope of the frenzied Arab mob speaking in unison (to choose kebabs rather than Kentucky Fried Chicken) renders slightly ludicrous many similar scenes and the narrowly repeated sounds that accompany them in recent mainstream Hollywood films. Unlike the representatives of American law and government agencies, who in a stream of films and television shows since 9/11 have declared that they "don't negotiate with terrorists," the Egyptian police, stationed in the minaret of a mosque from which the call to prayer is usually issued, decide that the demands of a terrorist and inflamed mob must be met, and so they order lunch. Hearing the ways in which such popular non-Hollywood films offer alternatives to Hollywood sound conventions is perhaps one way to begin to recognize that the sound of the "War on Terror" in American media has so far been drawn from an unnecessarily limited repertoire.

Notes

1   Jane M. Gaines, "The Production of Outrage: The Iraq War and the Radical Documentary Tradition," *Framework* 48:2 (2007): 36. Other valuable studies of the "War on Terror" as a "war of images" include the following: Nicholas Mirzoeff, *Watching Babylon: The War in Iraq and Global Visual Culture* (New York: Routledge, 2005); W.J.T. Mitchell, "Cloning Terror: The War of Images 2001–04," in Diarmuid Costello and Dominic Willsdon, eds, *The Life and Death of Images: Ethics and Aesthetics* (Ithaca: Cornell University Press, 2008), 179–207; Karen Engle, *Seeing Ghosts: 9/11 and the Visual Imagination* (Montreal and Kingston: McGill-Queen's University Press, 2009). I wish to supplement in this chapter the insightful but widespread attention to images in the "War on Terror" by focusing on the sounds of these images.
2   Susan Buck-Morss, *Thinking Past Terror: Islamism and Critical Theory on the Left* (London: Verso, 2003), 63–4.
3   Melani McAlister, *Epic Encounters: Culture, Media, and US Interests in the Middle East since 1945*, updated ed. (Berkeley: University of California Press, 2005), 269.
4   Dexter Filkins, *The Forever War* (New York: Random House, 2007), 193–4.
5   Jonathan Raban, *Surveillance* (New York: Pantheon, 2007), 3.
6   Norman Daniel, *Islam and the West: The Making of an Image* (1960; repr. Oxford: Oneworld Publications, 2009), 233.
7   Michel Chion, *The Voice in Cinema*, trans. Claudia Gorbman (New York: Columbia University Press, 2009), 24, 19.
8   See Flagg Miller, *The Moral Resonance of Arab Media: Audiocassette Poetry and Culture in Yemen* (Cambridge: Harvard University Press, 2007) and Charles Hirschkind, *The Ethical Soundscape: Cassette Sermons and Islamic Counterpublics* (New York: Columbia University Press, 2006). Both offer rich accounts of sound in Islamic cultures that challenge reductive treatments.
9   Zangana, 66.
10   Haifa Zangana, "Songs of Resistance," in *War With No End* (New York: Verso, 2007), 61–75. On popular music and 9/11, see Jeffrey Melnick, *9/11 Culture* (Malden, MA: Wiley-Blackwell, 2009).
11   On the common mistranslation of *jihad* as "holy war," see Talal Asad, *On Suicide Bombing* (New York: Columbia University Press, 2007), 11.
12   Steven W. Bender, "Sight, Sound, and Stereotype: The War on Terrorism and Its Consequences for Latinas/os," in *Oregon Law Review* 81 (2002): 1153–78.
13   Jack G. Shaheen, *Reel Bad Arabs: How Hollywood Vilifies a People* (New York: Olive

Branch Press, 2001), 404–6; Tim Jon Semmerling, *"Evil" Arabs in American Popular Film: Orientalist Fear* (Austin: University of Texas Press, 2006), 163–201. Semmerling is often attentive to film's sound and notes that William Friedkin began his earlier horror film *The Exorcist* (1973) in Iraq, with a muezzin's call.

14   Edward Said, *Orientalism* (1979; repr. New York: Vintage, 1994), 320–1.

15   Garrett Stewart notes a similar shift to silence in *The Battle for Haditha* (Nick Broomfield, 2007) in a brilliant essay otherwise focused on the role of digital images in "War on Terror" films. See Garrett Stewart, "Digital Fatigue: Imaging War in Recent American Film," *Film Quarterly* 62 no. 4 (2009): 45–55.

Visions of War and Terror

CHAPTER 8

Avatars of Destruction: Cheerleading and Deconstructing the "War on Terror" in Video Games

DAVID ANNANDALE

In November 2007, President George W. Bush visited wounded veterans of the Iraq War and played a video game with them: a shooter taking place in a simulated Baghdad.[1] Not long after, the Holiday issue of *Electronic Gaming Monthly* featured a review of *Call of Duty 4: Modern Warfare*. At one juncture, the reviewers describe a level where the player is in a C-130 gunship:

> ... manning weapons stations to blast ground vehicles and evildoers who appear as ghost-white stick figures in your whitewashed thermal vision. The plane's intercom crackles and pops with clipped, all-business crew conversation, seemingly out of place with the carnage on the ground ... Real-life military technology that for years has been described as "like a videogame" has wound up in a videogame that completely captures real life.[2]

These are but two examples of the intersection between video games and actual warfare that suggest a symbiotic relationship where war encourages an interest in its virtual representation and said representation encourages participation in (or, at the very least, support for) the real thing. In fact, the situation is rather more complex. Like the other forms of popular culture, video games have mirrored, tracked, and questioned the dreams and nightmares that have shaken the American psyche in the wake of 9/11—dreams and nightmares that have birthed dramatic actions in the arenas of domestic and foreign policy. A number of competing fantasies have emerged, embodied in the games as well as in the physical realities of the "War on Terror" itself. Video games by turns celebrate these fantasies and interrogate them, always in the most visceral terms. Further, McKenzie Wark proposes that games "are not representations of the world. They are more like allegories of a world made over as gamespace. They encode the abstract principles upon which decisions about the realness of this or that world are now decided."[3] Games are therefore engaged in a form of thought experiment, enacting different possible responses to 9/11, to tactics of the "War on Terror," and to the consequences of those tactics. Thanks to their immersive qualities, games give the players a much greater sense of actually performing an action rather than reading about it or seeing it, and thus the aforementioned tactics and consequences gather a concrete immediacy. However, though the players always have a certain latitude regarding the individual actions they take and decisions they make, each game's agenda circumscribes this choice. The implied rhetoric behind the same action will vary, depending on context, from game to game. Thus, in every case to be considered here, the players' avatars are involved in massively destructive acts, but those actions are in the service of wildly different ideological projects. The games become sites where the post-9/11 dreams of victory and nightmares of oppression are embodied.

Cheerleading

The games that I would describe as the cheerleaders of the "War on Terror" include those that happen to be its ideological allies (such as the *Ghost Recon* and *Rainbow Six* series) and those games that are actually produced in cooperation with the Armed Forces (*America's Army, Full Spectrum Warrior*). As a general rule, the more sympathetic the game is to the Bush conception of the "War on Terror," the closer the game comes to "realism," in the sense that the settings are recognizable (or at least not derived from science fiction or sword-and-sorcery narratives), the player's avatars are not inhumanly resistant to damage, and there is great pride taken in the accurate simulation of weaponry, whether actual or in development. Gonzalo Frasca defines simulation (in the specific context of video games) as the effort "to model a (source) system through a different system which maintains (for somebody) some of the behaviors of the original system."[4] Here, then, one sees a particularly detailed effort at physical simulation that incorporates a specific brand of ideological simulation. These games, in their relationship with the "War on Terror," are a perfect demonstration of Wark's contention that games are not "failed representations of the world, but quite the reverse . . . The world outside is a gamespace that appears as an imperfect form of the computer game."[5] In these games, not only has the perfect enemy been found, but the means of combating him/her are satisfyingly effective. Even as they reflect social fears about terrorism and envisage horrific scenarios, these games are often paradoxically optimistic as they present a fantasy that is a corrective to the messy reality in Iraq and elsewhere.

America's Army is arguably the most honest of this group, at least insofar as it has no need to disguise its role as propaganda. The Army released it in 2002 as a free download for the PC and aggressively marketed it at the 2003 Electronic Entertainment Expo (E3), the premier showcase for the video game industry.[6] Ubisoft reissued it commercially as *America's Army: Rise of a Soldier* in 2005 for the Xbox. In its original conception, the game was quite explicitly a recruiting tool, so one would be foolish to expect anything other than the glorification of its title subject. Much game time involves training the player in basic military tactics, weaponry, and discipline. But this attention to detail evaporates at the level of contextualizing the battles themselves. The campaign takes place in an unnamed nation where a dictator has recently been deposed. One of the urban missions occurs in the generically named "Old Town." The geography suggests the desert one moment (possibly revisiting painful memories of Somalia), but in the next, the player can be moving through a farmyard that might as well be in Kansas (perhaps conjuring for some players the paranoid/revenge fantasies of such films as John Milius's *Red Dawn* [1984]). Though the mission briefings mention the existence of a civilian population, there is no visible evidence of such during game play itself. There are only enemies, usually too distant to be more than anonymous silhouettes, speaking languages suggesting at times the Middle East and at others Russia. They are also unknowable in their motivations. At the end of the farmyard mission when one soldier wonders about the nonsensical nature of the attack that just took place, the commanding officer responds, "They were outlaws. I doubt we'll ever know what they were thinking." The enemy is, perhaps by virtue of being an enemy, irrational and mysterious, and one can properly deal with him only through the use of deadly force. In much the same way, one dismisses the idea of root causes and motives beyond pure evil with regard to terrorists. *America's Army* thus presents a conflict of varied anyplace battlefields, a conflict where the enemy remains Other, and where the rules are simple: follow orders, and kill anyone who is not part of your group.

The Institute for Creative Technologies, described by Ed Halter as a combination of "an animation studio, an academic research center, a video game developer . . . a special effects house [and] military think tank,"[7] collaborated with game developers THQ and Pandemic to create *Full Spectrum Warrior* (2004), which had both Army training aid and simplified commercial incarnations. Its setting is more defined than *America's Army*'s, but only just: it takes place in the fictional nation of Zekistan, located, according to the manual, "between modern day Afghanistan, Pakistan and China." It thus creates a fictional space sufficiently similar to actual locations to conjure them (Afghanistan in particular) but where fantasy shapes the nature of the conflict. Interesting, too, is what one discovers at the beginning of the campaign proper as the principal characters are introduced. First, the action is set in December 2004. Second, for one of the squad members, "Iraq was the most fun he's ever had. Ever." The inference, then, is that the war in Iraq is over, the mission accomplished. Gamers from 2004 on, playing in full knowledge of the game scenario being violently at odds with the actual state of affairs, must engage in a much more conscious effort of fantasy creation than the game might have intended. To return to Frasca, events not anticipated by the simulation's ideology strain the links to its original model. If the primary fantasy thrust seems to have been to refight battles in a part of the world that stands in for Afghanistan and Iraq in the comfort of believing the actual wars to be over, the game inadvertently sabotages its own project, as well as the ideological one of its makers. By referencing the real world, it highlights the slippage between fantasy and reality. This slippage was not enough to hurt the game's popularity (it spawned a sequel in 2006: *Full Spectrum Warrior: Ten Hammers*), but it does, I would argue, reinforce the imaginary nature of the action for the player, at the expense of the desired simulation.

In the "cheerleading" games, then, the players can take satisfaction in dishing out the kind of fantasy justice that the Bush administration promised but could never deliver, due to the imperfection of the real world. Even so, the absence of those very imperfections in the games effectively lays bare the fact that the worldview promoted by the Bush ideologues was just as fantastic as that offered by the games. The closer the games come to verisimilitude at the level of weapons, combat, and settings, the more actively the players must work to ignore the other absences. Therefore, in trying to support an ideological fantasy, the games ironically put players into the position of becoming much more explicitly aware that they are engaged in a fantasy, thus driving a wedge between the fantasy and the reality it is supposed to represent. Other games, however, hold a rather more jaundiced view and have no interest in propping up a dangerous set of beliefs in the first place.

Skepticism

In the publicity run-up to the release of the phenomenally successful *Halo 2* (2004), Joe Staten, the writer of the game and the director of its cinematography, said, "You could look at [the story] as a damning condemnation of the Bush administration's adventure in the Middle East."[8] This rare instance of a creator explicitly stating that a political subtext exists in a given game is worth examining. The *Halo* trilogy tells the tale of humanity's desperate fight against the numerically superior Covenant, a coalition of alien species. The inhumanity of the foes that the player guns down might, on the surface, appear to be the logical extension of the dehumanized portrayal of the terrorists/insurgents/what-have-you of the military games. In *Halo 2*, the Covenant attacks Earth itself, and the player, in the character of an armored super-solider known as the Master Chief (whose face is never seen), leads the resistance—at least at first. As the narrative progresses, complications arise. In the original *Halo* (2001), the Covenant's races speak in incomprehensible grunts. They are completely unknowable. Not so this time, as *Halo 2*'s opening cut scenes intercut between the opposing forces' reactions to the events of the previous game. The Covenant now speak English, and partway through the narrative the player begins playing alternating episodes, first as the Master Chief, then as the Arbiter, a disgraced Covenant commander (of a species known as the Elite) seeking redemption through suicidal missions. If we are to take Staten's comment at face value, then the Master Chief and Earth's forces, who, after all, are the invaded, do not represent the Bush administration. Taking on that role, instead, is the religiously driven Covenant, whose fundamentalist leaders (the "Prophets") are intent on triggering a galaxy-wide Apocalypse. In the Covenant's millenarian beliefs, there is more than a faint echo of the Christian Zionist movement whose support for Israel is predicated on the premise that the establishment of the Jewish state is a necessary prerequisite to the Second Coming.[9] Furthermore, the attack on Earth is a mistake in the sense that the Covenant leaders were not expecting humans to be there—a jab, perhaps, at the complete lack of preparation for completely foreseeable consequences (looting, infrastructure breakdown, and violent factionalism to name but three) that characterized the invasion of Iraq. These parallels, though, do not go much further than that. Rather than mount a direct attack on the "War on Terror" itself, *Halo 2* is more interested in questioning the black-and-white thinking that underpins any clash of fundamentalisms.

The principal tool in this approach is the character of the Arbiter. Having spent the length of *Halo* and the first portion of the sequel slaughtering the Elites, players might well suffer some confusion of sympathies when the game's point of view shifts and they find themselves, still in a first-person perspective, now in the body of the enemy. Adjustment to the new state of affairs is fairly easy, as the Arbiter is a likable character. In fact, with his doubts, confusion, and self-loathing, he is far more "human" than the emotionless, implacable Master Chief. The identification with the Arbiter is, however, itself tinted with unease as the two storylines gradually converge. In the closing level before the collision actually happens, the player, as the Arbiter, moves through corridors and hears, in the near distance, the shouts of human Marines, raising the uncomfortable possibility that they will become targets. The game stops short of presenting such a complete reversal to the player, and such a move is unnecessary. The point has been made, the doubts sown. The rejection of lethal binary oppositions is driven home by the scene where Gravemind, the collective intelligence of the parasite known as the Flood, holds the Master Chief and the Arbiter in its tentacles. Examining first one, then the other, Gravemind intones, "This one is machine and nerve and has its mind concluded. This one is but flesh and faith and is the more deluded." One might read, in the description of the Arbiter, a reference to foreign policies dictated not by fact but by belief. But the key here is that *both* characters are blinkered and are operating on black-and-white assumptions that are untenable in a complex world. At this moment of the narrative, *Halo 2* questions not a specific ideology, but ideological dogmatism of any stripe.

Subversion

The third type of response I want to consider is the direct attack by video games on specific aspects of the "War on Terror." Overtly political games are, at least in the mainstream world of consoles, relatively rare (though not unheard of, with the all-encompassing satire of the *Grand Theft Auto* games being a case in point). Thus, though I would argue that players would find it difficult to ignore the blurring of oppositions presented by *Halo 2*, they could easily miss Staten's Iraq War analogy. They have to look for it. The two games I wish to consider here—*Raze's Hell* (2005) and *Crackdown* (2006)—make their commentary on specific Bush administration actions unmistakable. The first eviscerates the logic and the rhetoric behind the war in Iraq. The second casts a withering eye on the erosion of civil liberties on the home front.

Raze's Hell begins in the form of a fairy tale, signaling the preposterous nature of the events it is about to narrate. A storybook opens and the narrator unfolds the story of the Kewletts, informing us that they were beings "who thought they had the perfect society, and it was hard to argue the point. They had wealth and privilege, and sheer, overwhelming numbers." Already, then, the Kewletts are surrogates for the developed nations and the pressure and arrogance of the face they present to the developing world. The ruling Princess announces to her subjects, "It is our solemn duty to bring our infinite bounty to those less fortunate than us. Let us go forth then and spread our message to the ignorant, to the primitive, to the ugly. I say to you, fear not, you will be saved." Here the game skewers the condescending, paternalistic attitude implicit in such claims as "bringing democracy" to Iraq. The Kewletts dub their invasion "Operation Fresh Hope," and it is nothing less than the wholesale slaughter of other species.[10] One member of "the ignorant, the primitive, and the ugly" is Raze: "[w]hen he returned to his village to find it being 'saved,' all he could do was stand there in shock and awe." The language is redolent of spin from the Afghanistan and Iraq wars, with a pointed reference to Vietnam being added to the mix. The saving of Raze's village is, of course, a massacre of unarmed civilians. During a later Kewlett news broadcast, the anchor reminds the troops, "Remember guys, you're bringing these people *freedom*," and extols a condominium construction site that will "bring hope to the hopeless." In the first place, the idea of an inappropriate, unwanted, unneeded project suggesting nothing more than wholesale corruption might well remind players of Halliburton and other such dubious figures of the Iraqi "reconstruction." Worse yet, though, is the fact that the only thing present at the site itself is a gigantic mortar cannon, guarded by two Kewletts who have the following exchange:

> "What do we need the mortars for? I thought this was a construction project."
> "Well, you can't make an omelet without breaking a few eggs."
> "What the hell is that supposed to mean?"
> "You can't wage a pre-emptive, expansionist war without some incidental collateral damage."
> "Well, why didn't you just say that?"

With the narrator punching up such expressions as "shock and awe," the game makes explicit the connection between the Kewletts' folly and the various invasions of the "War on Terror." It then puts the justifications of those wars in the mouths of jejune, genocidal creatures who appear to be quite honestly convinced that their interests inevitably coincide with everyone else's, even when those interests mean the extermination of everyone else. And yet, as shown by the conversation above, even the Kewletts do not fully believe the spin, though they never question their right to act as they wish.

Having established an analogy between Kewtopia and the United States, the game then introduces its protagonist. In stark contrast to the extremely white Kewletts, Raze's skin is a dark brown. It is difficult, then, for the players not to infer that they are playing the role that would have been designated by the likes of *Full Spectrum Warrior* as an insurgent. Though the storyline of *Raze's Hell* does not sustain this level of astringent satire throughout, losing some of its focus as it trots out Kewletts that are rather familiar Nazi parodies (German-accented criminal scientists), the overall premise, and the strategies that the game employs to establish it, are quite remarkable. The player is most likely to be a member of the culture that the game mocks, and the narrative conventions, including the dismayingly accurate caricatures of local news broadcasts (perfect hair, inane banter, unthinking jingoism), clearly denote a Western, and most particularly an American implied audience. But since the players are sympathizing with and embodying Raze, this recognizable culture they see is the enemy. The game presents to the players their own culture as a foreign, invading, unwelcome presence, in short, as Other. Simultaneously, players now identify with the foreign cultures designated by their own society as Other and understand their resistance.

Raze's Hell, then, looks at the foreign adventures of the "War on Terror" and, by extension, other self-interested interventions and sees only nonsense, finding a justifiable position with the victims of invasion and not the invaders. This is not to say that Raze becomes a disturbingly heroic vision of an al-Qaeda operative. He is not already a warrior at the start of the game. When first encountered, he is a defenseless civilian, watching the extermination of his village. He has no recourse but to flee into caves, and it is there that he acquires the means to fight back. It is, therefore, the invasion itself that politicizes him. The Kewletts create the means of their own defeat.

Raze's Hell and the other games discussed thus far stage their action in other countries, on other planets, but never in America itself. Their commentary, then, favorable or not, is on the external manifestations of the American reaction to 9/11. There are exceptions to this trend, however. *Tom Clancy's Rainbow Six: Vegas* (2006) deals with a terrorist attack on home soil, at once reactivating the nightmare fantasy that 9/11 embodied and imagining the means of retaliating in the person of the eponymous crack anti-terror warriors. *Crackdown*, however, presents a much darker fantasy. The game might appear, at first glance, to be imagining a scenario similar to that of *Rainbow Six: Vegas* (domestic terror), though in a much more comic-book fashion, with over-the-top explosions and an extremely flexible attitude toward the laws of physics. However, *Crackdown* is ultimately far more concerned with the darker implications of its title, and with the *internal* reaction to 9/11. It is about the distorting effects of the "War on Terror" on America itself.

Crackdown takes place in the imaginary Pacific City, a metropolis where crime has metastasized to the point that social order is undergoing complete collapse. Pacific City is a xenophobe's multicultural dystopia. It is ethnically segregated into three regions: La Mugre is Hispanic and so is its ruling criminal gang; the Den is populated by Eastern European refugees terrorized by the ex-military Volk; and the Corridor is run by a criminal corporation known as Shai-Gen. The player, whose avatar is a nameless, genetically modified super-policeman referred to only as "Agent," hears no English spoken on the streets or very little spoken by gang members for the first two-thirds of the game. The situation changes once the Agent arrives in the Corridor. By far the most affluent of the three districts, its inhabitants are English-speaking and Caucasian, while the leaders of Shai-Gen are a melting pot of ethnicities. What might appear to be a disturbing xenophobia on the part of the game (immigrants taking over "our" cities and bringing with them rampant crime) is in fact part of the *Crackdown*'s satirical strategy. The game makes stark socioeconomic divisions too striking to miss, as it does the implications of the law enforcement by rocket launchers in minority enclaves. The game trumpets its appeal on its case as "All justice. No restraints," but the conclusion reveals this slogan as bitterly ironic. The key to the satire is the omnipresent voice-over, acting as the contact between the Agent and the Agency. The contact comments on the Agent's activities, on the various crime lords, and on the environment of Pacific City with the clenched-teeth, jut-jawed urgency associated with movie trailers and propaganda films. At the game's conclusion, the contact praises the Agent's successful restoration of law and order, then chuckles and announces,

> It's taken years of meticulous planning and patience to reach this stage. But it was worth it. Who do you think supplied Los Muertos? Who do you think turned a blind eye to the Volk's activities? Who do you think was Shai-Gen's biggest supporter? Who do you think ran organized law enforcement and ran it into the ground? The people had to experience absolute anarchy before they would accept unconditional control. You are the portent of a new world order, Agent. Pacific City was only the beginning.

The conspiracy suggested here echoes the sentiment expressed in the now disbanded Project for the New American Century's infamous 2000 statement that "the process of transformation, even if it brings revolutionary change, is likely to be a long one, absent some catastrophic and catalyzing event—like a new Pearl Harbor."[11] But *Crackdown* is not suggesting that 9/11 was planned by the Bush administration. It is, however, itemizing a series of actions—alliances of opportunity with criminal thugs, unrestrained weapons dealing, gutted essential services—that inevitably lead to a catastrophic situation that empowers the very people who are responsible for it, deliberately (in the case of the game) or not.

The players' reaction to this turn of events might well be a pronounced feeling of betrayal on discovering that they have been furthering the aims of an authoritarian project all along. The warnings, however, are omnipresent, starting with the game's title, continuing on through the menacingly black Agency uniform, and the treatment of civilians. There is a penalty for killing them: the growth of the Agent's powers slows, and Agency forces become hostile. The penalty, however, is not severe, and this is precisely the point. If a grenade goes astray and blows up some innocents, the contact will admonish the Agent, but will also comment that civilians "are a barely tolerable nuisance." They are a nuisance because their presence interferes with the fantasy of justice with "no restraints," and thus they expose the falsity of the idea, just as civilian death tolls are conspicuous in their absence from the official narratives of the wars in Afghanistan and Iraq. "Justice" has nothing to do with anything in this world.

Crackdown's vision, then, is not, as it initially leads the players to believe, of an apocalyptic struggle between the forces of law and order and the forces of chaos. There is not even really a struggle between competing powers. There is only, quite simply, a power grab. A crackdown. The setting may be exaggerated, the comic-book sensibility enhanced by the cell-shaded art-style of the game, but the concerns of the society are still immediately recognizable as contemporary American ones. The game is a worst-case-scenario depiction of Homeland Security concerns trumping all other rights and doing so for entirely spurious reasons. Even if some of the actors—that is, the players—have the best of intentions, the result is still a tyranny. Furthermore, *Crackdown* does not let the players off the hook, since the signs are all-too apparent. In other words, the ending twist should not really be a surprise. The message to the player is *you should have known better*. Perhaps there lies another fantasy behind that message: the fantasy that the players now *do* know better and will resist the crackdown in the real world.

Crackdown explicitly embraces the fact that it is a fantasy—primarily of power, but also of vengeance. But it equally explicitly exposes the dangers of that fantasy. While the likes of *Full Spectrum Warrior* unintentionally expose the fault lines of their (and their society's) fantasies even as they attempt to shore up these fantasies, *Crackdown* and its ilk revel no less viscerally in the implosion of these fantasies. In their reactions to such concerted attacks, players might well be forced to show their own political hand, particularly to themselves. The visual/virtual destruction that their avatars engage in is nothing less than the metaphorical destruction of untenable ideologies.

Post-Bush Postscript

It is, as of this writing, too early for the mainstream game industry to reflect what changes to the "War on Terror" might be wrought by the Obama administration. But one might, perhaps, be able to see a consideration of the Bush legacy already present in two suggestive examples: *BlackSite: Area 51*, released in November 2007; and *Saints' Row 2*, from October 2008.

BlackSite is perhaps the first game to explicitly connect the war in Iraq with the home front. The opening act takes place not in an imaginary locale in the midst of a fictional-yet-familiar war but in Iraq itself with a Special Forces squad searching a bunker for nonexistent weapons of mass destruction but instead finding monsters linked to an alien artifact. The action then shifts to stateside three years later, with the war still ongoing, the draft re-instituted, and an eruption of the same monsters in Nevada. The game's chapters are a compendium of phrases associated with the war in Iraq: "Hearts and Minds," "Coalition of the Willing," "Mission Accomplished" (the title of the last chapter of the first act, when everything is clearly going badly wrong), "WMD MIA," "The Surge," "Regime Change" and so on. The destruction at home turns out to be the direct result of morally indefensible policies enacted domestically and abroad. The enemy troops—the "Reborn"—are resurrected corpses made up of the homeless, illegal immigrants and, primarily, KIA American soldiers. The idea behind the Reborn is to eliminate the phenomenon of "middle class kids coming home in body bags." Summers, a member of the protagonist's squad in Iraq, is the leader of the rebelling Reborn, and he seeks to achieve the regime change of the chapter title in the United States, defending the country, as he puts it, from tyrants foreign *or domestic*. While the player must defeat Summers in order to complete the game, there is a sense that there are no good choices here, no moral high ground to find. The final words of the game are that honor sometimes is not about doing the right thing but rather about "picking up the pieces." The game acts as a kind of snapshot of the widespread disillusion with the war in Iraq, as well as a pessimistic speculation not only on its dire consequences, but also on the various poor options that face those who must deal with what the Bush administration leaves in its wake.

Saints' Row 2, meanwhile, melds *Crackdown*'s cynicism with an amorality as cheerful as it is absolute. A sandbox game in the vein of *Grand Theft Auto* (*GTA*), it actually *is* the game that *GTA* is often accused of being. The "Mayhem" activity, for example, requires the player to cause as much devastation and loss of life as possible within a given time limit. The airport provides players with jet planes to play with as they see fit, and the climactic mission even involves flying a helicopter at the upper floor of a skyscraper. The vision here is of an American society broken beyond repair at every possible level, and thus the only sane response is to revel in the burning of Rome.

These digital dreams are dark ones. So are the times they mirror. It remains to be seen whether the legacy they reflect can be overcome. What is nevertheless encouraging is that while the medium provides the most visceral artistic experience yet of modern warfare and other forms of post 9/11 conflict, it is also, in some quarters, questioning the ideological underpinnings of these conflicts in ways that are just as visceral. If 9/11 and the "War on Terror" are being transformed into entertainment, the transformation is frequently accompanied by a thoughtfulness and an urgent sense of engagement. This is an engagement the player is invited to share and is one that goes far beyond managing a health bar.

Notes

1   "Bush Plays Video Games with Recovering War Veterans," *AFP*, November 9, 2007, http://afp.google.com/article/ALeqM5jExFefQsl8i87mwwcEqLxWdg1BVA (accessed July 15, 2009).

2   Crispin Boyer, Garnett Lee, and Andrew Pfister, "Review of *Call of Duty 4: Modern Warfare*," *Electronic Gaming Monthly* 223 (2007): 72.

3   Mackenzie Wark, *Gamer Theory* (Cambridge, MS: Harvard University Press, 2007), 20.

4   Gonzalo Frasca, "Simulation versus Narrative: Introduction to Ludology," in *The Video Game Theory Reader*, eds Mark J. P. Wolf and Bernard Perron (New York: Routledge, 2003), 223.

5   Wark, *Gamer Theory*, 22.

6   Ed Halter, *From Sun Tzu to Xbox: War and Video Games* (New York: Thunder's Mouth Press, 2006), viii.

7   Ibid., 208–9.

8   Geoff Keighley, "Hooray for Halowood," *Entertainment Weekly*, November 5, 2004, 48.

9   See Victoria Clark, *Allies for Armageddon: The Rise of Christian Zionism* (New Haven, CT: Yale University Press, 2007).

10 The name is tonally equivalent to "Operation Restore Hope" (Somalia), "Operation Enduring Freedom" (Afghanistan), and "Operation Iraqi Freedom."

11 See Thomas Donnelly, *Rebuilding America's Defenses: Strategy, Forces and Resources for a New Century*, Report of The Project for the New American Century, September, 2000, http://www.newamericancentury.org/RebuildingAmericasDefenses.pdf (accessed January 4, 2008).

CHAPTER 9

The Land of the Dead and the Home of the Brave: Romero's Vision of a Post-9/11 America

TERENCE MCSWEENEY

"The zombie films are what I perceive as my platform, a pulpit. They have given me an opportunity to at least, not necessarily express opinions or criticize, but observe what's going on in society."

—George Romero

The American film industry was initially reluctant to dramatize the events of September 11, 2001, and the subsequent "War on Terror." Despite many concurring that the spectacle was one of the most cinematic events in national history, it took five years for any film to portray the events directly. Although *United 93* (Paul Greengrass, 2006) and *World Trade Center* (*WTC*; Oliver Stone, 2006) were widely acclaimed for their realism, some challenge their fundamentally reactionary perspective. Slavoj Žižek argues,

> ... both films are restrained from taking a political stance and depicting the wider context of the events. Neither the passengers on *United 93* nor the policemen in *WTC* grasp the full picture ... The result is that the political message of the two films resides in their abstention from delivering a direct political message. It is the message of an implicit trust in one's government: when under attack, one just has to do one's duty.[1]

Žižek is one of many cultural commentators who have explored media depictions of what Jean Baudrillard called "the mother of all events."[2] This chapter argues that, while Hollywood initially refused to explore the turbulent political aftermath of the destruction of the Twin Towers in New York directly, a diverse range of films tackled these issues through subtext and allegory, and, in doing so, were able to take the "political stance" that Žižek described as missing in *United 93* and *World Trade Center*. Without being confined by issues of political correctness and the responsibilities that accompany depictions of real life events, these allegorical films become far more challenging and, ironically, directly political. Such films can be found across a diverse range of genres: historical dramas like *The New World* (Terrence

Malick, 2005), *Elizabeth: The Golden Years* (Shekhar Kapur, 2007), and *Apocalypto* (Mel Gibson, 2006); science fiction films like *War of the Worlds* (Steven Spielberg, 2005) and *Children of Men* (Alphonso Cuaron, 2006); horror films like *28 Days Later* ... (Danny Boyle, 2002) and *Planet Terror* (Richard Rodriguez, 2007); and even action films like *V for Vendetta* (James McTeigue, 2005) and *300* (Zack Snyder, 2007). All can be read allegorically, their texts redolent with images or situations reminiscent of America's political and social climate in the years since 2001.

Land of The Dead (Romero, 2005) is the fourth entry in Romero's acclaimed and influential zombie cycle of films, which began with *Night of the Living Dead* (1968) over 40 years ago. The first film of the series forged Romero's reputation as the "godfather" of the zombie subgenre and is often read as an allegory of the tumultuous social climate of 1960s America in the years of the Vietnam War and the Civil Rights Movement. The film's reception set a trend for sociopolitical analysis of horror movies in the years to come, and two sequels followed in the subsequent decades: *Dawn of the Dead* (1978) and *Day of the Dead* (1986). Critics have read these films from a diverse variety of critical perspectives: as critiques of capitalism, racism, and American conflict abroad.[3] Film theorist Robin Wood called the initial trilogy "[o]ne of the most remarkable and audacious achievements of modern American cinema."[4] Wood views the trilogy in Freudian terms, as a "return of the repressed" exploring through the horror narrative what happens when those aspects of our national ideology we have sublimated reemerge.

Romero did not return to the franchise for nearly two decades, yet in his absence zombies had become even more of a compelling cultural icon than ever, part of a new millennial zeitgeist through a proliferation of films, books, and video games. After the attacks on 9/11 and the escalation of the "War on Terror," it became difficult for any zombie text, be it film, book, or videogame, not to allude to 9/11 in some way. The term "living dead" also became part of the terminology in the "War on Terror" when then Secretary of Defense, Donald Rumsfeld, gave his infamous "unknown knowns" comments about, among other things, the fate of the prisoners in Guantánamo Bay.[5] He asserted that many of the prisoners, although they were technically alive, were officially "living dead" as they had been the intended targets of American bombs and could therefore be treated accordingly.

When Romero finally announced in 2002 that he would be creating a fourth film in the zombie cycle, he said, "We started sending the screenplay around right after 9/11, and everyone said, 'Ugh! We want to make soft and fuzzy movies now. Go home.' So I did. Then this post 9/11 mentality started to set in and I thought, 'This might be even better'; so I tried to relate this movie to the post-9/11 head in America."[6] When he revealed the official title of the film to be the evocative *Land of the Dead*, its allusion to the American national anthem suggested a broad attack on the cultural myths at the heart of the American experience.

When the film was finally released in the United States in June 2005, the "War on Terror" resonated around the globe, the Second Gulf War moved into its third year of conflict, and the Patriot Act and the general erosion of civil liberties under George W. Bush's presidential administration were two of the many factors contributing to Bush's popularity sinking from a 9/11 high of 90 percent to a historic low of

37 percent, the lowest of any second-term President for more than 50 years.[7] I argue in this chapter that *Land of the Dead* is one of the most scathing and implicitly political films of the post-9/11 period and a film that sees Romero audaciously reenact the lead-up to the events of September 11, climaxing with a symbolic reconstruction of the destruction of the World Trade Center itself.

The narrative of *Land of the Dead* takes place in an unnamed city, though one obviously modeled on Romero's hometown and habitual setting, Pittsburgh. In this apocalyptic scenario the zombies and the heavily outnumbered survivors have reached a partial détente. The undead have learned not to venture into the city, where they are shot on sight by a privately financed mercenary army. This Blackwater-esque force is financed by a group of individuals who have maintained their money and authority and who now live in an exclusive and heavily fortified tower called Fiddler's Green. With self-conscious echoes of a pre-9/11 America, those in power are under the impression that their superior military, their high-tech defenses, and their geographical placement make them impregnable.

These elites also finance nightly raids into zombie-populated territory, ostensibly to secure vital provisions and medicine but in reality to procure luxury goods for their own extravagant consumption. Far from being organized military operations, the raids demonstrate a flagrant disregard for property and propriety. The "army" is a marauding group of gung-ho mercenaries waving the Stars and Stripes and shouting macho war cries. One of their leaders is Cholo DeMora (John Leguizamo), a brutal and selfish Mexican-American with little regard for those around him. The zombies on the receiving end of these nightly incursions offer little in the way of resistance and are all dispatched easily with a disturbing relish. For Cholo and his team, war is sport and little more than target practice. One of the young soldiers under Cholo's command, a boy on his first mission outside the safety of the city, comments on the inadequacy of the zombie opposition: "I thought it was going to be a battle . . . It's a fucking massacre." Later, the same young boy will be killed because of Cholo's negligence.

On the particular night that opens the film, Cholo leads an attack on the zombie-populated Uniontown, a name with connotations of solidarity, which is decidedly absent in Fiddler's Green. As in all Romero zombie films, the zombies are generally a passive presence; they are almost even no longer a threat to the living unless provoked. They perform mindless tasks and recreate rituals of their former lives, milling around a church, a factory, a town center and a bandstand. Romero takes care to show the zombies as coming, quite distinctly, from a lower social demographic and from a variety of ethnic backgrounds. He presents an oppressed social and racial underclass and offers a critique of one of the quintessential myths that have long stood at the heart of American identity, that of the classless society.

However, the zombies of Uniontown *are* different than the previous zombies in Romero's films; they appear to be evolving, learning, and even developing a consciousness. One of the other commanders of the nightly raids, the conscientious, professional soldier and the superficial hero of the film, Riley Denbo (Simon Baker), is the only one aware of the change: "They are not just walking. It's like they are communicating, they are thinking, something's going on." For the first time in a Romero film, one of the zombies even emerges as a leader: Big Daddy (Eugene Clarke), the African-American owner of a small gas station.

As Cholo's marauders enter Uniontown, they shoot fireworks (nicknamed "Sky Flowers") from their giant war truck, a real weapon of mass destruction, called Dead Reckoning. The "Shock and Awe" tactics of the military paralyze the zombies, and Cholo's men move through their ranks and kill the undead with impunity. The zombies cannot see what is going on around them as they are distracted by the bright colors and loud noises that fill the sky. Unlike his distracted fellow zombies, Big Daddy is somehow impervious to their effect and unsuccessfully tries to rouse his compatriots. Powerless to prevent his fellow zombies from being butchered in such large numbers, for no purpose other than aggression and subjugation, he cries with pain and remorse.

Considering Big Daddy's leadership abilities and the sociopolitical commentary within the film, Romero characterizes the zombies in *Land* as "a little more organized. Big Daddy is not as instantly as sympathetic as Bub [the zombie from *Dawn* that began to evolve]. He is . . . Zapata."[8] By comparing Big Daddy to the Mexican revolutionary, Romero insists that the film be viewed from both class and racial perspectives. The raid on Uniontown is Romero's opening political gambit and is a rather unsubtle, but potent, allegory of America's self-proclaimed role as global policeman. Romero dramatizes a military power invading a much weaker opponent and overpowering them with superior force, thus relieving them of their resources under the guise of retrieving essential supplies. These aggressive actions are key, as they will trigger the zombies' desire to retaliate against their oppressors.

With the evolution of Big Daddy and, later, the other zombies, the film explores the fact that the distinction between zombie and human is no longer easy to make, just as the "War on Terror" provoked a reemergence of the discussion as to what constitutes a terrorist act and the morals of ignoring the Geneva Conventions' provisions. Noam Chomsky notes that, despite its aggressive anti-terrorist rhetoric, "The US is the only country that was condemned for international terrorism by the World Court and that rejected a Security Council resolution calling on states to observe international law."[9] When in April 2004 Bush stated that the difference between "Us and Them" was his belief that "We love freedom and they hate freedom—that's where the clash occurs," many commentators focused on his naïveté or his deliberate agenda. Romero explores the centrality of Bush's "Us and Them" rhetoric to the escalation of the "War on Terror" through the relationship between zombies and humans in *Land of the Dead*. The young boy who dies in the opening attack on Uniontown explains to Riley, "There's a big difference between us and them. They're dead. It's like they are pretending to be alive." To which Riley replies with a question, "Isn't that what we are doing?" The opening sequence concludes with Big Daddy convening an army of zombies who have "decided" to fight back against their oppressors. The undead stare up at an illuminated tower block in the distance, an imposing physical and psychological landmark that evokes the Twin Towers.

The grand skyscraper is Fiddler's Green, a luxurious building where the wealthy elite still live a life of extravagance. Despite the terror and poverty around them, they continue to live as if nothing has happened; they dine in fine restaurants and shop in indulgent and exclusive boutiques. Their sense of security derives from their isolation from undesirables (both the zombie hoard and the slum dwellers below) and also from the armed guards and electric fences. For these elite, states the tower's advertisement voice-over, "Life goes on at Fiddler's Green in the heart of one of America's oldest and greatest cities. Bordered on three sides by mighty rivers, Fiddler's Green offers luxury living in the grand old style." The language is a nostalgic evocation of a return to the past, couched in dialogue reminiscent of the Old South's melancholy toward the decline of the Confederacy. In Romero's hands this constitutes both a desire for pre-zombie days and for a return to a pre-9/11 US before "everything" changed. While superficially, life in Fiddler's Green seems perfect, appearances are deceptive; it is an artificially contrived utopia, which profits from the poverty, deaths, misery, and manipulation of others. The evocation of the Old South is heightened by the residents of the tower block being quite obviously from the privileged class and all white. Despite the harmony of Fiddler's Green, the world outside is changing, even if its residents are unaware of it. The advertisement for Fiddler's Green plays repeatedly on television screens, reminding them of something they already have. To further underline the point, as Romero's camera glides through the lavish halls of Fiddler's Green, it pauses for a brief moment on a bird in a gilded cage, an unsubtle indication of the tide of change that is about to sweep over them. Beyond their walls a war is being fought in their name, whether they are aware of it or not, and the battle is about to be brought to them.

The presentation of Fiddler's Green connotes echoes of both the World Trade Center and America itself. About the cultural resonance of the 9/11 targets, Jürgen Habermas has observed:

> What was new was the symbolic force of the targets struck. The attackers did not just physically cause the highest buildings in Manhattan to collapse; they destroyed an icon in the household imagery of the American nation. Only in the surge of patriotism that followed did one begin to recognise the central importance that the towers held in everyone's imagination, with their irreplaceable print on the Manhattan skyline and their powerful embodiment of economic strength and projection towards the future.[10]

Just as *Dawn of the Dead*'s shopping mall provided a telling emblem of capitalism in 1970s America, *Land of the Dead*'s skyscraper functions as an icon of American capital and cultural dominance.

A ruthless CEO called Paul Kaufman (Dennis Hopper), a thinly veiled portrait of George W. Bush with shades of Donald Rumsfeld, rules over Fiddler's Green. Kaufman wears a red tie and an American flag tie pin, and even his name offers echoes of the extreme forms of capitalism and the political ideology he represents.[11] One of the characters describes the economy of Fiddler's Green in colorfully fascist terms: "If you can drink it, shoot it up, fuck it or gamble on it, it belongs to him [Kaufman]." In the DVD's director's commentary, Romero relates a conversation he had with Hopper in which Hopper remarks, "I'll play him as Rumsfeld." Romero continues "That's exactly where I'm going. This *is* the Bush administration."

Throughout the narrative, Romero frequently juxtaposes the two leaders of the film, Kaufman and Big Daddy, and the "civilized" human being Kaufman is found wanting. He steals, manipulates, betrays, and murders, whereas Big Daddy displays courage, mercy, intelligence, and compassion, leading by example and even risking his "life" for his fellow zombies.

Kaufman's Fiddler's Green and his emperor-like status are two of several deliberate allusions to the decline of the Roman Empire, which Romero offers as a parallel to the current status of the so-called American Empire. This interpretation casts Kaufman (and, by extension, Bush) as a Nero-like figure, corrupt and depraved by power and money, and ultimately responsible for the demise of the empire. Bush, as his most recent predecessors have done, denied any ambition to create a *Pax Americana*, stating in June 2002, "America has no empire to extend or utopia to establish. We wish for others only what we wish for ourselves."[12] Bush continued "We're not an imperial power ... We're a liberating power."[13] Yet many have come to the opposite conclusion. Niall Ferguson states, "The United States is an empire in every sense but one, and that one sense is that it doesn't recognise itself as such."[14] Ferguson posits a pessimistic outlook for its future in the wake of America's continued reliance on foreign capital, its rapidly escalating manpower deficit, and the rising sense of anti-American sentiment spreading throughout the world.

Describing *Land*'s screenplay, Romero repeatedly and explicitly connects Fiddler's Green with America:

> Then 9/11 happened and I made it more political, more about what was turning into America's "new normal." You know, a government that had felt it was protected by water. The folly being that the "new normal" is not really normal at all. Is the fortified city of opportunities making money out of being surrounded by zombies an allegory for America living with terrorism and trying to keep the threat at bay? Is the Dennis Hopper character George Bush in disguise? Yes, is the simple answer.[15]

Fiddler's Green's resonance with Baghdad's "Green Zone" further extends the allegory. Outside of Fiddler's Green, but within the bases that surround it, is the third group of individuals that populate the film, the slum-dwelling, disenfranchised (but living) proletariat. They have no electricity and lack even the most basic food or medical supplies. The army, funded by Kaufman, polices the area. While their official mission is to keep the zombies out, there is a discernible sense that their real job is keeping the masses away from the tower itself.

They are discontented with their social situation, but they seem unable or unwilling to do anything about it; they look up at the tower and fantasize about social change but are preoccupied by Kaufman's myriad diversions. Kaufman provides entertainment to take their mind off their predicament, just as the zombies were distracted by the Sky Flowers. Kaufman supplies gambling, prostitution, and gladiatorial arenas (another allusion to the Roman Empire), which, at first, allow them to watch zombies fight over stray dogs. As their social situation worsens more extreme forms of entertainment emerge as "undesirable" humans find themselves in the arena too. These arenas have electricity, unlike the slums, and the richer inhabitants of Fiddler's Green attend the events to experience vicariously the thrills of lower-class life before returning to their luxurious suites in the tower.

Kaufman, like the Bush administration and the "War on Terror," was initially able to strike the delicate balance of convincing the slum dwellers that the zombies are simultaneously no threat to them but also something to be greatly feared. In the aftermath of the 9/11 attacks, America found itself living in a culture of fear which revolved around the phrase "War on Terror" itself. The cultivation of the culture of fear proved beneficial for the Bush administration in gaining support from Congress, which would have been severely hampered without the symbolic links that the administration drew between 9/11 and Iraq. Bush propelled through the 2004 elections by portraying himself as head of a nation at war. All the time this sense of fear was political currency. Kyle Bishop sees fear as central to the evolution of the zombie, evoking Freud's uncanny: "Zombies are not uncanny because of their humanistic qualities; they are uncanny because they are, in essence, a grotesque metaphor for humanity itself."[16] Kaufman parades the zombies, referred to in a racially motivated epithet as "stenches," through the camps, hanging them up, letting people have their photo taken with them, and shooting at them for target practice. Yet it is clear that outside the walls (which he repeatedly reminds those around him that he pays for) danger waits and that they should be thankful to him and him alone for keeping them safe.

The two leaders of the mercenaries, the brutal Cholo and the more humane Riley, come from the lower classes. Both are disillusioned with life in the city, but they have different ideas as to what constitutes freedom. Riley has a frontier fantasy of fleeing "civilization" for the open expanses of Canada, which he believes may be empty of both people and zombies. The irony is that traditionally those American citizens who have wished to avoid fighting for the Armed Forces have fled to the border for refuge in Canada, but as part of the Patriot Act, the border between the United States and Canada has been closed, and a passport is required for travel between the two. Riley repeats what could be a mantra for a post-9/11 America: "Nothing bad ever happened to me, until everything changed."

For Cholo, freedom is earning an apartment inside Fiddler's Green. Although he is twice separated from its residents, once by his race and again by his class, he believes his dirty work for Kaufman will get him access. For not only does Cholo retrieve luxury supplies for his master, he also disposes of political dissidents who oppose Kaufman's regime. Riley knows Cholo has no chance of acceptance into Fiddler's Green: "You're dreaming Cholo. They won't let you in there. They wouldn't let me in there. We're the wrong kind." The scene where Cholo visits his master in Kaufman's palatial presidential suite at the top of Fiddler's Green reveals Cholo's unsuitability. At first Kaufman seems pleased to see him. As a token of good faith and servitude, Cholo hands Kaufman a glass of champagne he has inadvertently placed in a whiskey glass. Unaware of social etiquette, he does not understand why Kaufman then pours the drink into a long necked champagne flute. In one subtle gesture Romero reveals that the two men inhabit different worlds and the doors of Fiddler's Green will never be open for someone like Cholo.

With his wish for an apartment summarily denied, Cholo sets course for revenge.

He steals Dead Reckoning and demands five million dollars, or he will launch a devastating salvo of missiles directly at Fiddler's Green. This violent plan evokes the exploited colonized seeking revenge on his colonizer and conjures a parallel to Islamic fundamentalist terrorists using the weapons and training of their previous sponsors, the United States, against them.[17] Romero analogizes Osama bin Laden to Cholo with his line, "I'm gonna do a jihad on his ass." A few moments later Kaufman tells his board of executives, "We don't negotiate with terrorists," a direct quotation of one of Bush's most famous comments about the "War on Terror." Fiddler's Green becomes a potent symbol to everyone in the film, something akin to another of the quintessential myths of the United States, the American Dream. Cholo believes that access to it will bring him happiness and acceptance, Kaufman believes he built it and it belongs to him, Big Daddy is drawn to it, and Riley wants, more than anything, to get away from it.

Cultural theorist Jean Baudrillard earned considerable scorn in the United States when he dared to assert, just a month after the event, that American foreign policy had itself played an instrumental role in provoking the attacks on 9/11:

> For it is this superpower [the US] that, through its unbearable power, is the secret case of all the violence percolating all over the world, and consequently of the terrorist imagination, which unbeknownst to us, inhabits our psyche. That we may have dreamed of that event, that everybody with out exception, dreamed of it because no one cannot dream of the destruction of a power that has become hegemonic to such a point, is unacceptable to Western moral consciousness. However, it is a fact that can be measured against the pathetic violence shown by all the speeches and discourses that want to erase the event. We could even go so far as to say that it is *they* who perpetrated the attack, but it was *we* who wished it.[18]

Baudrillard echoes Noam Chomsky's famous assertion that "We can think of the United States as an 'innocent victim' only if we adopt the convenient path of ignoring the record of its actions and those of its allies, which are, after all, hardly a secret."[19] Romero has dramatized what both Baudrillard and Chomsky suggested and what other films like *World Trade Center* and *United 93* are unable or unwilling to explore. When Žižek criticized them for their lack of political context, he pointed out their ideological message actually existed in the absence of an ideological message. Seemingly incidental details in the movies' subtexts reflect their conservative outlook and their unquestioning acceptance of societal norms, their traditional notions of heroism, their call to mythologize real life events, and their disturbingly framed concepts of what constitutes "the Other."

In contrast, *Land of the Dead* concludes with Big Daddy's army of zombies mobilizing, invading, and destroying Fiddler's Green and all who live there. They even cross the river, long thought to have been an impassable barrier for their kind, which the residents of Fiddler's Green considered a part of their security, just as America considered itself an isolated island because, until 9/11, there has been no attack on American soil since 1812. Fences and walls, which had once been protection for the survivors, now serve only to trap them and prevent them from being able to escape.

Used to the luxury of their surroundings, they are powerless to fight back and are butchered. Even though the zombies have no technology or weapons, it is their sheer hunger and determination that make them unbeatable foes.

While Riley may be the ostensible hero of the film, Big Daddy is the moral center. The zombie's actions are repeatedly intercut with Kaufman's frantic attempts to flee Fiddler's Green after he realizes that the tower is under attack. Kaufman steals funds from a safe and then murders his second in command. Escaping to the basement he comes face to face with Big Daddy and attempts several times to shoot him, only for his shots to comically miss his target. He melodramatically cries "How dare you!?" with the self-righteous tone of one who believes that all is owed to him. Cholo and Big Daddy finally dispatch Kaufman when he becomes trapped in his Lincoln Continental, a car that has become symbolic of American power, dominance, overconsumption, and lack of concern for the environment. Big Daddy first fills the inside of the car with gasoline, then returns to hurl a burning gas cylinder at the car, causing it to explode. The zombies, previously a mindless hoard who compulsively fed on their victims, have learned self-control. Big Daddy turns away from the burning car and the remains of Kaufman and makes his way back to lead his fellow zombies, more human than the humans who wish him dead.

For a film that spends much of its runtime deconstructing cultural myths, it ironically ends by reinforcing one. Riley returns to Dead Reckoning and leaves for the frontiers of Canada with his crew. Romero's endings have previously been unremittingly bleak and much more powerful for it. This optimistic conclusion suggests that there is always open space in which to find freedom. As Dead Reckoning leaves, one of the gunners prepares to fire the remaining missiles at the zombies, but Riley stops her, for the cycle of violence must end here: "They are just looking for a place to go. Same as us." Once again the boundaries between "Us and Them" continue to be blurred; we see ourselves in the enemy.

Notes

1 Slavoj Žižek, "On 9/11, New Yorkers Faced the Fire in the Minds of Men: Hollywood's Attempts to Mark the 2001 Attacks Ignore Their Political Context and the Return to History They Symbolise," *The Guardian*, September 11, 2006, 30.

2 Jean Baudrillard, *The Spirit of Terrorism and Other Essays*, trans. Chris Turner (New York: Verso, 2003), 4.

3 On the critique of capitalism, see R.H.W. Dillard, "*Night of the Living Dead*: It's Not Just a Wind That's Passing Through," in *American Horrors: Essays on the Modern American Horror Film*, ed. Gregory A. Waller (Chicago: University of Illinois Press, 1987), 14–29; on racism, see Richard Dyer, "White," *Screen* 29 no. 4 (1988), 59–63; on American foreign policy, see Sumiko Higashi, "A Horror Film about the Vietnam era," in *Hanoi to Hollywood: the Vietnam War in American Film*, eds Linda Dittmer and Gene Michaud (New Jersey: Rutgers University Press, 1990), 175–88; on the Vietnam War, see Karen Randell, "Lost Bodies/Lost Souls: MIA Narratives in *Night of the Living Dead*," *Film & History CD-ROM Annual (2004–2005)* (Oshkosh, WI: Center for the Study of Film and History, 2005).

4 Robin Wood, *Hollywood from Vietnam to Reagan* (New York: Columbia University Press, 2003), 267.

5 Donald Rumsfeld, "Defense Department Briefing," *Defense Link*, February 12, 2002),

http://www.defenselink.mil/transcripts/transcript.aspx?transcriptid=2636 (accessed January 22, 2009).

6   Graham Rae, "Dead Reckoning," *Cinefastique* 37 no. 4 (2005): 45.

7   Detailed information on Bush popularity ratings can be found at http://www.polling report.com/BushJob.htm (accessed October 14, 2009).

8   Giulia D'Agnolo-Vallan, "Let Them Eat Flesh," *Film Comment* 41 no. 4 (2005): 24.

9   Noam Chomsky, *9–11* (New York: Seven Stories Press, 2001), 44.

10   Jürgen Habermas, quoted in an excerpt of Giovanna Borradori, *Philosophy in a Time of Terror: Dialogues with Jürgen Habermas and Jacques Derrida* (Chicago: Chicago University Press, 2003), http://www.press.uchicago.edu/Misc/Chicago/066649.html (accessed January 9, 2009).

11   The German word "Kaufen" is the verb "to buy."

12   Jonathan Marcus, "America: An Empire to Rival Rome?" *BBC News*, January 26, 2004, http://news.bbc.co.uk/1/hi/world/americas/3430199.stm (accessed July 23, 2007).

13   Bush's speech is cited in Guy Raz, "World Sees 'Imperialism' in American Reach, Strength," *NPR*, November 2, 2006, http://www.npr.org/templates/story/story.php?storyId=6423000 (accessed January 7, 2009).

14   Niall Ferguson in Marcus, "America: An Empire to Rival Rome?"

15   Alan Jones, "George A. Romero. Dead Reckoning," *Film Review* 662 (2005): 64.

16   Kyle Bishop, "Raising the Dead," *Journal of Popular Film & Television* 33 no. 4 (2006): 196.

17   It is widely known that Osama bin Laden was one of many militant Islamic leaders trained, armed, and financed by the CIA to wage war against the Soviet Union in Afghanistan. After the withdrawal of Russian troops from Afghanistan, the sponsored acts of terrorism allegedly continued for many years in Tanzania, Kenya, Chechnya, and inside Russia. The conflict then turned against America in the light of perceived American aggression against the Muslim faith.

18   Baudrillard, "L'esprit du Terrorisme," trans. Michael Valentin, *South Atlantic Quarterly* 101 no. 2 (2002): 404.

19   Chomsky, *9–11*, 35.

CHAPTER 10

Superman *Is* the Faultline: Fissures in the Monomythic Man of Steel

ALEX EVANS

Robert Jewett and John Lawrence suggest that the superhero is ubiquitous enough in what they call the American civil religion to make it a "monomyth": a term which suggests monologic intransigence, monolithic politics, perhaps even a *monoculture*.[1] Aspects of comic book heroism since the 9/11 attacks, as we will see, certainly seem to confirm their assessment of the genre. And yet, while the ubiquity of the myth might be read in itself as monolithic, just as its occasional tendency to be used to justify hegemonic and imperialist projects of domination might suggest that it is innately reactionary, the superhero has always seen, and continues to demonstrate, a good deal of ideological battle across its myriad surfaces: it is not *just* a tool of hegemony and imperialism but also a site of considerable resistance and conflict. What close study shows, I would suggest, is just how fraught—and, perhaps, fragile—the ideological unity of *mainstream* American popular culture is, even in the wake of seemingly endless attempts at right-wing ideological unity in the Bush era. My feeling is that the real ideological work, and, hence, the real signs of splinter and dissent, are to be found at the coal face of hegemonic, mainstream, populist texts. As such, instead of concentrating on supposedly oppositional, "traditionally" subversive or "counter-cultural" comic books, such as the recent work of Art Spiegelman, this chapter analyzes conflicts in the figure of Superman—the oldest and surely traditionally considered the most hegemonic, central, quintessentially American of superheroes.[2]

Mythology

Myth, says Roland Barthes, is "frozen speech," which "at the moment of reaching me ... suspends itself, turns away and assumes the look of a generality: it stiffens, makes itself look neutral and innocent."[3] Myth, in other words, is a de-historicizing discourse, designed to elide the contingency of ideological constructs. It would be hard to think of a stiffer, more frozen discourse than the hugely popular comic art of Alex Ross. Ross's hyper-real images, drawn from life with the use of models and uniquely stylized lighting effects, are even collected in a hagiographic compendium entitled, incredibly appropriately, *Mythology: The Comic Book Art of Alex Ross*. A detailed three-dimensional statue of Superman designed by Ross in particular is, to this viewer at least, viscerally terrifying, overtly patriarchal: an elder statesman, thick-necked, intransigent, an aging good ol' boy.[4] And, in particular, from the beefy somatotype of the model (who seems to recall the George Reeves incarnation), to the cut of his hair, to the regular return to an earlier (in fact, 1930s) costume style, the Superman of Alex Ross is also the Superman of an American *always*. This is the Superman of your father's generation—but as such, it is also, for Ross's generation, the Superman who *is your father*. In the visual return to a nostalgic past, in terms of historical references to earlier versions of the hero, and to a patriarchal protector untroubled by the passage of time, this seems to seek to construct a Superman divested of the historical and political developments and fads of the last half-century. Superman is returned to safety in the ideological and historical fixity of mytho-poeic Americana, an America where it is always the 30s, the 50s, where Dad and Superman are always right, always strong, and always the same.

This is of course precisely a response to the tendency for Superman to change with the times, particularly since the early 1990s. Conservatives have long feared that the ideological changes of history will undo their hero. Republican conservative activist Herbert London, for example, opined on the death of Superman (a development in the mythology in the early 1990s, interestingly just as Clinton came to power),

> [i]t is understandable that Superman must go. His assets were inconsistent with an era of moral ambiguity and androgynous sexual leanings. [. . .] Superman is after all an anachronism, a model of a bygone era when virtue mattered, when morality wasn't relative [. . .] After all, Clark Kent was a simple man with a basic middle-American sense of justice. In his Kent persona Superman could be confused with Tom Sawyer, a kind of American Adam. [. . .] Superman was indeed a figure towering above the others, a hero to emulate. [. . .] Superman will be missed, but the virtue he embodied will be missed even more.[5]

This is the kind of conservatism that would no doubt have delighted 1950s anti-comic book campaigner Fredric Wertham, who equally feared the rise of such moral relativism and sexual androgyny.[6] Such overt de-historicizations of Superman are intended to serve as a bolster against the vicissitudes of shifting moral and political values (and, in particular, the legacy of the 1960s). But certainly, by the time of London's writing, this is part of a rear-guard maneuver by conservative ideology—a maneuver that, as we will see, continues as part of a wider battle for ideological control of a particularly valuable piece of American mythology. Superman is always in danger of getting away, becoming morally relative, of becoming "un-American."

On closer inspection, we find that, whatever London may think, the Man of Steel has in fact always shifted with an astonishing alacrity between political positions.

Before US involvement in World War II in 1939, Superman is strongly opposed to embroilment in Europe—a distinctly anti-capitalist imperialist hero (created, after all, by left-leaning New York Jews) foils a plot by fat-cat arms dealers to embroil nations in war: "But why should we fight?" asks one European leader. "We're not angry at each other," says another. "Gentlemen, it's obvious you've been fighting only to promote the sales of munitions!—Why not shake hands and make up?" suggests Superman.[7] By 1940, before the US has signed up to battle Hitler, Superman is bringing der Führer and Joe Stalin to trial before the League of Nations.[8] By 1941 he is enthusiastically supporting the war: beaming, he strides arm in arm with two cheerful military men on the cover of Superman #12. As mainstream US opinion has shifted at this point, so has Superman's, and, indeed, Superman is part of the apparatus being used to shift—and hold—that opinion.

Years later, our hero's position takes a more disturbing turn when, in the early 1990s, a union-busting Superman must defeat Demolitia, a Latin American, possibly lesbian, freedom fighter—that is, terrorist—who seeks the destruction of an armaments factory to stop the flow of US-made devices into the hands of the brutal military dictatorship in control of her home country. Cue much wagging of Kryptonian fingers: to close the arms factory, Superman says, would be to put good, honest Americans out of work. So while the factory owner is, says Demolitia to an Average Joe worker trying to stop her advance, "an evil monster," whom he "should be ashamed of trying to protect," the working man counters,

> Lady, what I'm tryin' ta protect—is us! All we're doin' is our jobs! We got mortgages, kids ta put through school! But your idea of justice is wreckin' this factory—an' our livelihoods with it! How're we supposed to survive, huh? Dijda think of that?[9]

Superman, then, is protecting ordinary Americans and their livelihoods, not just the interests of gigantic corporations profiting from human misery—since of course the interests of the working-class man and the capitalist warmongers are, in fact, the same. But the pages of Superman comics have also been a site of perhaps truly subversive conflict over American domestic political power and the role of capital in its assignment. In the 1990s, Lex Luthor was redrawn as, not a mad scientist or petty criminal, but a multi-billionaire Machiavellian capitalist. And then, soon after the 2000 presidential election, who should suddenly find himself in the Superman universe's White House but said evil genius and Machiavellian capitalist Lex Luthor![10] It would be very hard not to read this as some kind of critique. These are redolently subversive parallels with reality to say the least—even if the real-life Machiavellian capitalist president in question was by no means a genius and was not, after all, democratically elected.

What we are seeing here, at the very least, is ambivalence, and such a position has also been insistently present in renderings of Superman's geopolitical urges. In 1999 when the US was already bombing and terrorizing its military inferiors and had already suffered an abortive attempt to bring the concrete giants crashing down—Ross and writer Paul Dini collaborated on a series of large-format, storybook-style works, one of which was *Superman: Peace on Earth* (1998). As Henry

Jenkins notes, these works are almost prescient in their questioning of America's global role, and, although my sense is that their political positions are far more problematic than Jenkins allows, a clear movement within hegemony of sorts is very much visible.[11] After the fall of the Towers, the superhero became a figure of some focus for those seeking to express their grief, anger, and fear in the wake of the attacks. Galleries on superhero fan websites began to fill with home-made images of Superman—culled from various comic-book incarnations, or sometimes featuring already-fallen superman Christopher Reeve—portrayed standing ghostly and defiant by the still-standing Twin Towers[12] or mournfully by their iconic wreckage. One shows Superman carrying a dead firefighter, titled "Farewell to a real hero."[13] Of course, it is all too easy to balk at the sentimentalism of such outpourings of grief and mourning. But while much of the grief and outrage these images express is, let me be clear, quite real and appropriate, what discomfort over these images and other aspects of popular mourning since 9/11 proceeds from is an intertextual knowledge of their problematic interrelation with discourses of hatred and violent retribution so central to many popular US cultural items since the attacks—as well as their material practice in global policy.

And such an interrelation is clear in *Heroes: The World's Greatest Superhero Creators Honor the World's Greatest Heroes. 9.11.2001.* This Marvel Comics production, designed to produce income for the Twin Towers Fund shortly after the attacks, features many short pieces by well-known comic book artists. Some of these are of a fairly gentle mourning/nurturing/heroic type, featuring superheroes and firefighters working together to help those fallen in the attacks[14] or telegrammatic images of loss (a woman waiting by the phone for her pilot husband to call).[15] Others show a social renewal in liberal-pluralistic unity (children of all races coming together to remember the lost),[16] all races—including species from other worlds—giving blood together,[17] or schoolchildren "Ellen McKenzie" and "Fatima Jaffal" holding hands and crying together as they see the towers burn on TV in class.[18] Jenkins's suggestion is that it is these nurturing works which dominate responses,[19] and yet I would suggest that we must also take heed of the more problematic images, given their obvious intersection with mainstream political discourses at this point: images that take on a more chilling tone. In perhaps the most disturbing entry of this collection, Captain America stands, a ravaged flag fluttering still-erect in his hand, with an inscription by comics legend Stan Lee (creator of Spiderman and many others):

> A day there was of monumental villainy. A day when a great nation lost its innocence and naked evil stood revealed before a stunned and shattered world.
> A day there was when a serpent struck a sleeping giant, a giant who will sleep no more. Soon shall the serpent know the wrath of the mighty, the vengeance of the just.
> A day there was when liberty lost her heart—and found the strength within her soul.[20]

What this imagery and text most uncomfortably recalls is the confluence of sentimentality with intolerance and brutality, alongside a tendency to speak in lofty, near-meaningless, trans-historical abstracts, most characteristic of cultural aspects of fascism. Since 9/11 there have been, what we might read as perhaps anxious, attempts to fix and stabilize the Superman mythology. From early on, "Supes" became an occasional poster boy for the forthcoming "War on Terror," and the Anne Coulter-esque bravado[21] of Stan Lee's Captain America piece quoted above pales by comparison with DC artist Neal Adams's image of Superman prepared for one of two DC Comics coffee-table editions responding to 9/11. "Support your Red Cross," it suggests, above the flag-holding Superman, standing again in front of the iconic WTC rubble. To his left is Uncle Sam, sleeves rolled for business. At his feet is a plaque: "FIRST THINGS FIRST. THEN WE COME FOR YOU."

And then, the redoubling of such efforts seems particularly overt on the cover of the 600th anniversary issue of *The New Adventures of Superman* in March 2002. This striking image features Superman, again in a costume which returns to its earliest incarnation, hypertrophically proportioned and oleaginously bequiffed, carrying Old Glory, an offset clutch of serifed text reading:

"NOW MORE THAN EVER—
FOR TRUTH, JUSTICE AND THE AMERICAN WAY!"

We might be forgiven for a momentary shudder. But the cover is by Daniel Adel, a professional caricaturist. There is everything to suggest that this is mythologizing of the most quintessentially Barthesian sort: the trans-historical connection between *Now* and *Ever* reinforced at a clear point of the passage of time (an anniversary), which is yet all the more tremulous and clearly vulnerable for its hysterical insistence. This image is surely a carnivalesque exposition of the underside of Alex Ross's Superman—itself no less bizarre and infinitely more disturbing. And so, just at a point where ideological coherence might be expected to be strongest—and be ideologically *required* to be so—subversive forces take over, parodically transforming to-the-letter conformity through figurative and textual hyperbole. While we might suggest that different readings of this cover are taking place and that perhaps "real" Superman fans read it as sincere, as the following statement highlights, however, we should note that comics readers are not as "dumb" as some might like to think:

Oh, I'm sure the sophisticated Cool Cats of the *Rolling Stone* Magazine set enjoyed the cover's air of delicious irony, since the patriotic sentiment looks as flat-out foolish as Superman himself. But as for Superman fans at the time, it's fair to say most of us were pretty disappointed.[22]

They knew they were being had. But perhaps some of them—like me—rather liked it. Inside, the comic sees Superman still undergoing a crisis of conscience over Lex Luthor's presidency, only six months post-9/11.[23]

Faultlines

As a mythic palimpsest, the superhero is a particularly useful source for cultural studies: the tendency for the most popular figures in the genre to last for many years and go through various incarnations and revisionist "reboots" of their mythology,[24] as well as the connected fact that continuities in the comic book world are multiple and flexible—often making use of multiple divergent "universes" in different runs of a title and its offshoots—means that complications and contradictions become all the more possible and, indeed, clearly visible. Of course, Marvel and DC go to great lengths to control these universes and ensure that they remain coherent across titles, yet we have long been persuaded, after all, that texts are impossible to control; that their meanings are deployed *across their surfaces* and, as such, are impossible to centralize or constrict. This is surely all the more the case as the number of surfaces, and the "size" and spread of a text, increases all the more rhizomatically.

As cultural materialist scholar Alan Sinfield points out, the neo-Gramscian turn in cultural studies was designed in part to break the stranglehold of the "entrapment" model popularized by French late structuralist thinkers, particularly Louis Althusser.[25] This has provoked a necessary complication of our understanding of the ideological assignment of power. While the ruling ideas are indeed those of the ruling class, what this work has consistently reminded us is that, first, no ideological domination is total, and, second, that even hegemony itself is constantly fragmented, fraught, and in danger of losing its grip.[26] As such, it requires constant reinforcement, realignment, and defense, since, at the same time, we find that counter-hegemonic influences themselves are always struggling to achieve dominance. My feeling is that in popular culture in particular we are able to see this process in action, and most of all, perhaps, in those cultural texts which repeat—texts we might call myths, archetypes, or "generic." The reason is that their persistent (but flexible) shape and clear structural delineation allow us to see more clearly the points of breakage and shift in ideological formation that inevitably occur over the period of repetition. Indeed, rather than assuming that such texts are all the more monolithically ideological for their repetition, those texts are ironically the ones that allow us most clearly to recognize, first, the processes of history, and, second, connectedly, of shifting and contested ideological structures. In particular, in versions of Superman, we can see processes of dissidence, rupture, containment: dead-Superman meets Herbert-London-Superman; Alex-Ross-Superman meets Daniel-Adel-Superman.

Sinfield takes just such an approach in his seminal work, *Faultlines: Cultural Materialism and the Politics of Dissident Reading* (1992), proposing that we pay attention to what he calls "faultline stories."[27] These stories or mythologies serve as a crisis point, and, hence, a focus, for culture's "awkward, unresolved issues [that] require most assiduous and continuous reworking; they hinge upon a fundamental, unresolved ideological complication that finds its way [. . .] into texts."[28] In particular, Sinfield's approach is an attempt to find a way out of, first, models which presuppose the individual agency of an independent rational (or trans-historical) mind as a way of explaining the processes of cultural change, and, second, out of the aforementioned "entrapment" model.[29] Sinfield proposes instead that culture itself produces its own problems and contradictions, which manifest themselves in culture as sites of anxious repetition: the stories must be retold, reworked, rethought. At this point, they may be either returned to, and recuperated by, hegemonic ideology, or, instead, may be sizeably re-figured by non-hegemonic readings—or rewritings—in such a way that they actually produce some kind of cultural change. Sinfield's ideas are also greatly influenced by Foucault,[30] and his proposal of multiple sites of resistance rather than a single "great refusal"; the question, then, is where exactly these sites of cultural resistance can—and should—take place. The faultline story is one persuasive answer to that question.

The importance of Sinfield's faultline theory, to my mind, lies in its foregrounding of reiteration as a site for historical analysis of cultural and particularly ideological change, and this most of all in its potential to demonstrate more clearly than other forms of analysis the battleground nature of culture: a single site can be occupied simultaneously, or at least consecutively by numerous opposing readings and rewritings of a narrative and its attendant ideological formation. The task then becomes the analysis and cataloguing of those opposing formations: the trick in all cases is to analyze complexities, conflicts, breaks, and dissonances, as well as superficial coherences and repetitions. Such analyses might also help us to work out the way that those shifts in formation might be harnessed to *effect* further social change. Faultline stories, after all, might be seen as a highly useful place to direct cultural activism, since they are, by definition, points of weakness as well as points of contestation in dominant ideology. The superhero has always been, and remains, exactly such a point, even since what we might see—what we are encouraged to see—is the ideological watershed of 9/11.

What neo-Gramscian work shows us, then, and what Sinfield's work emphasizes, is that ideological hegemony itself is always split and divided—and always a temporary yoking together of disparate groups and interests. This means that we are always likely to find far more conflict and ambivalence at the center than we might otherwise have imagined. Despite Jewett and Lawrence's use of Marvel Comics' American icon, Captain America, as the quintessential example of monolithic cultural hegemony, and even despite Stan Lee's disturbingly vengeful salvo quoted above, such conflict and ambivalence has become central to the mythology: Cap has equally upset right-wing critics in daring to suggest that America may well have sown the seeds of terrorism elsewhere in the *Captain America: The New Deal* series:

> We might expect such blame-America logic from Hollywood activists, academic apologists [yes, us], or the angry protesters who regularly fill the streets of European capitals (and many major American cities). When such sentiments turn up, however, hidden within star-spangled, nostalgic packaging of comic books aimed at kids, we need to confront the deep cultural malaise afflicting the nation on the eve of war.[31]

And perhaps such a deep cultural malaise—or rather, a sense of changing political nuances, a deeply disturbing sense for the power elite that America may not be as ideologically centralized, harmonized, controlled as they would wish—has been in evidence in the Superman world too. More and more visibly, even the very central parts of the mythology are full of more possible faultlines and ideological fragmentations than we might imagine. Of course, it is debatable whether comics are really a mainstream form: Henry Jenkins, in his article on comic books post 9/11, makes the distinction that they are "popular" (that is, using the generic language of mainstream culture and being produced for entertainment) but are now not mainstream but a fringe medium that appeals mainly to college students and college-educated professionals.[32]

What we see in debates over the reading of Superman are heated battles, sometimes almost disturbing in their ideological fervor, and I suspect they are so often so ferocious because it is realized that this is one very promising place where cultural change might happen. We see here a constantly developing, constantly fragmenting mythology of Superman as it plays out in public discourse in arguments over meanings of preexisting texts, and this is precisely the kind of process that Sinfield maps out in his *Faultlines*. But one of the benefits of Superman over, say, Sinfield's focus, Shakespeare, is that the primary texts are still to play for, can be changed, reproduced and rewritten directly. There are political battles of reading—performatively, publicly—between fans, bloggers, journalists, but there are also those between, say, traditionalist and revisionist writers and artists. As Jenkins reminds us, we ought not to forget that often artists working within popular culture work for political ideals as well as economic imperatives.[33] Perhaps these revisionist superhero writers really are, as Silver Age hero artist Jim Steranko angrily suggested, "cultural terrorists."[34] I prefer the term "cultural activists," but it is interesting to hear such a loaded term being used—if the bandying about of "terrorist" in the context of comic books does not speak of the terrifyingly expandable nature of such a categorization in Bush's America, I don't know what does.

Conclusion

The neo-Gramscian and Foucauldian turn in cultural studies and, in particular, Sinfield's work was designed to tell us, at a point when resistance seemed futile—we were "entrapped"—how resistance might be produced and directed. Because, even if culture itself produces the faultlines, it is real men and women who will have to *stick a spade in them*, so to speak. A faultline—with the potential it offers splinter ideological groups to performatively reread or, indeed, *rewrite* that story to gain some kind of leverage, to stake a claim to the hegemony through the (re-)production of meaning—might be precisely where these cultural battles are most productively, if always awkwardly, anxiously, pursued. Overall, what I have tried to suggest is that, while some may imagine that the myth of Superman will heal America and repair the damage of any earth-shaking disaster, including the splinters and fissures of ideology, we find instead that Superman himself *is* a faultline. We find here a continuing story of dissidence and containment, and ongoing battles for control of his cultural and political energies may give us hope and, perhaps, direction in the pursuit of truth and justice—for all.

Notes

1   Robert Jewett and John Shelton Lawrence, *The Myth of the American Superhero* (Grand Rapids, Michigan: William B. Eerdmans Publishing Company, 2002), 28.

2   See Henry Jenkins, "Captain America Sheds His Mighty Tears: Comics and

September 11," in *Terror, Culture, Politics: Rethinking 9/11*, eds Daniel J. Sherman and Terry Nardini (Bloomington: Indiana University Press, 2006).

3   Roland Barthes, *Mythologies*, translated by Annette Lavers (London: Vintage, 2001), 125.

4   Chip Kidd and Geoff Spear, *Mythology: The DC Comics Art of Alex Ross*, reprint edn (New York: Pantheon, 2005).

5   Herbert London, "The Death of Superman," *First Things* # 31 (March 1993), http://www.firstthings.com/article/2008/05/003-the-death-of-superman-23 (accessed June 28, 2007).

6   See Andy Medhurst, "Batman, Deviance, and Camp," in *The Many Lives of the Batman—Critical Approaches to a Superhero*, eds Roberta E. Pearson and William Uricchio (New York: Routledge, 1991), 150–4; and Fredric Wertham, *Seduction of the Innocent* (London: Museum Press, 1955).

7   Jerome Siegel and Joe Schuster, untitled Superman strip, 1939, repr. in *Superman From the Thirties to the Seventies*, ed. E. Nelson Bridewell (New York: Spring Books, 1971), 50.

8   Jerry Siegel and Joe Schuster, Superman strip, *Look* (February 27, 1940), repr. at www.Superman.ws—the Superman Website: Superman through the ages, http://superman.ws/tales2/endsthewar/?page=3 (accessed June 28, 2007).

9   Micheline, Dwyer & Rodier, *Action Comics* # 718, "'Demolitia . . . She Plays For Keeps!!!'/By Darker Reason" (New York, DC Comics, 1996).

10   J.M. DeMatteis, *et al.*, *Superman: President Lex* (Book 5) (New York: DC Comics, 2003).

11   I do not want to leave unchallenged the notion that Superman is always acting with the best "intentions" (Kidd and Spear, *Mythology*).

12   Azie from Brooklyn, Composite digital image of Alex Ross's Superman ghosted in front of the Twin Towers, at Supermantv.net (2002), http://www.supermantv.net/wallpaperbattles/newsuperman/april2004/superman_wtc.jpg (accessed June 26, 2007).

13   Kevin Konrad, "Farewell to a Real Hero" (2002), www.superman.ws/FanArtWTC/Farewell_to_a_Real_Hero.bmp (accessed July 3, 2007).

14   Joseph Scott Campbell and Hi-Fi, untitled image, in *Heroes: The World's Greatest Superhero Creators Honor the World's Greatest Heroes, 9.11.2001*, ed. Rob Haynes, with Tim Townsend, Tim and David Self, second edn (New York: Marvel Comics, December 2001).

15   John Romita Sr. with Udon Studios, untitled image, in Haynes, *Heroes: The World's Greatest Superhero Creators*.

16   Salvador Larocca and Chris Clairemont, "Liquid!," image, in Haynes, *Heroes: The World's Greatest Superhero Creators*.

17   Mike Allred with Laura Allred, untitled image, in Haynes, *Heroes: The World's Greatest Superhero Creators*.

18   Patrick Zircher with Derek Fridolfs and Hi-Fi, text by Fabian Nicieza, untitled image in Haynes, *Heroes: The World's Greatest Superhero Creators*.

19   Jenkins, "Captain America," 79.

20   Stan Lee, Kyle Hotz and Hi-Fi, Plate 51 in Haynes, *Heroes: The World's Greatest Superhero Creators*.

21   "We should invade their countries, kill their leaders and convert them to Christianity. We weren't punctilious about locating and punishing only Hitler and his top officers. We carpet-bombed German cities; we killed civilians. That's war. And this is war." Anne Coulter, "This Is War. We Should Invade Their Countries," *National Review Online* (September 13, 2001) http://www.nationalreview.com/coulter/coulter.shtml (accessed July 10, 2007).

22   Mark Engblom, *Comic Coverage*. http://comiccoverage.typepad.com/comic_coverage/comic_coverage_blog/ (accessed October 16, 2009).

23   Joe Casey, Mike Wieringo, Jose Marzan, Jr., Tanya and Rich Horie, and Bill Oakley, "A Lex," in *Adventures of Superman* # 600, ed. Eddie Berganza (New York: DC Comics, 2002), 30.

24   Jeff Klock, *How to Read Superhero Comics and Why* (New York: Continuum, 2002).

25   Alan Sinfield, *Cultural Politics: Queer Reading* (London: Routledge, 1994), 24.

26   Raymond Williams, "Base and Superstructure in Marxist Cultural Theory," in *Problems in Materialism and Culture* (London and New York: Verso, 1980), 38.

27   Alan Sinfield, *Faultlines: Cultural Materialism and the Politics of Dissident Reading* (Berkeley: University of California Press, 1992).

28   Sinfield, *Cultural Politics*, 4.

29   Sinfield, *Faultlines*, 41.

30   Sinfield, *Cultural Politics*, 26.

31   Michael Medved, "Captain America, Traitor? The Comic Book Hero Goes Anti-American," http://www.nationalreview.com/comment/comment-medved040403.asp (accessed June 28, 2007).

32   Jenkins, "Captain America," 72–3.

33   Ibid., 98.

34   Ibid., 79.

CHAPTER 11

The Tools and Toys of (the) War (on Terror): Consumer Desire, Military Fetish, and Regime Change in *Batman Begins*

JUSTINE TOH

"Where does he get those wonderful toys?"

—The Joker, after Batman has foiled his plot in *Batman* (1989)

"I gotta get me one of those."

—Sergeant Gordon, after seeing the Batmobile in *Batman Begins* (2005)

"Does it come in black?"

—Bruce Wayne, after test-driving the future Batmobile in *Batman Begins*

The Hollywood adaptations of *Batman* promote a matrix of consumer desire, military fetish, and an ultimate reliance on force, not only feeding a taste for the tools and the toys of war but the desire to see them engaged in action. Above, the Joker expresses petulant jealousy of Batman's tools (toys?) that persistently frustrate the villain's plots. In his quote, Sergeant Gordon, representative of Gotham City's crime-fighting apparatus, sighs his admiration of the Batmobile. Even though the chance of "getting one of those" for himself is unlikely, by the end of *Batman Begins* he will have taken the Batmobile for a test drive. And, after experiencing the Batmobile's capabilities, Bruce Wayne bestows his approval upon it by appropriating the buyer's language of the car yard: it's a great car, but does it come in the color I want?

Thus the criminal and the law enforcer of Gotham City are equally courted in this matrix of consumer desire, but both lack the purchasing power of billionaire industrialist Bruce Wayne/Batman. *Batman Begins* delivers the ultimate lesson of war culture: those with the best toys/tools of war *win*. In the film, the misrecognition of tools of war as toys grants military hardware a consumer-friendly façade, further stoking consumer desire for future development of tools of war that may be consumed as toys. In this arrangement, one's enemies are a target and one's own people a target *market*. *Batman Begins* promotes a philosophy of political vigilantism, where the tools of military technoscience are engaged in "righteous," if not entirely legal, action. When war culture is more readily accepted at home in the US, this context provides a much greater scope in which to promote imperial adventures abroad, whether sanctioned by the international community or not.

This essay reads *Batman Begins* against the "War on Terror" (WOT) of the George W. Bush Administration (2001–09) by considering the military hardware—the toys and tools of war—that Batman enlists in his quest to save Gotham. I proceed in two parts: in the first, I discuss Batman's Batsuit and the Batmobile as emblems of the military-industrial-entertainment complex, arguing that their transformation into desirable consumer items encapsulates the militarization of popular culture. In the second part, I discuss the microwave emitter, a weapon used by the film's terrorists to vaporize Gotham's water supply. This discussion allows us an insight into the real-world practice of exporting democracy abroad at the point of a gun.

Hard Bodies and Hardware: Batman and His Toys

Nothing speeds up the development of technology like war.

—Jean-Louis DeGay[1]

War drives technological innovation, claims Jean-Louis DeGay, a project specialist with the Pentagon's Future Combat System Program (FCSP), a project dedicated to developing high-tech body armor for soldiers. His comment exemplifies the growth of the "military-industrial complex" that President Eisenhower cautioned against in 1961, alliances between the military and industry that could entrench a state in a permanent war economy.[2] However, the commercial opportunities of such technology make it irresistibly attractive for corporate investment. Indeed, Eisenhower's original term has expanded to refer to the involvement of the entertainment industry in the "military-industrial complex," given that the US Military employs video games for training and recruitment purposes.[3] In *Batman*, the Joker's characterization of Batman's tools as "wonderful toys" highlights a central aspect of play and consumer desire in the *Batman* universe, where much pleasure is derived from watching Batman's gadgets in action. The military origins of the tools of *Batman Begins*, however, disturb the easy pleasure of watching Batman's weapons at work, for Batman's body armor (the Batsuit) and the "Tumbler" (the Batmobile) expose the interdependence of consumer and military culture.

In *Batman Begins*, both the Batsuit and Batmobile are military prototypes that emerge from the Applied Sciences division of Wayne Enterprises, the company run by Thomas Wayne, Bruce's late father. Since Thomas's death, the company has taken on lucrative military contracts—work that contradicted the idealism of the Wayne patriarch. In contrast to his father, Bruce/Batman is more pragmatic, employing the tools in his fight to save Gotham, as if the "righteous" ends to which he will direct them redeem their manufacturing. He uses the Batsuit and the Batmobile to counteract the threat posed by the third toy in my discussion: the microwave emitter, also manufactured by Wayne Enterprises.

In order to explain to Lucius Fox what use Bruce has for the high-tech body armor, Bruce pretends to use it for cave-diving, playing off his image as a thrill-seeking rich kid in order to conceal his identity as Batman. Later, Bruce jokes about using a panic-inducing hallucinogen (that he discovers is part of a terrorist plot to destroy Gotham) as a party drug. Through these jokes, along with his "Does it come in black?" quip about the Batmobile, Bruce mocks his persona as a rich, prodigal playboy whose buying power is measured by his ability to play with high-tech machinery. That is, military machinery can moonlight as emblems of a privileged, consumer-driven lifestyle for those who can afford to consume such luxuries as toys. The Hummer, as I will discuss with reference to the Batmobile, global positioning systems (GPS), navigational equipment, and even the Internet and the humble computer, all have military origins. Caren Kaplan argues that the consumer appropriation of GPS suggests the militarization of everyday civilian life and its attendant consumer culture—more on this shortly.[4]

Batman's body armor is supplemented by his cape, obtained from Fox by Bruce who pretends to use it for base-jumping. The cape is manufactured out of "memory cloth," as Fox calls it, with an electric current running through the fabric, which allows it to hold any rigid shape. This feature allows Batman to glide through the air. Batman's "memory cloth" cape and his body armor merge to approximate real military technology, as developed by the FCSP. In 2010, the Pentagon's Future Warrior will be fortified with body armor outfitted with nanotechnology. Here, the "smart cloth" of the body armor will be soft and pliable when wearing. When it "senses" approaching bullets, it becomes rigid in order to deflect the bullet before softening again. Along with increasing the defenses of a soldier, the armor of the Future Warrior will provide physiological readings of a soldier's heart rate and other vital functions, to be transferred back to local command, allowing medics to remotely diagnose appropriate treatment in the event of injury during conflict. The Vision 2020 Future Warrior system, to be implemented a decade after the first wave of the FCSP, envisions the incorporation of "nanomuscle fibers" into body armor, which will allow soldiers to carry heavier loads. DeGay's vision is that soldiers will be able to improve their lifting ability by 300 percent, which will potentially facilitate the mounting of a weapon directly on the uniform system, turning the soldier into "a walking gun platform."[5]

Elsewhere in the same Army press release, DeGay refers to the future soldier as an "F-16 on legs" (an F-16 is an Air Force fighter jet). Such description portrays the soldier as a weapon and fetishizes hard bodies augmented by military hardware. That these types of developments in military innovation have been foreshadowed in films like *The Terminator* (1984), *RoboCop* (1987), and *Universal Soldier* (1992) illustrates a cross-pollination of images and ideas between the military, private industry, and entertainment. Colin Milburn demonstrated the extent of the interdependence between military technoscience and comic books in recounting an incident where MIT's Institute for Soldier Nanotechnologies submitted a tender for research funding to the US Military, accompanying their proposal with a graphic of a soldier in armor strikingly similar to that depicted in the comic book *Radix* (2005). For Milburn, this instance was one example of a shared cultural landscape between military innovation and entertainment, where "images of [the Predator] alien costume [could] not only serve as aesthetic guides to supersoldier design, but also provide a functioning imaginative context."[6] Such an example suggests the post-human context of military innovation (as explored by Chris Hables Gray[7]) that is concerned with the advances of the human-machine interface, but here I want to place more emphasis on Kenneth Saltman's critique of bodybuilding, given that Bruce/Batman is a mortal man.[8]

Bodybuilding and the Weapon-Commodity: Batman, Bale, and the Batmobile

> . . . to dream of becoming a bodybuilder, to dream of becoming a soldier, is to dream of being a human weapon.
>
> —Kenneth Saltman[9]

Saltman articulates bodybuilding as an activity that produces the human body as a weapon of war. When enhanced by superior military equipment, Batman becomes such a human-weapon. The physicality of Christian Bale, the latest actor to portray Bruce/Batman, is crucial in this context. Though Bale is not a bodybuilder, his film career has repeatedly demonstrated the lengths to which he will go for his craft—from shedding extreme weight for his roles in *The Machinist* (2004) and *Rescue Dawn* (2006) to bulking up to play Batman. His starring role in the controversial *American Psycho* (2000) is instructive in this regard. In that film, Bale plays narcissistic serial killer Patrick Bateman who spends much time caring for his body, treating it as a luxury item as he sculpts it into a weapon to murder people. Bateman consumes his body just as Batman consumes military gear, as a commodity-status symbol, though Bateman pushes this appetite to psychotic ends. Indeed, the film links Bateman's sociopathic tendencies to his obsession with consumerism.

With that in mind, consider Saltman, for whom bodybuilding symbolizes the purest expression of capitalism, where "the bodybuilder enacts the production process and makes himself the product . . . one's own body becomes both the locus for the process and the product."[10] The body is thus a commodity for those able to devote the necessary time and effort to its training; the body is at once its own end and the means to get there. In order to play Batman and Bateman, then, Bale brings physicality and martial prowess (where fitness training for his on-screen roles is "the production process") to his roles as human weapons ("the product"): in *Batman Begins* he is a disciplining weapon deployed against criminals, and in *American Psycho* a serial-killing weapon deployed against society. In constructing his own body and offering it for exhibition in films that become commodities for sale in the Hollywood marketplace, Bale is transformed into a specific kind of commodity: a weapon. But being an actor in a fictional film, Bale only needs this weaponized body-commodity for purposes of play and make-believe, mirroring Bruce/Batman's ability to consume tools of war as toys.

Saltman continues: while the image of the bodybuilder sells the fantasy of security and safety, the bodybuilder is at war with his or her own body. This body must be increasingly disciplined or supplemented with drugs in order to achieve its maximum potential.[11] This inner conflict is encapsulated by Bruce/Batman's war with his own fear. He says he seeks "the means to fight injustice. To turn fear against those who prey on the fearful." And later, when his butler Alfred inquires why Bruce has nominated a bat as his totem, he replies, "Bats frighten me. It's time my enemies share my dread." Batman's defensive armor evoking the sign of the bat thus betrays an edge of hysteria. Not only does the armor protect Batman's body, but it uses his own fear to frighten others. The psychologically complex *Batman Begins* thus holds its protagonist hostage to fear that he is not able to master. Indeed Bruce/Batman's fear is generative, as the more Batman endeavors to contain it, the more it spawns new threats to Gotham—of which more soon.

Derrida describes such a conundrum as an "autoimmunity complex": suicidal logic where a system attacks its own protection and reproduces ills in efforts dedicated to their eradication.[12] In the case of *Batman Begins*, Bruce/Batman's use of fear-based measures to enforce security produces instead still greater insecurity. This autoimmune disorder also underwrites the sports utility vehicle (SUV) or the "Hummer," commercially available vehicles of military origin. Stephen Graham recounts that after the first Iraq War, the US Army's "Humvee" assault vehicle was customized into the civilian "Hummer," with the first vehicle sold to Arnold Schwarzenegger.[13] Graham argues that these combative vehicles—with names like "Stealth" or "Warrior"—enforce a militaristic view of life for individuals desiring an armored car to traverse their neighborhoods, resignified as suburban combat zones. In the Hummer, domestic desire for comfort and safety relies on a consumer-friendly military solution, but one that enforces greater *in*security, not least because these vehicles are more than capable of terrorizing the streets upon which they are driven. While SUVs promise safety for the occupant of the vehicle, it is safety at the expense of other drivers on the road in less fortified cars, who are implicitly constituted as potential enemies.

The real-world context of the Humvee is evoked by the Batmobile in *Batman Begins*. In the film, Fox explains that the "Tumbler" possesses both defensive (its ability to deflect radar tracking) and offensive (missile-firing cannons) capabilities. Once converted into Batman's Batmobile, it becomes an effective and impressive weapon. For a policeman awed by its screaming rampage across Gotham, "tank" is the most appropriate label at hand. But this weapon is constantly referred to as a status symbol within the film. When a valet compliments Bruce's luxury car, Bruce murmurs, "You should see my other one," referring to his Batmobile. Significantly, on the DVD's special features, the film's co-writer describes the Batmobile as a cross between a Lamborghini and a Humvee, further attaching luxurious connotations to military might. In fact, the Hummer similarly evokes the bodybuilder inasmuch as the Hummer is to a regular car what the bodybuilder's physique is to a non-body-built human body. Both are luxury items which parade martial strength and dominance, yet both are icons of insecurity.

Weapons for Which We Kept the Receipts: The West's Inextricability from Its Enemy Others

The Batmobile and the Batsuit are two military prototypes that Batman uses for "good" in order to neutralize the menace posed by the microwave emitter. If the Batmobile and the Batsuit function as emblems of the military-industrial-entertainment complex, the microwave emitter, in its constitution as a "weapon of mass destruction" (WMD) invites the film to be read against its sociopolitical context: the Bush Administration's WOT. In this frame, Batman's righteous task is to clean up Gotham by removing its corrupt elements, a fictional parallel for the righteousness of the US's campaign to promote democracy in the Middle East. Most associated with the presidency of George W. Bush, key features of this WOT involve the removal of Middle Eastern tyrants: the Taliban in Afghanistan and Saddam Hussein in Iraq.

But really, Batman must save Gotham from a technology created by his own company, and one now exploited by Gotham's enemies. The real threat emerges from within, rather than without. The Tandberg cartoon (Figure 3) appeared in Australia's *The Age* newspaper in September 2002, during the US debate over Hussein's alleged possession of WMDs. The cartoon highlights the inextricability of the West from its so-called enemies by suggesting the hypocrisy of Western leaders who demonize political enemies while stocking their arsenals. In *Batman Begins*, though the microwave emitter was stolen by Ra's Al Ghul and thus may represent a hijacking of Western technology by "terrorists," this plot development opens up the points of contact between the West and its "terrorist" Other. Ra's Al Ghul and his League of Shadows bear more than a passing resemblance to Osama bin Laden and the shadowy al-Qaeda network—a network that struck New York City (often identified with Gotham City) on September 11, 2001.

Figure 3

This ambiguity is also reflected in Bruce/Batman's very formation: *Batman Begins* depicts Bruce/Batman as learning his trade at what is essentially a terrorist training camp, presided over by an extremist (Ra's Al Ghul) who plans to raze Gotham City as punishment for its decadence. Bruce/Batman's crime-fighting techniques thus equally suggest those of the terrorist. This connection is emphasized in the Batsuit, to which Bruce/Batman adds brass forearm gauntlets, modeled after the armor worn by the members of the League of Shadows. Thus he combines the technology of the West with those of its terrorist menace. Bruce's emergence as Batman via a training camp also reverses the real-life example of the Central Intelligence Agency having armed and trained Osama bin Laden in the US campaign against the Soviets in Afghanistan. Bin Laden is thus not an unknowable enemy representing an "evil other" and wholly distinct from the "civilized West," but one whose genesis is entangled with the West.

Political Vigilantism and Regime Change: Batman's New Covenant for the Post-9/11 Era

In *Batman Begins*, Fox explains that the microwave emitter is a weapon of infrastructural warfare that seeks the enemy's submission by vaporizing their water supply. And at the film's climax, Ra's places the microwave emitter on a train and sends it hurtling towards Wayne Tower—the same building that houses Gotham's central water utility. This weapon and how it is used thus evokes the twenty-first century context of asymmetric warfare where attacks on networked urban infrastructure (water, electricity, transport) make cities particularly vulnerable to attack.[14] The 9/11 terrorists exploited airplanes, while the Madrid 2004 and the London 2005 bombers delivered their attacks via trains and buses. The destruction of infrastructure is only one outcome of such attack; another result is the spreading of panic and fear throughout the populace.[15] This propagation of terror is literalized in *Batman Begins* where Ra's has added the weaponized hallucinogen to Gotham's water supply. He plans to vaporize it in order to release the panic-inducing gas into Gotham's atmosphere, causing its citizens to attack each other out of fear. *Batman Begins* thus depicts the potential of a city's disintegration through attacks on its infrastructure.

Wayne Tower literally shines in the darkness of the cityscape at night, the film's symbol of economic prosperity in the service of social liberalism. These values are given concrete form in the train, Thomas Wayne's urban regeneration project to encourage rich and poor to mingle in the same social space. In saving the tower yet crashing the train, Bruce/Batman establishes a fresh covenant for the post-9/11 era. His actions place more faith in political force (his vigilante identity as Batman) and sound economic management (in regaining control of his father's company) than he does in the utopian space of the train, represented by the well-meaning but weak-willed social liberalism of Thomas Wayne. That is, Bruce/Batman desires to continue his father's legacy of social responsibility inasmuch as that involves the business of cleaning up Gotham City, but he improves on the rhetoric by backing it up with unilateral force. Such action constitutes an analogy—and apologia—for forced regime change in the Middle East after 9/11. That Batman's vigilante actions ultimately rely on force, and by extension violence, evokes Richard Slotkin's thesis of "regeneration through violence."[16] For Slotkin, recourse to violence in the American imagination expresses a fundamental discontent with democracy as an instrument of progress, preferring instead to place faith in "a gun in the hands of the right man."[17] For Ra's Al Ghul, Thomas Wayne's reluctance to use force to defend his family (resulting in the orphaning of young Bruce) betrays a weakness of character that parallels the deterioration of Gotham. Though by the end of *Batman Begins* Bruce/ Batman commits himself to restoring his father's name through rebuilding Wayne Manor (destroyed after the terrorist incursion into Gotham), philosophically he aligns himself with his "other" father, Ra's. While Batman values justice and liberty, he bypasses the law by unilaterally enforcing both at the point of a gun. He could be considered to be a consensus builder as he establishes an alliance with Gordon, the only honest cop in Gotham, and the district attorney Rachel Dawes, but Batman is looking for minor partners in a "coalition of the willing" to grant legitimacy to his illegitimate use of force.

With the partnership of Gordon, who demolishes the struts of the train tracks courtesy of the weapons systems on the Batmobile, Bruce/Batman defeats Ra's and crashes the train. One military prototype, the Batmobile, is used to defeat another, the microwave emitter. The development of future weapons to counteract existing ones is circular logic designed to perpetuate the system. It offers a strange spin on the phenomenon of "disaster capitalism" that Naomi Klein[18] described as the George W. Bush Administration's practice of awarding reconstruction contracts in Iraq and Afghanistan to private contractors with ties to the Bush regime. Of course, this is after crucial infrastructure has been destroyed by the coalition's bombing campaigns. In this case, however, money is made by creating one weapon and then another to offset the initial threat. The underlying rationale of such an arrangement is that as long as such military technology remains in the "right" hands, all will be well.

But whose "right" hands? The Batsuit and the Batmobile are both represented in defensive, rather than offensive, terms. While enhanced body armor may better protect the soldier, or an armored car the driver, little attention is paid to the aggressive, combative connotations of heavily fortified cars or body armor. That is, the hard bodies of their existence expect assault. A similar doublethink accompanies the Strategic Defense Initiative (SDI). Carl Boggs argues that this "misnamed" initiative is "primarily an *offensive* weapons scheme ... central to a full-spectrum strategy that would enable the United States to counter Russian and Chinese military power" (original emphasis).[19] Speaking of the Initiative in 1985, President Reagan said:

> The Strategic Defense Initiative has been labeled *Star Wars*, but it isn't about war; it's about peace. It isn't about retaliation; it's about prevention. It isn't about fear; it's about hope. And in that struggle, if you'll pardon my stealing a film line: The force is with us.[20]

Reagan promoted the Initiative as investment in protecting freedom-loving people everywhere, but his rhetoric revealed the centrality of force to this desired constellation of twenty-first century security arrangements. Additionally, the allusion backfired. In referencing *Star Wars*, Reagan associated himself with the "good" side of the force by rephrasing the popular Jedi line. However, the SDI most resembles the "Death Star" of *Star Wars*, the principle weapon of the *evil* galactic empire—thus identifying the United States with imperial aggression and violence.

By the end of *Batman Begins*, Batman has initiated a judicial regime change and installed himself as the unofficial law of Gotham City. He has also regained control of his father's company and is thus in a position to steer Gotham's judicial and economic fortunes. Where Thomas Wayne may have seen fit to cancel the company's military research, it is patently obvious that Bruce will not, since the Batsuit and the Batmobile have proved so useful to him as Batman. This decision is sealed in the destruction of the train and yet the preservation of Wayne Enterprises indicates a preference for private industry to stimulate regrowth, rather than social welfare and public programs driving reform.

Graham warns that decreasing government investment in public infrastructure, paired with privatization of formerly public services, entails a loss of account-ability to the wider community.[21] Future *Batman* films will undoubtedly add more military hardware to Bruce/Batman's arsenal for his vigilante quest for justice. It is less certain, however, that Bruce's plan to save Gotham will involve more legitimate avenues of social reform. Saltman writes:

> The militarized body aims at ever greater control over the physical world and results only in ever-greater estrangement from it . . . The built body promises safety, security, and freedom while contributing to the militarization of civil society—a process at odds with democratization.[22]

Saltman's critique of bodybuilding essentially argues that the (over)built body is a trope for a body at war against itself. If we apply such critique to a post-9/11, security-conscious context, we find that a perpetually expanding defense budget diverts public money and government attention away from endemic and entrenched inequality. The resultant systematic poverty engenders challenges to the state, encouraging criminality at home and terrorism abroad, an autoimmune disorder of Derridean variety. Victor Archibong and Paul Leslie argue that with civic services sapped of funds, disadvantaged citizens seek employment in the military, where they are called upon to fight to protect elite privilege. Evoking Eisenhower's fears of the permanent war economy, they conclude: "the conditions produced by the military-industrial complex foster a tacit conspiracy which both leads us to armed conflict and maintains the system itself."[23]

Though Bruce/Batman's dedication to Gotham bodes well for the city, it sits uneasily that this benevolent tyrant betrays similarities to Ra's Al Ghul. Bruce/Batman's plan to revitalize Gotham and save it is not, fundamentally, that different from the film's "terrorist," for both ultimately rely on force as the impetus of social change. Bruce/Batman is in a unique position to enable this to happen, as Bruce Wayne is the "apotheosis of the New Right."[24] He represents a political regime that regards its body politic as the "great unwashed," where citizens are incapable of governing their own affairs and need a strong, conservative leader. Batman fights to preserve the status quo, in effect protecting the structural inequality of the system that upholds his privilege. Under Batman's tenure, democracy transmutes into authoritarianism, as Tim Blackmore[25] recognized in Frank Miller's 1991 *Batman: The Dark Knight Returns*.

However, embedded in the reactionary politics of *Batman Begins* is recognition that Batman is part of the problem he attempts to eradicate in Gotham. Gordon raises the question of escalation:

Gordon: And what about escalation?

Batman: Escalation?

Gordon: We get semi-automatic weapons, they get automatics. We get Kevlar body armor, they get armor-piercing rounds. And you're wearing a mask and jumping off rooftops. Take this guy. Armed robbery, double homicide, has a taste for theatrics, like you. He leaves a calling card. (GORDON hands BATMAN a clear plastic evidence bag with a playing card inside it.)

Batman: (BATMAN turns the card over to reveal a Joker card) I'll look into it.

Gordon: (BATMAN turns to leave) I never got to say thank you.

Batman: And you'll never have to.

This sequence identifies two aspects of escalation. Firstly, Batman's theatricality in using fear as a weapon against evil in turn unleashes it anew on a civilian population as his nemeses develop personas to match him. Secondly, Gordon speculates that criminals will attempt to meet the purchasing power of Bruce/Batman in order to even the playing field between Gotham's law enforcement and its outlaws. Remember, those with the best tools and toys of war win. In this scene, Batman is forced to acknowledge the indefinite nature of his quest to restore justice to Gotham. His preoccupation with fear, combined with the vast resources available to him in order to fortify himself against this fear, lock him into Derrida's autoimmune contract, which reproduces ills in efforts dedicated to their eradication. In the film's sequel, *The Dark Knight* (2008), District Attorney Harvey Dent foreshadows Batman's ultimate fate in saying, "You die a hero, or you live long enough to see yourself become the villain." Dent's quote encapsulates the quandary facing Batman in this last scene from *Batman Begins*: that Batman's vigilantism does not ultimately work and cannot produce real safety or freedom. Instead, Batman's preference for force destines him to become what he most despises: a villain. The film displays a self-critical awareness that, far from solving Gotham's problems, Batman instead recreates the conditions for their reproduction.

Conclusion: Buying Ideology—*Batman Begins* as Commodity

Without super villains there would be no Batman, or at any rate, no meaningful existence for Batman.

—Richard Reynolds[25]

Have we already been drafted?

—Colin Milburn[26]

If we look beyond the film's diegesis and consider the film as a commodity for sale, we realize that Batman's makers have a vested interest in assuring Gotham is never entirely cleansed of crime. The enduring popularity of the comic book and the previous Batman films (1989, 1992, 1995, and 1997) already testified to the Caped Crusader's ability to spin a profit. *Batman Begins'* numerous merchandising tie-ins marketed to children, the obligatory computer game, and special edition DVD crammed with special features herald the film as the first installment of what may prove to be a very profitable renewed franchise. Eileen Meehan writes, "as we ... approach *Batman*, Bat-mania, and Bat-audiences, our discussion of economics reminds us that text, intertext, and audiences are simultaneously commodity, product line, and consumer."[28] This extra-diegetic context of Hollywood as a business dictates that, at the level of the film's diegetic reality, Batman needs to keep doling out justice to Gotham's criminals. A safe Gotham City, its criminal elements eradicated, is bad for Hollywood's business because it renders obsolete a franchise about the Dark Knight's agitations for justice. This should make clear that *inbuilt in the film-as-commodity are the conditions that perpetuate the military-industrial-entertainment complex.* Just as Batman's toys and tools of war merge to become talismans of consumer desire, *Batman Begins* is itself a commodity selling a product: not only the merchandising attached to the film, but a political ideology that pairs the righteous use of force with a fetish for the hard body of military culture.

Milburn's question above echoes Kaplan's concern raised earlier: is the consumer mobilized into militarized modes of being through the purchase of particular products? For Milburn, the most mundane activity (such as his purchase of "Gap nanopants"—trousers made with "smart" fabric not unlike a primitive version of Batman's "memory cloth") symbolizes an everyday existence marked by the increasing confluence of militarized, consumer and civilian identities.[29] This confluence is encouraged by the US military's practice of training and enlisting soldiers through electronic gaming. Ed Halter recounts an online recruitment advertisement that courted potential recruits with the invitation: "If you're ready to stop playing games, we're ready for you."[30]

If we understand the *Batman* franchise as a commodity that in order to remain profitable must throw up new challenges to Batman's rule, transferring this debate to the real world should make us question the feasibility of the WOT. Does the state instead produce terror, or have a vested interest in producing it or at least seeing it continue? Critics argue that such a nebulous label as the WOT heralds both an unending war and one that can never be decisively lost or won. Following Richard

Reynolds,[31] we may argue that without super villains (like Osama bin Laden) in the "real" world, there would be no meaningful existence for a regime that devotes itself to his capture and the supposed eradication of terror. As *Batman Begins* demonstrates, the effort to fight crime from a bastion of social privilege, and one that promotes the development of future weapons effectively, props up existing power structures and furthers the military-industrial-entertainment complex. In doing so, it reproduces the ills of the system instead of offering a real alternative for the liberation of all.

Given the psychological complexity of *Batman Begins*, with Bruce constantly at war with his own fear, it is no surprise that the Joker and Two-Face were chosen to star in *The Dark Knight*. Both villains reflect crucial aspects of Bruce/Batman's internal conflict:

> The Joker epitomizes the dark and negative side of the personal obsessions which fuel Batman's crimefighting career: the Joker is a constant reminder that strength which derives from traumatic experience can be turned towards evil as easily as good. Two-Face redoubles the force of this assertion, the more so because his split personality (itself mirroring the Bruce Wayne/Batman duality) belongs to an individual who was once an officer of the law.[32]

The war machine grinds on. In purchasing a ticket to *Batman Begins* and any ensuing sequels, we may do well to reflect on exactly what political ideology we are drafted (or courted?) into buying.

Notes

1   Matthew Hickley, "US Military Develops Robocop Armor for Soldiers," *The Daily Mail*, April 11, 2007, http://www.dailymail.co.uk/pages/live/articles/technology/technology. html?in_page_id=1965&in_article_id=447631 (accessed October 16, 2009).

2   Dwight Eisenhower, "Farewell Radio and Television Address to the American People," *The Dwight D. Eisenhower Presidential Library*, http://www.eisenhower.archives.gov/ farewell.htm (accessed October 16, 2009).

3   James Der Derian, *Virtuous War: Mapping the Military-Industrial-Media-Entertainment Network* (New York, Basic, 2001); Ed Halter, *From Sun Tzu to Xbox: War and Video Games* (New York: Thunder's Mouth Press, 2006).

4   Caren Kaplan, "Precision Targets: GPS and the Militarization of US Consumer Identity," *American Quarterly* 58.3 (2006): 693–713.

5   Phil Copeland, "Future Warrior Exhibits Super Powers," *American Forces Press Service*, *US Department of Defence*, July 27, 2004, http://www.defenselink.mil/news/newsarticle. aspx?id=25636 (accessed October 16, 2009).

6   Colin Milburn, "Nanowarriors: Military Nanotechnology and Comic Books," *Intertexts* 9.2 (2005): 90.

7   Chris Hables Gray, *Postmodern War: The New Politics of Conflict* (London: Routledge, 1997).

8   Kenneth J. Saltman, "The Strong Arm of the Law," *Body and Society* 9.4 (2003): 49–67.

9   Ibid., 50.

10   Ibid.

11   Ibid., 52.

12   Giovanna Borradori, *Philosophy in a Time of Terror: Dialogues with Jürgen Habermas and Jacques Derrida* (Chicago: University of Chicago Press, 2003), 99.

13   Stephen Graham, "Postmortem City: Towards an Urban Geopolitics," *City* 8.2 (2004): 165–96.

14   Stephen Graham, "Switching Cities Off: Urban Infrastructure and US Air Power," *City* 9.2 (2005): 169–94; Graham, "Postmortem City."

15   Graham, "Postmortem City," 172.

16   Richard Slotkin, *Gunfighter Nation: The Myth of the Frontier in Twentieth Century America* (New York: Atheneum, 1992).

17   Ibid., 396.

18   Naomi Klein, "The Rise of Disaster Capitalism," *No Logo*, April 15, 2005, www.nologo.org (accessed October 16, 2009).

19   Carl Boggs, "Pentagon Strategy, Hollywood, and Technowar," *New Politics* 9.1 (2006), http://www.wpunj.edu/newpol/issue41/Boggs41.htm (accessed October 16, 2009).

20   Ronald Reagan, "Remarks at the National Space Club Luncheon," *The Ronald Reagan Presidential Library Archives*, 1985, http://www.reagan.utexas.edu/ archives/speeches/1985/32985b.htm (paragraph 10), (accessed October 16, 2009).

21   Graham, "Switching Cities Off," 172–3.

22   Saltman, "The Strong Arm," 50.

23   Victor Archibong and Paul Leslie, "The Military-Industrial Complex and the Persian Gulf War: Ike's Caveat," in *The Gulf War as Popular Entertainment: An Analysis of the Military-Industrial Media Complex*, edited by Paul Leslie (New York: Edwin Mellen Press, 1997), 39.

24   Anne Cranny-Francis, "*Batman*: Hollywood and the Postmodern," *Social Semiotics* 1.1 (1991): 19, 26.

25   Tim Blackmore, "The Dark Knight of Democracy: Tocqueville and Miller Cast Some Light on the Subject," *Journal of American Culture* 14, no. 1(1991): 37-56

26   Richard Reynolds, *Super Heroes: A Modern Mythology* (London: B.T. Batsford, 1992), 103.

27   Milburn, "Nanowarriors," 99.

28   Eileen R. Meehan, "'Holy Commodity Fetish, Batman!' The Political Economy of a Commercial Intertext," in *The Many Lives of the Batman: Critical Approaches to a Superhero and his Media*, edited by Roberta E. Pearson and William Uricchio (New York: Routledge, 1991), 61.

29   Milburn, "Nanowarriors," 99.

30   Halter, *From Sun Tzu to Xbox*, xvi.

31   Reynolds, *Super Heroes*, 103.

32   Ibid., 68.

CHAPTER 12

"It Was Like a Movie": The Impossibility of Representation in Oliver Stone's *World Trade Center*

KAREN RANDELL

"Was it a dream?" Michael Moore's wistful voice-over at the start of *Fahrenheit 9/11* (2004) sets up a viewing experience for its audience predicated on fantasy: the joyful scene of Al Gore accepting Florida's vote, on election night 2000, amid banners and fireworks belies the truth: as we now know, Florida was called for Bush. Live televised images then, Moore shows us, are powerful signs: we believe what we see, it's happening now, it must be true . . . but Gore didn't win. Such a paradox between the live image and the reality of the situation is played out here with an ironic (if somewhat bitter) tone and provides a false start to *Fahrenheit 9/11*. Ten minutes into the film the title credits appear on screen; the mood abruptly changes from exuberance to discomfort as we see President Bush and network anchor men prepare for the 9/11 announcement: the film is beginning again. What we have seen before is a preamble to what is the central focus of the film: the dual plane crash into the twin towers of the World Trade Center in New York City on 11 September 2001.

The formal properties of the film's double-start function to engage and prompt our memory, insist that we make a connection between what we have seen before (in the first ten minutes) and what we are watching now: we are encouraged to be active viewers, making connections as we go along. Now the camera pans out on a shot of the White House: fade to black. There are no images for the next two minutes; instead, we hear the drone of a descending aircraft and a deafening crash; a woman's voice, shocked, says, "Oh my God!" We hear another fast descending plane, crash, fire truck sirens, again, "Oh my God!" People screaming, the sound of a helicopter, a man's voice shouts, "Let's go!" There is a long reverberating crash.

This two-part structure to the opening of the film presents a viewing dilemma. Seeing is not believing; with Gore's election "win" the image could not be trusted: whereas, by removing the visualization of the 9/11 catastrophe, the power of the image cannot deceive. This disruption to the film form denies the power of the image and replaces it instead with the invocation of memory. Why no image?

Perhaps Moore did not want to seem gratuitous in showing this oft-repeated tele-vised event? Perhaps the image is too traumatic to show again? Maybe so, but what it does do is to make the memory of this event personal. With no screen image present, the image that we must imagine is ours, evoked from our first sight of the catastro-phe as it played out before us on a television screen.[1] It does not matter if this was synchronous with the event or later on a cable news broadcast or a TV documentary. It does not matter if we viewed this in New York, San Francisco, or Southampton, England; no one film or image can replicate our first memory of the event.[2]

The absence of image invites two assumptions: that the audience has viewed the destruction of the World Trade Center *and* that they will have a personal response, constructed through that memory, to the catastrophe. These assumptions lead me to make another: Moore acknowledges that the 9/11 event is a collective trauma, one in which we can all share, no matter whether we are a New Yorker or a world citizen. There is an assumption here that there is no ambivalence or ambiguity to this shared memory. This is problematic. The notion of consensus attached to these memories denies the possibility of multiple ways in which to engage with the event—there is only one dominant narrative of the day. And Hollywood has claimed it. Earlier inde-pendent films that engaged with the "other side" of the event, for instance, Antonia Bird's *Hamburg Cell* (2004), which concentrates on the hijackers, did not receive a general release even after its rave reviews at the 2004 Edinburgh Film Festival. Nor have Steven Rosenbaum's *7 Days in September* (2002) or Jules and Gédéon Naudet's film *9/11* (2002), arguably the most useful in terms of understanding the trauma of the day for those involved in the rescue of the trapped. Indeed this film had much difficulty in being aired due to its "profane" language (used by the rescue crews)[3]—this idea of what is considered profane perhaps undermining the notion of trauma that the film encompassed. The difficulty for Hollywood filmmakers in representing the World Trade Center catastrophe is that the notion of a consensus of memory of 9/11 seems to render the image beyond the conventional models of representation. How do you make a movie of a day that already played out like a movie?

Oliver Stone's answer to this in *World Trade Center* (2006) is to re-create the events of that day as if it were already a disaster movie. The film follows the entrap-ment and rescue of Port Authority Officers Sgt. John McLoughlin (Nicolas Cage) and Will Jimeno (Michael Peña). It begins with a close-up of a digital clock, the red figures showing 3:29. John McLoughlin stretches over to turn off the alarm clock—does he do this before the 3:30 alarm as a consideration to his sleeping wife or is McLoughlin an anxious man—awake and thinking? The film sets up its nar-rative around the husband and wife relationship that Stone asserts drives the rescue narrative. This beginning also echoes the start of *Independence Day* (1996), already suggesting the generic conventions that this film will employ. What follows is a silent montage of McLoughlin showering, preparing for work, driving in the darkened suburban streets of New York: a working-class man going about his daily routine. This is followed by images of what we later learn are members of his Port Authority team; arriving for work on the subway, by foot, on the Staten island ferry—the World Trade Center towers clearly visible in the early morning light—a poetic and senti-mental vision to establish a comparison to the later scenes of destruction. Finally

Will Jimeno is seen driving into New York City in his truck listening to Brooks and Dunne's "Only in America"—offering an opportunity for one last glistening look at the New York skyline. Already the audience is invited to feel a yearning nostalgia for a skyline that does not now exist. Just 24 minutes of screen-time later, Jimeno and McLoughlin will be trapped inside the collapsed concourse between the two towers.

Stone has described his film as being "very tightly connected, emotional, in the tradition of Hollywood, the tightly connected emotions of four characters. Two wives, two husbands."[4] Thus Stone does not seek to politicize the event but uses the trope of a family in crisis and the heroic rescue narrative as potentially comforting devices to represent what many still find to be a traumatic day. Nicolas Cage states:

> I really don't want to attach politics to this movie. This movie is a triumph of the human spirit, it's about survival, it's about courage, and I think trying to link it to anything else right now, would take away from what the movie is really about . . . it's not a downer, you walk out feeling like yeah, angels do exist, these people are heroes.[5]

Here, Cage invokes the notion of rescue as the uplifting denouement to a traumatic event: an event that might legitimately be considered as the most significant political protest in this century. In many ways it is hard to understand how a film about this event isn't a "downer." However, genre is a powerful tool in restoring safety to its audiences. As Steve Neale reminds us:

> [T]he existence of the Hollywood genres means that the spectator, precisely, will know that everything will be "made right in the end"—that everything will cohere, that any threat or any danger in the narrative process itself will always be contained.[6]

As I will explore, the tropes of the Hollywood disaster movie are variously employed in *World Trade Center* to enable a traumatic event to be represented with some notion of resolution—*even if* scriptwriter Andrea Berkoff has created a narrative that moves away from the event of disaster and instead places ordinary people in extraordinary situations through its rescue narrative. Although her decision to tell the events of 9/11 through the eyes of two survivors most certainly does give a sense of the "everyman" to the events of the day, the narrative and cinematic form fulfill the characteristics of the disaster genre. Stephen Keane asserts that "Whether human or environmental, alien or accidental, most of all disaster movies provide for solutions in the form of a representative group of characters making their way towards survival."[7] The pleasures, then, for the audience of the disaster genre are within the spectacle and special effects of the catastrophe and the plot-line, which sets up a "who will survive" mystery.[8]

In *World Trade Center* the pleasure of this active engagement for the audience is certainly disrupted by the historical and biographical nature of the narrative (it is clear from pre-advertising for the film that Jimeno and McLoughlin are the only two survivors from this Port Authority team); however, the "how" of their heroic and dangerous rescue is central to the narrative. As I will discuss, the form and rhythm of the film pick up the characteristics of the 1970s disaster movie, providing a familiar and nostalgic "hook" for its audience—as Nicolas Cage identifies—this will be a feel-good movie no matter what the reality of the scenario. Nick Roddick states that the disaster movie should not "just be a movie with a disaster in it; it must be 'about' the disaster."[9] As Keane identifies, Roddick's nosology for the disaster movie is useful in understanding the conventions and scale of the complexities of the 1970s version of the genre (for instance, *The Poseidon Adventure*, Neame, 1972; *The Towering Inferno*, Guillemin and Allen, 1972; *Earthquake*, Robson, 1974); however, in the post-9/11 environment Roddick's list becomes an ironic description of the actual catastrophic event in New York City. He suggests that the disaster must be "diegetically central," "factually possible," "largely indiscriminate," "unexpected (although not necessarily unpredicted)," "all encompassing," and "people must believe 'it' could—indeed, very well might—happen to them."[10] It's a chilling list. For a filmmaker the scene is already set; 9/11 is already a movie, waiting to be made—so why isn't anyone in Hollywood (except Stone) making it?[11]

Debates in trauma theory can help us to interrogate this question; Thomas Elsaesser has argued that "traumatic events for contemporary culture turn around the question of how to represent the unrepresentable, or how—he suggests, in Samuel Beckett's words—to name the unnamable."[12] In its very absence a trauma can seem present in the gaps and elisions of narrative. In film it is often the absence of an action or logical plot-line or causality that alerts us to the presence of a trauma.[13] In this respect, in my opening example, the absence of the actual sight of the 9/11 trauma in *Fahrenheit 9/11* draws our attention to the "unrepresentable" status of the attack. This notion of the impossibility of the traumatic image can be found in both the critical media and audience responses to *World Trade Center* and draws attention to the ways in which the event is being processed.

A web respondent to the *Rolling Stone* review by Peter Travis asks a question that is often formulated around the memory of the 9/11 disaster: "How can any American be ready to go back [to the WTC site], and see how it was for those thousands of people that perished in the rubble? ... it is inconceivable and, of course, will never be known."[14] This respondent voices a key concern here of the early audiences for *World Trade Center*—however, other reviews from both critics and public are often more ambivalent to representations of the event. Audience responses range from the incredulous, "this movie should not have been made for another ten years in respect for the families of those killed in the WTC attacks," to the impressed, "this [film] is not in the least bit offensive to those who suffer in the disaster."[15] The disaster movie conventions are not lost on Roger Ebert who views this film as an "attempt to deal with a galvanizing tragedy" but that this is really no more than an "average TV movie"; or to the British *Guardian* newspaper reviewer Peter Bradshaw who is outraged by the film and describes it as "grotesquely boring and badly acted." [16]

The notion that audiences need at least "ten years" in which to process the trauma of 9/11 is pertinent. Two major events of the twentieth century required much time before they were explicitly represented by mainstream cinema. There was not, for example, an *explicit* combat film made for seven years after the First World War and for 13 years after the Vietnam War.[17] This gap, I would argue, is symptomatic of the cultural climate that exists after a national traumatic event and can also be understood in terms of the need for temporal space in which to assimilate its various traumas. The *Rolling Stone* contributor's notion of "ten years" does not appear to be an arbitrary time frame but one that is understood in terms of past precedents in Hollywood cinema. It is a precedent, I would argue, of Hollywood producers relying on indicators of the cultural climate and consensual discourse around an event before they can commit to economic investment.

National traumas such as the Vietnam War were dealt with cautiously by Hollywood until there was a political climate appropriate to production.[18] Thus, I would argue that the range of explicit Vietnam War films made during the 1980s (*Platoon*, Stone, 1986; *Full Metal Jacket*, Kubrick, 1987; *Casualties of War*, de Palma, 1989) were enabled by such indicators as the naming of post-traumatic stress disorder in the *Diagnostic Statistical Manual-III* in 1980 (and thus providing a language to "explain" the inappropriate actions of some troops during the war and some veterans since the war) and the dedication of the Vietnam War memorial (the Wall) in Washington, DC in 1982. Whether this is a commonsense approach from the industry to an event or a cynical business strategy, the results are the same; no films are made of events that the public deems too sensitive to pay money to view.[19]

Cathy Caruth has argued that "a traumatic event cannot be 'assimilated' or experienced fully at the time, but only *belatedly*, in its repeated possession of the one who experiences it."[20] This notion of trauma is useful in understanding the ways in which Hollywood *has* responded to 9/11. Representations of that day have been repeatedly returned to—one could say neurotically returned to—not through explicit narrative but through a referentiality that allows its audiences to assimilate events via mediated images, dialogues, and echoes of the attack. A film such as *Spider-Man 2* (Sam Raimi, 2004), for instance, denotes New York City under attack; its *mise-en-scène* insists that we remember the vulnerability of the high-rise glass-fronted office buildings, and Peter's continued battle with the "hero within" becomes a reference point for the heroic actions of those who perished and survived that day. *Collateral Damage* (Andrew Davis, 2002) echoes the fear of terrorism and the emotional effects of its actions on the bereaved family—as well as bringing the revenge narrative into the fore. Whereas *We Were Soldiers* (Randell Wallace, 2002) pays tribute to the American soldiers who fought in Vietnam and pertinently suggests to its audiences that necessary and worthwhile sacrifices may now need to be made in times of war, *Ladder 49* (Jay Russell, 2004) reminds its audiences of the heroic efforts of the fire crews within the two towers, whilst safely situating itself in Baltimore and its rescue narratives staying within the realms of domestic situations.

These narratives, then, displace trauma, and the audience is situated in a cyclical motion of return to the attack and to New York City. Such narratives take the viewer back to the moment of the event, back, if you like, to the site of trauma. This backward motion, whilst undermining the linear notion of history—an event can be resolved in the future—provides a useful way to think about the apparent void in production of the 9/11 narrative within the dominant Hollywood film form. Hollywood film since 2002 has been saturated by narratives surrounding the events of 9/11: of national pride (*We Were Soldiers*), critique and parody (*W.*, Oliver Stone, 2008), attack (*Collateral Damage*) and heroism (*Ladder 49*). These discourses offer Hollywood audiences an opportunity to return again and again to the 9/11 site. They also offer the audiences a familiar generic language (particularly of heroes and villains) with which to realize this psychological return.[21] It is a mediated return to a mediated event.

Such a complex structure for the reparation of trauma here relies on a nostalgia of the film form and a knowledge of the 9/11 event. There is nothing unexpected or unfamiliar to be found in the structure of *World Trade Center*. The introduction of the main characters and the establishing shots of the site of disaster not only engage with the classical model of exposition, but it also exposes a poignant (and glittering) reminder for the audience of what has already been lost; to all intents and purposes the ending of this film has already been written—and *World Trade Center*'s narrative relies on its audiences to fill in the scriptwriter's gaps. That is, the spectacle of the twin towers collapse is already understood to be imprinted on the audience's memory. Thus, like Moore's film, the impact of the planes and the collapse of the towers remain invisible to the main characters, the second hit viewed only by the remaining Port Authority crews watching a small-screen TV showing CNN coverage.

The only glimpse of what caused the catastrophe is the shadow of the first plane cast on the walls of neighbouring skyscrapers—the audience is guided upwards by Will's POV of this fleeting moment. Scriptwriter Berkoff has been directed by the narratives of Jimeno and McLoughlin and has understood that the men did not "see" the hit. But this casting of the shadow becomes a moment of "poetic cinema" that echoes the spectre of the horror genre (and the looming shadow of Nosferatu) or the expressionistic light and shade of noir. The sunlight is literally blocked from Will's face for an instant. He has a moment of wonder, an aura of anticipation before he hears the crash and chaos hits the streets. He is shocked back into reality. He cannot think what it was that he thought he saw—he must do his job and get citizens to safety. This visual gap for the character highlights the gap in understanding, of assimilation of the 9/11 event within the general discourse surrounding that day; it is part of what can "never be known." It is a moment of stillness in the film that allows for a brief contemplation of the event but also of something else—it is the moment "before" the world changed; the "WOT"; the Iraq and Afghanistan death toll; the Patriot Act; the "one percent rule"; the list goes on.

This one glimpse is all the audience has to understand the predicament that the men find themselves in throughout the rest of the film. As Slavoj Žižek has noted, "one can easily imagine exactly the same film in which the twin towers would have collapsed as the result of an earthquake"[22] as the remaining two hours of screen time focus on the day and night in which the two men are trapped beneath the rubble and successfully rescued. This comment takes into account the lack of political rhetoric and context within the film but it is also pertinent to my argument concerning trauma: the lack of knowledge that the men had of the reasons for their entrapment—and as an audience member it is easy to forget too—finds its reference in the lack of understanding within the dominant discourse around the attack; it's still incomprehensible. It did happen but the film is littered with statements of disbelief.

As one of the Port Authority Officers states in the first ten minutes "what schmuck would fly a plane into the World Trade Center?" Throughout the film those watching and waiting continue to utter their disbelief—and the film does not attempt to recuperate this.

Žižek's comment also nods to the formulaic way in which the film plays out: the rhythm of the film moves between the trapped men as they struggle to stay alive by talking, shouting and, at one point, singing (the *Starsky and Hutch* theme) and their wives (rather than the rescuers) as they wait for news. Reminiscent of the passive wives in Ron Howard's *Apollo 13*, the women are little more than emotional gauges of those who watched the events unfold on TV that morning. Stone has stated that he wanted to create a rhythm of dark and light—to move from the darkness of the hole in which the men were trapped to the brightness of the homes—which later becomes reversed as darkness falls outside but the searchlights are brought into the site. And this rhythm of danger and safety can be found in films such as *The Towering Inferno*. The telephone conversation is used as a means to move between the two spaces (above and below) as the sweating and dirty Fire Chief O'Hallorhan (Steve McQueen) at the top of the tower is instructed about details of the building by the calm and clean architect, Doug Roberts (Paul Newman). The telephone links the two spaces and sets up the symbiotic relationship for the audience; these two characters (and stars) will need to work together to bring resolution to this situation. In *World Trade Center* this trope is utilized to enable the rhythm of dark and light that Stone desires but also to set up the emotional identification for the audience.

As the pregnant Alison Jimeno (Maggie Gyllenhaal) holds onto the hope that her husband will be rescued successfully, the audience is reminded of the conversation he is holding with McLoughlin about naming the baby. This visual trope then reassures by moving the action away from the danger area but creates tension by placing the identification with those who can only look on.

Stephen Keane suggests that the use of stars and its classical film form (cause and effect narrative) make *The Towering Inferno* one of the most "reassuring disaster movies of the 1970s";[23] the theatrical posters aid this by giving the audience ways in which to read the film and to play the "Disaster Movie Game" (who will die next). The poster for *The Towering Inferno* shows the faces of the two stars, McQueen and Newman, who will necessarily work together; the very nature of their star status ensuring that they will survive.[24]

This type of reassurance is at play too in the advertising for *World Trade Center*. An early poster for the film shows the still-standing twin towers looming large over two male figures who are staggering forward, the tag line: "A true story of courage and survival." All notion of disaster here is undermined by the erect towers, the quality of courage, and the certainty of an uplifting end—survival. Without memory or knowledge of 9/11 these images have no negative connotations. A later poster, though, (and the image that has been chosen for the US and Europe DVD release) uses the star image to contain and "bookend" the now iconic image of the mangled metal of the World Trade Center. Nicolas Cage and Maggie Gyllenhaal are placed on the outside of Michael Peña and Maria Bello (less well-known actors), and the images of searchers in the debris are dwarfed by the larger determined faces of

Figure 5: Alison Jimeno waits for news

Figure 6: Doug Roberts instructs the Chief

McLoughlin (Cage) and Jimeno (Peña). The reassuring faces of the star personas here undermine the huge death toll of 9/11; that particular trauma is not engaged. This film is about two men who survived—the tag line appears unnecessary.

In terms of traumatic memory, perhaps the most significant representation in *World Trade Center* is—like *Fahrenheit 9/11*—a memory evoked for the audience through an aural stimulus. The unpalatable narrative of those who fell (or jumped) from the two towers is not made explicit in the film (although there is one lone jumper seen by Jimeno and the crew before they enter the concourse); sickening thuds are heard by the Port Authority team before the second tower collapses. Jimeno asks the security guard "what is that?" The guard's answering frown suggests that he has seen what he will not tell. The most incomprehensible events of that day are again left to personal memory. Here, though, is where the relative comfort of the genre conventions gives way to the revulsion of the special effects from previous disaster movie incarnations. The unspoken horror for those who witnessed the falling people from the World Trade Center is underpinned by the imagination of what they fell from; how awful must it be to consider jumping? Placing the image of "the falling man" beside the image of the character of Lorrie (Susan Flannery) falling from the burning building in *The Towering Inferno* produces a distressing comparison. Here the tropes of the disaster movie with its ideological narrative reasons (adultery) for the early demise of a boss and his secretary become rewritten as a horrifying reminder of what disaster can do.

The site of the World Trade Center remains one of anxiety; a leading article in the *New York Times* on 14 March 2004 suggests that the building of the Freedom Tower at the site has brought a new dimension to these anxieties: Chief Engineer John McCormick recognizes that the new tower could be a new target for terrorists, and states that ". . . the engineers and architects are *thinking the unthinkable* [my emphasis], and playing out their visions of catastrophe, often on computers." Their work therefore continues to be shrouded in secrecy. "Thinking the unthinkable," even now that the "unthinkable has happened," there is still a rhetoric of disbelief, of incomprehension, of impossibility. The assimilation that Caruth suggests as necessary for reparation can be seen to be situated within the very structure of Hollywood's production cycles. The production of displacement narratives is reminiscent of traumatic memory (apparent in post-traumatic stress disorder) where events and places that evoke memories can move one back in time to the moment of original trauma; in these terms Hollywood cinema becomes part of the process of memory retrieval, driving its audiences ever closer to an assimilation of a cultural trauma through a repetitive and fragmented production of the 9/11 story.

Stephen Keane ends his book on the disaster movie by suggesting that in a post-9/11 environment a hybrid disaster genre will emerge, may even be necessary. The disaster movie has, he suggests, "a new responsibility to take on or provide an alternative to: not the seduction but the involvement in spectacle; intelligence and empathy rather than functionality and simple entertainment."[25] *World Trade Center* does not use the *vérité* style of camera work that Paul Greengrass engages in *United 93* to involve its audience, but the reliance on nostalgia for the generic form and memory of 9/11 is suggestive that a new type of disaster film is emerging.

Figure 7: The "Falling Man"

Figure 8: Lorrie falls

A cultural mark of resolution, such as the commemoration of the Washington memorial provided for the Vietnam era, would signal a sea change in public opinion and send a green light to Hollywood to continue its production cycle. Perhaps then the industry will produce the ultimate, explicit 9/11 story, perhaps after the completion and dedication of the Freedom Tower in New York City. Until then Hollywood relies on the familiarity and nostalgia that genre films such as *World Trade Center* offer audiences with all the knowing certainties of character, plot and resolution.

Notes

1 And much could be made of an analysis of this event via psychoanalytical thought, in particular Freud's notion of "screen memories" (1899), but this is beyond my interest in genre and effect here.

2 A version of this analysis of the opening of *Fahrenheit 9/11* also appears in Karen Randell, "Speaking the Unspeakable: Invisibility and Trauma after 9/11," in *Art in the Age of Terrorism*, eds Graham Coulter-Smith and Maurice Owen (London: Holberton Publication, 2005).

3 A federal court decision in 2006 finally allowed the film to be aired on network television. Other independent films that did not get wide release include *11'09"01* (2002) as discussed in the introduction to this collection and *7 Days in September* (Steve Rosenbaum, 2002).

4 "Oliver Stone and Nicolas Cage Discuss World Trade Center" http://movieweb.com/news/NELeULLPWHi4PS (accessed 22 November 2009).

5 Ibid.

6 Steve Neale, *Genre* (London: BFI, 1980), 28.

7 Stephen Keane, *Disaster Movies: The Cinema of Catastrophe* (London: Wallflower, 2006), 5.

8 Ibid.

9 Nick Roddick, "Only the Stars Survive: Disaster Movies in the Seventies" in *Performance and Politics in Popular Drama: Aspects of Popular Entertainment in Theatre, Film and Television 1800–1976*, ed. D. Brady (Cambridge: Cambridge University Press, 1980), 246.

10 Ibid.

11 Paul Greengrass's *United 93* (2006) is, of course, a 9/11 film, but its action does not take place around the site—rather it involves another site of trauma, an airplane as a potential weapon of destruction.

12 Thomas Elsaesser, "Postmodernism as Mourning Work," *Screen* 42 no. 2 (Summer 2001): 195.

13 For a fuller discussion of this notion see Karen Randell, "Masking the Horror of Trauma: The Hysterical Body of Lon Chaney," *Screen* 44 no. 2 (Summer 2003): 216–21.

14 http://www.rollingstone.com/reviews/movie/7667716/review/11077386/world_trade_center (accessed 17 March 2008).

15 Both reviews from www.rollingstone.com (accessed 20 March 2008).

16 Peter Bradshaw, "World Trade Center." Review. http://www.guardian.co.uk/film/2006/sep/29/actionandadventure (accessed 22 November 2009).

17 Those films are *The Big Parade* (King Vidor, 1925) and *Platoon* (Oliver Stone, 1986). *Go Tell the Spartans* (Post, 1978), *The Deer Hunter* (Cimino, 1978), and *Apocalypse Now* (Coppola, 1979) are not, in my opinion, true combat films but are important to my argument that there is a gradual return to the site of trauma.

18 See Oliver Stone's difficulty in getting *Platoon* made in James Riordan, *Stone, A Biography of Oliver Stone: The Controversies, Excesses and Exploits of a Radical Filmmaker* (New York: Aurum Press, 1996).

19 Television has not been so reticent to represent the events of 9/11; for a wider discussion of this see Randell, "Speaking the Unspeakable" and Wheeler Winston Dixon, ed., *Film & Television after 9/11* (Carbondale: Southern Illinois UP, 2004).

20 Cathy Caruth, *Trauma: Explorations in Memory* (London: John Hopkins UP, 1995), 4.

21 More recent films such as *Grand Torino* (Clint Eastwood, 2008), *Cloverfield* (Matt Reeves, 2008), and *The Dark Knight* (Christopher Nolan, 2008) have moved the 9/11 "story" into problematic areas of "right" and "wrong" that suggest that Hollywood is entering a new cycle of process in its engagement with post-9/11 issues.

22 Slavoj Žižek, "On 9/11, New Yorkers Faced the Fire in the Minds of Men," *Guardian*, 11 September 2006, www.guardian.co.uk/commentisfree/2006/Sep11/comment.september11 (accessed 30 May 2009).

23 Keane, *Disaster Movies: The Cinema of Catastrophe*, 38.
24 See Richard Dyer, "American Cinema in the '70s: *The Towering Inferno*," *Movie* 21 (1975): 30–3.
25 Keane, *Disaster Movies: The Cinema of Catastrophe*, 107.

CHAPTER 13

The Contemporary Politics of the Western Form: Bush, *Saving Jessica Lynch*, and *Deadwood*

STACY TAKACS

As Susan Faludi has argued, the "terror dream" that gripped the United States in the wake of 9/11 took the peculiar form of a Wild West fantasy of frontier violence, captivity, and rescue.[1] Politicians and pundits alike depicted Americans as innocents besieged by wild savages and desperate for strong men with guns to rescue them. President George W. Bush, in particular, laced his public performances with frontier "folkisms" calculated to reassure the public that he was a strong, capable leader. He described the terrorists as irrational, called for the capture of Osama bin Laden "Dead or Alive," and portrayed the US as a reluctant gunslinger forced by circumstances to resort to violence.[2] Such rhetoric reduced complex geopolitical realities to a simple Manichean morality tale in which the US could do no wrong because its mission was "defensive."

This chapter examines the construction, dissemination, and contestation of this legitimating narrative through the examination of two recent incarnations of the TV Western: the NBC made-for-TV movie *Saving Jessica Lynch* (2003) and the HBO series *Deadwood* (2004–06). The former, though not technically a western, used Western imagery to frame the invasion of Iraq as a defensive struggle to rescue civilization from savagery. *Deadwood*, on the other hand, used Western conventions to interrogate the logics of Manichean morality and militarized heroism underwriting the Bush administration's turn to war as an instrument of peace. Its anti-heroic depiction of life on the frontier challenged the ideology of American exceptionalism and gave viewers a rare opportunity to contemplate the costs and consequences of US foreign policy.

The comparison demonstrates TV's importance as a site of ideological struggle in the post-9/11 context. The Bush administration frequently used TV programming to communicate political messages, providing access, information, and production assistance to *Saving Jessica Lynch* and a number of other series (most notably *Profiles from the Front Line* [2003], *JAG* [1995–2005], and *24* [2001–present]).[3] Yet, the commercial nature of the medium and the multiplicity of available channels virtually ensured the official version of events would be contested elsewhere on the dial.[4]

Deadwood's controversial reframing of frontier discourse, for example, was made possible by the different political economy of subscription television. Unlike NBC, HBO is not subject to FCC regulation and does not need to attract a mass audience to finance its productions. This gives the network the freedom to encourage aesthetic experimentation and court controversy as a branding strategy. These structural differences guarantee a certain amount of ideological complexity within the television medium. Indeed, as this chapter will demonstrate, TV has functioned admirably as a "cultural forum" for the ethical contemplation of dilemmas raised by the Bush Doctrine.[5] Since it was also one of the *only* sites available for such contemplation, its role in framing and re-framing 9/11 and its aftermath is of vital concern.

The utility of frontier rhetoric to the project of political legitimation was demonstrated most forcefully in regard to the War in Iraq, which was, after all, an unprovoked assault on a nation with no connection to the terrorists who attacked the US on 9/11. The Bush administration manufactured evidence of a direct threat to the nation (WMDs), then clarified the moral stakes of the battle by lumping Iraq into an "Axis of Evil," the existence of which seemed to demand a forceful solution. When the US finally invaded, the vulnerability of US troops to counterassault provided new, more compelling opportunities to brand the invasion a defensive maneuver. The captivity and rescue of Pfc. Jessica Lynch, in particular, gave military spin doctors a chance to reverse the positions of aggressor and aggrieved and paint the US military as the group besieged. Lynch was a member of the 507th Maintenance Unit of the US Army, which came under attack in An-Nasariyah on March 23, 2003. Eleven members of the unit were killed, five were taken hostage, and Lynch was sent to Saddam General Hospital for the treatment of wounds suffered during the battle. On April 1 she was "rescued" in a spectacular (but unnecessary) raid by US Special Forces. The story of the "ambush" and "rescue" invoked the tradition of the Western captivity narrative to code the Iraqis as aggressors and justify the continued use of force. Lynch was perfectly cast as the damsel-in-distress because of her devastating injuries, petite stature, and all-American good looks (i.e. her whiteness).[6] Her literal need for rescue would lend credence to the Bush administration's depiction of the invasion as a humanitarian intervention to secure Iraqi liberation.

NBC's made-for-TV movie version of the events, *Saving Jessica Lynch* (*SJL*), deployed Western imagery quite overtly to call up the cultural fantasy of regeneration-through-violence activated by the captivity narrative.[7] The film opens like a Western with shots of a desert landscape whose scope and barrenness foreshadow the suffering and death to come. Images of strange beasts (camels and nomads) and malevolent natural forces (sandstorms) code Iraq as an inhospitable and utterly alien terrain. Lynch (Laura Regan) and her companions are both literally and figuratively lost in this menacing landscape, and the sense of disorientation is heightened through contrasting shots of Lynch's serene and supportive home life. In flashback, we meet her loving family and learn "why we fight"—to protect and defend this bastion of civilization. The scene reassures viewers that US motives are pure: we want nothing more than to eliminate the "bad guys" and then "come home."

The assault on the convoy extends the frontier motif by paying visual homage to John Ford's *Stagecoach*. As in that film, the representatives of civilization travel

Figure 9: Feminizing Private Lynch

Figure 10: A Wild West standoff

through hostile territory and are attacked by an undifferentiated mass of savages. In a parody of the Western shootout, the leader of the attackers locks eyes with Lynch, then strides down the main street with a rifle on his hip. Lynch is aggressively feminized in the sequence so that the attack may seem all the more unwarranted. While she cowers on the floor of the Humvee, shrieking, crying and praying, a subjective camera aligns the viewer with her perspective and affirms her status as "innocent victim." Lynch's weakness and passivity are underscored by her inability to fire her weapon and by her "blackout" at the conclusion of the scene. For the remainder of the film, her injuries render her literally helpless, completing her shift from soldier to damsel-in-distress and transforming the invasion of Iraq into a literal rescue mission.

The conclusion of the film can be summarized in this way: with the aid of a loyal Indian scout, the cavalry locates the missing captive and swoops in to save the day. This "scout" is Mohammed al-Rehaif, the Iraqi lawyer who conveyed Lynch's whereabouts to the Marine Corps and whose book formed the basis of the teleplay. In the film, he is carefully distinguished from the mass of "evil" Iraqis by virtue of his hatred for the Fedayeen and his alignment with American popular culture and family values. When al-Rehaief (Nicholas Guilak) first sees Lynch, she is being beaten by an Iraqi interrogator; he vows to help her because "she's just a girl, a child." This paternalism aligns al-Rehaief with the values espoused by Lynch's own father earlier in the film and identifies him with the "good guys." When al-Rehaief insists on helping Lynch, his wife blames American Westerns: "your mother poisoned your mind with all of those John Wayne movies." Al-Rehaief's association with the militarized masculinity of Wayne prepares the audience to accept him as the hero of the rescue narrative. The film concludes with the double rescue of Lynch from Saddam General Hospital and al-Rehaief and family from Iraq. The redemption of Lynch facilitates the redemption of al-Rehaief, which, in turn, redeems the US mission in Iraq, and, in a final nod to the Western, Al-Rehaief and family ride off into the sunset in a US helicopter.

The use of Western motifs in *SJL* seems calculated to reinforce the Bush administration's depiction of the War in Iraq as a showdown between good and evil, civilization and savagery. Because the filmmakers received assistance from the Department of Defense, this is not at all surprising. *SJL* was little more than a propaganda piece inviting Americans to view themselves as the good guys and their military exploits as redemptive. As the human and material costs of the war mounted, however, alternative ideas about militarized masculinity and moral authority began to emerge in popular culture. Film and TV scholars are careful to note, the Western genre is neither monolithic nor ideologically uniform. All Westerns may take male heroism and righteous violence as their primary subject matter, but they often handle these subjects in unexpected ways.[8] HBO's series *Deadwood* took the demystification of Western mythology as its starting point. By challenging virtually every convention of the Western genre, *Deadwood* called into question the Manichean morality undergirding the militarized model of security promoted by the Bush administration and texts like *Saving Jessica Lynch*. Its graphic depiction of the costs of militarized violence seemed calculated to cool the "righteous ecstasy" invoked by 9/11 and to encourage consideration of alternative ways of being in the world.

According to the show's creator, David Milch, the central theme of the program was "society trying to find its organizing principles in the absence of law."[9] In 1876, when the series opens, Deadwood is a society whose principal organizing force is force itself. It is an illegal settlement established by renegade whites in anticipation of a treaty with the Indians, who own the territory. By making everyone in the town technically an outlaw, *Deadwood* evacuates the traditional Western's pretensions to moral clarity at the outset. The people in this town are not just illegal; they do everything they can to avoid becoming legal. They delay creating a local government, refuse to identify a sheriff, and resist garrisoning the military. If they do any of these things, it is from self-interest, rather than public spirit. Über-villain and town strongman Al Swearengen (Ian McShane) only gets the men together to establish a local government when it seems the federal government might step in and do it for them. Positions in the nascent government are handed out at random, and public monies are used to bribe the magistrates to keep it that way. Thus, money and power, rather than the Law, are what organize this society, at least initially.

"The repressed dimension of Westerns," according to Stanley Corkin, "is their relationship to imperialism."[10] The genre mystifies economic goals by associating them "with character traits that resonate within the national mythos," specifically "'freedom' and 'individualism.'"[11] President Bush's explanation of American hegemony as a benevolent form of empire designed to spread "freedom and democracy," rather than harvest gain, certainly profits from this Western legacy. As an exploration of capitalist development, specifically of the moment of "primitive accumulation," when resources and peoples are first incorporated into the capitalist system, *Deadwood* foregoes the mystification, exposing the imperial heart of the civilizing mission. Deadwood's citizens blatantly rape the land for economic purposes and in the name of progress. There is no pretense here of higher morality or honor. Milch believes that "most moral codes are elevated expressions of economic necessity," and *Deadwood* illustrates that belief.[12]

Deadwood gives us an image of what "freedom and democracy" look like when they are conceived in overly economic terms, as free trade and freedom of consumer choice rather than the freedom to shape government and society in the people's interests. It presents a fully realized vision of neoliberal economic principles run amok. Virtually anything is permissible in the world of Deadwood in pursuit of the almighty dollar. The righteous violence sanctioned by the traditional Western is unmasked here as but the swiftest means of procuring a competitive advantage. In the pilot episode, for example, Al cons Brom Garrett (Timothy Omundson), a tenderfoot from the East, into overpaying for a mine claim Al thinks is worthless. When one of the parties to the con ups the price without authorization, Al, first, intimidates him into relinquishing his cut of the proceeds, then has his bartender, Dan Dority (W. Earl Brown), stab the man to death. They dispose of the body using Mr. Wu's (Keone Young) carnivorous pigs—a colorful plot device that is also a fitting metaphor for the capitalists themselves. When the tenderfoot begins to smell the con, Al has him thrown off a cliff. On the way down to recover the body, Dan discovers a rich vein of gold on the property and reports it to Al, who then tries to con the widow out of her claim. Thus, Al gets the lion's share of the con and first dibs on the claim (though he never actually acquires it), and it is violence that secures his competitive advantage.

The program rarely depicts force as righteous or tidy. Instead it is intimate, brutal, petty, and leaves nasty stains on the floor (characters are forever scrubbing up pools of blood). By unmasking its characters' economic motivations, *Deadwood* acknowledges that "the passion for profit . . . was the passion at the core of the Western adventure."[13] It challenges the mythic construction of the West as a site where worldly success was a reward for right living and resources were divinely ordained to fall to the hard working pioneer. *Deadwood* harbors no illusion that claims to resources or profits are adjudicated fairly or honestly. Instead, it reveals Western settlement to be a naked form of primitive accumulation organized through the violent suppression of competing claims and claimants.

The brutal treatment of women, the Chinese community, and the neighboring Indians in *Deadwood* offers a case in point. Because "Natural Law" dictates that "adult white males [are] on top with everyone else in descending order beneath,"[14] Indians, women, and the Chinese are all subject, like nature itself, to commodification and exploitation. In the first episode, for example, Al plays upon the miners' racism to deflect attention from his own complicity in the massacre of a Swedish family. He suggests the Sioux, whom he refers to as "Godless bloodthirsty heathens," are responsible for the assault and offers a bounty of $50 for any Indian head brought into the camp "with no upper limit." Thus, the Sioux begin the series as tokens of exchange cementing relations between white men, and they rarely appear as anything else. Women, too, serve this mediating function, and their social roles are largely limited to whore or madam. Even the proper Victorian marriage between Brom and Alma Garrett (Molly Parker) is a monetary exchange: Alma agreed to the marriage as a means of alleviating her father's debts ("I can never repay you for what you've done for me," he tells her, "but I can repay everyone else"). As commodities, women have little power and are regularly subject to abuse. When one of Al's favorite whores is assaulted by a customer and shoots him in self-defense, for example, Al does not rise to her defense; instead he drives her head into a wall and threatens to kill her because her resistance to male domination is "bad for business." Finally, the Chinese are referred to as "Chinks" and forced to live in an over-crowded ghetto on the margins of society. The white men mock their cultural habits and forbid them from entering white businesses or exacting "justice" on white men who wrong them. This puts the Chinese at an extreme disadvantage in a town where the ability to protect one's economic interests requires the exercise of both preemptive and retaliatory violence. The routine nature of such exploitation in *Deadwood* reveals the "natural order," so highly touted in Western myth, to be a social construction facilitating the smooth operation of capitalism. Racism and sexism are not expressions of individual pathology, the program suggests; they are structural techniques for administering the distribution of power and resources.

Deadwood also challenges the "naturalness" of this order by attacking the model of masculine authority that sustains and profits from it. The men who exercise power in *Deadwood* challenge every convention of heroics established by the Western form. They are not chiseled monuments to physical prowess; they are never silent or stoic; and they are far too pragmatic to be unforgiving. Most importantly, their capitalist desires and close proximity to others create entanglements that prevent them from acting completely autonomously. They can neither remain isolated nor evade the consequences of their actions in the tight quarters of Deadwood. Ultimately, the rejection of the disciplinary model of Western heroism leads to the emergence of alternative forms of civilization organized around values like empathy, reciprocity, and mutual support.

Deadwood's treatment of the traditional gunslinger illustrates its contempt for the two-dimensional caricature of masculinity preferred by traditional Westerns. The legendary gunslinger Wild Bill Hickok (Keith Carradine) enters Deadwood, an alcoholic gambler on his last legs. Though the town's citizens treat him as royalty, he shows himself to be little more than a lousy card player and habitual drunkard. In contrast to the rest of the characters, Hickok is laconic and avoids entanglements. He refuses to assist the tenderfoot when he suspects Al has cheated him, and, though he rides out with the posse that rescues a young Swedish girl from the massacre site, it is Seth Bullock (Tim Olyphant) who initiates the gunfight that results in "justice" being served. Hickok is tired of embodying heroic masculinity and openly pleads with his traveling companion, Charlie Utter (Dayton Callie), to let "me go to hell the way I want to." His death in the fourth episode is both anti-climactic and anti-heroic: he is shot in the back of the head by a half-witted gambler named Jack McCall (Garret Dillahunt). By murdering its gunslinger in such an unromantic fashion, *Deadwood* violates every expectation of the genre and marks the ideals of autonomous masculinity and rugged individualism as nostalgic and outmoded.

Though the show establishes Seth Bullock as the successor to Wild Bill's legacy, Bullock is a far more complex, morally ambiguous character. By the time Bullock assumes the position of town sheriff at the end of season one, both he and the role have been severely compromised. For one thing, the sheriff in Deadwood is not democratically elected but appointed by Al. The first sheriff is the aptly named Con Stapleton (Peter Jason) who, as Bullock says, can be bought "for the price of bacon grease" ("Sold Under Sin"). Disgusted with Con's refusal to arrest a white man for the murder of a Chinese man, Bullock throws Stapleton's badge in the mud, providing a visual metaphor for the compromised status of the role. He later picks the badge up and absent-mindedly fingers it while suggesting to Dan that it would be in Al's best interest to kill Alma Garrett's greedy father, Otis Russell (William Russ), who has arrived to exploit her new wealth. Dan looks at the badge and says: "You ought to pin that on your chest. You hypocrite enough to wear it." Bullock's heroic status is further undercut when he confronts Alma's father at the end of the episode and brutally beats him to near death. This incident suggests that the Western hero's reflexive resort to violence is, in fact, sociopathic. Even Bullock wonders, "What kind of man have I become?"

When Bullock finally says, "I'll be the fucking sheriff," it is because he recognizes his fitness for the role within the morally ambiguous world of Deadwood. He has abandoned his illusions that either he or the law could be pure and uncompromised.

It is better, he decides, to have a "man . . . who understands the dangers of his own temperament" in the role than one of Al's lackeys. *Deadwood* offers no illusion that things will change, however. Al lets Bullock take up the badge as a hedge against Cy Tolliver (Powers Boothe), but he reaffirms his control over the town by daring Bullock to arrest him for the murder of a federal magistrate: "Well, Sheriff, I'm going to step over that blood stain that mysteriously appeared [on my floor] and see to my interests." Bullock responds, "Take your time." This depiction of morality as situational and dependent on shifting alignments presents a much more realistic picture of how communal security may be created and sustained over the long term.

The sympathetic portrayal of the villain, Al Swearengen, further complicates the moral order of *Deadwood* and proves that even the most rugged individualist is still a social being beholden to others. Al is both a hardened swindler and a sentimental fool. He buys all of his whores from the same orphanage where he was raised in order to redeem them from a life of chronic poverty. He is also emotionally involved with a whore named Trixie (Paula Malcomson) without whom he cannot seem to function. In the first season, Trixie has a love tryst with hardware store proprietor Sol Starr (John Hawkes), and when Al finds out about it in "Jewel's Boot is Made For Walking," he openly acknowledges his need for human connection: "What can any one of us ever really hope for except for a moment here and there with a person who doesn't want to rob, steal, or murder us. Everybody needs that. It becomes precious to 'em. They don't want to see it fucked with." Trixie's act denies Al the illusion of intimacy that had sustained him. To avenge the betrayal, he deprives Trixie of a comparable connection by making Starr pay for her services and insisting future "business" be conducted at the Saloon. In subsequent episodes, Al tries to renounce his dependence on Trixie by forcing her to "sleep with [her] own" and calling her "that other one," but he is clearly afflicted by her absence. He cannot sleep without her in his bed, and, though other whores can meet his physical needs, no one else satisfies his need for rapport. Al's paradoxical mixture of self-interest and compassion for others culminates in the mercy killing of the ailing Reverend Smith (Ray McKinnon) at the end of season one. When no other character can bring him or herself to put the reverend out of his misery, Al gently cradles the man's head, soothes his fears, and smothers the life out of him, all while explaining to his new road agent how to make a "good seal" over the mouth to ensure the kill.

The acknowledgment of moral ambiguity in *Deadwood* ultimately enables the assertion of a different set of social priorities and values. The program's unconventional use of language, for example, inverts the gendered dichotomy of the Western, reasserts the primacy of diplomacy over gunplay, and opens men, in particular, to connection with others. By making men speak and speak eloquently (if profanely), *Deadwood* dismisses the illusion of masculine integrity and autonomy preserved, in typical Westerns, through the weapon of silence. As Jane Tompkins explains, "To speak is literally to open the body to penetration by opening an orifice . . . it suggests a certain incompleteness, a need to be in relation. Speech relates the person who is speaking to other people . . . It requires acknowledging their existence and, by extension, their parity."[15] In *Deadwood*, men are encouraged to be open to the existence and humanity of others even as they routinely fail to rise to this challenge.

The possibility of transcending their sense of themselves as alone is always an option, however, even when it is not taken up. This suggests *Deadwood* may be doing more than just knocking the Western hero off his high horse. It may be making a case for the reprioritization of communication, empathy, negotiation, and compromise—all of those "feminine" values eschewed by the Bush administration in the wake of 9/11—over violence as a means of resolving conflict.[16]

The conclusion of season one would seem to affirm such an allegorical reading, for it culminates in a less than subtle indictment of the role of the military in securing "civilization." When Gen. George Crook's Army unit, known as "Custer's Avengers," enters Deadwood looking for rest and relaxation after a "victorious" battle against the Sioux, the town throws them a parade. General Crook's speech extolling the virility and sacrifice of his men during the battle is a paean to empire, but its celebratory message is undercut in significant ways. First, Director Davis Guggenheim literally obscures the message by positioning the General so that he faces away from both the crowd and the television audience. Second, the elevated language of the speech makes it clear this is a rhetorical performance, not a factual account ("The march through the mud was a trial sent by God, and harsh necessity required of us much suffering and great sacrifice," and so on). The ranting of a traumatized veteran exposes the self-serving nature of this performance, for just as the General says, "Their resistance was overcome. There were no prisoners," the soldier blurts out a reference to "every man, woman, and child." The soldier thus acknowledges what Gen. Crook's use of passive voice is meant to deny: that the battle was really a massacre of civilians. When Crook subsequently dedicates the massacre "to the progress of the United States," members of both audiences are supposed to be sickened. The scene demonstrates not only how dependent civilization is on acts of barbarism but also how important "the power to narrate or to block others' narratives from forming and emerging" is to the propagation of empire.[17]

In place of the moral clarity of the traditional Western, *Deadwood* offers moral confusion and implies that dialogue may be a healthier, more reasonable response to vulnerability than retaliation. The show's obsession with the costs and consequences of violence makes the zero sum logic of war inescapable and begs for a consideration of other methods of securing the peace. Rev. Smith's eulogy for Wild Bill Hickok in "The Trial of Jack McCall" makes this point abundantly clear by reminding the attendants of their mutual interconnection and dependency:

> The body is not one member but many. The eye cannot say unto the hand, I have no need of thee. Nor, again, the head to the feet, I have no need of thee. Nay, much more those members of the body, which seem to be more feeble, and those members of the body which we think of as less honorable. All are necessary . . . There should be no schism in the body but . . . the members should have the same care one to another, and whether one member suffer, *all* the members suffer with it.

A paraphrase of 1 Corinthians 12, the eulogy marks the passing of both Hickok and the "go it alone" philosophy of the Western gunslinger he embodies. It challenges viewers to think of other humans not as enemies but as neighbors in a global community, and it asks whether militarized conflict is a sustainable method of security under these conditions. The lesson, as Milch puts it, is this: "respect the humanity of your fellow man ... don't eat your own species."[18]

By challenging the chauvinistic conception of "civilization" proposed by President Bush and reinforced in texts like *Saving Jessica Lynch*, *Deadwood* pushed individuals to reconsider the righteousness of American policies in Iraq and elsewhere. While it may not have moved individuals to take direct political action, it did prod them to ask questions and entertain doubts at a time when such activities were being discouraged in official political culture. This ultimately is what it means to describe TV as a "cultural forum." It is not that TV serves as a national public sphere or provides a space for meaningful public debate on social issues; it is, rather, that TV, by constantly re-articulating the central beliefs of the society, gives individuals a chance to assess the validity and efficacy of those tenets and to imagine alternatives. While the radical effects of any single TV program are likely to be limited, the medium as a whole testifies to the constructed nature of social priorities and, in doing so, suggests they might be amenable to reconstruction. In times of crisis, this is an important political service in and of itself, for it reminds individuals that the mechanisms of social control are never as monolithic or all-powerful as they seem. Indeed, as HBO's *Deadwood* illustrates, the various control mechanisms may sometimes conflict with each other in ways that open spaces for the articulation of counter-narratives. It remains to be seen whether these counter-narratives will engender a shift in social priorities and practices over the long term, but the election of the more diplomatically inclined Barack Obama to the US presidency in 2008 seems a good omen.

Notes

1   See Susan Faludi, *The Terror Dream: Fear and Fantasy in Post-9/11 America* (New York: Metropolitan Books, 2007).
2   See Ryan Malphurs, "The Media's Frontier Construction of President George W. Bush," *The Journal of American Culture* 31 no. 2 (2008): 185–201.
3   See Katherine Q. Seelye, "Pentagon Plays Role in Fictional Terror Drama," *New York Times*, March 31, 2002, A12; and Neil Hickey, "Access Denied: Pentagon's War Reporting Rules are Toughest Ever," *Columbia Journalism Review* 40 no. 5 (2002): 26–31.
4   See Lynn Spigel, "Entertainment Wars: Television Culture After 9/11," *American Quarterly* 56 no. 2 (2004): 235–70.
5   See Amanda Lotz, "Using 'Network' Theory in the Post-Network Era: Fictional 9/11 US Television Discourse as a 'Cultural Forum,'" *Screen* 45 no. 4 (2004): 423–38; and Horace Newcomb and Paul Hirsch, "Television as a Cultural Forum," in *Television: The Critical View*, 6th ed., ed. Horace Newcomb (New York: Oxford University Press, 2000).
6   See Stacy Takacs, "Jessica Lynch and the Regeneration of American Identity and Power Post-9/11," *Feminist Media Studies* 5 no. 3 (2005): 297–310.
7   See Richard Slotkin, *Regeneration Through Violence: The Mythology of the American Frontier, 1600–1860* (Middletown, CT: Wesleyan University Press, 1973).
8   See Stanley Corkin, *Cowboys and Cold Warriors: The Western and US History* (Philadelphia: Temple University Press, 2004); and Horace Newcomb, "The Opening of America: Meaningful Difference in 1950s Television," in *The Other Fifties: Interrogating Midcentury American Icons*, ed. Joel Foreman (Urbana, IL: Univ. of Illinois Press, 1997).

9   See David Milch, "Director's Commentary: Episode One," *Deadwood: The Complete First Season*, DVD, directed by David Milch (2004; Burbank, CA: HBO Video, 2005).

10 Corkin, *Cowboys and Cold Warriors*, 24.

11 Ibid., 25.

12 See Michael Schwarz, "The New Language of the Old West," *Deadwood: The Complete First Season*, DVD, directed by David Milch (2004; Burbank, CA: HBO Video, 2005).

13 Patricia Nelson Limerick, *The Legacy of Conquest: The Unbroken Past of the American West* (New York: W.W. Norton, 1987), 77.

14 Jane Tompkins, *West of Everything: The Inner Life of Westerns*, (New York: Oxford University Press, 1992), 73.

15 Ibid., 56.

16 See Julie Drew, "Identity Crisis: Gender, Public Discourse and 9/11," *Women & Language* 27 no. 2 (2004): 71–8; and Faludi, *The Terror Dream*.

17 Edward Said, *Culture and Imperialism* (New York: Vintage, 1993), xiii.

18 Michael Schwarz, "An Imaginative Reality," *Deadwood: The Complete First Season*, DVD, directed by David Milch (2004; Burbank, CA: HBO Video, 2005).

Prophetic Narratives

CHAPTER 14

Governing Fear in the Iron Cage of Rationalism: Terry Gilliam's *Brazil* through the 9/11 Looking Glass[1]

DAVID H. PRICE

Terry Gilliam's 1985 film, *Brazil*, presents a stunning dystopic vision of a totalitarian world bureaucratically fighting a terror war that bears a striking, darkly tragic resemblance to post-9/11 America.[2] Using fictional abstractions of a nonspecific nation and time, *Brazil*'s world prefigures many of the fundamental dynamics, threats, and bureaucratic terrors gripping America and the post-9/11 world. Gilliam's vision so aligns with the world promulgated by the Bush administration in post-9/11 America that Gilliam recently joked that he was going to sue Bush "for the illegal and unauthorized remake of *Brazil*, the reality TV show."[3]

Gilliam's prescience came not from some mystical ability providing him with the ability to see the future but from his keen understanding of the dark nature of his world, an ability to embrace the absurdity of everyday interactions, and an artist's inkling of the next iterations that cultural trajectories might produce. This essay compares prominent thematic features of Gilliam's *Brazil* with shifts in post-9/11 America, focusing on structural, bureaucratic, and ideological similarities between these two worlds. I close with a consideration of the narrative structure of the "Love Conquers All" happy-ending vision that Universal studios attempted to release as the American version of *Brazil*. I compare the studio's dishonest representation of *Brazil*'s world with representations of post-9/11 America, as presented by the Bush Administration and its media-spinning supporters who justified shifts in American governmental reliance on surveillance, torture, and un-freedom.

Brazil, Story and Setting

Brazil's plot is complex, but the basic narrative follows Sam Lowry, a daydreaming, underachieving, functionary everyman working for the Ministry of Records in a world embroiled in an ongoing terror war against vaguely unspecific terrorists. A

bureaucratic mix-up of the names Buttle and Tuttle leads to the mistaken detention, torture, and murder of a citizen named Archibald Buttle. Buttle's neighbor, Jill,
turns out to be the woman of Sam's dreams, and Sam's efforts to find Jill lead him
to transfer his job to the Ministry of Information Retrieval (where rendered citizens
are interrogated) where he locates Jill and becomes identified as a wanted terrorist.
Sam is eventually captured, processed, interrogated, and tortured by the Ministry of
Information Retrieval. During this final interrogation, even as he is being brutally
tortured, Sam mentally escapes his captors by regressing into a fantasy of his own
rescue by a group of anti-state rebels. Sam Lowry's mental escape is a dark key to
the film; according to Gilliam, *Brazil* explores the question of "can one make a film
where the happy ending is a man going insane?"[4]

Brazil's mixing of technologies, styles, designs, and limited specifics on the exact
nature of this world's political economy gave the film its strength of representative
vision at the time of its initial release. These elements still give *Brazil* an authority
of abstract realism in post-9/11 America, as the US mixed torture with the values
of public amnesia, denial of civil rights, the sanctification of consumer culture in a
world where a collage of atrocities blur across national media backdrops, while those
who contribute to this state of affairs find rewards of occupational advancement
and secure credit lines.

Some critics and viewers were confused by Gilliam's decision to set *Brazil* in an
unspecified time and place—no doubt, the title (referring to Ary Barroso's samba,
"Aquarela do Brasil" and *not* the South American nation) contributed to this confusion, but the non-specified temporal or geographical location of Gilliam's vision
helps us see how his vision overlays with post-9/11 America. The retro-futuristic
technology supporting Gilliam's world confirms that the story is set not so much
in a known place living within the bounds of technological evolution shared by
our world (ducts, tubing, and retro-magnification computer screens dominate the
technological landscape following evolutionary paths not selected in our world) and
are instead an amalgamation from another world. Gilliam's prescient vision relied
on his interpretations of the present, not on the sort of wild sense of the imagined
hi-tech future found in poorly aging sci-fi films like Truffaut's *Fahrenheit 451*; he
merely followed the visible bureaucratic trajectories found in his present to their
extended horizons, and decorated the background of this world with clumsy retro-
technology that mirrors larger social dysfunctions.

Many of *Brazil*'s dystopian motifs are of the variety commonly stocked in post-
Orwellian totalitarian fiction: bleak monolithic architecture, hegemonic slogans, a
social climate of distrust, loss of privacy, and individual rights, and a surrender to the
glorification of state terror in the name of freedom. With a nod to Orwell, *Brazil*'s
offices and public spaces display posters declaring slogans like: "suspicion breeds
confidence," "don't suspect a friend, report him," "trust in haste, regret at leisure."

Brazil's obscurantist bureaucratic language helps state agents remove themselves
from stark admissions that they tortured Buttle to death, as each governmental
ministry reframes this act with its own bureaucratic euphemism to describe his murder in the hands of the Ministry of Information. When Lowry and his boss search
ministry records to locate Buttle they see him catalogued under various terms: the

"Population Census has him down as *dormanted*"; "the central collective storehouse computer's got him down as *deleted*"; "information retrieval has got him down as *inoperative*"; "Security has got him down as *excised*"; and "administration has got him down as *completed*."⁵ Lowry looks up Buttle on a computer and is surprised to discover that these terms mean that he's dead—a concept that had escaped both of them in the maze of distancing bureaucratese.

Rather than clarifying what behaviors are being linguistically represented, the linguistic shifts of *Brazil* and post-9/11 America shield the populous from confronting what specific actions are occurring. Like Orwellian doublespeak, the euphemisms deployed in both worlds disguise rather than reveal. America's terror war transforms American English in Orwellian forms of linguistic torture as citizens find themselves rapidly pressed to absorb a steady stream of undefined terms used in new, uncritical ways. Post-9/11 America has been transformed by phrases like: terrorist, War on Terror, asymmetrical warfare,⁶ the Long War, WOT, enemy combatant, kill chain, Islamofascism, ghost flights, renditions, WMDs, embedded reporting, shock and awe, radical cleric, Homeland Security, stop loss orders, and national security letters. The American Dialectic Society announced that the 2007 "euphemism of the year" was the US Army's "Human Terrain Teams," newly formed weaponized anthropological cultural advisors used by the Army in battlefield settings.⁷ The phrase Human Terrain suggests sanitized geographic sorting exercises rather than more threatening processes of using ethnographic knowledge to label populations in dangerous battlefields in ways that could endanger or increase their likelihood of survival.

Language is not the only force used to distance individuals from behaviors and responsibilities. Bureaucratic structures insert the desires of state into the lives of all. *Brazil*'s oppressive bureaucratic structures dominate a world where individual love is difficult, and heroic dreams and fantasies are the remaining refuge of escape for malcontents wishing to escape tyrannical realities. But it is in the film's understated details and ambient attitudes that Gilliam makes his most persuasive statements about the nature of oppression in modern surveillance states. Gilliam mixes dark humor with a pessimistic triumphalism in a world where even small heroic gestures doom actors whose choice of inaction or compliance to the needs of bureaucratic careerism would otherwise lead to relatively comfortable lives, elevated social status, and improved credit ratings.

One of the reasons that post-9/11 America connects so well to *Brazil* is that the film's totalitarian inventions are rooted not in absurdist fantasies, but in the mundane experiences and practices of everyday life. Gilliam notes:

Most of the details that I got about the tortures and the arrests were very commonplace in most of the other countries in the world. There was very little invented. I kept telling people: this film is really a documentary, I've invented nothing, these are only things that I have observed.⁸

Post-9/11 America adopted more openly *Brazil*-like tactics such as disappearing hooded detainees denied of civil rights and due process so that they may be tortured at undisclosed locales. While news images of such unsettling acts spark occasional discomfort in the American public, there have been consistent bipartisan efforts and willing media (both news and entertainment) campaigns to lull the American people into a compliant dreamlike state where such acts can be seen as necessary. Citizens must struggle on their own to recall an age where such depravities were not background elements of daily life. During the Bush years, claims of necessity helped justify a lack of critical attention; under Obama, slogans of change divert attentions from the many policy continuities remaining in place from the Bush years.

Brazil's world is marked with failing technology, and odd conglomerations of retrofits. Just as ducts mar the retrofitted interiors of *Brazil*'s beautifully designed interiors, torture and bureaucratic tyranny crudely overlay and re-channel the flow of whatever system of justice, order, and due process once, if ever, ruled this land. Order and due process are replaced by the bureaucratic, which creates its own order. Gilliam's world is an apt metaphor for a post-9/11 America where everything from the Bill of Rights to the streets of Washington, DC are retrofitted to meet newly claimed "security" needs in ways that deny not only elegance, but also designed intent.

Brazil's retrofits stress not only a devaluation of aesthetics, but they provide a record that this is a world where a clumsy police state has been overlaid atop what was once a more elegant and open society. Retrofitted ducts tarnish the interiors of most buildings. Telephones, computers, and other human-environmental inter-faces appear to be retro-adaptations of 1950s designs crudely merged with more modern devices such as desktop computers. Sam's office at Information Retrieval is a retro-subdivision of an office in which he shares half his desk through a wall with the adjoining office. The state's security apparatus has been retrofitted to building entrances and passageways—this world was not always plunged into its endless terror war, and the state's apparatus overlays environments in ill-fitting and awkward ways.

The security apparatus of post-9/11 America is retrofitted to architectural features of government buildings, airports, even private shopping centers, as metal detectors and X-ray machines take over the entrances to our public spaces: in the name of security, crude function trumps form. With little resistance, Americans now surrender themselves and their possessions to mysterious technologies and allow strangers to pry into their lives and possessions. Airport hallways designed for walking or the display of public art are transformed into networks of cattle lines through which human beings must navigate and surrender bodies and baggage to state inspection. These retrofitted spaces create their own warped ambiance in which it would not seem completely out of place for post-9/11 retrofitted airport security functionaries to conduct full cavity searches in crowded airport hallways designed for walking, not rectal exams.

Brazil's technological failures are artifacts of an empire in a state of slow col-lapse—though the population's attention directed towards the terror war keeps it from focusing on state failures and corruptions. Things don't work as the engineers envisioned: the floor-plugs designed to readily fill holes drilled when capturing prisoners are the wrong size; heating systems fluctuate; elevators malfunction; even the food is unappetizing. Some of the technology used to detect terrorism appears to be fake: when entering public buildings and restaurants all but the state is obliged to pass bag and packages though X-ray machines—but these machines offer the public false assurances, as the exact same x-rayed contents appear on the monitoring screens regardless of what bag has been passed through them.[9] This is a technology of control, though those controlled are not apparently real or imagined terrorists; they are the public who believe this controlling, invasive state is needed to protect their freedom and privacy.

State Power, State Lies

The identity or cause of *Brazil*'s alleged terrorists is unclear, but each attack strengthens governmental power and authority, as the fear accompanying the attacks reinforces justifications for harsh state actions. The opening scene shows the Ministry of Information Deputy Minister, Eugene Helpman, being asked in a televised interview if he believes "that the government is winning the battle against terrorists." Helpman replies with a familiar sort of sports metaphor, saying: "Oh yes. Our morale is much higher than theirs. We're fielding all their strokes, running a lot of them out, and pretty consistently knocking them for six. I'd say they're nearly out of the game."[10]

When asked about the motivation of the recent terrorist attacks, the Deputy Minister Helpman replies: "Bad sportsmanship. A ruthless minority of people seems to have forgotten certain good old-fashioned virtues. They just can't stand seeing the other fellow win. If these people would just play the game . . ."[11] It was this same logic claiming that "terrorists don't play by the rules" that was used by the Bush administration to justify extreme renditions and other forms of torture and abuse of "terror suspects," as if the only way to win against a cheating opponent is to also cheat—and once cheating becomes normalized, it is no longer seen as cheating.

While the state violates the rule of law, citizens are expected to blindly obey all laws. Expectations that people will "follow the rules" are the foundation of social life in *Brazil*. When bureaucrats violate the rules by kidnapping and killing the wrong citizen, other rules must be violated to establish a paper trail of bureaucratic legitimacy. In *Brazil*, Lowry becomes expendable to maintain the myth that rules are being followed. Despite the state's obvious failures, its authority in *Brazil* is supreme; Tuttle becomes an enemy of state because he deviates from state protocols by repairing broken heating equipment using techniques not sanctioned by the state. Tuttle's actions inform us that terrorism has become any non-state sanctioned act. Unauthorized repairs become "sabotage" and transform Tuttle into "a freelance subversive."

In *Brazil*, the state appears to gain more strength with every claimed terror attack, but as the charges levied against Sam Lowry indicate, there are good reasons to doubt state claims of widespread terrorism. In post-9/11 America, every claimed advance against terrorism (captured documents, claims of thwarted plans, heightened terror alert levels following presidential approval slumps) empowers and apparently justifies the expansion of Homeland Security and other national and domestic security agencies.

Terror attacks do not in themselves reduce freedom, but they can clear the way for state responses that do. The greater the representations of threats, the more power can be taken by state authority. States battling terrorism create self-fulfilling prophecies as standard forms of deviance are reclassified as terror crimes, and all who undertake anti-state activities are seen as being "with the terrorists."

In some sense, in both worlds, it does not matter who the terrorists are, for the power and reach of the state is intensified with each terror attack, real or perceived. *Brazil* raises questions about who is behind the terror campaigns strengthening the government's power. Outside of the film, Gilliam discussed whether the state is responsible for the terror attacks:

> [The] question that always came up in these discussions was: are the terrorists real? To which I would always say that I don't know if they are, because this huge organization has to survive at all costs, so if there is no real terrorism it has to invent terrorists to maintain itself—that's what organizations do. This always came as a big surprise to them, and they wanted answers: was the explosion in the restaurant a terrorist one? Again, I said I didn't know, it might just be part of the system that went bang, which happens all the time.[12]

While the US government has not perpetrated similar acts of domestic terror, it has usurped new centralized powers by exploiting fears of such attacks. Functionally, it doesn't matter that the state did not undertake the attacks of 9/11; it used the fear generated by these events to further expand its power and control.[13]

Nice People and Torture

America's post-9/11 reliance on torture, secret prisons, kidnappings, and renditions connects our world with *Brazil*—but even more significantly, there is a thematic similarity in the pleasantness surrounding individual interactions of members of a society so committed to performing and ignoring acts of dehumanization.

Prisoners being transported in hooded suits fill the background of *Brazil*. We see vans with hooded prisoners, even children playing interrogation in the streets using paper bags to cover prisoners' heads. These scenes conjure images of Guantánamo, Abu Ghraib and the CIA's kidnappings, called "secret renditions."

Brazil depicts how "nice people" with families, pets, and pleasant manners engage in heartless acts of inhumanity as part of their daily duties at work—work from which they disassociate any personal responsibility, instead rationalizing their participation as the normalized social functions required of them. As individuals, these are "nice" people in much the same way that American slave owners were, as described by Chomsky in the film *The Corporation* (2003): many individuals have been "nice people" engaged in a social system based on the ownership of human beings as property. "Nice people" are socialized to distance themselves and their sense of self from the inevitable negative impacts of what they do to the world they inhabit.

The clinically white, sanitary hallway of the 50th Floor of the Ministry of Information Retrieval has a single red drop of blood on the floor. A smiling, big-haired secretary is seen typing transcripts of an interrogation session in which she transcribes: "Why am I here? . . . [What] is that you are putting on my head? . . . Ahhhhh, oh god . . . no, don't . . . ohh, please . . . Stop! . . . I can't stand . . . Aiiiieeeeee . . . oooohhh . . . ahhhhh . . . please . . ." Gilliam described this motherly secretary as:

> . . . the cheeriest, the sweetest woman that we could find, yet doing this [e.g., tran-scribing a torture session] with no sense of what it means, [with] no sense of the awfulness. That's one of the things that amazes me about the human animal: how it can separate its mind from reality and from awfulness and carry on . . .. these are the "survivors," these are the ones that keep the species going. They don't think about things, they just accept things or they approach them with positive joy . . . I'm sure these people exist all around the world, in every secret service organization; the CIA has got those people—they're out there—they do the job, they don't think about it, they do the paperwork. I think everybody in this world is doing it.[14]

In interrogator Jack Lint's comfortably decorated office, his daughter sits playing with toys while her father tortures people in the next room, fulfilling his job and duties at the Ministry of Information Retrieval. There's nothing personal about any of this; Lint is just doing his job. As Gilliam observed:

> We were talking about [Jack Lint, Michael Palin's character] being a father and husband, an all-round nice guy, but we weren't showing it. So we brought in my three-year-old-daughter, Holly, to play his daughter. Same dialogue, but now he's down there playing with bricks and blocks and she's got her little lines, and the scene just goes *whoosh*, because now he's talking about torture while playing with a kid.[15]

Over the past half-century a wide range of social psychological experiments establish how social circumstances conspire to turn "good people" into agents of circum-stance, surrendering their authority to other forces. Stanley Milgram's experimental examination of how authoritarian situations will lead most people to administer what they believe are harmful, even possibly lethal, shocks, tells us that research subjects will surrender to administrators overseeing the experiments if they believe it is all part of an accepted system. Solomon Asch demonstrated how individuals suppress their own interpretations of events to coalesce with group interpretations that are clearly in error. And Irving Janis's conception of "groupthink" explained how institutional settings develop their own mindset that coaxes the silencing of dissent and helps develop and maintain institutional limits that shape the range of perceived options for dealing with a particular problem.[16] Through such processes, social formations normalize and rationalize the inhumane and irrational in ways that come to make sense to those in these worlds.

The reliance on and forms of state torture in *Brazil* have striking parallels in post-9/11 America. All interrogation methods (even forms of coercive interrogation) are

designed to coax subjects into coming around to providing interrogators with information that they don't want to give up. Torture is generally ineffective as a means
of gaining information from uncooperative individuals. But torture is also effective
in getting individuals to make private or public "confessions," though torture can
only be considered "effective" if one cares only about the act of confession and not
the truth of the confession.

The effectiveness of torture and interrogation methods has been studied by the
CIA for decades.[17] One of the consistent findings of the CIA's interrogation studies
is that while some "coercive interrogation" techniques can produce decent flows of
information (these techniques include depriving subjects of regular sleep, placing
them in positions in which they cause themselves harm, asking questions in gibberish, etc.), the sort of torture techniques depicted in *Brazil* and practiced in Abu
Ghraib and during extreme renditions generally can get individuals subjected to
these techniques to *confess* to acts but they do not necessarily lead to the extraction
of true information that subjects do not wish to disclose. The CIA's 1963 *Kubark*
manual found that the sort of blunt force and direct pain depicted in *Brazil* could
lead prisoners to make confessions, but the truth of these confessions was unknown;
while more refined techniques relying less on physical pain and more on skillful
manipulations and questioning in environments marked by minor discomforts
elicited much more truthful information.[18]

Using torture to elicit (false) confessions makes logical sense in the twisted world
of *Brazil* where interrogators are more interested in establishing blame than they
are in finding truth—utilizing similar practices in our world suggests a similarity
of intent and must give us pause.

The State's Panoptical View

In both post-9/11 America and *Brazil*, fears of terrorism are used to allow the state
to extend its panoptical view into the lives of all. One cut dream sequence from
Brazil contained a segment known as the "eyeball sequence" in which Sam Lowry
dreams he is soaring across the sky and encounters a horizon filled with eyeballs
looking skyward. A stone tower protrudes upward amongst the eyes, and, as flying
Lowry approaches, each of the eyeballs independently follow him as he flies to the
top of the tower.

Brazil is full of clumsy machines with cameras dangling from accordion-
protruding arms that press up against, inspect, and invade people entering ministry
buildings. State surveillance apparatus is everywhere. Even private spaces require
individuals to surrender their privacy and dignity, as X-ray machines inspect packages, purses, and hand-held items. Metal detectors and bomb detecting devices
screen everyone entering restaurants and other public spaces. These screening
devices have become part of the background ambience of this world, and, while they
are shown to be ineffective (by the continued detonation of bombs in public spaces),
the ubiquitous presence of these machines serves as an advertisement for the need
of the totalitarian state, while forcing all citizens to participate in daily humiliation

rituals in which their private personhood is surrendered to a state ready to degrade them with invasions, all in the name of the public good.[19]

Sam Lowry acts with an awareness that there is no real privacy, that all acts and all intentions must be negotiated within view of the state. *Brazil*'s world has surrendered to the inevitability of panopticism. There is no space which can be assumed to be out of view; yet the inefficiency and stupidity of the state offers its own twisted hope of freedom as omnipresence is not the same thing as omnipotence.

The spread and acceptance of state surveillance cameras in post-9/11 British and American cities marks a transition of boundaries where once private spheres become public, and desires for privacy generate suspicions. The UK now boasts over four million closed-circuit surveillance cameras (that works out to about one camera for every 14 people)—many capable of remote control and zooming, some with speakers allowing remote agents of state to command those under surveillance to perform desired behaviors. Chicago, America's surveillance capital, trails far behind, with about 600 hi-tech, computer-driven cameras capable of identifying and tracking individuals and car license plates—but for Chicago proper this is still only one camera per 5,000 people.[20] Surely, eyeball-affixed surveillance cameras at the entrance to all public buildings cannot be far behind.

Police States and the Bureaucracy of Fear

Fear empowers *Brazil*'s leaders to justify whatever actions they desire. Nothing is *supposed* to be safe. If it were, there would be no need for this state, itself a fear-based Hobbsian Leviathan whose members surrender their rights to reap presumed protections—but such surrenders paradoxically create the need for protection from these very states. In *Brazil* these conditions have formed a self-reinforcing möbius loop of dependency and co-evolution in which the more fear and tension is generated, the stronger the state becomes. Gilliam saw *Brazil*'s government as being driven by the peoples' fears of terror, which in turn fueled a dynamic where fear of terrorism was more powerful than actual terrorism. Gilliam recalls that:

> In my original ideas about the film, the Ministry didn't know whether there were terrorists out there or not because over the years they had so many counter-agents and counter-counter-agents out there and agent provocateurs who maybe set explosions to lure people in, that people lost track of whether there really were terrorists or not. But the most important thing was that the belief in terrorists had to be maintained to allow the Ministry to continue to survive.[21]

In *Brazil*, bureaucracy, paper, and accountability direct actions more than any sense of duty or right and wrong. The Ministry of Information is filled with busy-looking bureaucrats occupying crowded work stations, pretending to work at their computers while actually watching cowboy and Indian dramas on their screens. One can easily imagine parallel scenes routinely occurring deep within the bowels of Homeland Security where rows of functionaries hide screens with YouTube, Twitter,

Facebook, and network circus extravaganzas from patrolling managers. On a daily basis, the mundane business of the terror war has only a passing concern so far as it gives the office of both worlds a purpose for existence, regardless of outcomes.

One measure of the gravitational force inflicted by *Brazil*'s bureaucratic governmental structures (where employees worry more about adjusting to fit bureaucratic structures than about terrorists) is seen in a party scene where Jack Lint's wife Allison is mistakenly called "Barbara" by his boss. Lint not only does not correct his boss, but in a later scene he refers to his wife as "Barbara," so as not make his boss aware of this mistake. When Lowry asks him if he's going to keep calling her Barbara, Lint says, "Why ever not? Barbara's a perfectly good name isn't it?"

Brazil's terror state is justified with the same McCarthyistic false choices President Bush used to pitch his terror war months after the 9/11 attacks when he declared: "you are either with us or you are with the terrorists."[22] When Jill asks Sam, "doesn't it bother you, the sort of things you do in Information Retrieval?" Sam avoids confronting his own complicity in a system that will ultimately destroy him and automatically replies: "What? I suppose you'd rather have terrorists?" Such false choices are taught through the indoctrinations of state and obscure the ways that engaging in torture and other atrocities converts individuals and governments into agencies of state terror.

After Sam Lowry is arrested and placed in a hooded canvas-bag that looks like a mailbag, he is brought before the law where he is advised of his charges—most of which, ironically, stem from his efforts to assist his boss, Mr. Kurtzmann, in resolving the unfortunate Tuttle/Buttle matter. Lowry is then offered a number of financial options relating to the payment of his coming trial and interrogation should he not confess to the charges against him. The scene is shown through Sam's eye, looking through the slot in the hooded prisoner suit he wears, as his canvas-bag is hung from a track on the ceiling. In the distant background viewers can just make out shadowed outlines of prisoners hanging from the ceiling as they are brought before similar desks for processing and then moved down the line like a cattle carcass in a slaughterhouse. A kindly functionary advises Lowry to "plead guilty, it's easier and cheaper for everyone." Sam has been transformed into an object in the bureaucratic processes in which he has been a detached functionary for years.

It was the historical precedence of this practice of charging prisoners for their own interrogation that initially inspired Gilliam to construct this world where one's credit would be used to fund their own torture. Gilliam reports that,

> ... the initial spark for *Brazil* really came from a seventeenth-century document I stumbled across from a time when witch-hunts were at their height. This was a chart of the costs of different tortures and you had to pay for those inflicted on you; if you were found guilty and sentenced to death, you had to pay for every bundle of faggots that burned you. I started thinking about the guy who was a clerk in the court and had to be present while the tortures were going on, to take down testimonies. It's an awful job, but this man has a wife and kids to support, so how does he deal with it? That's actually where *Brazil* really started.[23]

If one accepts capitalism's fundamental premise that markets are capable of taking care of human needs, then it is hardly an excess of logical efficiency to propose not only that all individuals, including children, be responsible for financing their own medical care, but also the financing of their own interrogation, imprisonment, or even execution. Such extensions of the logic of market forces continue rather than reformulate fundamental elements of our social formulations of the rights and duties of *Homo economicus*.

The market forces and economic needs weigh heavily on the actions and consciousness of the inhabitants of post-9/11 America and *Brazil*. And both of these worlds share similar expectations of economic consumption as duties to be upheld by all members of society, not as an act of self-gratification, but as a commitment to a greater good.

Consumerism and Business as Usual

Brazil's inhabitants work to find distractions from the fear, alienation, and terror permeating their world; these distractions help "responsible" people learn to not think about what is going on. Plastic surgery is a primary obsession of citizens, itself a means of diverting one's attention and outward appearance. When the pleasant tune of the song "Brazil" is interrupted on Sam Lowry's car radio with a news bulletin of a terrorist bombing, he just changes the station to another, seeking more distracting music. When a bomb blast rips through an elegant restaurant and shrapnel kills and maims diners in one section of the room, the gunpowder-charred string quartet continues to play while unscathed diners resume their meal beside the carnage. *Brazil*'s war without end rages as the appearance of middle class life as usual dominates the foreground and lives of the populous. With wounded diners in the background, the blather of consumer culture continues as Sam's mother tells her friend: "I saw the most wonderful idea for Christmas presents at the chemists: gift tokens, medical gift tokens!" The maître d' profusely apologizes for the ruckus and a folding screen is dragged out and set next to the table so that the diners do not have to view the mayhem. The maintenance of consumer normalcy is a vital background feature of *Brazil*'s terror war.

Consumerism helps citizens avoid coping with the contradictions posed by the terror war. Advertisements for luxury items and vacation escapes populate the background and periphery of scenes. Fear is used to market products to *Brazil*'s consumers. In the background of one scene a poster advertises a high-security luxury cruise vacation on an extravagant cruise ship with a squadron of retro-aircraft flying watch overhead. The poster's slogan reads: "Mellowfields, Top Security Holiday Camps. Luxury without fear. Fun without suspicion. Relax in a panic-free atmosphere." In the film scene's foreground, five children play a game in which they imitate the police. One child uses a toy machine gun to capture another, as a third child stands wrapped up with a bag over his head, like the adult prisoners packed by the state. The child says with playful conviction: "I'll never confess." The children are mimicking scenes in which parents and other loved ones have been kidnapped and murdered by the bureaucratic state that envelops their lives. These are the playful fantasies of children living in a society where reminders of the terror war are everywhere. In post-9/11 America, the terror war's reach became so far-reaching that fears of terrorists took over the imaginations of the children of South Park.[24]

American corporate and governmental reactions to 9/11 transformed America's economy by commodifying fear and promises of safety in new ways. Surveillance gear, protective clothing, crazed sales of plastic tarps and duct tape (for jerry-rigged "biosafe rooms"), weapons sales, and a new prevalence of tank-like cars mark American efforts to buy and sell, based on promises of safety. The post-9/11 world brought increases in criminal background checks for employment, renting homes, school attendance, public parenting, and even dating.[25] All forms of public and private engagements with the world began to subject all to new losses of privacy and increased public scrutiny.

Brazil's world merges religion, state, and consumerism towards a common purpose. In a Christmas street scene, a group of people in a public square march down the street under a banner reading "Consumers for Christ," with a standard depicting a cross with a dollar sign affixed.[26] When Santa Claus asks a child what she wants for Christmas, she replies, "my own credit card." As *Brazil*'s endless war wages onward, citizens are expected to shop.

The 9/11 attacks initially brought an economic downturn as airlines and other sectors absorbed the economic blow. Under a banner of patriotism, President Bush urged Americans to consume at pre-attack levels, encouraging citizen-consumers to take extravagant trips to Disney World and to consume mass qualities of durable goods as a means of reviving the lagging economy. One 2003 Bush initiative mailed American families with children checks made out for $400 per child, as a "bonus" to help push the economy back on track—though, as many disgruntled families later discovered, this "bonus" was only an advance on the tax exemption refund they would have received later the next year when they completed their tax returns. This governmental incentive transformed consumption from an economic choice into a patriotic duty—as if circulating one's own money were a means of transforming consumption into a sacrament of state.

Three months after 9/11, Stuart Elliott wrote a cutting piece in the *New York Times* examining how political and economic forces were converging to mix patriotism, consumerism, and civic duty.[27] Elliott contrasted the current era with World War II campaigns which unified national action, noting that:

> Compared with the high-minded work that agencies created during World War II, much of it demanding sacrifice from citizens, today's advertising relies far more on reassurances that victory is achievable through sybaritism. The mantra of the booming economy of the 1990s, 'Shop till you drop,' has been replaced with a millennium mutation: 'Shop till Osama drops.'[28]

Elliott analyzed several grotesque national advertising campaigns exploiting the national tragedy by conflating consumerism and patriotic duty:

Take for instance the campaign for General Motors carrying the theme "Keep America rolling," which sought successfully to stimulate automobile sales after Sept. 11 with zero percent loans. The first print ad spent two paragraphs recounting how "the world as we knew it came to a halt" and how the attacks "shook us to our very core."

Then the ad shrewdly took a brisk U-turn: "Now it's time to move forward. For years, the auto industry has played a crucial role in our economy. General Motors takes that responsibility seriously." The ad, by the Troy, Mich., office of McCann-Erickson Worldwide Advertising, concluded with this deft blend of selflessness and self-interest: "This may very well be the most serious crisis our nation has ever faced. In this time of terrible adversity, let's stand together. And keep America rolling."[29]

This process merged Brand America with Brand GM—united by fear and a patriotic duty to keep the economy rolling: perhaps the only missing feature of this arrangement that would connect our world with that of *Brazil* is found in this advertisement's restraint from claiming that Jesus himself would have driven a GM car, if given the opportunity.

The ability to continue high mass consumption is all-important in both worlds. In *Brazil*, a guard lashing Sam Lowry's arm to an interrogation chair in the Ministry of Information Retrieval earnestly advises him: "Don't fight it son. Confess quickly! If you hold out too long, you could jeopardize your credit rating." Sam Lowry's arrest and booking process includes discussing financial options and implications derived from the expenses of his own upcoming interrogation.

Conclusions: "That's the beauty of it"

When Universal Studios head, Sid Sheinberg, realized what a long, dark movie *Brazil* had become, he demanded that a shorter, happier version of the film be released. Gilliam fought back in an intense public campaign demanding the release of the film he'd made; the fight culminated in Gilliam's victory, after he screened a stolen print of his version to film critics assembled in a USC classroom.[30] Though Gilliam's version was released to American audiences, Sheinberg's more upbeat "Love Conquers All" version has been shown on network television broadcasts and was released in VCR and DVD versions. In this alternate reality, Sam Lowry escapes his tortures; various elements of *Brazil*'s world are altered or hidden from the audience, creating a more hopeful viewing experience of this totalitarian world where Sam is also not culpable for any of his world's atrocities.

Perhaps one other way that *Brazil* provides a lens through which we can view the trajectories and false fronts of post-9/11 America is to consider Sheinberg's warped re-envisionment of how Gilliam's nightmare could be sweetened into a false representation of an oppressive world. While Sheinberg's "Love Conquers All" version destroyed the integrity of *Brazil*, it does provide us with an artifact of false representation of the brutal nature of *Brazil*'s world in a way that helps us understand how Bush and others strove to misrepresent the post-9/11 world.

Because one of the studio's roles is to provide escape, the cuts they chose in the "Love Conquers All" version provide information on specific cultural discomforts. Studio editors were worried about the social discomfort created by a bleak totalitarian world dominated in this fictional terror war, and what they cut informs us about what we don't want to know about worlds like *Brazil*—perhaps what they cut can alert us to the sort of painful features of America's post-9/11 predicament that its leaders likewise strove to eliminate from public narratives.

The "Love Conquers All" studio edit reshaped the story so that Sam was no longer seen to be an active contributor to the totalitarian state's oppressive machinery—even Sam's knowledge of the state's murder of Buttle was removed. Sam's mother's manipulation of his personal and professional life was excised, along with our view into his rich escapist fantasy life; Tuttle is represented as part of an actual terrorist/resistance network. But the most egregious misrepresentation in this version was the false idea that Sam had successfully fought the oppressive state and escaped to freedom—instead of being tortured to death as part of a petty administrative cover-up.

These studio cuts inform us of what we aren't supposed to realize about *Brazil*'s world, but they also parallel what we aren't supposed to think about in post-9/11 America. What Sheinberg redacts bleeds over into our world, a world where we are reluctant to see that: we all have a supportive role in the state; we all know that bad things are happening and our everyday interactions tame us and get us to go along with them; even our silence is a form of participation; we are not free to choose many of our most personal matters; most of us can only dream of heroic anti-state acts; resistance to the state is futile; and those like Tuttle who do not do things in accordance with state protocols are suspect as being "with the terrorists." These edits turn Sam into a heroic character fighting back rather than revealing him to be a hapless everyman who would go along with it all if not for his love. But most significantly, all of these cuts and edits deny the viewer from seeing just how deep the world of hurt that Sam Lowry is, and by extension *we* are, in.

Brazil displays the logical extension of common bureaucratic state formations leading toward what Max Weber described as "the iron cage of rationality," where contingencies of interlocked rules and structures remove individuals from taking responsibility for their actions and outcomes. *Brazil* depicts a world where people have been socialized to become Weberian "specialists without spirit, sensualists without hearts," and it is Lowry's individualistic movement towards love—to become a sensualist with a heart—that sets him on his doomed heroic course.[31]

Finally, if *Brazil* offers a prophetic (if not poetically un-concrete) commentary on post-9/11 America, we obviously have much to be concerned about. *Brazil* depicts a familiar world marked by loss of personal freedoms and privacy, the creation of bureaucratic social structures demanding increasing compliance, and the empowerment of a centralized surveillance state. In post-9/11 America, then, one of our chief concerns should be to try and imagine how a self-fueling, self-justifying, non-falsifiable terror war like that in *Brazil* could ever end. Terror wars seem to offer no self-controlling dynamic to limit or curtail the ever-increasing power of a centralized state that both creates and feeds on fear, while using fear to justify atrocities both mundane and horrific. If *Brazil* is any guide to elements of our world, it is difficult to imagine an endgame for such a terror war.

As Jack Lint observes, almost as a declaration of faith: "Everything's connected—all along the line. Cause and effect. That's the beauty of it. Our job [at Information Retrieval] is to trace the connections and reveal them." It does not matter that the "connections" between Tuttle and Jill are imaginary; their connections will still be traced in ways similar to the Bush administration's fantastical claims that there are connections between the attacks of 9/11 and Saddam Hussein. Terror wars by their very nature feed on unverifiable speculation, and lack of proof means nothing to those driving terror war crusades that are inherently unfalsifiable.

Post-9/11 America finds itself with a frighteningly expanding Homeland Security state, the curtailment of which seems unfathomable because a lack of terrorist attacks is used to justify the success of programs based on massive totalitarian assaults of privacy and civil rights, just as the occurrence of terrorist attacks is used to justify these same programs. This dynamic leads to a lack of consequences and obvious checks and balances that could subdue the spread and reach of the terror state, unless individuals within the system seek solutions by rising up in Tuttle-like rebellion, or escaping to an inward refuge like Sam Lowry.

Notes

1   My interpretation of *Brazil* benefited from discussion with Thomas Abel, Thomas Anson, Jeff Birkenstein, Alex Cockburn, Marvin Harris, Midge Price, and Lisa Queen.
2   Cited Versions of *Brazil*: BDC *Brazil, Director's Commentary* (Criterion Collection Disk One) and BLCA *Brazil, "Love Conquers All" Version* (Criterion Collection, Disk Three).
3   See 10/4/06 http://www.youtube.com/watch?v=1dC1GAIHMOo (accessed October 16, 2009).
4   David Cowen, "*Brazil* (Movie, 1985) Frequently Asked Questions v1.3," 1996, http://www.faqs.org/faqs/movies/brazil-faq/(accessed October 16, 2009).
5   *Brazil* [BDC], DVD, directed by Terry Gilliam (1985; New York: Criterion Collection, 2006), 36:30.
6   When illegally held detainees at Gitmo (Guantánamo Bay) committed suicide, Rear Admiral Harry Harris claimed such suicides were acts of asymmetrical warfare (Timothy Lynch, *Doublespeak and the War on Terrorism*, CATO Institute Briefing Paper 98, September 6, 2006: 4).
7   American Dialect Society, "Word of the Year Press Release," January 4, 2008, http://www.americandialect.org/Word-of-the-Year_2007.pdf (accessed October 16, 2009).
8   *Brazil* BDC, 0:05.
9   Ibid., 18:33 and 18:49.
10   Jack Mathews, *The Battle of* Brazil (New York: Applause, 1987), 186.
11   Ibid., 185.
12   Terry Gilliam and Ian Christie (ed.), *Gilliam on Gilliam* (London: Faber and Faber Limited), 131–2.
13   David Altheide, *Terrorism and the Politics of Fear* (Lanham, MD: Alta Mira Press, 2006).
14   *Brazil* BDC, 1:16.
15   Gilliam and Christie, *Gilliam on Gilliam*, 127.
16   Irving Janis, *Victims of Groupthink* (Boston: Houghton Mifflin, 1972); Stanley Milgram, "Some Conditions of Obedience and Disobedience to Authority," *Human Relations* 18 (1965): 57–76; Philip Zimbardo, *The Lucifer Effect* (New York: Random House, 2007).

17   Alfred McCoy, *A Question of Torture: CIA Interrogation from the Cold War to the War on Terror* (New York: Macmillan, 2006); David Price, "Buying a Piece of Anthropology, Part Two: The CIA and Our Tortured Past," *Anthropology Today* 23.5 (2007): 17–22.

18   CIA, *Kubark Counterintelligence Interrogation* [Manual], July 1963 [Declassified]; CIA, *Human Resource Exploitation Training Manual*, 1983 [Declassified].

19   Harold Garfinkel, "Conditions of Successful Degradation Ceremonies," *American Journal of Sociology* 61.1 (1956): 420–4; David Price, *Threatening Anthropology* (Durham: Duke University Press), 23–6.

20   David Schaper, "Chicago's Video Surveillance Gets Smarter," NPR, *All Things Considered*, October 26, 2007).

21   *Brazil* BDC, 1:40.

22   George W. Bush, "Address to a Joint Session of Congress and the American People," *Whitehouse.gov*, September 20, 2001.

23   Gilliam, *Gilliam on Gilliam*, 132.

24   Trey Parker, "Imaginationland," *South Park*, Season 11, Episode 2, first aired October 17, 2007.

25   Altheide, *Terrorism and the Politics of Fear.*

26   *Brazil* BDC, 1:37.

27   Stuart Elliott, "The Media Business: Advertising; Madison Ave. Grapples with Post-Sept 11 Era," *New York Times*, December 11, 2001.

28   Ibid.

29   Ibid.

30   Mathews, *Battle of* Brazil.

31   Max Weber, *The Protestant Ethic and the Spirit of Capitalism* (New York: Scribners & Sons, 1904 [1958]), 182.

CHAPTER 15

Cultural Anxiety, Moral Clarity, and Willful Amnesia: Filming Philip K. Dick After 9/11

LANCE RUBIN

"We're an empire now, and when we act we create our own reality. And while you're studying that reality—judiciously, as you will—we'll act again, creating other new realities, which you can study too."[1]

—Senior advisor to George W. Bush, 2004

Though Philip K. Dick struggled to find a wider audience in his lifetime, twenty-first century audiences have found his work to be a prescient commentary on the nature of reality, identity, history, and power. To date, Dick's fiction has been adapted into five major motion pictures since 2001: Steven Spielberg's *Minority Report* (2002), Gary Fleder's *Imposter* (2002), John Woo's *Paycheck* (2003), Richard Linklater's *A Scanner Darkly* (2006), and Lee Tamahori's *Next* (2007).[2] While *Blade Runner* (Ridley Scott, 1982) and *Total Recall* (Paul Verhoeven, 1990) prompted a fresh look at his perceptive vision of the not-so-distant future, many perceptions of the world after September 11, 2001, have come to mirror the cultural machinations Dick prefigured in his writing. His Cold War-era stories are finding a second life since 9/11 and the Bush administration's "War on Terror"[3] because of their engagement with remarkably similar central debates and characteristic obsessions of their cultures.[4] Both Dick's fiction and their film adaptations can be evaluated through what Clifford Geertz calls the "thick description" of culture, the sustained and complex positions in relation to the discourse of their respective Americas.[5] The films discussed in this essay are not simply reflections of events and conditions but participate in shaping audience judgments surrounding the manipulation of memory and identity, social cohesion and class, and political and military power.

After 9/11, the Bush administration scripted official explanations for the attacks and the nation's response to them: "the construction of an enemy image; the avoidance of blame on any other than the enemy; a definition of core values that were at risk; and a claim to global leadership."[6] A largely obedient media ignored how these narratives—millennial beliefs of a world divided between Good and Evil; an eschatology seeing liberal democracy as the only blueprint for all nations; a desire for American military power to influence foreign policy—were being constructed from subjective political and teleological ideologies held by "neoconservative" groups like the American Enterprise Institute and Project for the New American Century. Their missionary politics were immediately "championed as the logical solution [of] a new world," while their messianic discourse "enshrined a referential framework in which official interpretations [of American response to 9/11] received the benefit of the doubt to the exclusion of other more moderate responses."[7] The strategy included stoking fervent nationalism, establishing a demonic enemy, and "reinterpreting or downright falsifying history" so dogmatically that "debate (let alone dissent) is chilled."[8]

These post-9/11 political maneuverings were also on full display during the Cold War, and they fascinated Dick. His work returns constantly to the manipulation of truth and the subtle tyranny maintained by nationalism, fear, and religious conviction.[9] Marked by amnesia, false memory, splintered identity, Dick's protagonists stand as powerful allegories for the confusion, paranoia, and phenomenological uncertainly about memory and identity in post-9/11 America. Rather than externalizing threats in the Manichean mantra of "with us or against us," *Minority Report*, *Imposter*, *Paycheck*, and *A Scanner Darkly* suggest that the menaces to freedom are much closer. They articulate an internalization of the "War on Terror," the willful forfeiture of our humanity to those who would manipulate our memories and identities for political ideals that disregard the lives of individuals in the name of a professed greater good.

"The New and Improved Clarity": Pre-Crime and Preemptive War

Spielberg's *Minority Report* (2002) is a prescient exploration of the neoconservative discourse that influenced American attitudes after 9/11, especially the policy of preemption. Set in the mid-twenty-first century, John Anderton (Tom Cruise) heads the Washington, DC, department of Pre-Crime, which imprisons would-be criminals before they act. Pre-Crime centers on three clairvoyants (called "Precogs") who are immobilized in a drug-laced pool, their brains wired to machines that read their future visions of violent crimes. Washington's murder rate is almost nonexistent under Pre-Crime, and its co-founder, now District Attorney Lamar Burgess (Max Von Sydow) is close to getting national approval for the program when Anderton himself appears in the Precogs' memory of the future. As he flees, Anderton tries to find who he is predicted to kill and why. Through Pre-Crime's other co-founder, Iris Hineman (Lois Smith), Anderton learns that the Precogs sometimes disagree about the future. When they do, the dissenting forecast—the "minority report," usually seen by the female Precog Agatha (Samantha Morton)—is suppressed so as to make the system look flawless. Freeing Agatha to help solve his future crime, Anderton eventually finds Leo Crow (Mike Binder), who appears to have killed Anderton's son Sean. Though Anderton resists revenge, Crow shoots himself with Anderton's gun, but not before he reveals he has been set up; that Burgess himself has orchestrated Sean's death, knowing Anderton would become an unwavering supporter of

Pre-Crime. In addition, Burgess has suppressed a minority report of his own murder of Agatha's mother Ann Lively so as to keep her precognitive daughter enslaved in the name of national security. Pre-Crime is thus exposed as morally corrupt, despite the noble intentions upon which it is founded.

Pre-Crime's appearance of success, predicated on silencing voices articulating alternative outcomes about the future, makes for a number of rich connections to America's "War on Terror." Scared, anxious, and angry, Americans after 9/11, like those in *Minority Report*'s future America, sought an outlet for their vengeance and newfound vulnerability. Glossing over the details of how the government was assuring safety, they embraced policies of preemption. Pre-Crime's arrest of would-be murderers, like the rationale for preemptive strikes on Iraq, is predicated on the need, as President Bush proclaimed in 2002, to "take the battle to the enemy": "If we wait for threats to fully materialize, we will have waited too long."[10] Three months later, the *National Security Strategy of the United States* (NSS) announced the policy of preemption by redefining the idea of "imminence" from visible confirmation of military forces preparing for attack to intelligence suggesting "rogue states" or "terrorists" may, eventually, attack America. The NSS policy was championed as the only rational form of national defense in an age of terrorism and bolstered by Dick Cheney's so-called "one percent doctrine." Told of the possibility that al-Qaeda was in contact with Pakistani nuclear scientists, Cheney responded, "If there's a one percent chance" that the report is true, "we have to treat it as a certainty in terms of our response. It's not about our analysis, or finding a preponderance of evidence."[11] With one percent likelihood as the new threshold, America would now act on all conceivable threats as if they were certain to happen rather than analyze the probabilities.

The assertiveness with which these policies were announced echoes Pre-Crime's confidence in its system. "The commission of the crime is absolute metaphysics," Officer Fletcher (Neal McDonough) tells Danny Witwer (Colin Farrell), a Department of Justice agent questioning the legality of "arresting individuals who have broken no laws."[12] The "absolute metaphysics" of both Pre-Crime's mission and the NSS policy, however, is dependent upon conclusive, corroborated data forecasting an impending act of aggression. But as the Precogs' vision of Anderton's guilt and Ann Lively's murder contained minority reports, the CIA's post-9/11 intelligence on Iraq was far from conclusive. In the same way Burgess suppresses Pre-Crime's ambiguity, the White House manipulated forecasts of the future to meet their own predetermined decisions. Without clear evidence that Iraq had the means to attack America, Donald Rumsfeld and Paul Wolfowitz created the Office of Special Plans, which offered its own assessment of the data. As Gerald Huiskamp documents, any conclusions in the intelligence reports that contradicted "the corresponding preferred policy of regime change . . . [were] erased from the public record" before "any seeds of insidious doubt might be sown."[13] These real life minority reports withheld evidence while the White House "made allegations depicting Iraq's nuclear weapons program as more active, more certain, and more imminent in its threat than the data they had would support."[14] Forecasts of a military "cakewalk" and American soldiers being greeted as liberators were propelled to the realm of "absolute metaphysics" through a docile media that had been cowed into compliance since 9/11 for fear of appearing unpatriotic.

In the buildup to war, the White House also positioned preemption as a moral obligation, using "aspirations to greater 'moral clarity' as the guiding light for US benevolent global hegemony."[15] In 1996, Kristol and Kagan's call for "moral clarity" in "Toward a Neo-Reaganite Foreign Policy" was a seminal moment in uniting neo-conservative desire for a "sense of the heroic" in America's conduct abroad.[16] Charles Krauthammer's "We Need Moral Clarity" (2001), David Limbaugh's "President Bush's Moral Clarity" (2001), William Bennett's *Why We Fight: Moral Clarity and the War on Terror* (2002), and Rod Martin's "September 11: Moral Clarity and the War on Terror" (2006) are but a fraction of the articles that praise George W. Bush's moral vision while advocating a preemptive strike on Iraq as part of a larger "just" war.[17] At a 2004 commencement address at Liberty University, Karl Rove also lauded Bush's "moral clarity and courage to do what's right," while Senator John McCain praised Bush's "great moral clarity" in a 2004 campaign ad.

As Anderton looks for the truth, he exposes the boundary where the "moral clarity" of Pre-Crime becomes delusion and blindness. With his son dead and his wife gone, Anderton routinely uses a drug called neuroin as he watches holographic videos of his family. In an early scene, he scours the slums of DC, called The Sprawl, looking for his eyeless neuroin dealer, who calls to Anderton from the darkness. Anderton hurriedly says, "I just need a little clarity," to which the dealer asks, "You want the customary clarity or the new and improved kind of clarity?" Anderton opts for "the new stuff." Anderton's drug-induced "clarity" is linked with Pre-Crime: as the Precogs lie suspended in a drug-filled bath reliving memories of the future, Anderton wallows in a narcotic nostalgia, reliving memories of the past to cope with the trauma of his son's death. Likewise, Pre-Crime provides an illusory sense of comfort for the citizens of Washington, DC. But both are artificial and Pre-Crime is eventually exposed as "a false justice served by artificial clarity."[18] The policy of preemption is a similar restorative remedy for the widespread sense of loss and anger after the 9/11 attacks.[19] Because our "moral clarity" was tainted with political ideology and false claims of imminence, the "War on Terror" can be seen in the same light as Pre-Crime. The "new and improved kind of clarity" where only suspicion is required is also a euphoric fantasy that provides temporary comfort but does nothing to solve the larger, systemic causes of terrorism and hatred.

The film inexorably builds to a confrontation between Anderton and Burgess, who tells Anderton early in the film that the nation admires his "absolute belief" that is "born of pain, not politics." We do not yet see the cynicism of these platitudes, but once Anderton unravels the mystery of his future, he exposes Burgess, raging against the manipulation of his memory: "You used the memory of my dead son to set me up! You knew that was the one thing that would drive me to murder." In much the same way, America's own memories of 9/11 were cynically used in the invasion of Iraq. Though the White House insisted they never explicitly connected Saddam Hussein with al-Qaeda and 9/11, it repeatedly linked them in speeches and interviews uncritically examined by the approving press, reinforcing an impression that the Iraqi dictator played a direct role on 9/11. In polling right after 9/11 attacks, asking open-ended questions about who carried them out, only 3 percent mentioned Iraq or Hussein. But by January of 2003, 44 percent of Americans reported that either "most" or "some" of the 9/11 hijackers were Iraqi citizens.[20] June 2007 polls revealed 41 percent of Americans still believed Hussein was involved in planning or financing 9/11, while 30 percent believed weapons of mass destruction were found in Iraq.[21]

Clearly, the discourse coming from the White House contributes to these false memories. Memory researcher Elizabeth Loftus has confirmed how easy it is to "distort" or "to plant false memories."[22] Many factors, including the opinions of authority figures, information repeated in the culture, the emotional intensity of the event, or an individual's internal desire to conform, all contribute to what Loftus calls "post-event information"—ideas and suggestions introduced after an event that are integrated into memory, modifying beliefs in what individuals saw, heard, or experienced. Over time, integrating post-event information with information gathered at the time of the event can combine into one seamless memory.

"It's a Good Life": Willful Amnesia in *Paycheck*

Of course, claiming Americans had their memories manipulated by the White House metanarrative about 9/11 and Iraq may be too simplistic. While the public relations campaign for war was unrelenting, John Carlos Rowe argues that the "cultural preparations for a 'just war'" relied upon "a willing audience, already prepared for certain cultural semantics adaptable to new political circumstances."[23] That is, free-trade capitalism, cultural hegemony, and military intervention appeared so natural that Americans accepted imperial practices without examining possible repercussions. So long as we were kept safe and the economy grew, we were willing to sustain our "chronic ignorance of world events" that "reinforces that the US is the center of the world."[24] Gore Vidal has renamed America the "United States of Amnesia" for its myopic perspective and unwillingness to put 9/11 into a coherent historical context. Asking certain questions would require answers that put our self-identities and complacency at risk.

Michael Jennings (Ben Affleck) in Woo's *Paycheck* registers the United States of Amnesia. Rich, confident, and healthy, Jennings is satisfied to live an unexamined life, but his comfortable existence is maintained by a purposeful amnesia. Jennings is a "reverse-engineer" who pirates new technology for other corporations to avoid copyright infringements. His activities are illegal, but he is free from this knowledge because after every project, his memories of his involvement are erased in exchange for a paycheck. Woo's film centers on Jennings' deal with college friend James Rethrick (Aaron Eckhart), owner of the Allcom corporation, who recruits Jennings to work on a three-year project, after which, in exchange for his amnesia, he will be paid nearly $100 million. Suspecting a dubious reason for the prolonged memory loss, Jennings nonetheless accepts the assignment, ignoring Rethrick's cryptic reminder of their one-time desire "to change the world." After Jennings reminds him, "I thought we wanted to *save* the world," Rethrick mutters, "Well, that's semantics." His distinction between "changing" and "saving" the world indexes the dual nature of the policy of "regime change" in Iraq after 9/11. While packaged as a mission to "save" the Iraqis (once weapons of mass destruction were not found), the 2003 Iraq invasion was ultimately motivated by the desire to "change" the Middle East to a liberal democracy receptive to global capitalism. That is, cloaked in the discourse of divine benevolence, America's messianic mission has been a boondoggle for multinational corporations and neoconservative interest groups less interested in "saving" the world than "changing" it for their benefit.[25]

Jennings' reaction to Rethrick's semantics is much like the nation's acceptance of the administration's shifting rationale for invasion. As long as Jennings reaps the rewards of forgetting work so secret even he cannot know what it is (a machine that can see into the future) he is willing to forget about the results of his complicity. Indeed, Jennings initially convinces himself that his amnesia means nothing. When his friend Shorty (Paul Giamatti) asks if he is curious about his lost memories, Jennings shrugs uncomfortably, feigning indifference to the past's significance: "What's to know?" he asks, noting the material rewards of his amnesia: "You know what the last thing I remember is? Driving in Spain in the Aston Martin. Learning to dive in Belize with what's-her-name? The seven stadiums in seven days trip . . . It's a good life." However, Jennings can live "the good life" only by allowing himself to forget the work he does for corporations like Allcom. His stance about what is worth remembering and forgetting is a fitting metaphor for America's blissfully unaware stance toward its complicity in the working of its government and corporations; actions that may have led to 9/11.[26] As Catherine Lutz claims, Americans live "with the work of forgetting required by what has been done in our names in faraway places."[27]

Indeed, since WWII, America has attempted to bring down more than 40 foreign governments and to crush more than 30 populist-nationalist movements attempting to depose insufferable regimes, while it has bombed over 20 countries and tampered in the elections and economies of dozens.[28] Americans have also traded memory for financial gain and comfort by ignoring how "the US military keeps regimes like the Saudis' in power in exchange for cheaper oil" and that our cost of living "would be higher if the United States did not train and equip the militaries that repress labor organizing in countries where the clothing is made."[29] This amnesia is reinforced by advertisers for those products. Myra Stark, a researcher for Saatchi and Saatchi, explained to clients how "Americans now have a Pre-9/11 Self and a Post-9/11 Self. They yearn to get back to their Pre-self, but when they move too far in that direction, their Post-self reacts with guilt." She advises companies to associate products with images of comfort, safety, and nostalgia. Ignoring the possibility that the multinational corporations she counsels play a role in the mounting global anger against America, Stark strengthens collective amnesia by discouraging consumers from questioning their economic behavior with images of simplicity and nostalgia. She echoes Bush's post-9/11 call to shop and to fly to Disney World; to keep the nation's economy moving rather than have real discussions about why 9/11 happened.

Our collective amnesia on the current Iraq War is similar. Through our media, Americans learn almost nothing about no-bid contracts given to corporations to rebuild Iraq, the woeful state of the Iraqi infrastructure, or the forced privatization of over 200 formerly centrally-controlled Iraqi enterprises. MSNBC reporter Ashleigh Banfield, fired for publicly speaking about the carnage that the press was suppressing, claimed that the war looked "glorious and courageous" on television: "We got rid of a dictator . . . but we didn't see what it took to do that" ("MSNBC's Ashleigh"). Likewise, Marine Staff Sergeant Jimmy Massey said Americans "need to know [that] we killed a lot of innocent people" in Iraq using depleted uranium and cluster bombs.[30] We were forbidden to see the flag-draped coffins of American soldiers, though the made-for-TV sensationalism of Jessica Lynch and Pat Tillman was encouraged.[31] The majority of Americans do not seem to mind. So long as we continue to live the "good life," we are likely to be kept—and keep ourselves—in a willing state of forgetfulness. But we do so at our own peril. Indeed, in *Paycheck*, Jennings finds himself the target of both the FBI and an assassin for Allcom (Colm Feore) who wants to assure the time machine remains secret. But Jennings has no idea why any of this is happening because of his amnesia, an analogue to the questions posed after 9/11: "Why do they hate us? Why were we attacked?" While in no way attempting to justify the murders of that day, those questions stem from an amnesiac culture which has willingly or otherwise forgotten significant memories of its past.

As the film reveals, Jennings' pre-amnesiac self found Allcom's project morally reprehensible. Eventually learning that his machine will trigger a cycle of preemption and retaliation that ends in nuclear war, he leaves clues for his post-amnesiac self to piece together, including images of future newspaper headlines proclaiming "World Leaders Condemn Allcom Innovation: 'Knowledge of the future holds terrible consequences'" and "President Orders Preemptive Strike on Enemy Targets Citing Allcom's Predictive Technology." The final image shows a nuclear explosion in Seattle, and Jennings understands what his pre-amnesiac self realized: "The machine predicts a war, we go to war to prevent it. It predicts a plague and we horde all the sick together, and create a plague. Whatever future this predicts we make happen. We give control of our lives completely." As in *Minority Report*, *Paycheck* undermines the logic of preemption. Jennings reverses his cavalier attitude about the past, understanding how his amnesia and his complicity would have created untold misery and profound catastrophe for millions of people.

"What Does a Scanner See?": Cultural Schizophrenia in *A Scanner Darkly*

A Scanner Darkly is perhaps the most cautionary take on Dick's concern about the human costs of unchecked, ideologically driven power. Linklater notes the urgency of Dick's message to post-9/11 America: "a future where the endless unwinnable drug war would sort of meld in with the endless unwinnable War on Terror – and how governments and corporations profiteer and the effects of that on the individual."[32] The film centers on federal agent Robert Arctor (Keanu Reeves), assigned to find the source of Substance D, a hallucinogenic drug made from blue flowers that has 20 percent of Americans addicted. When Arctor is at headquarters, he is known as "Agent Fred," his identity shielded through a computerized "scramble suit," a constantly shifting composite of over a million facial and voice characteristics. Everyone in the agency, including Fred's supervisor "Hank," wears scramble suits to protect their identities. Posing as a user of D, however, Arctor becomes addicted to the drug. Hank, unaware that Arctor and Fred are the same person, eventually orders Fred to set up surveillance (scanners) inside Arctor's house to spy on his housemates James Barris (Robert Downey, Jr.) and Ernie Luckman (Woody Harrelson), and his would-be girlfriend Donna Hawthorne (Winona Ryder). Running surveillance on himself, Arctor, increasingly dependent on Substance D, forgets that he is spying on his own house. Hank later tells Fred that he has figured out he is Arctor. Increasingly disorientated, Arctor is shocked and confused and finally breaks down completely. Donna takes him to New Path, a corporation that runs rehabilitation clinics. However, we learn that Donna herself is "Hank" and is part of a larger operation to penetrate New Path, suspected to be the actual source of the drug. Arctor had been set up to become addicted to Substance D so he could infiltrate New Path with the hope that he could remember enough of his former identity to expose the corruption.

While the film does not glamorize drugs, Linklater explores the effects of declaring nebulous wars (on "drugs" or "terror") that inevitably increase the power of the state and corporations at the expense of personal freedom. The "War on Terror" resonates in an opening scene of Agent Fred delivering a speech emphasizing battles with "drug terrorists" in the countries producing Substance D: "And while our troops are down there fighting for us, it is up to each and every one of us here to do our part in eliminating the demand for this drug. It is important that you as citizens report all suspicious activities and individuals." Aside from the obvious echoes of calls to "be vigilant," the "small, highly toxic flower" Fred shows while talking about supporting the troops conjures the resurgent poppy crop in Afghanistan. Since late 2001, poppy growth has more than quadrupled, accounting for 95 percent of the world's heroin supply, its value estimated at over $3 billion.[33] The US military tacitly endorses the poppy growers, looking the other way for concerns that "raids will drive farmers with no other income to join extremists."[34] This is significant in the film's revelation that New Path itself is the source of Substance D. The cynicism of starting a drug epidemic in order for the corporation with the monopoly on rehabilitation clinics to profit has an uncomfortable parallel on the corporate benefits of the terror war, especially those profiting from the increased privatization of the military, prisons, and security.[35]

The spread of addiction also legitimates increased intervention of law enforcement and surveillance, further strengthening the power structures in place. Arctor's scramble suit, coupled with his mission to spy on himself, illustrate how the paranoia of the culture can render power automatic and self-perpetuating. Wearing the scramble suit Agent Fred is called "the ultimate everyman." With no name and a "constantly shifting" physical appearance, the idea is not only that whoever wears the scramble suit could be anyone, thereby increasing the surveillance society, but that he is, in a sense, everyone. The film updates Foucault's notion of the panopticon, whereby individuals, forced to act as if being watched all the time, internalize and perpetuate the normative discourse and desired conformity of those in power. The individual under surveillance, like Arctor, "assumes responsibility for the constraints of power," thereby inscribing "the power relation in which he simultaneously plays both roles; he becomes the principle of his own subjugation."[36] Scanners, phone taps, and the scramble suit—the ultimate metaphor of unlocatable and internalized power—not only alters behavior, but regulates individuals into behaving according to the dominant definitions of normality. Motivated by the fear of acting "suspicious," we internalize the external discipline and become our own police, betraying, like Arctor, our individuality to those in power.

Arctor's slide from drug enforcement agent to incoherent schizophrenic reflects the contradictory expectations of post-9/11 culture. The cultural enforcement of the normalizing with-us-or-against-us judgment is enacted as Agent Fred meets with psychologists at the agency, who administer tests to those acting out of the ordinary. Asked to identify certain objects, Fred is told of the test's lack of ambiguity: "It's not interpretive. There are many wrongs, but only one right. You either get it or you don't and if you show a run of not getting it, then we have a fix on a functional impairment." The doctors diagnose Arctor with "competition phenomenon," whereby the two halves of his brain split and compete to determine reality. He has "two signals that interfere with each other by carrying conflicting information." Multiple or conflicting opinions are not permitted; the black-and-white paradigm is strictly enforced.

This test is another insightful metaphor to thinking about the War on Terror. Like Fred/Arctor, who acts as both police and criminal, post-9/11 America can be seen as suffering from "competition phenomenon" in the manner we endorse the methods of fighting ill-defined wars. These tactics are also displayed in the revelation that Hank *is* Donna (whose real name is Audrey). She has been covertly addicting Arctor to Substance D in order to infiltrate New Path, but by the film's end he is an empty cipher, causing her to question the ethics of the operation. "Shit, we're colder than they [New Path] are," she tells her partner Mike, whose reply echoes the neoconservative rhetoric of moral certainty: "I believe God's M.O. is to transmit evil into good, and if He's active here He's doing that now. Although our eyes can't perceive it. The whole process is hidden beneath the surface of our reality. It will only be revealed later." In the same way that the Precogs are enslaved, Arctor has been sacrificed so that a larger "war" can be won. Mike echoes the messianic discourse circulating today. Any rights that are eroded or "collateral damage" we inflict is all for the greater good, which we cannot see but are asked to believe in.

However, Mike's vision of the future does not take into account the damage done, not only to individuals, but to the character of the country in whose name this "war" is being waged. Using absolutist, messianic rhetoric to rationalize the distressing pictures of torture and humiliation of Iraqis at Abu Ghraib reveals something tragic, says David Griffith, in the way "we see ourselves as innocent and exceptional—a chosen people ordained by God to rid the earth of evil in a War on Terror." But the revelation of those photographs," he contends, is "evidence of the subterranean flaw beneath our benevolent, Christian surface."[37] Understanding that images of tortured Arabs provide catharsis for some Americans, they nonetheless mirror a terrorist mindset by "memorializing the negation of humanity and the incremental undoing of the world."[38] At stake is the ability of Americans to judge themselves and the world "clearly," as opposed to "darkly." In *A Scanner Darkly*'s most moving scene, Arctor, struggling to keep his identity straight, reflects on the personal toll of a security-obsessed power structure that demands outward conformity:

What does a scanner see? Into the head? Down into the heart? Does it see into me, into us? Clearly or darkly? I hope it sees clearly, because I can't any longer see into myself. I see only murk. I hope for everyone's sake the scanners do better. Because if the scanner sees only darkly, the way I do, then I'm cursed.

Arctor despairs of the idea that his only identity is what the scanner sees, the outward behavior that does not define who he is. Arctor is lost, no longer knowing who he is, but not liking what he sees.

Do Americans like who they are, what they have become during the "War on Terror"? Do we consider how much of our integral identity is being replaced by darkness and "murk," particularly after 9/11, when fear prompts us to take the same tactics as those we claim to abhor? Do we recognize ourselves amidst all of the fear and self-censorship that passes as moral clarity, but which really tears us apart, both individually and collectively? All of the Dick-adapted films ask these questions of their audiences. While the post-9/11 discourse emphasizes the terrorists' Otherness, these adaptations suggest that the atmosphere of paranoia and fear marking post-9/11 America can lead to the kind of fanaticism and destructiveness that the 9/11 attacks exposed. Anderton, Jennings, and Arctor are ultimately presented as sympathetic figures, the films highlighting their disturbing Everyman quality, an ambiguous line in between criminal and victim. While the official rhetoric of the post-9/11 "War on Terror" demanded that one choose to be "with the terrorists or against them," Dick's work thrives in the post-9/11 era because his vision powerfully undermines these dichotomies that have been discursively constructed over the last few years. These films demonstrate that any "War on Terror" must prompt us to examine the practices of our culture and our selves.

Notes

1   Quoted in Ron Suskind, "Without a Doubt," *New York Times Online*, October 17, 2004, http://www.hereinstead.com/Suskind-WithoutaDoubt.htm (accessed October 19, 2007).

2   According to Dick's official website (philipkdick.com), there are more on the way, with the rights to *Time out of Joint, Valis, Radio Free Albemuth*, and *Flow My Tears the Policeman Said* all being sold.

3   The Obama administration has since dropped this term.

4   Dick's fingerprints can be seen in a great deal of turn-of-the-century film. In addition to the adaptations of his own work, Dick's themes are unmistakable in several films over the past ten-plus years, including Terry Gilliam's *Twelve Monkeys* (1995), Kathryn Bigelow's *Strange Days* (1995), Alex Proyas's *Dark City* (1998), Peter Weir's *The Truman Show* (1998), Andy and Larry Wachowski's *The Matrix* (1999), and Michel Gondry's *Eternal Sunshine of the Spotless Mind* (2004).

5   Clifford Geertz, *The Interpretation of Cultures* (New York: Basic Books, 1973), 10. I am not breaking new ground by positioning these films as political allegories of the present. There is an abundance of scholarship on these issues that make it redundant for me to fully rehearse them here. I have found the following particularly helpful: David Seed's *American Science Fiction and the Cold War: Literature and Film* (Chicago and London: Fitzroy & Dearborn, 1999); Karen Sayer and John Morre's collection *Science Fiction, Critical Frontiers* (New York: St. Martin's Press, 2000); Gary Westfahl and George Slusser's collection *Science Fiction, Canonization, Marginalization, and the*

Academy (Westport, CT: Greenwood Press, 2002); and Michael Pinsky's *Future Present: Ethics and/as Science Fiction* (Madison, NJ: Farleigh Dickinson University Press, 2003).

6   Stuart Croft, *Culture, Crisis, and America's War on Terror* (Cambridge: Cambridge University Press, 2006), 69.

7   Stefan Halper and Jonathan Clarke, *America Alone: The Neo-Conservatives and the Global Order* (Cambridge: Cambridge University Press, 2004), 207. The list of neo-conservative (or neo-Reaganite, as they prefer) officials include former Vice President Cheney, former Secretary of Defense Donald Rumsfeld, Paul Wolfowitz, William Kristol, Elliott Abrams, Lewis "Scooter" Libby, Ken Adelman, Robert Kagan, Douglas Feith, Clifford May, and Richard Perle. It is important to note that Halper worked for the White House and the State Department under Nixon, Ford, and Reagan, while Clarke is a Foreign Affairs Scholar at the CATO Institute.

8   Ibid., 10.

9   Leo Strauss is often credited with modernizing the Platonic necessity for the "noble lie" in his *The City and Man* (Chicago: Rand McNally, 1964). For an excellent analysis of Strauss's influence on post-9/11 policies and neoconservative ideology, see John Gray's *Black Mass: Apocalyptic Religion and the Death of Utopia* (New York: Farrar, Straus and Giroux, 2007), especially Chapter 4, "The Americanization of the Apocalypse," 107–45.

10 Ron Suskind, *The One Percent Doctrine: Deep Inside America's Pursuit of Its Enemies Since 9/11* (New York: Simon and Schuster, 2006), 49–150.

11 Ibid., 62.

12 The religious discourse surrounding Pre-Crime is also seen in the Precogs' chamber being called The Temple, while would-be criminals are "haloed."

13 Gerard Huiskamp, "*Minority Report* on the Bush Doctrine," in Joseph G. Peschek ed., *Politics of Empire: War Terror and Hegemony* (London: Routledge, 2006), 133.

14 Barton Gellman and Walter Pincus, Iraq's Nuclear File: Inside the Prewar Debate, "Depiction of Threat Outgrew Supporting Evidence," *Washington Post*, August 10, 2003, A1.

15 Huiskamp, "*Minority Report* on the Bush Doctrine," 134.

16 William Kristol and Robert Kagan, "Toward a Neo-Reaganite Foreign Policy," http://www.carnegieendowment.org/publications/index.cfm?fa=view&id=276&prog=zgp&proj=zusr&zoom_highlight=Kristol+Kagan+Toward (accessed June 28, 2009).

17 In a fascinating interpretation of American origin, Martin makes the claim that 9/11 "triggered a revolution in our foreign policy, aligning it more with our founding principles and Declaration of Independence."

18 Huiskamp, "*Minority Report* on the Bush Doctrine," 125.

19 As Fredric Jameson quips, "All Americans are now receiving therapy, and it is called war (or more officially, 'the war on terrorism')" ("Symptom of Theory or Symptoms for Theory," *Critical Inquiry* 30:2 Winter, 2003, 57).

20 Lisa Feldmann, "The Impact of Bush Linking 9/11 and Iraq," *The Christian Science Monitor*, March 1, 2003, http://www.csmonitor.com/2003/0314/p02s01-woiq.htm (accessed July 12, 2007). Similarly, a survey by the Pew Research Center and the Council on Foreign Relations released in February 2003 found that 57 percent of those polled believed Saddam Hussein helped terrorists involved with the 9/11 attacks, while March 7–9, 2003 New York Times/CBS News Poll showed that 45 percent of interviewees agreed that "Saddam Hussein was personally involved in the Sept. 11 terrorist attacks." A March 2003 CNN/USA Today/Gallup poll found this impression held by 51 percent.

21 Brian Braiker, "What American's (Don't) Know," *MSNBC*, June 23, 2007, http://www.msnbc.msn.com/id/19390791/site/newsweek/ (accessed July 22, 2007).

22 In Laura Spinney, "We Can Implant Entirely False Memories," *Guardian*, July 12, 2003.

23 John Carlos Rowe, "Culture, US Imperialism, and Globalization," *American Literary History* 16.4 (2004): 575–95.

24 Ibid: 586.

25 Indeed, the Iraq War has financially benefited a number of corporations. Lockheed

Martin's stock increased 300 percent between 2000–04, with 80 percent of its revenue coming from the government, and others, like Northrup-Grumman, Kellogg, Brown & Root, and Halliburton have seen similar extraordinary spikes in revenue (Peter Phillips *et al.*, "The Global Dominance Group: A Sociological Case for Impeachment of George W. Bush and Richard Cheney," in *Impeach the President: The Case Against Bush and Cheney* (New York: Seven Stories Press, 2006), 253–92).

26   Benjamin Barber's *Jihad vs. McWorld: Terrorism's Challenge to Democracy* (New York: Ballantine, 1995) is an excellent introduction to the symbiotic relationship between free-market capitalism and the rise of fundamentalist reactions.

27   Catherine Lutz, "The Wars Less Known," in *Dissent from the Homeland: Essays After September 11*, eds Stanley Hauerwas and Frank Lentricchia (Durham, NC: Duke University Press, 2003), 50.

28   See William Blum's *Killing Hope: US Military and CIA Interventions Since WWII* (Monroe, ME: Common Courage Press, 1995) and *Rogue State: A Guide to the World's Only Superpower* (Monroe, ME: Common Courage Press, 2000), as well as John Perkins' *Confessions of an Economic Hit Man* (San Francisco: Berrett-Koehler, 2004).

29   Catherine Lutz, "The Wars Less Known," 49.

30   Americans are also kept ignorant about the actual death toll of Iraqi citizens. Whereas Bush offered a figure of 30,000 since the invasion in 2003, several sources, including the Johns Hopkins School of Public Health (2006), have put the number over 600,000, to include those who would not have died had Iraqi infrastructure remained intact.

31   Anna Froula, "Lynch `N England: Figuring Females as the US at War," *Global Media Journal* 5.9 (Fall 2006), http://lass.calumet.purdue.edu/cca/gmj/fa06/graduatefa06/gmj_grad_fa06_froula.htm (accessed June 22, 2007).

32   Paul Joseph Watson, "Linklater On a Scanner Darkly: It's the World We're Living In," July 12, 2006, http://infowars.com/articles/media/scanner_darkly_linklater_its_world_were_living_in.htm (accessed November 22, 2009).

33   "Afghan Poppy Crop Sets Another Record," *MSNBC*, August 4, 2007, http://msnbc.msn.com/id/12480416 (accessed July 30, 2007).

34   Ibid.

35   See Jeremy Scahill's *Blackwater: The Rise of the World's Most Powerful Mercenary Army* (New York: Nation Books, 2007).

36   Michel Foucault, *Discipline and Punish* (New York: Vintage Books, 1979), 202.

37   David Griffith, *A Good War is Hard to Find: The Art of Violence in America* (New York: Soft Skull Press, 2007), 35–6.

38   Ibid., 83.

CHAPTER 16

Prolepsis and the "War on Terror": Zombie Pathology and the Culture of Fear in *28 Days Later* . . .

ANNA FROULA

"Terrorism, like a virus, is everywhere. Immersed globally, terrorism, like the shadow of any system of domination, is ready everywhere to emerge."

—Jean Baudrillard

Introduction

Danny Boyle's *28 Days Later* . . . (2002), one of the first post-9/11 horror movies, imagines England decimated by a synthetic biological contagion known as the "rage virus." Writer Alex Garland envisions the movie as "an oblique war film, relayed via seventies zombies movies," which Boyle incorporates into his study of the modern phenomenon of social rage— "road rage, air rage, hospital rage, even supermarket rage."[1] Though not explicitly about social rage against George W. Bush's presidential administration's policies on terrorism, the film presciently envisions the anger evidenced in worldwide protests against the Iraq invasion and Bush-era policies of torture and rendition. Zombie films have long been indices of cultural anxiety about global events, such as colonialism, controversial wars, space exploration, and atomic threats. I argue here that the figure of the zombie in post-9/11 cinema re-animates the ramifications of US foreign policies in the Middle East in particular and is a dominant cultural metaphor within American culture in general. In its exploration of social anger run amok, *28 Days Later* . . . dramatizes the imperialist worldview and the material realities that informed the Bush Doctrine of preemptive war and the conditions of the Iraq invasion and occupation.[2] Anchored by visual analogues to late twentieth and early twenty-first century wars and genocide, the film anticipates that doctrine's dependency on a culture of fear of ever-looming biological warfare, terrorism, and pandemic disease. While concerned with various forms of violence in the world that bloodily embody social injustice, the film's zombie allegory operates as a proleptic mirror of the ways in which the Bush administration conceived of and spoke about terror, terrorists, and terrorism throughout its tenure.

The proletariat underclass of cinematic monsters, zombies lack the sensual cunning of the vampire and the functioning human counterpart of the werewolf or serial killer.[3] Rather, they are both victim and monster, dramatizing the horrors of brainwashing and enslavement. Movies have portrayed zombies as victims of diabolically imperial masters through the 1930s and 1940s and ghouls radiating fears of communist invasion and atomic annihilation in the 1950s. Whether serving as warnings against future world war, such as in Abel Gance's *J'Accuse!* (1938), or providing an exotic background to a gothic love story, such as in Jacques Tourneur's *I Walked With a Zombie* (1943), zombies in classical Hollywood primarily remained under the control of a master until their eventual emancipation by George A. Romero. His *Night of the Living Dead* (1968) recast the zombie's origin as a wayward result of exploring the "final frontier"—a returning US space probe from Venus that crashes in Pennsylvania. During the Vietnam War, zombies in films were ghoulish referents to casualties, both killed and missing in action in John F. Kennedy's "New Frontier" in Vietnam. They continue to be powerful metaphors of bodies consumed and destroyed by imperialist warfare.[4] Like others before it, the post-9/11 cycle of zombie films evokes the compulsive and repetitive nature of trauma, which, at its core, is that which cannot be articulated or assimilated into personal history as non-traumatic experiences are.[5]

As Gregory A. Waller explains, the fear that zombies inspire originates in the uncanny confrontation with people we *know* and perhaps love, who want nothing but to "feed on us, and, with no malice and no grand design, to reach out and pull us into their ranks."[6] Zombies depict fates worse than death, such as lifetimes of enslavement or of mindless cannibalism without the release of the grave. Whereas the rhetoric of war-making insists on the demonization of the Other and state propaganda delineates the oppositions between "us" and "them," zombies negate those differences. They blur the boundary between life and death by pitting us against ourselves and by confronting us with the abject corpse we will all one day become, whether we benefit from empire, suffer under its rule, or both. As contemporary allegories of global trauma and unrest, zombies dramatize our social anxieties, fears, and sense of helplessness *through* violent encounters with soulless monsters that look human.[7] To watch a zombie movie is to watch humans try to kill recognizably human forms, often with more barbaric and brutal tactics than the zombie possesses, whether it lumbers or frenetically charges its intended victim.

9/11 and the Allegorical Moment

Since *28 Days Later . . .* was made before, during, and after 9/11 (released in the UK on November 1, 2002, and in the USA in January 2003), it does not embody but nonetheless does conjure up the occupation of Afghanistan in the name of the "Global War on Terror," the still-unsolved anthrax attacks that heightened the American public's fears of the Bush Administration's depiction of Saddam Hussein's "weapons of mass destruction," and the shocked citizenry submitting to the dismantling of the Bill of Rights.[8] The film opens in the Cambridge Primate Research Centre, a bleaker and darker version of Kubrick's Ludovico treatment center in *A Clockwork Orange* (1971). The audience's initial perspective is that of a primate being tortured in an inescapable spectator's position, watching unending coverage of human violence. The archive footage of actual—and seemingly commonplace—torture and human brutality, riots, explosions, and fighting anticipates the atrocities of the "War on Terror," signified most prominently by Guantánamo Bay, Abu Ghraib and Haditha, and serves as a reminder that "everything" did not change on September 11, 2001. Rather, it underscores how typical it is for individuals and communities to commit and to experience terrors, trauma, and tragedy, highlighted in this scene by the sheer anonymity and excess of images.

The camera moves jerkily over the initial victims in the screened footage, anticipating the movement of the "infected" that updates the lurching ghouls of earlier zombie films with adrenaline-filled berserkers. A dark-skinned man hunches and covers his head just before a crowd of marauding men and boys waving sticks enters the frame; a veiled Middle Eastern woman wails as she clutches and rocks the swaddled bundle of a dead child. Scenes of marching policemen in riot gear cut to Middle Eastern men cheering the sight of a dead man dangling from a noose. Men

Figure 11: **Creating the social rage virus**

in turbans strike the swinging body, graphically matched to the following shot of police in riot gear kicking and striking demonstrators. The camera cranes from the screaming faces, explosions, beatings, and hordes of humans running from armed riot police to reveal that we are watching multiple, conjoined screens through the eyes of one primate test subject. Boyle's apocalyptic nightmare transforms Kubrick's vision of the effects of social conditioning *against* violence into a rage-causing contagion in the blood. Unlike Malcolm McDowell's Alex, the test subjects are not granted redemption, even when a small group of animal rights activists attempts to free the "torture victims," ignorant that—in doing so—they release the synthetic virus that rampages through the UK. As the hand-held camera documents, the virus is extremely contagious and fast-acting, passing through saliva and the blood, recalling cultural fears about AIDS transmission as well as embodying the post-9/11 panics over anthrax and the SARS, West Nile, Avian, and Swine flu viruses.[9]

Boyle does not show us the decimation of England. Rather, four weeks after the initial infection, the film's emaciated protagonist Jim (Cillian Murphy) awakens from a coma in a hospital bed, hooked to machines. Indeed, our Adamic hero has slept through the day that changed everything. Jim walks through deserted London, calling out forlorn and uncomprehending "hellos" before finding an *Evening Standard* at Churchill's Corner that describes the horror that occurred while he lay unconscious. The front page outlines the global displacement that occurs when national catastrophe spreads across international borders: "The exodus of British

Figure 12: Ground Zero, London

people causes global chaos . . . Blair declares a state of emergency . . . Military ordered 'shoot to kill' . . . UN to build giant refugee camp." Jim pauses at a Piccadilly Circus kiosk that was modeled on a photograph from an earthquake in China, which none-theless allegorically evokes Manhattan immediately after 9/11 with its handwritten notices, photographs of missing loved ones, and desperate pleas for information.[10]

After encountering his first infected, a frothing priest in need of perverted Eucharist, Jim meets up with two other survivors—Mark (Noah Huntley) and Selena (Naomie Harris)—who teach him how to survive in post-apocalyptic London. As they hide in a snack shop after blowing up a gas station and several pur-suing infected, Selena rehearses the history of England's domestic terror, its ground zero from within: "It started as rioting, and right from the beginning you knew this was different 'cause it was happening in small villages. Market towns"—not, she implies, in major cities such as New York City or London. She describes the horrors of life in a biological war zone—evacuation attempts, overrun military blockades, panicked citizens, and eventual silencing of government propaganda on the air-waves: "The day before the TV and radio stopped broadcasting there were reports of infection in Paris and New York. You didn't hear any more after that." When Jim asks about state authorities Selena replies, "There's no government." "Of course there's a government," Jim responds in angry disbelief, "There's always a government." He then names the actual locales of Vice President Richard Cheney and President Bush immediately after the attacks on 9/11: "They're in a bunker or a plane."

Jim's desire for state protection marks him as Lauren Berlant's infantile citizen who cannot shed his privilege of childlike innocence or his faith in protective state institutions to comprehend how drastically his world has changed nor initially adopt the new tactics required for survival.[11] He insists on visiting his parents despite Selena's assurances that they are dead, and they arrive the next day to find the Volvo still sitting in the suburban driveway in a tableau of middle-class security. Jim's parents are indeed dead via suicide, as the prescription bottle indicates. Yet even this information cannot bring him to accept the danger of the world he inhabits. While sleeplessly wandering through the kitchen and hallucinating a happier memory with his parents, Jim lights a candle that attracts the vengeful hunger of a neighboring infected. Mark and Selena spring into defensive action and slaughter the attacker, but Mark is left examining a gaping wound on his arm. Selena brutally kills him with her machete before he "turns." This visceral portrayal of human violence establishes that to survive the apocalypse and triumph over terror means to kill swiftly and decisively. Foreshadowing the logic of 9/11, the response to the threat must be as or more barbaric than the threat itself. Though the pretensions to the tools of "civilized warfare" long enjoyed by the US-British Coalition—including long-range missiles, "smart bombs," and bunker busters dropped from the relative safety of the air—are absent from this scene, empire by force is not. Rather, the grisly hand-to-hand slaughter with a machete evokes the jungle combat in developing countries that are cinematically associated with zombies because of oppression, overpopulation, and imperial pasts. Such images of combat conjure the blazing Haiti of Faulkner's *Absalom, Absalom!*, "when the niggers rushed at [Sutpen] with their machetes," and surrealistic Cambodia, where Willard in Coppola's *Apocalypse Now*

(1979) slaughters Kurtz like a rogue beast.[12] These images animalize the dark bodies subject to European and American colonial practices that have historically served as justifications for military interventions.

Released before the machinations of President Bush's "War on Terror" emerged fully into public view, the movie as a whole belies the very logic that sustains the Iraq and Afghanistan occupations: the fantasy that terrorism can be contained and defeated by superior military power without addressing its root causes and specific regional grievances. Whereas the Bush administration promised a state of security in exchange for faith in its often secret methods, *28 Days Later . . .* warns of the dangers of trusting government propaganda and martial law. The film's visual representations of the city abandoned by a panicked population, of a government that responded too late to the monstrous return of its own creation, and the notices for information regarding missing loved ones resonate with images that became iconic of September 11, 2001, and subsequent days. Bush's fantasy holds that terrorism emerges from a mindless hatred of "freedom" rather than from within the very systems of neocolonial power that, as Naomi Klein has documented, cast the entire Middle East as a "potential terrorist breeding ground" that the United States military can suppress with its bloody and "messy" delivery of democracy.[13]

Zombies and Imperialism

The post-9/11 increase in zombie and infection films presents us with what Adam Lowenstein terms an "allegorical moment," characterized by "collisions" of past events with contemporary popular texts that confront hegemonic narratives with the collective traumas they try to suppress.[14] Writes Lowenstein, "9/11" is comprised of a "still-unfolding series of events" in which the "past" painfully collides into the "present" via the representation of historical events that resonate in contemporary culture. For example, *We Were Soldiers* (Randall Wallace, 2002), a Vietnam War movie, was made before but released in the aftermath of 9/11 and is read within the context of the invasion of Afghanistan.[15] Allegorical moments confound attempts to portray history as linear, mythic, or predestined. As Lowenstein notes, Walter Benjamin locates the death head at "the heart of the allegorical way of seeing."[16] Like the red-streaked eyes of an infected staring from *28 Days Later . . .* promotional posters, Benjamin's death head, the human skull, condenses into a human face "everything about history that from the very beginning has been untimely, sorrowful, unsuccessful."[17] Lowenstein concludes that "allegorical images" depict meaning as a fluid quantity that can transform within the image itself, for these images "exist in the allegorical moment *between* being and appearance, *between* subject and object, *between* life and death," much like the zombie itself.[18]

So it is, then, that in his "zombiepocalypse," Boyle purposefully incorporates several visual allusions to specific, horrific historical events from the recent past: Jim gathering wads of useless currency outside Buckingham Palace, which visually invokes scenes of the Khmer Rouge's abandonment of Phnom Penh; Jim stepping into a church and seeing piles of bodies, which visually quotes images of Rwandan genocide; Jim encountering a dead mother clinging to her dead child, which evokes a photograph from Saddam Hussein's gassing of the Kurds.[19] Since I see the post-9/11 zombie renaissance as a *memento mori* unto itself, *28 Days Later . . .* is an allegory in which the colonial origins of both zombies and zombie movies collide with contemporary neocolonial events and with the material reality of those who suffer and/or resist imperial violence. In other words, watching *28 Days Later . . .* after 9/11 marries globalized trauma to this British film and further informs the cultural moment of neocolonialism for the viewer.

Zombies also embody contemporary anxieties of empire because of both their origin myths and the origins of zombie films. As Jamie Russell notes, "the zombie was a powerful symbol of fear, misery, and doom" in Haiti, where the modern concept of the walking dead originates. European slave traders who brought African slaves to San Domingo translated the word into the Creole *zôbi*, which evolved into the modern *zombie*. In the West Indies—especially Haiti—and in New Orleans, voodoo spiritualism amalgamated with Catholicism, literalizing the resurrection of the body. Slave owners believed that conversion to Catholicism would tame their "savage labor force" of enslaved West Africans and their descendents, who were brought to Haiti to work the sugar plantations after European colonizers destroyed the island's native population with brutality and bioweaponry.[20]

Hence, the infection in *28 Days Later . . .* is historically inflected by both zombie origins and a much earlier "coalition of the willing" that profited from the London-based Royal African Company of slave traders and American plantation-made goods. For US popular rhetoric at the turn of the nineteenth century cast the San Domingo Revolution (1791–1802) as a metaphoric contagion of insurrection threatening the American slavocracy as well as the commercial interests of European empires. The former slave Toussaint successfully led the liberation of the colony, the "crown jewel" of the sugar trade, from French planters, British and Spanish forces, and the "allegedly invincible armies of Napoleon Bonaparte" and renamed it Haiti, the first "Black Republic" in the Western Hemisphere.[21] The revolution threatened Europe's slave-trade-based commercial interests and haunted American northerners and southerners alike with images of landless white planters fleeing from savage bloodshed.

Similar to the specter of Iraq in the minds of the Bush administration, Haiti embodied for Thomas Jefferson and other members of the ruling class a pervasive danger from which America needed protection. In 1791 George Washington had "urged that the United States render every possible aid to France to help 'crush the alarming insurrection of the Negroes in St. Domingo.'"[22] In other words, the US government hoped to fight slave insurgency *over there* so the US would not have to fight it *here*; likewise, Bush frequently defended the occupation of Iraq in such terms as taking "the fight to the terrorists abroad, so we don't have to face them here at home."[23] Eight years after Washington's warning, Jefferson nervously described Toussaint and his forces as prototypical zombies—the "cannibals of the terrible Republic"—capable of "sweeping the globe" with "revolutionary storm."[24] This global threat grew increasingly virulent when it crossed the Caribbean Sea to inspire other slave revolt conspiracies in the 1820s and 1830s. Americans feared that Creoles were carriers of "traces and taints" that could poison America's "own redemptive mission in the New World."[25] As Russell argues, the cannibal cycle of the zombie film envisions this historical horror on the big screen as "an apocalypse in which the Third World's dead rise up against white, Western civilisation in bloody revenge for centuries of imperial conquest."[26] Implicitly, *28 Days Later . . .* dramatizes the rhetoric and underlying racism made explicit in the Western empires' response to the colony's revolt for freedom by graphically emphasizing the blood-borne contagion.

Other allegorical moments in zombie film history reveal traces of this historical violence at play in *28 Days Later . . .* Early Hollywood's zombie tales implicitly mediate this racial history during a period when the US was not only militarily occupying Haiti but also enacting what Douglas Blackmon terms "neo-slavery," the systemic re-enslavement of African Americans via post-Reconstruction laws and complicit Southern municipal governments.[27] In 1932, when Victor Halperin released *White Zombie*, Hollywood's first zombie movie that was set in Haiti, the US had been occupying Haiti for 17 years to protect its commercial interests, namely the Haitian American Sugar Company, as well as its military dominance, preventing nations such as Germany from establishing bases so terrifyingly close to the US.[28] *White Zombie* dramatizes the Vodoun religion by foregrounding the plight of the white zombie, an American woman enjoying a destination wedding in the tropics, who is zombified by white men who want to steal her from her bridegroom. Bela Lugosi's wild-eyed mystic Murder Legendre is the zombie master, creating automaton servants to work his sugar mill. The film thus depicts via the horror genre the ugly underside of exploitative capitalism amid Great Depression-era uncertainty. When one zombie falls into the mill's gears, the rest of the slaves continue laboring without missing one lurching step. The image of the gears crushing the body as sugar production continues constitutes an ominous metaphor of endless misery unabated by death for a shell-shocked, Depression-era labor force, a military-occupied island, and African-American men in forced-labor camps throughout the southern United States.

In one especially disturbing scene in *28 Days Later . . .*, PFC Mailer (Marvin Campbell), an infected black soldier, haunts the screen with the repressed memory of black slaves in chains to revivify what "living dead" means. At this point in the movie, Selena and Jim have traveled with young Hannah (Megan Burns) to a military base outside Manchester that broadcasts its claim of possessing "the answer to infection" on short wave radio. Reminiscent of the virus's origins in a lab filled with imprisoned primates, base commander Major West (Christopher Eccleston) keeps Mailer alive in his courtyard prison to learn how long it will take him to starve to death. As West explains this experiment to a cowering Jim, the infected soldier falls to the ground and vomits blood before reaching pitifully to Jim. Not only does the captive Mailer's dark skin signify the terrors of the US-UK slave trade, but his tortured form also allegorizes the condition of the prisoners of the "War on Terror," those the Bush administration renamed "detainees" and "enemy combatants." Regarding Guantánamo Bay's Camp X-Ray, Anne McClintock writes that the innocent prisoners, which the Red Cross estimates to be roughly 90 percent of the total prison population, are "reduced to zombies, unpeopled bodies, dead men walking, bodies as imperial property."[29] The scene's opening subjective shot from Mailer's perspective and his soldier's uniform warn of the permeable boundary between being an agent of military rule and being a body policed by it.

Landmines, concertina wire, and a sophisticated alarm system protect the military base from the infected, but no sooner do our protagonists catch their breaths and eat a meal than the horrors of imperial military rule emerge. West shows off his team's defense system to Jim during an attack by a handful of infected. Fresh from the victorious skirmish, the soldiers are ready to celebrate by claiming the sexual rewards promised by West from Hannah and Selena, having stripped Selena of her weapon. As the men leer at the women, one announces, "I'm going to have the black one. And I'm gonna make her squirm." Though quick-thinking Selena and her civilized insistence on politeness buy enough time to provide Hannah some medication "to make her not care," this turn of events underscores Major West's earlier claim that humanity's long history of "people killing people" is status quo, that uninfected humans are as brutal and violent about satisfying their biological appetites as the infected ones are.

Futilely resisting the women's sexual enslavement, Jim is beaten and escorted to military prison in the basement with Farrell, who is imprisoned for advancing the conspiracy theory that life is going on as normal elsewhere in the world, while this "diseased little island" is quarantined until the infection and the infected die out completely. Both men are dragged to the compound's concertina-wire-protected

Figure 13: Torturing the walking dead

edge for execution, but the captors fight among themselves. Capitalizing on their indecisiveness, Jim breaks free and escapes over the wall. As the two soldiers bicker, Jim lies bleeding on the forest ground, catching his breath. A subjective shot catches the silent flight of a jet over the quarantined island.

Like the opening scene that serenely juxtaposes the chaos of social rage with the civilized structure of the primate lab, this image of jet contrails reminds us how any community that poses a threat to dominant power structures is expendable, and, thus, "collateral damage." For Jim, the airplane is both a confirmation of his government's lies about the infection spreading throughout the world and a hopeful sign that, despite "rumors of infection in New York and Paris," there is an orderly world that could rescue him and his friends both from the horror of infection and the military's plan to repopulate the UK through rape. However, one online reviewer notes the horrifying "contrast between the apocalyptic violence on the ground and the image of the jet streaming peacefully overhead. What makes it horrific is that this is not just something invented by the film, but is in actuality a[n] occurring event. All around the world jets full of businessmen and tourists coast blissfully unaware of the struggles for basic survival that rage below."[30] This description of a zombified national conscience, or unconsciousness, serenely ignorant of or genially unfocused on the all-too-real horrors of daily life emphasizes the banality of imperial privilege in context of the oppressed.

Though Boyle initially expressed concern that zombie fans would be disappointed by his apocalyptic film, *28 Days Later* . . . helped inaugurate a new wave of the zombie/

Figure 14: "The banality of imperial privilege over one 'diseased little island'"

infection horror genre that has proliferated in the age of post-9/11 US foreign policy and the subsequent "War on Terror."[31] Later films explicitly connect zombie horror to the terrifying experiences of US soldiers and Iraqi civilians in the distant theaters of the "War on Terror." Examples include Showtime's *Masters of Horror* television episode "Homecoming" (Joe Dante, 2005), which depicts US soldiers who died in Iraq returning from the grave to vote against the Bush administration in 2004, and *Stir of Echoes II: The Homecoming* (Ernie Barbarash, 2007), which aligns domestic incidents of intimidation and terror against American civilians who "look" Middle Eastern with both the killing of Iraqi civilians overseas and the combat trauma of those American soldiers who do the killing. University of Alabama instructor Sean Hoade, who has taught a course on zombie films, suggests that zombies "act as a mirror for Americans, not only as we see ourselves but also as the rest of the world [saw] America in the time of George W. Bush: as a roaming, voracious killer turning its victims into soulless creatures like itself."[32] Along with the recent surge of such horror shows, zombie culture is also on the rise, as the sheer numbers of apocalyptic zombie video games, organized "zombie mobs," the use of "zombie" as an adjective for banks that are worth less than nothing or for lies that do not "die" once debunked, and courses on zombie culture, literature, and film all indicate.

The recent resurgence of zombie films and their infected cinematic cousins speaks to the uncanny knack of empires to imagine their own destruction through popular culture.[33] As the gut-level response of many eyewitnesses to the destruction of the World Trade Center suggests, the spectacle of the transformation of commercial airplanes into explosive missiles was "something out of the movies." According to David Altheide in this volume, the United States' larger goal within the rubric of the "War on Terror" is to maintain its precarious position as *the* world's military power. The Bush doctrine was designed to protect US global dominance from major international treaties that would legally prevent the US from engaging in preemptive attacks against and invasions into any country with a one percent chance of attacking the US with any WMDs that might rival the American collection.[34] Though there were few opportunities to dissent on corporate airwaves in the lead-up to the invasion of Iraq, as Altheide argues, the Bush administration's logic of "with us or against us" cast any forms of resistance to the "War on Terror" into the faceless mass of worldwide protestors, raving anti-Americans driven by rage, or zombies. Though President Bush swore that the War on Terror would rid the world of the evil of terrorism, *28 Days Later . . .* insists that the potential for "evil," that is, acting against American, Western, or, more broadly, imperial interests, lies dormant within each of us.[35] This stance is illustrated most viscerally in Jim's revenge on Major West's squad after he returns, frees Mailer, and kills the soldiers so brutally that both Selena and Hannah think he is infected.

There is a wide range of allegorical possibilities for the cinematic zombies that rampaged through Bush's presidency. Most chilling is McClintock's observation that in order to "legitimize" the ongoing occupation, "The US state *had to turn ordinary people into enemy bodies* . . . and put [them] on display for retaliation."[36] Boyle's frenetic ghouls articulate in particular the cultural fears that supported the Bush administration's justification for preemptively invading and occupying Iraq, that is, "they" hate "us" for our freedoms. They connote the absent bodies of the 9/11 terrorists, tauntingly evading the possibilities of American military vengeance, those "disappeared" into CIA prisons in Syria, Egypt, Morocco, Jordan, or elsewhere, and those endlessly detained and "interrogated" without access to legal representation in Bagram Air Base, Abu Ghraib, or Guantánamo Bay. As McSweeney notes in this volume, the term "living dead" has become part of the "War on Terror" lexicon, specifically in Donald Rumsfeld's categorizing the Guantánamo Bay inmates as technically alive but, as designated targets of American ordnance, "living dead." Despite the Obama administration's plans to try the captives, they remain in legal no-man's-land. Boyle's zombies also anticipate the US military casualties that arrive in Dover Air Force Base under cover of darkness, and the hidden wounded not counted in the American death toll. These include the heavily medicated, those suffering from post-traumatic stress disorder, the rising number of veteran suicides, veterans caught in VA purgatory, and those with invisible injuries such as traumatic brain injury, the "signature injury" of the War in Iraq, which results in the uncanny human—transformed on the inside but appearing the same on the outside.

More crucially, *28 Days Later . . .* warns of the inevitable consequences of empire and how quickly even a former empire can be reduced to "third world" conditions as a consequence of social rage in the age of globalization. On September 12, 2001, Simon Jenkins, former editor of the London *Times*, wrote, "The message of yesterday's incident is that, for all its horror, it does not and must not be allowed to matter. It is a human disaster, an outrage, an atrocity, an unleashing of the madness of which the world will never be rid."[37] Jenkins goes on to warn, as Boyle does, that Western nations have the choice whether to destroy their own democracies in response or to wait in zombified horror for the next attack to come.

Notes

1   Twentieth Century Fox, "*28 Days Later . . .* Production Notes," in *The Cillian Site*, http://www.cilliansite.com/production-notes/28-days-later-prod-notes.pdf (accessed June 20, 2009), 4–5.

2   The "Bush Doctrine" refers to policies codified in the 2002 *National Security Strategy of the United States*. See The George W. Bush White House, *National Security Strategy of the United States*, in *The George W. Bush White House*, http://georgewbush-whitehouse.archives.gov/nsc/nss/2002/index.html (accessed July 5, 2009).

3   Jamie Russell, *Book of the Dead: The Complete History of Zombie Cinema* (Ann Arbor: University of Michigan Press, 2005), 7.

4   See Gregory Waller, *The Living and Undead: From Stoker's* Dracula *to Romero's* Dawn of the Dead (Urbana: University of Illinois Press, 1987); Sumiko Higashi, "A Horror Film About the Vietnam Era," in *Hanoi to Hollywood: The Vietnam War in American Film*, eds Linda Dittmar and Gene Michaud (New Brunswick, NJ: Rutgers University Press, 1990), 175–88; and Karen Randell, "Lost Bodies/Lost Souls: MIA Narratives in *Night of the Living Dead*," *Film & History CD-ROM Annual, 2004–2005* (Oshkosh, WI: Center for the Study of Film and History, 2005).

5   See Sigmund Freud, *Moses and Monotheism* (New York: Vintage, 1955); Cathy Caruth, "Introduction," in *Trauma: Explorations in Memory*, ed. Cathy Caruth (Baltimore, MD: Johns Hopkins Press, 1995), 3–12; and E. Ann Kaplan's *Trauma Culture: The Politics of Terror and Loss in Media and Literature* (New Brunswick, NJ: Rutgers University Press, 2005).

6   Waller, *The Living and Undead*, 275.

7   See Annalee Newitz, *Pretend We're Dead: Capitalist Monsters in American Pop Culture* (Durham, NC: Duke University Press, 2006).

8   On being shocked into submission to a state, see Naomi Klein, *The Shock Doctrine: The Rise of Disaster Capitalism* (New York: Henry Holt, 2007).

9   See Priscilla Wald, *Contagious: Cultures, Carriers and the Outbreak Narrative* (Durham, NC: Duke University Press, 2008).

10 "*28 Days Later . . .* Production Notes," 11.

11 Lauren Berlant, *The Queen of America Goes to Washington City: Essays on Sex and Citizenship* (Durham, NC: Duke University Press, 1997), 21.

12 William Faulkner, *Absalom, Absalom!* (1936; repr., New York: Vintage, 1986), 201.

13 Klein, *The Shock Doctrine*, 327.

14 Adam Lowenstein, *Shocking Representations: Historical Trauma, National Cinema, and the Modern Horror Film* (New York: Columbia University Press, 2005), 177–81. See also Newitz, "Social Upheaval," for a list of zombie feature films from 2002–8.

15 Lowenstein, *Shocking Representations*, 177.

16 Ibid., 13.

17 Ibid., 183.

18 Ibid., 13, emphasis in original.

19 Kim Newman, "This Diseased World," in *Filmmaker Magazine*, Summer 2003, http://www.filmmakermagazine.com/summer2003/features/diseased_world.php (accessed September 29, 2007).

20 Russell, *Book of the Dead*, 11.

21 George F. Tyson, ed., *Toussaint L'Ouverture* (Englewood Cliffs: Prentice-Hall, 1973), 1.

22 Ibid., 93.

23 The George W. Bush White House, "President Signs Intelligence Reform and Terrorism Prevention Act," *The George W. Bush White House Archives*, December 17, 2004, http://georgewbush-whitehouse.archives.gov/news/releases/2004/12/20041217-1.html (accessed July 14, 2009).

24 Tyson, *Toussaint L'Ouverture*, 93; Eric J. Sundquist, "Benito Cereno and New World Slavery," in *Reconstructing American Literary History*, ed. Sacvan Bercovitch (Cambridge: Harvard University Press, 1986), 103.

25 I am borrowing Barbara Ladd's words from "'The Direction of the Howling': Nationalism and the Color Line in *Absalom, Absalom!*," *American Literature* 66 no. 3 (1994): 530.

26 Russell, *Book of the Dead*, 143.

27 Douglas Blackmon, *Slavery by Another Name: The Re-Enslavement of Black Americans from the Civil War to World War II* (New York: Doubleday, 2008), 1.

28 Russell, *Book of the Dead*, 16.

29 Anne McClintock, "Paranoid Empire: Specters from Guantánamo and Abu Ghraib," *Small Axe* 28 (2009): 65.

30 Unemployed Negativity, "The Zombie as Critic," June 11, 2007, http://unemployed negativity.blogspot.com/2007/06/zombie-as-critic.html (accessed September 15, 2007).

31 Newman, "This Diseased World."

32 Karina Wilson, "Zombie Walks," in *Horror Film History*, 2007, http://www.horrorfilm-history.com/index.php?pageID=ZombieWalk (accessed September 3, 2008).

33 Jean Baudrillard, "L'esprit du Terrorisme," trans. Michael Valentin, in *South Atlantic Quarterly* 101 no. 2 (2002): 404.

34 See Ron Suskind, *The One Percent Doctrine: Deep Inside America's Pursuit of Its Enemies Since 9/11* (New York: Simon and Schuster, 2006).

35 The George W. Bush White House, "President Declares 'Freedom at War with Fear,'" *The George W. Bush White House Archives*, September 20, 2001, http://

georgewbush-whitehouse.archives.gov/news/releases/2001/09/20010920-8.html (accessed July 10, 2009).

36   McClintock, "Paranoid Empire," 57, emphasis in original.

37   Chalmers Johnson, *Nemesis: The Last Days of the American Republic* (New York: Henry Holt, 2008), 4.

Afterword

JOHN G. CAWELTI

The first decade of the twenty-first century may have been an important turning point in American history, but it is still difficult to say what sort of transformation those years brought about. The decade began with a highly problematic Supreme Court decision awarding the election to George W. Bush over Al Gore. Though Bush hardly had anything resembling a mandate, he acted as though he did and the 9/11 attack on the World Trade Center unified the country behind him. 9/11 enabled the administration to attempt the enactment of its vision of a Christian, capitalist America dominating the world. These actions not only led to an increasing isolation of America from its former world allies but to the further decay of the environment and the country's infrastructure, which became increasingly obsolete as a result of Bush's policies. In addition, the country found itself dealing with increasing economic difficulties resulting from massive military spending, a growing gap between rich and poor, and the havoc wrought by untrammeled and unregulated greed on the part of major financial and corporate institutions.

The decade ended with the election of Barack Obama amid accelerating economic problems. It might seem, therefore, that the American people have decisively repudiated the Bush vision of an American empire. Yet for eight years Americans generally accepted, if they did not wholeheartedly support, such keystones of Bush policy as the war on Iraq, the end of government regulation of unrestrained capitalism, and the rejection of any attempts to deal with the growing environmental crisis. Actually, the Bush policies had a long foreground. As David Altheide shows, planning for the Iraq War and the idea of preemptive strikes against anti-American regimes went back at least to the first Bush administration and was articulated in the Project for the New American Century (PNAC) formulated by members of the second Bush administration in collaboration with neoconservative ideologists and think tanks. But the source of the ideology of the new American imperium goes back to the Cold War and the increasing influence of the military-industrial complex that President Eisenhower warned against in his 1961 farewell address. When the Cold War ended, the vision of America as the great bulwark against communist world domination came into serious question. Those who were ideologically committed to American supremacy in the world, as well as the corporate and military interests that had profited greatly from the Cold War, needed to find new enemies and new rhetoric to justify the maintenance of a huge military establishment in the face of arguments for the transfer of some portion of military expenditures into social welfare—guns into butter, as it were.

Several of the essays in this volume show how the American public's reaction to 9/11 was the perfect vehicle for the promotion of these ideologies. Public trauma enabled the Bush administration to generate a pervasive fear of terrorism, which supported worldwide expansion of American power and led to such policies as the preemptive invasion of Iraq, the detention and torture of war prisoners, and increasing indifference to the attitudes of important former allies like Germany and France. So shocked was the public by 9/11 that many Americans came to feel that criticism of the Bush administration's actions was supportive of terrorism. Instead, as several essays indicate, some of the most powerful criticism of the "War on Terror" had to be made in the indirect and symbolic form of movies like George Romero's *Land of the Dead* and Danny Boyle's *28 Days Later*... As Karen Randell's and Stacy Takacs' essays suggest, even those movies that directly dealt with 9/11 or the Iraq War presented these traumatic events in terms of traditional Hollywood genres like the disaster movie or the Indian captivity narrative.

The Bush administration's position that serious criticism of its policies was both dangerous and immoral was based in part on the administration's connection to fundamentalist evangelical Protestantism and the new kind of religious institutions and ideologies this movement generated. While fundamentalism had been an increasing influence in American religion throughout the twentieth century, the rise of fundamentalist megachurches and the new political activism of these churches were important features of American popular culture in the 1980s and 1990s. The fundamentalist worldview with its apocalyptic vision of Armageddon and its Manichean tendency to see world history in terms of Christians against the Antichrist is particularly highlighted in Jonathan Vincent's essay on the apocalyptic *Left Behind* novels of Tim LaHaye and Jerry B. Jenkins. The enormous readership of these books suggests how deeply seated these attitudes have become in American culture.

9/11 may have been an important turning point in another way. The first decade of the twenty-first century was also a period in which new structures of public communication became more important in American popular culture than the established institutions and communication patterns of the "mass media" that had dominated the second half of the twentieth century. These changes are so far-reaching and fundamental that it is difficult to predict how they will ultimately affect America's basic institutions of politics, economics, religion, and culture. It is even hard to be certain about which of these recent changes will ultimately prove to be the most important.

It would seem at this point that the most significant of these changes results from the continued attrition of the monopoly over much of American public communications once held by the mass media. Though never as monolithic as some of its critics suggested, the mass media of the second half of the twentieth century, driven by the tremendous influence and power of network television, strongly shaped American perceptions and ideologies. Many central events of the period—such as the Civil Rights movement, the political assassinations of the 1960s, the Vietnam

War and the protests against it, and the Watergate scandal—virtually played out on major network television.

Along with the impact of network television, metropolitan daily newspapers became increasingly centralized during the second half of the twentieth century, a development that resulted from their increasing loss of readership and influence. Where earlier newspapers had often reflected particular political parties and ideologies (for example, the *Chicago Tribune* was deeply conservative and republican, while the *Chicago Sun-Times* was liberal and democratic) the larger newspaper consolidations tended increasingly to downplay particular political affiliations in search of broader readership in a period when television news reporting increasingly drew readers away from printed newspapers.

Since the mass media tried to draw the broadest possible audience, its content generally reflected a broad centrist perspective. Other important features of the media were their tendency to avoid controversial stands and treat their audience as spectators rather than active participants. Perhaps the ultimate expression of this was the media coverage of the assassination of President John F. Kennedy when a large proportion of the population was glued to the television screen. These characteristics of the mass media helped support the widespread impression that the vast majority of the American public were neither liberal nor conservative but "centrist" in their beliefs, and that interest in significant political change was minimal. It was during this period that the "consensus" theory of American culture—the view that American history was shaped by a slowly evolving general agreement rather than the clash of political and economic interests—became highly popular among both politicians and historians.

In contrast, in the first decade of the twenty-first century Americans became highly polarized and divided in their attitudes. A number of important changes in the structure of public communications and popular culture seemed to have facilitated this change. The most significant of these was the increasing importance of the computer and the Internet. Unlike the mass media, the Internet was audience-centered rather than network-dominated. It responded directly to the interests of individuals and small groups in multiple combinations and as a result led to decentralization, specialization, diversity, and the creation of many different patterns of communication. Its users were activists rather than spectators since each individual had to originate and shape the pattern of communication that he or she preferred.

The more diverse, specialized, and fragmented modes of communication encouraged by the Internet were reinforced by other new technologies, ideologies, and institutional changes in American culture. Thanks above all to the enormous success of popular ideologues like Rush Limbaugh, the rebirth of radio as a major medium of political and cultural controversy made possible the expression of more extreme views, especially of intense conservative discontent, than would have been acceptable in the mass media. The increasing use of cell phones and associated wireless communications further diversified the available communication channels, as did the proliferation on cable television of an increasing array of specialized television channels ranging from CNN, whose news coverage increasingly eclipsed that of the major networks, to the Food Channel, premium movie channels, a spate of religious-oriented channels, and many more special-interest programs. The land-mark 2009 abandonment of analog television signals symbolized the final eclipse of a system of television dominated by a few major networks. Furthermore, adoption of on-demand television gave communication through television something of the same flexibility and direct response to audience interests as the computer and the Internet. It is crucial for those scholars studying popular culture to keep track of these changes—however nuanced—in our bid to understand the ways in which dominant discourses prevail and alternative voices can be heard: *Reframing 9/11: Film, Popular Culture and the "War on Terror"* is a vital part of that ongoing work.

The fragmentation of audiences and the expression of polarizing ideologies made possible by the new structures of public communication also related to new developments in American religious institutions. Giant megachurches, often based on extreme fundamentalist ideologies and tending toward a high degree of political activism, increasingly drew membership away from the mainline denominations. These new fundamentalist churches used the technological possibilities of the computer and cable television to create total communities within which members could close themselves off from the rest of the world in much the same way as the gated suburban communities, which also proliferated during the first decade of the twenty-first century.

The Bush administration was able to use the ideological fragmentation and polarization encouraged by some of these new cultural and technological patterns to intensify the public's fear and uncertainty in the aftermath of 9/11. In this context, what had been viewed as extreme positions and policies became acceptable and, in some cases, such as the Iraq War, were made to seem inevitable. Unquestionably, the Bush administration's "War on Terror" and its "culture of fear" gained further sup-port through the influence of radio demagogues, an Internet culture of conservative bloggers, and the power of fundamentalist megachurches to control the attitudes and perceptions of their membership. These extremist attitudes are still present among a sizable minority of the American public and further terrorist attacks may bring them to the fore again.

However, though cultural fragmentation and political polarization were enhanced by the specialization and separatism of new communication patterns, other possible outcomes became clear toward the end of the decade. Obama's successful campaign depended on the exploitation of new communication possibilities to contact and involve in the political process an extraordinarily wide spectrum of the American public. Obama's complex grassroots organizations effectively coordinated fundrais-ing and campaign events in such a way that more and more Americans were actively drawn into the political process, if only through the contribution of small amounts of money. In contrast to the tendency of the mass media to define audiences as spectators, the Internet, cell phones, and other new communications technology and programs increased active participation in the political process. Internet institutions like YouTube, Facebook, and Twitter depend completely on active postings by par-ticipants, as does that remarkable organ of Internet "reference," Wikipedia. Thus the new communication patterns not only encourage specialization and fragmentation but make possible new and more complex levels of interchange and consolidation and new kinds of communities and collectivities. In many ways Obama's victory was a repudiation of extremism and polarization using the possibilities of rational discussion and consensus-building available through new techniques of communication. One can only hope that in the aftermath of further terrorist attacks, these new patterns of popular culture will help to control and allay the kind of hysteria and trauma that transformed the reaction to 9/11 into a justification for imperialistic war and the erosion of American democracy.

Contributors

David L. Altheide is Regents' Professor in the School of Justice and Social Inquiry at Arizona State University. Two recent books that examine the role of the mass media and propaganda in promoting fear and social control received the Cooley Award from the Society for the Study of Symbolic Interaction: *Creating Fear: News and the Construction of Crisis* (Aldine de Gruyter/Transaction, 2002) and *Terrorism and the Politics of Fear* (AltaMira, 2006). Altheide received the 2005 George Herbert Mead Award for lifetime contributions from the Society for the Study of Symbolic Interaction and this academic society's Mentor Excellence Award in 2007.

David Annandale holds a PhD in horror fiction and film from the University of Alberta. He teaches literature and film at the University of Manitoba. His novels are *Crown Fire* (Turnstone Press, 2002) and *Kornukopia* (Turnstone Press, 2002). His articles include "Guerrilla Vamping: *Vampyros Lesbos*, Becoming-Woman and the Unravelling of the Male Gaze" in *Paradoxa* 17 2002, and "The Subversive Carnival of *Grand Theft Auto: San Andreas*" in *The Meaning and Culture of Grand Theft Auto* (ed. Nate Garrelts, McFarlane, 2006). He is currently working on a book-length study of video games.

Reza Aslan, an internationally acclaimed writer and scholar of religions, is a columnist at *The Daily Beast*. Aslan has degrees in religions from Santa Clara University, Harvard University, and the University of California, Santa Barbara, as well as a Master of Fine Arts from the University of Iowa, where he was named the Truman Capote Fellow in Fiction. He is a member of the Council on Foreign Relations, the Los Angeles Institute for the Humanities, and the Pacific Council on International Policy. He serves on the board of directors for both the Ploughshares Fund, which gives grants for peace and security issues, Abraham's Vision, an interfaith peace organization, and PEN USA. Aslan's first book is the *New York Times* bestseller, *No god but God: The Origins, Evolution, and Future of Islam*, which has been translated into 13 languages, short-listed for the Guardian First Book Award in the UK, and nominated for a PEN USA award for research non-fiction. His most recent book is *How to Win a Cosmic War: God, Globalization, and the End of the War on Terror*, followed by an edited anthology, *Words Without Borders: Writings from the Middle East*, which will be published by Norton in 2010. Aslan is co-founder and Chief Creative Officer of BoomGen Studios, a hub for creative content from and about the Middle East, as well as Editorial Executive of *Mecca.com*. Born in Iran, he now lives in Los Angeles where he is Assistant Professor of Creative Writing at the University of California, Riverside.

Jeff Birkenstein is Associate Professor at Saint Martin's University in Lacey, Washington. He received his PhD from the University of Kentucky in 2003; he has a second MA in Teaching English as a Second/Other Language. His major interests lie in American and world short stories, the short story sequence, and food and cultural criticism. His chapter, "'Should I Stay or Should I Go?' American Restlessness in the Short-Story Cycle" is in the forthcoming book, *A Companion to the American Short Story* (eds Alfred Bendixen and James Nagel, Blackwell, 2010). He is working concurrently on *Cultural Representation in the International Short Story Sequence*, co-edited with Robert M. Luscher, and a manuscript on "Significant Food" in the short story. He teaches a range of classes, from Freshman Seminar and Composition to The Short Story, Food & Fiction, and Narratives from the Aftermath of 9/11.

John G. Cawelti taught at the University of Chicago from 1957–79 and in 1980 became Professor of English at the University of Kentucky, from which he retired in June 2000. He has published ten books, the most important of which are *Apostles of the Self-Made Man* (University of Chicago Press, 1965), *Adventure, Mystery and Romance* (University of Chicago Press, 1976), *The Spy Story* (University of Chicago Press, 1987), *Leon Forrest: Introductions and Interpretations* (Popular Press, 1997), and *The Six-Gun Mystique Sequel* (Popular Press, 1999). He is widely published in the fields of American literature, cultural history, and popular culture, where he has been particularly concerned with the analysis of popular genres or formulas. Most recently, he co-edited Leon Forrest's last novel, *Meteor in the Madhouse* (Northwestern University Press, 2001) and published his own book *Mystery, Violence and Popular Culture*, in the spring of 2004 (University of Wisconsin Press).

Corey K. Creekmur is Associate Professor of English and Film Studies at the University of Iowa, where he also directs the Institute for Cinema and Culture. He is the author of a forthcoming study of gender and sexuality in the Western, and co-editor of *Out in Culture: Gay, Lesbian, and Queer Essays on Popular Culture* (Duke University Press, 1995), *Cinema, Law and the State in Asia* (Palgrave, 2007), and *The International Film Musical* (Edinburgh, 2010). He is also the author of numerous essays on American cinema, film music, and popular Hindi cinema.

Alex Evans is an independent scholar. His research focuses on culture and politics, with a particular focus on sexuality, cultural theory, and the politics of sexual health. After completing his PhD at the University of Sussex and a lectureship at the University of Canterbury, New Zealand, he now works in the fields of sexual health and social exclusion in the public sector.

Anna Froula is Assistant Professor of Film Studies at East Carolina University in Greenville, North Carolina. Her research interests include war, gender, zombies, and trauma. She has published on Pfc. Jessica Lynch and Pvt. Lynndie England, Arundhati Roy's *The God of Small Things*, *Team America*, *World Police*, and on representations of American servicewomen in World War II popular culture. She is working on a manuscript exploring the representation of US servicewomen in popular culture from World War II to the present.

Terence McSweeney is a writer and lecturer in Film Studies and History. He completed his PhD on Andrei Tarkovsky at the University of Essex, UK. He is the co-editor of *Millennial Cinema: Representations of Memory in Contemporary Film* (Wallflower Press, 2009).

John Mead is currently finishing his doctorate at the University of Illinois at Chicago; his dissertation research is on John Brown and abolitionist literature. He teaches literature, writing, and history in Chicago; he also teaches rock 'n' roll guitar at the Old Town School of Folk Music.

Mathias Nilges is an Assistant Professor at St. Francis Xavier University in Canada where he teaches American literature and critical theory. He has published articles on contemporary American literature, African-American literature, Marxism and critical theory, post-9/11 US culture, and graphic novels. He is currently finishing a book-length manuscript entitled *Nostalgia for the Future: Post-Fordist US Literature and Culture.*

David H. Price is Professor at St. Martin's University in Lacey, Washington, where he teaches courses in anthropology and social justice. His research uses the Freedom of Information Act, archives, and interviews to document historical interactions between anthropologists and intelligence agencies. He is the author of *Threatening Anthropology* (Duke, 2004), and *Anthropological Intelligence: The Deployment and Neglect of American Anthropology During the Second World War* (Duke, 2008).

Karen Randell is Principal Lecturer in Film and Program Leader for Film and Television at Southampton Solent University, UK. Her research interests include images of trauma, Lon Chaney, the war genre, post-9/11 popular culture, and issues of gender in film. She is published in *Screen* (Summer 2003), *Film History* (2005) and *Art in the Age of Terrorism* (Holberton Publications, 2005). She is co-author of *Screen Methods: Comparative Readings in Film Studies* (Wallflower Press, 2005) with Jacqueline Furby (SSU) and *The War Body on Screen* (Continuum, 2008) with Sean Redmond (Victoria University of Wellington, NZ).

Lance Rubin is Chair of the Humanities Department at Arapahoe Community College in Littleton, Colorado. He is the author of *William Dean Howells and the American Memory Crisis* (Cambria, 2008) and co-editor of *Reading Chuck Palahniuk: American Monsters and Literary Mayhem* (Routledge, 2009).

Stacy Takacs is Associate Professor of American Studies at Oklahoma State University. Her research focuses on the intersection of popular and political cultures in the contemporary US, and she has published numerous essays on the subject in journals such as *Cultural Critique, Feminist Media Studies, The Journal of Popular*

Culture, Spectator: Journal of Film and Television Criticism, and *Cultural Studies*. She is currently at work on a book-length manuscript that examines the mediation of the War on Terrorism in US television.

Justine Toh recently completed her PhD in Critical and Cultural Studies at Macquarie University, Australia. Her thesis examines how narratives of American exceptionalism construct the cultural memory of 9/11, as explored through Hollywood cinema and American memorial culture. The Dark Knight is her favorite American superhero.

Sara Upstone is Lecturer in English Literature at Kingston University, London. She specializes in contemporary postcolonial, black British, and British Asian fiction. She is the author of *Spatial Politics in the Postcolonial Novel* (Ashgate, 2009), as well as numerous articles. She is currently working on a study of contemporary British Asian fiction.

Jonathan Vincent is a researcher on the subject of American war culture, the militarization of liberalism, and the discourse of national security. He is currently completing the last stages of his dissertation at the University of Illinois, a project that examines these subjects in the period spanning the end of Reconstruction in 1877 to the advent of the "Global War on Terror" in our own time. His working title is "Preparedness Nation: War, Literature, and the American Political Imagination."

Bibliography

11'09"01—September 11. DVD. Directed by Alejandro González Iñárritu *et al.* 2002; New York: First Run Features, 2004.

24. Live television. Created by Robert Cochran and Joel Surnow. FOX, 2001–present.

28 Days Later . . . DVD. Directed by Danny Boyle. 2002; Burbank, CA: Twentieth Century Fox.

7 Days in September. Directed by Steve Rosenbaum. 2002; New York, NY: Cameraplanet. com, 2002.

Abbas, Tahir. "British South Asian Muslims: Before and After September 11." In *Muslims in Britain: Communities Under Pressure*, ed. Tahir Abbas, 3–17. London: Zed, 2005.

ABC News. "The Plan," *Nightline*, March 5, 2003.

Abdel-Fattah, Randa. *Does My Head Look Big in This?* London: Scholastic, 2006.

Aboulela, Leila. *Islamophobia: A Challenge for Us All.* London: Runnymede Trust, 2005.

——. *Minaret.* London: Bloomsbury, 2005.

Adams, Neal. Untitled image (Superman). *9–11: September 11, 2001: Stories to Remember*, Volume 2. New York: DC Comics, 2002.

Adams, Tim. "When Saturday Comes." *Observer*, Sunday January 30, 2005. http://books. guardian.co.uk/reviews/generalfiction/0,1401445,00.html (accessed March 30, 2007).

Adams, William C. *Television Coverage of the Middle East.* Norwood, NJ: Ablex Pub. Corp., 1981.

——. *Television Coverage of International Affairs.* Norwood, NJ: Ablex Pub. Corp., 1982.

Advertising Research Foundation. "The ARF Supports Ad Council Coalition against Terrorism." *Informed*, December 2001. http:// www.arfsite.org/Webpages/informed/ vol14-np6/page (accessed June 20, 2002).

"A Fatal Triumph of Privatization and Faith-Based Initiatives." *Blah3.com*, August 16, 2006. http://www.blah3.com/article.php?story=20060816100036444 (accessed June 11, 2008).

"Afghan Poppy Crop Sets Another Record." *MSNBC*, August 4, 2007. http://msnbc.msn.com/ id/12480416 (accessed July 30, 2007).

Aglietta, Michel. *A Theory of Capitalist Regulation.* New York: Verso, 2000.

Ahsan, M.M., and A.R. Kidwai, eds *Sacrilege Versus Civility: Muslim Perspectives on The Satanic Verses Affair.* Revised Expanded Edition. Leicester: The Islamic Foundation, 1993.

Ali, Monica. *Brick Lane.* London: Doubleday, 2003.

Allan, Stuart, and Barbie Zelizer. *Reporting War: Journalism in Wartime.* London: Routledge, 2004.

Allen, Chris. "From Race to Religion: the New Face of Discrimination." In *Muslims in Britain: Communities Under Pressure*, ed. Tahir Abbas, 49–65. London: Zed, 2005.

Allen, Thomas. "Bush Administration: What War on Terror? Bring in More Immigrants!" *Vdare.com*, August 28, 2006. http://vdare.com/allen/060828_bush.htm (accessed January 4, 2008).

Allred, Mike, with Laura Allred. Untitled image. In *Heroes: The World's Greatest Superhero Creators Honor the World's Greatest Heroes, 9.11.2001*, ed. Rob Haynes, with Tim Townsend, Tim and David Self, second edn (New York: Marvel Comics, December 2001).

Altheide, David L. "Consuming Terrorism." *Symbolic Interaction* 27 (2004): 289–308.

——. *Creating Fear: News and the Construction of Crisis.* Hawthorne, NY: Aldine de Gruyter, 2002.

——. "Iran Vs. US TV News! The Hostage Story out of Context." In *TV Coverage of the Middle East*, ed. William C. Adams, 128–58. Norwood, NJ: Ablex Pub. Corp., 1981.

——. *Terrorism and the Politics of Fear*. Lanham, MD: Alta Mira Press, 2006.

——. "Three-in-One News: Network Coverage of Iran." *Journalism Quarterly* Fall 1982: 482–6.

——. "To Die for a Mystique." *American Conservative*, May 18, 2009, 20–1.

Altheide, David L., and Jennifer N. Grimes. "War Programming: The Propaganda Project and the Iraq War." *Sociological Quarterly* 46 (2005): 617–43.

"Altman Says Hollywood 'Created Atmosphere' for September 11," *The Guardian*, October 18, 2001. http://www.guardian.co.uk/film/2001/oct/18/news2 (accessed October 2, 2009).

American Dad. Live television. Created by Seth MacFarlane. FOX, 1999–present.

American Dialect Society [ADS]. "Word of the Year Press Release." January 4, 2008. http://americandialect.org/Word-of-the-Year_2007.pdf (accessed October 19, 2009).

American Psycho. DVD. Directed by Mary Harron. 2000; Santa Monica, CA: Lions Gate Films, 2003.

America's Army: Rise of a Soldier. Xbox. San Francisco, CA: Ubisoft, 2005.

Ansari, Humayun. *The Infidel Within: Muslims in Britain Since 1800*. London: Hurst and Company, 2004.

Apocalypse Now. DVD. Directed by Frances Ford Coppola. 1979; Burbank, CA: Paramount Home Video, 1999.

Apuzzo, Jason. "Superman Returns. Libertas—A Forum for Conservative Thought on Film." June, 2006. http://www.libertyfilmfestival.com/libertas/?p=1659 (accessed June 28, 2007).

Archibong, Victor, and Paul Leslie. "The Military-Industrial Complex and the Persian Gulf War: Ike's Caveat." In *The Gulf War as Popular Entertainment: An Analysis of the Military-Industrial Media Complex*, ed. Paul Leslie, 33–43. New York: Edwin Mellen Press, 1997.

Armstrong, David. "Dick Cheney's Song of America: Drafting a Plan for Global Dominance." *Harper's Magazine* October 2002: 76–83.

Asad, Talal. *On Suicide Bombing*. New York: Columbia University Press, 2007.

"Ashcroft." *Star Tribune*, December 9, 2001.

Aslam, Nadeem. *Maps for Lost Lovers*. London: Faber, 2004.

Aslan, Reza. *How to Win a Cosmic War: God, Globalization, and the End of the War on Terror*. New York: Random House, 2009.

Azie from Brooklyn. Composite digital image of Alex Ross's Superman Ghosted in front of the Twin Towers, at *Supermantv.net* (fansite) (2002). http://www.supermantv.net/wallpaperbattles/newsuperman/april2004/superman_wtc.jpg (accessed June 26, 2007).

Bacevich, Andrew. *American Empire: The Realities and Consequences of US Diplomacy*. Cambridge, MA: Harvard University Press, 2002.

——. *The New American Militarism: How Americans Are Seduced by War*. New York: Oxford University Press, 2005.

Baer, Justin, and William J. Chambliss. "Generating Fear: The Politics of Crime Reporting." *Crime, Law and Social Change* 27 (1997): 87–107

Bailey, Frankie Y., and Donna C. Hale. *Popular Culture, Crime, and Justice*. Belmont: Wadsworth Pub. Co., 1998.

Barber, Benjamin R. *Fear's Empire: War, Terrorism, and Democracy*. New York: W.W. Norton & Co., 2003.

——. *Jihad vs. McWorld: Terrorism's Challenge to Democracy*. New York: Ballantine, 1995.

Barthes, Roland. *Mythologies*. Trans. Annette Lavers. London: Vintage, 2000.

Batman. DVD. Directed by Tim Burton. 1989; Burbank, CA: Warner Bros. Pictures, 2008.

Batman and Robin. DVD. Directed by Joel Schumacher. 1997; Burbank, CA: Warner Bros. Pictures, 1997.

Batman Begins. DVD. Directed by Christopher Nolan. 2005; Burbank, CA: Warner Bros. Pictures, 2005.

Batman Forever. DVD. Directed by Joel Schumacher. 1995; Burbank, CA: Warner Bros. Pictures, 1997.

Batman Returns. DVD. Directed by Tim Burton. 1992; Burbank, CA: Warner Bros. Pictures, 1995.

Baudrillard, Jean. "L'esprit du Terrorisme." Trans. Michael Valentin. *South Atlantic Quarterly* 101, no. 2 (2002): 403–15.

———. *Simulacra and Simulation.* Ann Arbor: University of Michigan Press, 1995.

———. *The Spirit of Terrorism and Other Essays.* Trans. Chris Turner. New York: Verso, 2003.

Bauman, Zygmunt. *Liquid Times: Living in an Age of Uncertainty.* Cambridge: Polity, 2007.

Bender, Steven W. "Sight, Sound, and Stereotype: The War on Terrorism and Its Consequences for Latinas/os." *Oregon Law Review* 81 (2002): 1153–78.

Bennett, W. Lance. *News: The Politics of Illusion.* New York: Pearson/Longman, 2005.

Berlant, Lauren. *The Queen of America Goes to Washington City: Essays on Sex and Citizenship.* Durham, NC: Duke University Press. 1997.

Bethel Academy. http://www.bethelacademy.org/discipline.html (accessed June 11, 2008).

Big Parade, The. DVD. Directed by King Vidor. 1925; Burbank, CA; Warner Home Video, 1992.

Birth of a Nation, The. DVD. Directed by D.W. Griffith. 1915; Des Moines, IA: Triad Productions, 2008.

Bishop, Kyle. "Raising the Dead." *Journal of Popular Film & Television* 33, no. 4 (2006): 196–205.

Black Hawk Down. DVD. Directed by Ridley Scott. 2002; Culver City, CA.: Columbia TriStar Home Entertainment, 2002.

Blackmon, Douglas. *Slavery by Another Name: The Re-Enslavement of Black Americans from the Civil War to World War II.* New York: Doubleday, 2008.

Blackmore, Tim. 1991. "The Dark Knight of Democracy: Tocqueville and Miller Cast Some Light on the Subject." *Journal of American Culture* 14, no. 1 (1991): 37–56.

BlackSite: Area 51. Xbox 360. San Diego, CA: Midway, 2007.

Blade Runner. DVD. Directed by Ridley Scott. 1982; Burbank, CA: Warner Home Video, 2006.

Blum, William. *Killing Hope: US Military and CIA Interventions Since WWII.* Monroe, ME: Common Courage Press, 1995.

———. *Rogue State: A Guide to the World's Only Superpower.* Monroe, ME: Common Courage Press, 2000.

Boggs, Carl. "Pentagon Strategy, Hollywood, and Technowar." *New Politics* 9.1 (2006). http://www.wpunj.edu/newpol/issue41/Boggs41.htm (accessed October 20, 2009).

Borradori, Giovanna. *Philosophy in a Time of Terror: Dialogues with Jürgen Habermas and Jacques Derrida.* Chicago: University of Chicago Press, 2003.

Boyer, Crispin, Garnett Lee, and Andrew Pfister. "Review of *Call of Duty 4: Modern Warfare.*" *Electronic Gaming Monthly* 223 (2007): 70–3.

Boyer, Paul. *When Time Shall Be No More: Prophesy Belief in Modern American Culture.* Cambridge: Harvard University Press, 1992.

———. "When US Foreign Policy Meets Biblical Prophesy." *Alternet.* February 20, 2003. http://www.alternet.org/story/15221 (accessed July 14, 2006).

Braiker, Brian. "What Americans (Don't) Know." (June 23, 2007). http://www.msnbc.msn.com/id/19390791/site/newsweek/ (accessed July 22, 2007).

Brazil. DVD. Directed by Terry Gilliam. 1985; New York: Criterion Collection, 2006.

Brennan, Timothy. *Wars of Position: The Cultural Politics of Left and Right.* New York: Columbia University Press, 2006.

Brothers Judd, The. "Review of *Master and Commander: The Far Side of the World.*" Brothersjudd.com. April 24, 2004. http://brothersjudd.com/index.cfm/fuseaction/reviews.moviedetail/movie_id/83/Master%20and%20Commander:%20The%20Far%20Side%20of%20the%20World.htm (accessed February 7, 2009).

Brown, Malcolm D. "Orientalism and Resistance to Orientalism: Muslim Identities in Contemporary Western Europe." In *Practicing Identities: Power and Resistance*, eds Sasha Roseneil and Julie Seymour, 180–98. Basingstoke: Palgrave Macmillan, 1999.

Brown, Wendy. *Edgework: Critical Essays on Knowledge and Politics*. Princeton: Princeton University Press, 2005.

Buck-Morss, Susan. *Thinking Past Terror: Islamism and Critical Theory on the Left*. London: Verso, 2003.

Bush, George W. "Address to a Joint Session of Congress and the American People." *Whitehouse. gov*, September 20, 2001. http://www.whitehouse.gov/news/releases/2001/09/20010920-8. html (accessed October 20, 2009).

——. "Bush Raps 'Revisionist Historians' on Iraq." *Cnn.com*, June 16, 2003. http://www.cnn. com/2003/ALLPOLITICS/06/16/bush.iraq/ (accessed October 20, 2009).

——. "Text: President Bush Addresses the Nation." *Washington Post*, September 20, 2001. http://www.washingtonpost.com/wp-srv/nation/specials/attacked/transcripts/ bushad-dress_092001.html (accessed February 7, 2009).

——. "Transition of Power: President-Elect Bush Meets With Congressional Leaders on Capitol Hill." *CNN.com*, December 18, 2000. http://transcripts.cnn.com/TRANSCRIPTS/ 0012/18/nd.01.html (accessed December 1, 2008).

"Bush Plays Video Games with Recovering War Veterans." *AFP*, November 9, 2007. http:// afp.google.com/article/ALeqM5jExFefQsl8i87mwwcEqLxWdg1BVA (accessed October 20, 2009).

Call of Duty 4: Modern Warfare. Xbox 360. Los Angeles, CA: Activision, 2007.

Campbell, David. *Writing Security: United States Foreign Policy and the Politics of Identity*. Minneapolis: University of Minnesota Press, 1998.

Campbell, Joseph Scott, and Hi-Fi. Untitled image. In *Heroes: The World's Greatest Superhero Creators Honor the World's Greatest Heroes, 9.11.2001*, ed. Rob Haynes, with Tim Townsend, Tim and David Self, second edn (New York: Marvel Comics, December 2001).

Captain Horatio Hornblower. DVD. Directed by Raoul Walsh. 1951; Burbank, CA: Warner Home Video, 2007.

Caruth, Cathy, ed. *Trauma: Explorations in Memory*. Baltimore, MD: Johns Hopkins Press, 1995.

Casey, Joe, Mike Wieringo, Jose Marzan, Jr., Tanya Horie, Rich Horie, and Bill Oakley. "A Lex." In *Adventures of Superman # 600*, ed. Eddie Berganza. New York: DC Comics, 2002.

Cerulo, Karen A. "Individualism Pro Tem: Reconsidering US Social Relations." In *Culture in Mind: Toward a Sociology of Culture and Cognition*, ed. Karen A. Cerulo, 135–71. New York: Routledge, 2002.

Chermak, Steven. *Victims in the News: Crime and the American News Media*. Boulder, CO: Westview Press, 1995.

Chion, Michel. *The Voice in Cinema*. Trans. Claudia Gorbman. New York: Columbia University Press, 2009.

Chomsky, Noam. *9–11*. New York: Seven Stories Press, 2001.

CIA. *Kubark Counterintelligence Interrogation* [Manual]. July 1963. [Declassified].

——. *Human Resource Exploitation Training Manual*. 1983. [Declassified].

Clark, Victoria. *Allies for Armageddon: The Rise of Christian Zionism*. New Haven, CT: Yale University Press, 2007.

Clockwork Orange, A. DVD. Directed by Stanley Kubrick. 1971; Burbank, CA: Warner Home Video, 2001.

Cloverfield. DVD. Directed by Matt Reeves. 2008; Los Angeles, CA: Paramount Pictures, 2009

Coghlan, Andy. "Obama to Restore Science to Its Rightful Place." *New Scientist* (January 20, 2009). http://www.newscientist.com/article/dn16452-obama-to-restore-science-to-its-rightful-place.html (accessed October 20, 2009).

Collateral Damage. Directed by Andrew Davis. Los Angeles: Warner Bros. Pictures, 2002.

Commission on British Muslims and Islamophobia. *Islamophobia: A Challenge for Us All*. London: Runnymede Trust, 1997.

Cooper, Richard T. "General Casts War in Religious Terms." *Common Dreams*, October 16, 2003. http://www.commondreams.org/headlines03/1016-01.htm (accessed July 12, 2009).

Copeland, Phil. 2004. "Future Warrior Exhibits Super Powers." *American Forces Press Service, US Department of Defense,* July 27, 2004. http://www.defenselink.mil/news/newsarticle. aspx?id=25636 (accessed October 20, 2009).

Corkin, Stanley. *Cowboys and Cold Warriors: The Western and US History.* Philadelphia: Temple University Press, 2004.

Coulter, Anne "This Is War. We Should Invade Their Countries." *National Review Online,* September 13, 2001. http://www.nationalreview.com/coulter/coulter.shtml (accessed July 10, 2007).

Cowen, David. "*Brazil* (Movie, 1985): Frequently Asked Questions, v1.3." 1996. http://www. faqs.org/faqs/movies/brazil-faq/ (accessed October 20, 2009).

Crackdown. Xbox 360. Redmond, WA: Microsoft, 2006.

Cranny-Francis, Anne. "*Batman*: Hollywood and the Postmodern." *Social Semiotics* 1, no. 1 (1991): 4–29.

Cray, Charlie. "The 10 Most Brazen War Profiteers." *AlterNet.org,* September 5, 2006. http:// www.alternet.org/waroniraq/41083/ (accessed July 30, 2007).

Croft, Stuart. *Culture, Crisis, and America's War on Terror.* Cambridge: Cambridge University Press, 2006.

Crumley, Andrew. "Perils of Seizing the Day." *Scotsman on Sunday,* February 6, 2005. http:// living.scotsman.com/books.cfm?id=139472005 (accessed March 30, 2007).

D'Agnolo-Vallan, Giulia. "Let Them Eat Flesh." *Film Comment* 41, no. 4 (2005): 23–24.

Daniel, Norman. *Islam and the West: The Making of an Image.* 1960; Reprint, Oxford: Oneworld Publications, 2009.

Dark City. DVD. Directed by Alex Proyas. 1998; Australia: Mystery Clock Cinema, 1998.

Dark Knight, The. DVD. Directed by Christopher Nolan. 2008; Burbank, CA: Warner Bros. Pictures, 2008.

Davies, Frank. "Many Americans Believe There Was a Link Between Iraq, Sept. 11." *San Jose Mercury News,* September 11, 2007.

Day After, The. DVD. Directed by Nicholas Meyer. 1983; Burbank, CA: MGM, 2004.

Day After Tomorrow, The. DVD. Directed by Roland Emmerich. 2004; Burbank, CA: Twentieth Century Fox, 2004.

Deadliest Catch, The. Live television. Produced by Brian Catalina. Discovery Channel, 2005–present.

Deadwood. Live television. Created by David Milch. Home Box Office, 2004–06.

de Certeau, Michel. *The Certeau Reader.* Ed. Graham Ward. New York: Blackwell, 2000.

Deer Hunter, The. DVD. Directed by Michael Cimino. 1978; Burbank, CA: Warner Home Video, 2003.

de la Vega, Elizabeth. *The United States v. George W. Bush et al.* New York: Seven Stories Press, 2006.

DeMatteis, J.M., Joe Kelly, Jeph Loeb, *et al. Superman: President Lex (Book 5).* New York: DC Comics, 2003.

Der Derian, James. *Virtuous War: Mapping the Military-Industrial-Media-Entertainment Network.* Colorado: Westview, 2001.

Dershowitz, Alan M. "Want to Torture? Get a Warrant." *San Francisco Chronicle,* January 22, 2002. http://www.sfgate.com/cgi-bin/article.cgi?file=/chronicle/archive/2002/01/22/ ED5329.DTL (accessed May 7, 2009).

Diamond, Sara. *Roads to Dominion: Right Wing Movements and Political Power in the United States.* New York: Guilford Press, 1995.

Di Certo, David. "Review of *Master and Commander: The Far Side of the World.*" *Christianitytoday.com.* http://www.christianitytoday.com/movies/reviews/2003/mas-terandcommander.html?start=3 (accessed October 20, 2009).

Dick, Philip K. "How to Build a Universe That Doesn't Fall Apart Two Days Later." In *The Shifting Realities of Philip K. Dick: Selected Literary and Philosophic Writings,* ed. Lawrence Sutin. New York: Vintage Books, 1978.

Dillard, R.H.W. "*Night of the Living Dead*: It's Not Just a Wind That's Passing Through." In

American Horrors: Essays on the Modern American Horror Film, ed. Gregory A. Waller, 14–29. Chicago: University of Illinois Press, 1987.

Dini, Paul, and Alex Ross. *Superman: Peace on Earth*. New York: DC Comics, 1998.

Dirda, Michael. "Shattered." *Washington Post*, Sunday, March 20, 2005, T01.

Dirty Jobs. Live television. Directed by Mikkel Beha Erichsen. Discovery Channel, 2003–present.

Dixon, Wheeler Winston, ed. *Film & Television After 9/11*. Carbondale: Southern Illinois UP, 2004.

Dodge, Catherine. "Cheney Defends Iraq War, Says World Safer Today." *Bloomberg*, September 10, 2006. http://www.bloomberg.com/apps/news?pid=20601170&sid=aMuFuSmq5znA& refer=special_report (accessed October 20, 2009).

Donnelly, Thomas. "Rebuilding America's Defenses: Strategy, Forces and Resources for a New Century." Report of The Project for The New American Century, http://www.newamericancentury.org/RebuildingAmericasDefenses.pdf (accessed January 4, 2008).

Douthat, Ross. "So, You Want to Win the Culture Wars? It Would Help to Engage in a Little Culture." *Theamericanscene.com*, December 13, 2004. http://theamerican scene.com/pubs/nr121304.html (accessed September 10, 2006).

Drew, Julie. "Identity Crisis: Gender, Public Discourse and 9/11." *Women & Language* 27, no. 2 (2004): 71–8.

Dreyfus, Robert. "Reverend Doomsday." *Rolling Stone*, January 8, 2004. http://www.rolling-stone.com/politics/story/5939999/reverend_doomsday/ (accessed December 14, 2007).

Duralde, Alonso. "How Gay is Superman?/What I learned from Superman." *Advocate*, May 23, 2006.

Dyer, Richard. "American Cinema in the '70s: *The Towering Inferno*." *Movie* 21 (1975): 30–3.

———. "White." *Screen* 29, no. 4 (1988): 59–63.

Eagan, Timothy. "In Sacramento, a Publisher's Questions Draw the Wrath of the Crowd." *New York Times*, December 21, 2001. Late Edition (East Coast).

Eisenhower, Dwight. 1961, "Farewell Radio and Television Address to the American People." *The Dwight D. Eisenhower Presidential Library*, http://www.eisenhower.archives.gov/ all_about_ike/Speeches/Farewell_Address.pdf (accessed October 20, 2009).

Elijah Generation International. http://www.spiritualbootcamp.org/ (accessed June 11, 2008).

Elliott, Stuart. 2001. "The Media Business: Advertising; Madison Ave. Grapples with Post-Sept 11 Era." *New York Times*, December 11, 2001.

Elsaesser, Thomas. "Postmodernism as Mourning Work." *Screen* 42, no. 2 (Summer 2001): 193–201.

Engblom, Mark. *Comic Coverage*, http://comiccoverage.typepad.com/comic_cover-age/2006/11/during_the_feve.html (accessed October 16, 2009).

Engel, Matthew. "War on Afghanistan: American Media Cowed by Patriotic Fever, Says Network News Veteran." *Guardian*, May 17, 2002, 4.

Engelhardt, Tom. *The End of Victory Culture: Cold War America and the Disillusioning of a Generation*. New York: Harper Collins, 1995.

Engle, Karen. *Seeing Ghosts: 9/11 and the Visual Imagination*. Montreal and Kingston: McGill-Queen's University Press, 2009.

Epstein, Edward J. *News from Nowhere*. New York: Random House, 1973.

Ericson, Richard V., Patricia M. Baranek, and Janet B.L. Chan. *Representing Order: Crime, Law and Justice in the News Media*. Toronto: University of Toronto Press, 1991.

———. *Visualizing Deviance: A Study of News Organization*. Toronto: University of Toronto Press, 1987.

Eternal Sunshine of the Spotless Mind. DVD. Directed by Michel Gondry. 2004; Los Angeles, CA: Universal Studies, 2004.

Evans, Alex. "Cultural Politics and the Gay Fantasia: Transcending and Ending Queer Crises in 90s North American and British Culture." PhD diss., University of Sussex, 2005.

Fahrenheit 9/11. DVD. Directed by Michael Moore. 2004; New York: Weinstein Company, 2007.

Fairness and Accuracy in Reporting [FAIR]. "In Iraq Crisis, Networks are Megaphones for

Official Views." *FAIR*, March 18, 2003, http://www.fair.org/reports/iraq-sources.html (accessed October 20, 2009).

Faludi, Susan. *Stiffed: The Betrayal of the Modern Man*. London: Chatton & Windus, 1999.

———. *The Terror Dream: Fear and Fantasy in Post-9/11 America*. New York: Metropolitan Books, 2007.

Family Guy. Live television. Created by Seth MacFarlane. FOX, 2005–present.

Faulkner, William. *Absalom, Absalom!* 1936. Reprint, New York: Vintage, 1986.

Feldmann, Lisa. "The Impact of Bush Linking 9/11 and Iraq." *Christian Science Monitor*, March 1, 2003. http://www.csmonitor.com/2003/0314/p02s01-woiq.htm (accessed July 12, 2007).

Fight Club. DVD. Directed by David Fincher. 1999; Burbank, CA: Twentieth Century Fox, 2000.

Filkins, Dexter. *The Forever War*. New York: Random House, 2007.

Force Ministries. http://www.forceministries.com/ (accessed June 11, 2008).

Foster, Thomas. "Cynical Nationalism." In *The Selling of 9/11: How a National Tragedy Became a Commodity*, ed. Dana Heller, 254–87. New York: Palgrave Macmillan, 2005.

Foucault, Michel. *Discipline and Punish*. Vintage Books: New York, 1979.

Frasca, Gonzalo. "Simulation Versus Narrative: Introduction to Ludology." In *The Video Game Theory Reader*, eds Mark J.P. Wolf and Bernard Perron, 221–35. New York: Routledge, 2003.

Freud, Sigmund. *Moses and Monotheism*. New York: Vintage, 1955.

Friedman, Roger. "'Superman' Struggles at Box Office." *Fox News*, July 1, 2006. http://www.foxnews.com/story/0,2933,201814,00.html (accessed June 26, 2007).

Froula, Anna. "Lynch `N England: Figuring Females as the US at War." *Global Media Journal* 5, no. 9 (Fall 2006). http://lass.calumet.purdue.edu/cca/gmj/fa06/graduatefa06/gmj_grad_fa06froula (accessed June 22, 2007).

Frykholm, Amy Johnson. *Rapture Culture: Left Behind in Evangelical America*. New York: Oxford University Press, 2004.

Full Spectrum Warrior. Xbox. Calabasas Hills, CA: THQ, 2004.

Full Spectrum Warrior: Ten Hammers. Xbox. Calabasas Hills, CA: THQ, 2006.

Furedi, Frank. *Culture of Fear: Risk-Taking and the Morality of Low Expectation*. London: Cassell, 1997.

Gaines, Jane M. "The Production of Outrage: The Iraq War and the Radical Documentary Tradition." *Framework* 48, no. 2 (2007): 36–55.

Garfinkel, Harold. "Conditions of Successful Degradation Ceremonies." *American Journal of Sociology* 61, no. 1 (1956): 420–4.

Garland, David. *The Culture of Control: Crime and Social Order in Contemporary Society*. Chicago: University of Chicago Press, 2001.

Geertz, Clifford. *The Interpretation of Cultures*. New York: Basic Books, 1973.

Gellman, Barton, and Walter Pincus. Iraq's Nuclear File: Inside the Prewar Debate, "Depiction of Threat Outgrew Supporting Evidence," *Washington Post*, August 10, 2003, A1.

George W. Bush White House, The. *National Security Strategy of the United States*. In *The George W. Bush White House Archives 2002*. http://georgewbush-whitehouse.archives.gov/nsc/nss/2002/index.html (accessed July 5, 2009).

———. "President Declares 'Freedom At War With Fear.'" In *The George W. Bush White House Archives 2001*. September 20, 2001. http://georgewbush-whitehouse.archives.gov/news/releases/2001/09/20010920-8.html (accessed July 10, 2009).

———. "President Signs Intelligence Reform and Terrorism Prevention Act," *The George W. Bush White House Archives* December 17, 2004. http://georgewbush-whitehouse.archives.gov/news/releases/2004/12/20041217-1.html (accessed July 14, 2009).

Gibbs, Nancy. "Apocalypse Now." *Time*. July 1, 2002. http://www.time.com/time/covers/1101020701/story.html (accessed July 15, 2009).

Gilliam, Terry and Ian Christie, ed. *Gilliam on Gilliam*. London: Faber and Faber Limited, 1999.

Gladiator. DVD. Directed by Ridley Scott. 2000; Universal City: Dreamworks Video, 2000.

Glasgow University Media Group. *Bad News*. London: Routledge & Kegan Paul, 1976.

Glassner, Barry. *The Culture of Fear: Why Americans Are Afraid of the Wrong Things*. New York: Basic Books, 1999.

Goldberg, Michelle. *Kingdom Coming: The Rise of Christian Nationalism*. New York: Norton Publishing, 2006.

Goldstein, Richard. "Neo-Macho Man: Pop Culture and Post-9/11 Politics." *Nation*, March 24, 2003, 16–19.

Gordimer, Nadine. *The Pickup*. London: Bloomsbury, 2001.

Gordon, Greg, and Marisa Taylor. "US Interrogators May Not Be in the Clear Yet; Bill on Abuses Won't Stop Prosecutions in Other Countries, Experts Warn." *Sacramento Bee*, September 30, 2006, p. A16.

Gordon, Michael R., and Jim Rutenberg. "Bush Links Al Qaeda in Iraq to 9/11; Critics Reject Connection." *New York Times*, July 13, 2007. http://www.nytimes.com/2007/07/13/world/africa/13iht-qaeda.1.6641919.html (accessed October 20, 2009).

Go Tell the Spartans. DVD. Directed by Ted Post. 1978; Burbank, CA: HBO Home Video, 2005.

Gough, Bob. "Is Superman's Bulge a CGI Fabrication?" *CBM*, December 13, 2005. http://www.comicbookmovie.com/news/articles/2462.asp (accessed June 28, 2007).

Gowan, Peter. "The Bush Turn and the Drive for Primacy." In *The War on Terrorism and the American 'Empire' after the Cold War*, eds Alejandro Colas and Richard Saull, 131–53. New York: Routledge, 2006.

Graham, Stephen. "Postmortem City: Towards an Urban Geopolitics." *City* 8, no. 2 (2004): 165–96.

———. "Switching Cities off: Urban Infrastructure and US Air Power." *City* 9, no. 2 (2005): 169–94.

———. "Man Plus: Enhanced Cyborgs and the Construction of the Future Masculine." *Science as Culture* 9, no. 3 (2000): 277–99.

Grand Theft Auto: San Andreas. Xbox. New York: Rockstar, 2005.

Grand Theft Auto IV. Xbox 360. New York: Rockstar, 2008.

Gran Torino. DVD. Directed by Clint Eastwood. 2008; Burbank, CA: Warner Home Video, 2009.

Gray, Chris Hables. *Postmodern War: The New Politics of Conflict*. London: Routledge, 1997.

Gray, John. *Black Mass: Apocalyptic Religion and the Death of Utopia*. New York: Farrar, Straus, and Giroux, 2007.

Gray, Mitchell, and Elvin Wyly. "The Terror City Hypothesis." In *Violent Geographies: Fear, Terror, and Political Violence*, ed. Derek Gregory and Allan Pred, 329–48. New York: Routledge, 2007.

Green Berets, The. DVD. Directed by Ray Kellogg *et al.* 1968; Burbank, CA: Warner Home Video, 1997).

Gregory, Derek, and Allan Pred. "Introduction." *Violent Geographies: Fear, Terror, and Political Violence*, ed. Derek Gregory and Allan Pred, 1–6. New York: Routledge, 2007.

Griffith, David. *A Good War is Hard to Find: The Art of Violence in America*. New York: Soft Skull Press, 2007.

Halliday, Fred. "West Encountering Islam: Islamophobia Reconsidered." In *Islam Encountering Globalization*, ed. Ali Mohammadi, 14–35. London: Routledge Curzon, 2002.

Halo. Xbox. Redmond, WA: Microsoft, 2001.

Halo 2. Xbox. Redmond, WA: Microsoft, 2004.

Halper, Stefan, and Jonathan Clarke. *America Alone: The Neo-Conservatives and the Global Order*. Cambridge: Cambridge University Press, 2004.

Halter, Ed. *From Sun Tzu to Xbox: War and Video Games*. New York: Thunder's Mouth Press, 2006.

Hank. "It's a Bird . . . It's a Plane . . . It's a Deadbeat Dad?" (Thursday, June 15, 2006). http://www.federalreview.com/2006/06/its-birdits-planeits-deadbeat-dad.htm (accessed June 26, 2007).

Harding, Susan. *The Book of Jerry Falwell: Fundamentalist Language and Politics*. Princeton: Princeton University Press. 2000.

Harnden, Toby. "Bin Laden Is Wanted: Dead or Alive, Says Bush." *Telegraph.co.uk*, September 18, 2001. http://www.telegraph.co.uk/news/worldnews/asia/afghanistan/1340895/Bin-Laden-is-wanted-dead-or-alive-says-Bush.html (accessed October 20, 2009).

Hartung, William D. "Making Money on Terrorism." *Nation*, February 5, 2004. http://www.thenation.com/doc/20040223/hartung (accessed July 30, 2007).

Harvey, David. *The New Imperialism*. New York: Oxford University Press. 2003.

Haynes, Rob, (ed.), with Tim Townsend and David Self. *Heroes: The World's Greatest Superhero Creators Honor the World's Greatest Heroes. 9.11.2001*. Second edn. New York: Marvel Comics, 2001.

Hedges, Chris. *War Is a Force That Gives Us Meaning*. New York: Anchor, 2003.

Hendershot, Heather. *Shaking the World for Jesus: Media and Conservative Evangelical Culture*. Chicago: University of Chicago Press, 2004.

Hess, Stephen. *International News & Foreign Correspondents*. Washington, DC: Brookings Institution, 1996.

Hickey, Neil. "Access Denied: Pentagon's War Reporting Rules are Toughest Ever." *Columbia Journalism Review* 40, no. 5 (2002): 26–31.

Hickley, Matthew. "US Military Develops Robocop Armor for Soldiers." *The Daily Mail*, April 11, 2007. http://www.dailymail.co.uk/pages/live/articles/technology/technology.html?in_page_id=1965&in_article_id=447631 (accessed October 20, 2009).

Higashi, Sumiko. "A Horror Film About the Vietnam Era." In *Hanoi to Hollywood: The Vietnam War in American Film*, eds Linda Dittmar and Gene Michaud, 175–88. Rutgers, NJ: Rutgers University Press. 1990.

Hirschkind, Charles. *The Ethical Soundscape: Cassette Sermons and Islamic Counterpublics*. New York: Columbia University Press, 2006.

Hitchens, Christopher. "Empire Falls: How *Master and Commander* Gets Patrick O'Brian Wrong." *Slate.com*, November 14, 2008. http://www.slate.com/id/2091249/ (accessed October 8, 2006).

Holmlund, Chris. *Impossible Bodies: Femininity and Masculinity at the Movies*. London: Routledge, 2002.

"Homecoming," *Masters of Horror*. Live television. Directed by Joe Dante. Showtime, 2005.

Huiskamp, Gerard. "*Minority Report* on the Bush Doctrine." In *Politics of Empire*, ed. Joseph G. Peschek. London: Routledge, 2005.

Huntington, Samuel. *The Soldier and the State: The Theory and Politics of Civil-Military Relations*. Cambridge: Harvard University Press, 1981.

——. *The Clash of Civilizations and the Remaking of World Order*. New York: Simon and Schuster, 1996.

Hussain, Yasmin. *Writing Diaspora: South Asian Women, Culture and Ethnicity*. Hampshire: Ashgate, 2005.

I Am Legend. DVD. Directed by Francis Lawrence. 2007; Burbank, CA: Warner Bros. Pictures, 2008.

Ignatieff, Michael. *Virtual War: Kosovo and Beyond*. New York: Metropolitan, 2000.

Imposter. DVD. Directed by Gary Fleder. 2002; Enfield Mddx, UK: Prism Leisure, 2003.

Institute for the Study of Islam and Christianity. *Islam in Britain: The British Muslim Community in February 2005*. Wiltshire: Isaac Publishing, 2005.

In the Valley of Elah. DVD. Directed by Paul Haggis. 2007; Burbank, CA: Warner Home Video, 2007.

Invasion. Live television. Produced by Shaun Cassidy. ABC, 2005–6.

Iraq for Sale: The War Profiteers. DVD. Directed by Robert Greenwald. 2006. Culver City, CA: Brave New Films, 2006.

I Walked with a Zombie. DVD. Directed by Jacques Tourneur. 1943; Atlanta, GA: Turner Home Entertainment, 2005.

J'Accuse. VHS. Directed by Abel Gance. 1938; Burbank, CA: Connoisseur Video, 1994.

Jackall, Robert, and Janice M. Hirota. *Image Makers: Advertising, Public Relations, and the Ethos of Advocacy*. Chicago: University of Chicago Press, 2000.

Jameson, Fredric. *Postmodernism or, The Cultural Logic of Late Capitalism*. Durham, NC: Duke University Press, 1991.

———. *The Seeds of Time*. New York: Columbia University Press, 1994.

———. "Symptom of Theory or Symptoms for Theory." *Critical Inquiry* 30, no. 2 Winter, 2003.

Janis, Irving. *Victims of Groupthink*. Boston: Houghton Mifflin, 1972.

Jehl, Douglas, and David Johnston. "Rule Change Lets C.I.A. Freely Send Suspects Abroad to Jails." *New York Times*, March 6, 2005. http://www.nytimes.com/2005/03/06/politics/06intel.html?ex=1110776400&en=e36cc36fc5ef2f81&ei=5070 (accessed October 20, 2009).

Jenkins, Henry. "Captain America Sheds His Mighty Tears: Comics and September 11." In *Terror, Culture, Politics: Rethinking 9/11*, eds Daniel J. Sherman and Terry Nardini. Bloomington: Indiana University Press, 2006.

Jericho. Live television. Directed by Guy Norman Bee. CBS, 2006–08.

Jesus Camp. DVD. Directed by Heidi Ewing and Rachel Grady. 2006; New York and Austin: Magnolia Home Entertainment, 2007.

Jewett, Robert and John Shelton Lawrence. *Captain America and the Crusade Against Evil: The Dilemma of Zealous Nationalism*. London: William B. Eerdmans Publishing Company, 2003.

———. *Captain America and the Crusade Against Evil: The Dilemma of Zealous Nationalism*. Grand Rapids, Michigan: William B. Eerdmans Publishing Company, 2002a.

———. *The Myth of the American Superhero*. Grand Rapids, MI: William B. Eerdmans Publishing Company, 2002b.

Johnson, Chalmers A. *Blowback: The Costs and Consequences of American Empire*. New York: Metropolitan Books, 2000.

———. *Nemesis: The Last Days of the American Republic*. New York: Metropolitan Books, 2008.

———. *The Sorrows of Empire: Militarism, Secrecy, and the End of the Republic*. New York: Metropolitan Books, 2004.

Jones, Alan. "George A. Romero. *Dead Reckoning*." *Film Review* 662 (2005): 64.

Kagan, Robert. *Of Paradise and Power: America and Europe in the New World Order*. New York: Knopf, 2003.

Kagan, Robert, and William Kristol. *Present Dangers: Crisis and Opportunity in American Foreign and Defense Policy*. San Francisco: Encounter Books, 2000.

Kaplan, Caren. 2006. "Precision Targets: GPS and the Militarization of US Consumer Identity." *American Quarterly* 58, no. 3 (2006): 693–713.

Kaplan, E. Ann. *Trauma Culture: The Politics of Terror and Loss in Media and Literature*. New Brunswick, NJ: Rutgers University Press, 2005.

Kaplan, Robert D. "Supremacy by Stealth: Ten Rules for Managing the World." *Atlantic* July/August 2003: 66–90.

Kappeler, Victor E., Mark Blumberg, and Gary W. Potter. *The Mythology of Crime and Criminal Justice*. Prospect Heights, IL: Waveland Press, 1999.

Katz, Cindi. "Banal Terrorism: Spatial Fetishism and Everyday Insecurity." In *Violent Geographies: Fear, Terror and Political Violence*, eds Derek Gregory and Allan Pred, 349–61. New York: Routledge, 2007.

Keane, Stephen. *Disaster Movies: The Cinema of Catastrophe*. London: Wallflower, 2006.

Keighley, Geoff. "Hooray for Halowood." *Entertainment Weekly*, November 5, 2004, 46–8.

Kellner, Douglas. *From 9/11 to Terror War: The Dangers of the Bush Legacy*. Lanham, MD: Rowman & Littlefield, 2003.

———. "Media Propaganda and Spectacle in the War on Iraq: A Critique of US Broadcasting Networks." *Cultural Studies/Critical Methodologies* 4 (2004): 329–38.

Khatman. "The True Heroes of September 11, 2001." Image at *Supermancollector.com*, 2003. http://www.supermancollector.com/americanway/americanspiritkhatman.jpg (accessed June 26, 2007).

Kidd, Chip, and Geoff Spear. *Mythology: The DC Comics Art of Alex Ross*. Reprint edition. New York: Pantheon, 2005.

Klein, Naomi. *The Shock Doctrine: The Rise of Disaster Capitalism*. New York: Metropolitan Books, 2007. http://www.naomiklein.org/main (accessed October 20, 2009).

Klock, Jeff. *How to Read Superhero Comics and Why*. New York: Continuum, 2002.

Konrad, Kevin. "Farewell to a Real Hero." Image at *Superman.ws*, 2002. www.superman.ws/ FanArtWTC/Farewell_to_a_Real_Hero.bmp (accessed July 3, 2007).

Krauthammer, Charles. "*Master and Commander*: Success on the High Seas." *Jewishworldreview. com*, November 14, 2003. http://www.jewishworldreview.com/cols/krauthammer111403. asp (accessed February 7, 2009).

Kristol, William, and Robert Kagan. "Toward a Neo-Reaganite Foreign Policy." http://www. carnegieendowment.org/publications/index.cfm?fa=view&id=276&prog=zgp&proj=zus r&zoom_highlight=Kristol+Kagan+Toward (accessed June 28, 2009).

Kumar, Krishan. "Apocalypse, Millennium, and Utopia Today." In *Apocalypse Theory and the Ends of the World*, ed. Malcolm Bull, 200–24. Cambridge, MA: Blackwell Publishers, 1995.

Kureishi, Hanif. *The Black Album*. London: Faber, 1995.

——. "My Son the Fanatic." In *Love in a Blue Time*, 119–31. London: Faber, 1997.

——. 1998. "The Road Exactly." In "Introduction to *My Son the Fanatic* screenplay." *The Word and the Bomb*, 53–9. London: Faber, 2005.

——. "The Carnival of Culture." In *The Word and the Bomb*, 97–100. London: Faber, 2005.

Ladd, Barbara. "'The Direction of the Howling': Nationalism and the Color Line in *Absalom, Absalom!*" *American Literature* 66, no. 3 (1994): 525–55.

Lagouranis, Tony, and Allen Mikaelian. *Fear Up Harsh: An Army Interrogator's Dark Journey Through Iraq*. New York: NAL, 2007.

LaHaye, Tim, and Jerry B. Jenkins. *Left Behind: A Novel of the Earth's Last Days*. Wheaton: Tyndale House, 1995.

Langewiesche, William. "American Ground: Unbuilding the World Trade Center, Part One: The Inner World." *Atlantic* 290, no. 1 (July/August 2002):42–79.

——. "American Ground: Unbuilding the World Trade Center, Part Two: The Rush to Recover." *Atlantic* 290, no. 2 (September 2002): 48–79.

——. "American Ground: Unbuilding the World Trade Center, Part Three: The Dance of the Dinosaurs." *Atlantic* 290, no. 3 (October 2002): 92–126.

Larocca, Salvador, and Chris Clairemont. "Liquid!" Image. In *Heroes: The World's Greatest Superhero Creators Honor the World's Greatest Heroes, 9.11.2001*, ed. Rob Haynes, with Tim Townsend, Tim and David Self, second edn (New York: Marvel Comics, December 2001).

Lears, T.J. Jackson. *No Place of Grace: Antimodernism and the Transformation of American Culture, 1880–1920*. Chicago: University of Chicago Press, 1994.

Ledman, Melinda. "Review of *Master and Commander: The Far Side of the World*." *Hollywood Jesus*, November 7, 2003. http://www.hollywoodjesus.com/master_commander.htm (accessed February 9, 2009).

Lee, Stan, Kyle Hotz, and Hi-Fi. Plate 59. In *Heroes: The World's Greatest Superhero Creators Honor the World's Greatest Heroes, 9.11.2001*, ed. Rob Haynes, with Tim Townsend, Tim and David Self, second edn (New York: Marvel Comics, December 2001).

Lenoir, Timothy. "All But War Is Simulation: The Military-Entertainment Complex." *Configurations* 8, no. 3 (2000): 289–335.

Levitz, Jay. "Review of *Master and Commander: The Far Side of the World*." *Christiananswers. com*. http://christiananswers.net/spotlight/movies/2003/masterandcommander. html?zoom_highlight=master+and+commander (accessed February 8, 2009).

Lim, Dennis. "The Life of Brain." *Village Voice*, March 15, 2005. http://www.villagevoice.com/ books/0511,bklim,62101,10.html (accessed March 30, 2007).

"Limbaugh on Torture of Iraqis: US Guards Were 'Having a Good Time,' 'Blow[ing] Some Steam Off.'" *Media Matters for America*, May 5, 2004. http://mediamatters.org/research/200405050003 (accessed October 20, 2009).

Limerick, Patricia Nelson. *The Legacy of Conquest: The Unbroken Past of the American West.* New York: W.W. Norton, 1987.

Lindsay, Robert. "'The Sutras of Abu Ghraib' by Aidan Delgado." Posting to http://robertlindsay.blogspot.com/2007/10/sutras-of-abu-ghraib-by-aidan-delgado.html (accessed January 3, 2008).

Lions for Lambs. DVD. Directed by Robert Redford. 2007; Century City, CA: United Artists, 2007.

Live Free or Die Hard. DVD. Directed by Len Wiseman. 2007; Burbank, CA: Twentieth Century Fox, 2007.

London, Herbert. "The Death of Superman." *First Things* # 31, March, 1993. http://www.firstthings.com/article/2008/05/003-the-death-of-superman-23 (accessed June 28, 2007).

Lost. Live television. Created by J.J. Abrams. ABC, 2004–7.

Lotz, Amanda. "Using 'Network' Theory in the Post-Network Era: Fictional 9/11 US Television Discourse as a 'Cultural Forum.'" *Screen* 45, no. 4 (2004): 423–38.

Lowenstein, Adam. *Shocking Representations: Historical Trauma, National Cinema, and the Modern Horror Film.* New York: Columbia University Press. 2005.

Lutz, Catherine. "The Wars Less Known," in *Dissent from the Homeland: Essays After September 11*, eds Stanley Hauerwas and Frank Lentricchia. Durham, NC: Duke University Press, 2003.

Lynch, Timothy. *Doublespeak and the War on Terrorism*. CATO Institute Briefing Paper 98, September 6, 2006. http://www.cato.org/pubs/bp/bp98.pdf (accessed October 20, 2009).

MacArthur, John R. "The Lies We Bought: The Unchallenged 'Evidence' for War." *Common Dreams*, May 1, 2003. http://www.commondreams.org/views03/0605-02.htm (accessed November 23, 2009).

MacDonald, Heather. "The Illegal-Alien Crime Wave." *City Journal*, Winter, 2004. http://www.city-journal.org/html/14_1_the_illegal_alien.html (accessed January 4, 2008).

Machinist, The. DVD. Directed by Brad Anderson. 2004; Madrid: Filmax Group, 2005.

Malphurs, Ryan. "The Media's Frontier Construction of President George W. Bush." *Journal of American Culture* 31, no. 2 (2008): 185–201.

Manhunt 2. PSP. London: Rockstar, 2007.

Mann, Michael. *Incoherent Empire*. London: Verso, 2003.

Man vs. Wild. Live television. Narrated by Bear Grylls. Discovery Channel, 2006–present.

Marcus, Greil. *Shape of Things to Come: New Sculptures*. New York: Rizzoli, 2009.

Marcus, Jonathan. "America: An Empire to Rival Rome?" *BBC News*, January 26, 2004. http://news.bbc.co.uk/1/hi/world/americas/3430199.stm. (accessed July 23, 2007).

Master and Commander: The Far Side of the World. DVD. Directed by Peter Weir. 2003; Los Angeles: Twentieth Century Fox, 2004.

Masugi, Ken. "Review of *Master and Commander: The Far Side of the World*." *Claremont Institute*, December 5, 2003. http://www.claremont.org/publications/pubid.314/pub_detail.asp (accessed February 9, 2009).

Mathews, Jack. *The Battle of Brazil*. New York: Applause, 1987.

Matrix, The. DVD. Directed by Andy and Larry Wachowski. 1999; Burbank, CA: Warner Home Video, 1999.

Mazzetti, Mark, and Johnston, David. "Bush Weighed Using Military in Arrests," *New York Times*, July 25, 2009, A01.

McAlister, Melani. *Epic Encounters: Culture, Media, and US Interests in the Middle East, 1945–2000*. Berkeley, CA: University of California Press, 2001.

——. *Epic Encounters: Culture, Media, and US Interests in the Middle East since 1945*. Updated edn. Berkeley, CA: University of California Press, 2005.

McClintock, Anne. "Paranoid Empire: Specters from Guantánamo and Abu Ghraib." *Small Axe* 28 (2009): 50–74.

McClure, Holly. "Review of *Master and Commander: The Far Side of the World*." *Crosswalk. com*, November 14, 2003. http://www.crosswalk.com/movies/1231139/ (accessed February 8, 2009).

McCoy, Alfred. *A Question of Torture: CIA Interrogation from the Cold War to the War on Terror*. New York: Macmillan, 2006.

McEwan, Ian. "Only Love and Then Oblivion. Love Was All They Had to Set Against Their Murderers." *Guardian*, September 15, 2001. http://www.guardian.co.uk/wtccrash/story/0,1300,552408,00.html (accessed March 30, 2007).

———. *Saturday*. London: Jonathan Cape. 2005.

Medhurst, Andy. "Batman, Deviance, and Camp." In *The Many Lives of the Batman—Critical Approaches to a Superhero*, eds Roberta E. Pearson and William Uricchio. New York: Routledge, 1991.

Medved, Michael. "Captain America, Traitor? The Comic Book Hero Goes Anti-American." *Nationalreview.com*. http://www.nationalreview.com/comment/comment-medved 040403.asp (accessed June 28, 2007).

Meehan, Eileen R. "'Holy Commodity Fetish, Batman!' The Political Economy of a Commercial Intertext." In *The Many Lives of the Batman: Critical Approaches to a Superhero and His Media*, ed. Roberta E. Pearson and William Uricchio, 47–65. New York: Routledge, 1991.

Melnick, Jeffrey. *9/11 Culture*. Malden, MA: Wiley-Blackwell, 2009.

Micheline, Dwyer and Rodier. "'Demolitia . . . She Plays For Keeps!!!'/ By Darker Reason." *Action Comics # 718*. New York: DC Comics, 1996.

Milburn, Colin. "Nanowarriors: Military Nanotechnology and Comic Books." *Intertexts* 9, no. 1 (2005): 77–103.

Milch, David. "Director's Commentary: Episode One." *Deadwood: The Complete First Season*. DVD. Directed by David Milch. 2004; Burbank, CA: HBO Video, 2005.

Milgram, Stanley. "Some Conditions of Obedience and Disobedience to Authority." *Human Relations* 18 (1965): 57–76.

Miller, Flagg. *The Moral Resonance of Arab Media: Audiocassette Poetry and Culture in Yemen*. Cambridge: Harvard University Press, 2007.

Minority Report. Directed by Stephen Spielberg. Los Angeles: Dreamworks, 2002.

Mirzoeff, Nicholas. *Watching Babylon: The War in Iraq and Global Visual Culture*. New York: Routledge, 2005.

Mitchell, W.J.T. "Cloning Terror: The War of Images 2001–04." In *The Life and Death of Images: Ethics and Aesthetics*, eds Diarmuid Costello and Dominic Willsdon, 179–207. Ithaca: Cornell University Press, 2008.

Monahan, Torin. *Surveillance and Security: Technological Politics and Power in Everyday Life*. New York: Routledge, 2006.

"MSNBC's Ashleigh Banfield Slams War Coverage." *AlterNet*, April 19, 2003. http://alternet.org/story/15778 (accessed July 2, 2007).

Nash, Geoffrey. "Re-siting Religion and Creating Feminised Space in the Fiction of Ahdaf Soueif and Leila Aboulela." *Wasafiri* 35 (2002): 28–31.

Neale, Steve. *Genre*. London: BFI, 1980.

Newcomb, Horace. "The Opening of America: Meaningful Difference in 1950s Television." In *The Other Fifties: Interrogating Midcentury American Icons*, ed. Joel Foreman, 103–23. Urbana, IL: University of Illinois Press, 1997.

Newcomb, Horace, and Paul M. Hirsch. "Television as a Cultural Forum." In *Television: The Critical View*, sixth edn, ed. Horace Newcomb. New York: Oxford University Press, 2000.

Newitz, Annalee. *Pretend We're Dead: Capitalist Monsters in American Pop Culture*. Durham, NC: Duke University Press. 2006.

———. "Social Upheaval Causes Spikes in Zombie Production." *io9*, October 29, 2008. http://io9.com/5070243/war-and-social-upheaval-cause-spikes-in-zombie-movie-production (accessed June 5, 2009).

Newman, Kim. "This Diseased World." In *Filmmaker Magazine*, Summer 2003. http://www.filmmakermagazine.com/summer2003/features/diseased_world.php (accessed September 29, 2007).

Newman, Rachel. "The Day the World Changed, I Did, Too." *Newsweek*, October 1, 2001, 9.

Next. DVD. Directed by Lee Tamahori. 2007; Los Angeles, CA: Paramount, 2007.

Nightline. "The Plan." ABC News, March 5, 2003.

Night of the Living Dead. Directed by George A. Romero. 1968; Burbank, CA: Twentieth Century Fox Home Entertainment, 2004.

Overstreet, Jeffrey. "Review of *Master and Commander: The Far Side of the World*." *Christianitytoday.com*. http://www.christianitytoday.com/movies/filmforum/031120.html (accessed February 8, 2009).

Paik, Peter Yoonsuk. "Smart Bombs, Serial Killing, and the Rapture." *Postmodern Culture* 14, no. 1. http://muse.jhu.edu/journals/postmodern_culture/v014/14.1paik.html (accessed October 15, 2006).

Pareles, Jon. "His Kind of Heroes, His Kind of Songs." *New York Times*, July 14, 2009. http://www.nytimes.com/2002/07/14/arts/music-his-kind-of-heroes-his-kind-of-songs.html (accessed October 20, 2009).

Parker, Trey. "Imaginationland." *South Park*. Season 11, Episode 2, 2007. First aired October 17, 2007.

Paycheck. Directed by John Woo. DVD. Burbank, CA: Paramount Pictures, 2003.

Pearl Harbor. Blu-ray. Directed by Michael Bay. 2001; Buena Vista Home Entertainment, 2006.

Perkins, John. *Confessions of an Economic Hit Man*. New York: Berrett-Koehler, 2006.

Perkovich, George. 2003. "Bush's Nuclear Revolution: A Regime Change in Nonproliferation." *Foreign Affairs* (March/April 2003). http://www.foreignaffairs.org/20030301facomment10334/george-perkovich/bush-s-nuclear-revolution-a-regime-change-in-nonproliferation.html (accessed October 20, 2009).

Phillips, Cheryl, Steve Miletich, and Ken Armstrong. "Airport-Security System in US Riddled With Failures." *Seattle Times*, July 11, 2004. http://community.seattletimes.nwsource.com/archive/?date=20040711&slug=tsa11 (accessed October 20, 2009).

Phillips, Melanie. *Londonistan: How Britain is Creating a Terror State Within*. London: Gibson House, 2006.

Phillips, Peter, Bridget Thornton, Lew Brown, and Andrew Sloan. "The Global Dominance Group: A Sociological Case for Impeachment of George W. Bush and Richard Cheney." In *Impeach the President: The Case Against Bush and Cheney*, eds Dennis Loo and Peter Phillips. New York: Seven Stories Press, 2006.

Philo, Greg, and Glasgow University Media Group. *Really Bad News*. London: Writers and Readers, 1982.

Pieterse, Jan Nederveen. "Scenarios of Power." In *The War on Terrorism and the American 'Empire' After the Cold War*, eds Alejandro Colas and Richard Saull, 180–93. New York: Routledge Press, 2006.

Pilger, John. "Axis of Evil; John Pilger Exposes the Frightening Agenda in Washington That is Behind the United States Threat to World Peace." *Morning Star*, December 14, 2002, 19.

Pinsky, Michael. *Future Present: Ethics and/as Science Fiction*. Madison, NJ: Farleigh Dickinson University Press, 2003.

Platoon. DVD. Directed by Oliver Stone. 1986; Los Angeles, CA: MGM; 2001.

Poole, Elizabeth. *Reporting Islam*. London: I.B. Tauris, 2002.

Pred, Allan. "Situated Ignorance and State Terrorism." In *Violent Geographies: Fear, Terror, and Political Violence*, eds Derek Gregory and Allan Pred, 363–84. New York: Routledge, 2007.

Price, David. *Threatening Anthropology*. Durham, NC: Duke University Press, 2004.

———. "Buying a Piece of Anthropology, Part Two: The CIA and Our Tortured Past." *Anthropology Today* 23, no. 5 (2007): 17–22.

Prince, Stephen. *Visions of Empire: Political Imagery in Contemporary American Film*. New York: Praeger, 1992.

Project for the New American Century. "Statement of Principles." June 3, 1997. http://www. newamericancentury.org/statementofprinciples.htm (accessed June 11, 2007).

Putney, Clifford. *Muscular Christianity: Manhood and Sports in Protestant America, 1880–1920*. Cambridge: Harvard University Press, 2001.

Quinby, Lee. *Anti-Apocalypse: Exercises in Genealogical Criticism*. Minneapolis: University of Minnesota Press, 1994.

Raban, Jonathan. *Surveillance*. New York: Pantheon, 2007.

Rae, Graham. "Dead Reckoning." *Cinefastique* 37, no. 4 (2005): 44–51.

Ramsey-Kurz, Helga. "Humouring the Terrorists or the Terrorised? Militant Muslims in Salman Rushdie, Zadie Smith, and Hanif Kureishi." In *Cheeky Fictions: Laughter and the Postcolonial*, ed. Susanne Reichl and Mark Stein, 73–86. Amsterdam: Rodopi, 2005.

Randell, Karen. "Masking the Horror of Trauma: The Hysterical Body of Lon Chaney." *Screen* 44, no. 2 (Summer 2003): 216–21.

——. "Lost Bodies/Lost Souls: MIA Narratives in *Night of the Living Dead*." *Film & History CD-ROM Annual, 2004–2005*. Oshkosh, WI: Center for the Study of Film and History, 2005).

——. "Speaking the Unspeakable: Invisibility and Trauma after 9/11." In *Art in the Age of Terrorism*, eds Graham Coulter-Smith and Maurice Owen. London: Holberton Publications: 2005.

Raz, Guy. "World Sees 'Imperialism' in American Reach, Strength," *NPR*, November 2, 2006. http://www.npr.org/templates/story/story.php?storyId=6423000 (accessed January 7, 2009).

Raze's Hell. Xbox. Edison, NJ: Majesco, 2005.

Reagan, Ronald. 1985. "Remarks at the National Space Club Luncheon." *Ronald Reagan Presidential Library Archives*, 1985. http://www.reagan.utexas.edu/archives/speeches/1985/32985b.htm (accessed October 20, 2009).

Real Time with Bill Maher. Live television. Hosted by Bill Maher. HBO studios, May 8, 2009.

Redacted. DVD. Directed by Brian De Palma. 2007; New York: Magnolia, 2007.

Red Dawn. DVD. Directed by John Milius. Century City, CA: United Artists, 1984.

Rendition. DVD. Directed by Gavin Hood. 2007; New York: New Line Home Video, 2007.

Rescue Dawn. DVD. Directed by Werner Herzog. 2006; West Hollywood, CA: Gibraltar Films, 2007.

Reynolds, Richard. *Super Heroes: A Modern Mythology*. London: B.T. Batsford, 1992.

Riordan, James. *Stone, A Biography of Oliver Stone: The Controversies, Excesses and Exploits of a Radical Filmmaker*. New York: Aurum Press, 1996.

RoboCop. DVD. Directed by Paul Verhoeven. 1987; Los Angeles: Orion Pictures Corporation, 2001.

Roddick, Nick. "Only the Stars Survive: Disaster Movies in the Seventies." In *Performance and Politics in Popular Drama: Aspects of Popular Entertainment in Theatre, Film and Television 1800–1976*, ed. D. Brady. Cambridge: Cambridge University Press, 1980.

Romita, John Snr. with Udon Studios. Untitled image. In *Heroes: The World's Greatest Superhero Creators Honor the World's Greatest Heroes, 9.11.2001*, ed. Rob Haynes, with Tim Townsend, Tim and David Self, second edn (New York: Marvel Comics, December 2001).

Rosenblatt, Roger. "The Age of Irony Comes to an End." *Time.com*. http://www.time.com/time/covers/1101010924/esroger.html (accessed October 20, 2009).

Rowe, John Carlos. "Culture, US Imperialism, and Globalization." *American Literary History* 16, no. 4 (2004): 575–95.

Rumsfeld, Donald. "Defense Department Briefing." *Defense Link*, February 12, 2002. http://www.defenselink.mil/transcripts/transcript.aspx? transcriptid=2636 (accessed January 22, 2009).

Russell, Jamie. *Book of the Dead: The Complete History of Zombie Cinema*. Ann Arbor: University of Michigan Press. 2005.

Rutenberg, Jim and Bill Carter. "Draping Newscasts with the Flag." *New York Times*, September 20, 2001, C8.

Said, Edward. *Culture and Imperialism*. New York: Vintage, 1993.

——. *Orientalism*. 1978 and 1979. Reprint, New York: Vintage, 1994.

——. *Covering Islam: How the Media and the Experts Determine How We See the Rest of the World*. London: Routledge and Kegan Paul, 1978.

Sailer, Steve. "Review of *Master and Commander: The Far Side of the World*." *American Conservative*, December 1, 2003, 24–5.

Salaita, Steven. "Beyond Orientalism and Islamophobia: 9/11, Anti-Arab Racism, and the Mythos of National Pride." *New Centennial Review* 6.2 (2006): 245–66.

Saltman, Kenneth J. "The Strong Arm of the Law." *Body and Society* 9, no. 4 (2003): 49–67.

Sardar, Ziauddin. *Orientalism*. Buckingham: Open University Press, 1999.

Saving Jessica Lynch. Live television. Directed by Peter Markle. NBC, November 23, 2009.

Sayer, Karen, and John Morre (eds). *Science Fiction, Critical Frontiers*. New York: St. Martin's Press, 2000.

Scahill, Jeremy. *Blackwater: The Rise of the World's Most Powerful Mercenary Army*. New York: Nation Books, 2007.

Scanner Darkly, A. Directed by Richard Linklater [film]. Burbank, CA: Warner Independent Pictures, 2006.

Schaper, David. 2007. "Chicago's Video Surveillance Gets Smarter." *NPR*, October 26, 2007. http://www.npr.org/templates/story/story.php?storyId=15673544 (accessed October 20, 2009).

Schwartz, Ben. "'It Seems Like Exactly the Wrong Film to Make.'" *Salon.com*, October 15, 2002. http://dir.salon.com/story/ent/movies/int/2002/10/15/avary/index.html (accessed October 20, 2009).

Schwarz, Michael. "An Imaginative Reality." *Deadwood: The Complete First Season*. DVD. Directed by David Milch. 2004; Burbank, CA: HBO Video, 2005.

——. "The New Language of the Old West." *Deadwood: The Complete First Season*. DVD. Directed by David Milch. 2004; Burbank, CA: HBO Video, 2005.

Sciolino, Elaine, and Alison Mitchell. "Calls for New Push Into Iraq Gain Power in Washington." *New York Times*, December 3, 2001, 9.

Scott, A.O. "Master of the Sea (and the French)." *New York Times*, November 14, 2003.

Seed, David. *American Science Fiction and the Cold War: Literature and Film*. Chicago and London: Fitzroy & Dearborn, 1999.

Seelye, Katherine Q. "Pentagon Plays Role in Fictional Terror Drama." *New York Times*, March 31, 2002. A12.

Semmerling, Tim Jon. *"Evil" Arabs in American Popular Film: Orientalist Fear*. Austin: University of Texas Press, 2006.

Sennett, Richard. *The Culture of the New Capitalism*. New Haven and London: Yale University Press, 2006.

Shaheen, Jack G. *Reel Bad Arabs: How Hollywood Vilifies a People*. New York: Olive Branch Press, 2001.

Shepherd, Laura J. "Constructions of Gender in the Bush Administration Discourse on the Attacks of Afghanistan Post-9/11." *International Feminist Journal of Politics* 8, no. 1 (March 2006): 19–41.

Shuck, Glenn. *Marks of the Beast: The Left Behind and the Struggle for Evangelical Identity*. New York: NYU Press, 2004.

Siegel, Jerome and Joe Schuster. Untitled Superman strip, 1939. Repr. in *Superman from the Thirties to the Seventies*, ed. E. Nelson Bridewell. New York: Spring Books, 1971,

——. Superman strip, *Look*, February 27, 1940. repr. at www.Superman.ws—the Superman Website: Superman through the ages. http://superman.ws/tales2/endsthewar/?page=3 (accessed June 28, 2007).

Siegel, Lee. "The Imagination of Disaster." *Nation*, April 11 2005. http://www.thenation.com/docprint.mhtml?i=20050411&s=siegel article (accessed March 30, 2007).

Sinfield, Alan. *Cultural Politics: Queer Reading*. London: Routledge, 1994.

——. *Faultlines: Cultural Materialism and the Politics of Dissident Reading*. Berkeley: University of California Press, 1992.

Sleeper Cell. Live Television. Created by Ethan Reiff and Cyrus Voris. Showtime. 2005–2006.

Slotkin, Richard. *Gunfighter Nation: The Myth of the Frontier in Twentieth Century America*. New York: Atheneum, 1992.

——. *Regeneration Through Violence: The Mythology of the American Frontier, 1600–1860*. Middletown, CT: Wesleyan University Press, 1973.

Slouka, Mark. "A Year Later: Notes of America's Intimations of Mortality." *Harper's* September 2002: 35–43.

Smith, Neil. "Afterword." In *War, Citizenship, Territory*, eds Deborah Cowen and Emily Gilbert, 385–92. New York: Routledge, 2008.

Smith, Zadie. *White Teeth*, London: Hamish Hamilton, 2000.

Soguk, Nevzat. "Reflections on the 'Orientalised Orientals.'" *Alternatives* 18 (1993) 361–84.

Spiegelman, Art. *In The Shadow of No Towers*. New York: Pantheon, 2004.

Spigel, Lynn. "Entertainment Wars: Television Culture After 9/11." *American Quarterly* 56, no. 2 (2004): 235–70.

Spinney, Laura. "We Can Implant Entirely False Memories." *Guardian*, July 12, 2003.

Standard Operating Procedure. DVD. Directed by Errol Morris. 2008; Culver City, CA: Sony Pictures, 2008.

Stark, Myra. "State of the Consumer—2003: The Consumer Context." www.saatchikevin.com/download/pdf/myra_stark_consumer_context_2003.pdf (accessed December 21, 2004).

Star Wars: Episode IV—A New Hope. DVD. Directed by George Lucas. 1977; Los Angeles: Twentieth Century Fox, 2006.

Stauber, John, and Sheldon Rampton. *Toxic Sludge is Good for You: Lies, Damn Lies and the Public Relations Industry*. Monroe, ME: Common Courage Press, 1995.

Stein, Mark. *Black British Literature: Novels of Transformation*. Ohio: Ohio State University Press, 2004.

Stewart, Garrett. "Digital Fatigue: Imaging War in Recent American Film." *Film Quarterly* 62, no. 4 (2009): 45–55.

Stir of Echoes II: The Homecoming. DVD. Directed by Ernie Barbarash. 2007; Sydney, Australia: Sony Pictures Home Entertainment, 2008.

Stolberg, Sheryl Gay. "President Signs New Rules To Prosecute Terror Suspects." *New York Times*, October 17, 2006, 20. http://query.nytimes.com/gst/fullpage.html?res=990DE1D71E30F93BA25753C1A9609C8B63&sec=&spon=&&scp=2&sq=Stolberg%20President%20signs%20new%20rules%20to&st=cse (accessed October 20, 2009).

Strange Days. DVD. Directed by Kathryn Bigelow. 1995; Los Angeles, CA: 20th Century Fox, 2002.

Strauss, Leo. *The City and Man*. Chicago: Rand McNally, 1964.

Strombeck, Andrew. "Invest in Jesus: Neoliberalism and the *Left Behind* Novels." *Cultural Critique* 64 (2006): 161–95.

Sundquist, Eric J. "Benito Cereno and New World Slavery." In *Reconstructing American Literary History*, ed. Sacvan Bercovitch, 93–122. Cambridge: Harvard University Press. 1986.

"The Superman Patriot Image Gallery" (2003). Images at www.supermancollectors.com/nowmorethanever.html (accessed June 26, 2007).

"Superman Returns, Crashes, Burns at Box Office (Liberal Hollywood Once Again Turns off America?)" *Federalreview.com*. Conservative news, blog, and criticism forum, July, 2 2006. http://www.freerepublic.com/focus/fnews/1659311/posts (accessed June, 2007).

Superman Returns. Directed by Bryan Singer. Sydney, Australia: Warner Bros. Pictures, 2006.

"*Superman Returns* Director Gets Defensive About Gay Rumors." *Advocate.com*, June 10, 2006. http://www.advocate.com/news_detail_ektid32138.asp (accessed July 6, 2007).

Surette, Ray. *Media, Crime and Criminal Justice: Images and Realities*. Belmont, CA: West/Wadsworth, 1998.

Survivor. Live television. Created by Charlie Parsons. CBS, 2000–present.

Survivorman. Live television. Directed by Les Stroud. Discovery Channel, 2004–present.

Suskind, Ron. *The One Percent Doctrine: Deep Inside America's Pursuit of Its Enemies Since 9/11.* New York: Simon and Schuster, 2006.

——. "Without a Doubt." *New York Times,* October 17, 2004. http://www.cs.umass.edu/~immerman/play/opinion05/WithoutADoubt.html (accessed July 31, 2007).

Syriana. DVD. Directed by Stephen Gaghan. 2005; Burbank, CA: Warner Home Video, 2006.

Takacs, Stacy. "Jessica Lynch and the Regeneration of American Identity and Power Post-9/11." *Feminist Media Studies* 5, no. 3 (2005): 297–310.

Tapper, Jake. "How Gay Is Superman? Or Jewish. Or Christ-Like. The Battle to Claim Superman as an Icon." *ABC News,* June 19, 2006. http://sendtofriend.abcnews.go.com/print?id=2094503 (accessed June 26, 2007).

Taxi to the Dark Side. DVD. Directed by Alex Gibney. 2007; Santa Monica, CA: Velocity/ Thinkfilm, 2008.

Temple-Raston, Dina. "Enemy Within? Not Quite." *Washington Post,* September 9, 2007, B01.

——. *The Jihad Next Door: The Lackawanna Six and Rough Justice in an Age of Terror.* New York: Public Affairs, 2007.

Terminator, The. DVD. Directed by James Cameron. 1984; Los Angeles: Orion Pictures Corporation, 2007.

Thompson, Peter. "Review of *Master and Commander: The Far Side of the World.*" http://sunday.ninemsn.com.au/sunday/film_reviews/article_1458.asp?s=1 (accessed October 8, 2006).

Three Kings. DVD. Directed by David O. Russell. 1999; Burbank CA: Warner Home Video, 2000).

Tibi, Bassam. *Islam: Between Culture and Politics.* Second edn. Basingstoke: Palgrave Macmillan, 2005.

Tickner, J. Ann. "Feminist Perspectives on 9/11." *International Studies Perspectives* 3 (2002): 333–50.

Tom Clancy's Ghost Recon: Advanced Warfighter. Xbox 360. San Francisco, CA: Ubisoft, 2006.

Tom Clancy's Rainbow Six: Vegas. Xbox 360. San Francisco, CA: Ubisoft, 2006.

Tompkins, Jane. *West of Everything: The Inner Life of Westerns.* New York: Oxford University Press, 1992.

Top Gun. DVD. Directed by Tony Scott. 1986; Burbank, CA: Paramount, 1998.

Total Recall. DVD. Directed by Paul Verhoeven. 1990; Santa Monica, CA: Lions Gate, 2005.

Towering Inferno, The. DVD. Directed by John Guillermin and Irwin Allen. 1974; Burbank, CA: Twentieth Century Fox, 2006.

Triumph of the Will. DVD. Directed by Leni Riefenstahl. 1935; Novi, MI: Synapse Films, 2006.

Truman Show, The. DVD. Directed by Peter Weir. 1998; Burbank, CA; Paramount Films, 2005.

Twelve Monkeys. DVD. Directed by Terry Gilliam. 1995; Hollywood, CA,: Universal Pictures, 2005.

Twentieth Century Fox, "*28 Days Later . . .* Production Notes." *The Cillian Site,* http://www.cilliansite.com/production-notes/28-days-later-prod-notes.pdf (accessed June 20, 2009).

Tyson, George F., ed. *Toussaint L'Ouverture.* Englewood Cliffs: Prentice-Hall. 1973.

United 93. Directed by Paul Greengrass. 2006; Hollywood, CA: Universal Pictures, 2006.

Universal Soldier. DVD. Directed by Roland Emmerich. 1992; Culver City, CA: Columbia TriStar Film, 2004.

"US is 'Battling Satan' Says General." *BBC News,* Friday, 17 October, 2003. http://news.bbc.co.uk/2/hi/americas/3199212.stm (accessed June 3, 2009).

Vågnes, Øyvind. "'Chosen to be Witness': The Exceptionalism of 9/11." In *The Selling of 9/11: How a National Tragedy Became a Commodity,*" ed. Dana Heller. New York: Palgrave Macmillan. 54–74.

Virilio, Paul. *War and Cinema: The Logistics of Perception.* Trans. Patrick Camiller. London: Verso, 1989.

Wald, Priscilla. *Contagious: Cultures, Carriers and the Outbreak Narrative.* Durham, NC: Duke University Press, 2008.

Waller, Gregory A. *The Living and Undead: From Stoker's* Dracula *to Romero's* Dawn of the Dead. Urbana: University of Illinois Press, 1987.

Wallis, Jim. "Contesting a Theology of War Confessing Christ in a World of Violence." *Catholic New Times,* December 5, 2004. http://findarticles.com/p/articles/mi_m0MKY/is_19_28/ai_n8698007 (accessed June 15, 2006).

Wark, Mackenzie. *Gamer Theory.* Cambridge, MA: Harvard University Press, 2007.

Wasburn, Philo C. *The Social Construction of International News: We're Talking about Them, They're Talking about Us.* Westport, CT: Praeger, 2002.

Watson, Paul Joseph. "Linklater on *A Scanner Darkly*: 'It's The World We're Living In.'" *PrisonPlanet.com,* July 12, 2006. http://www.prisonplanet.com/articles/july2006/120706scannerdarkly.htm (accessed July 22, 2007).

Watts, Michael. "Revolutionary Islam: A Geography of Modern Terror." In *Violent Geographies: Fear, Terror, and Political Violence,* eds Derek Gregory and Allan Pred, 175–203. New York: Routledge, 2007.

Weber, Max. *The Protestant Ethic and the Spirit of Capitalism.* 1904. Reprint New York: Scribners & Sons, 1958.

Weber, Timothy. "On the Road to Armageddon." *Beliefnet.com,* June 20, 2006. www.beliefnet.com/story/151/story_15165.html (accessed June 15, 2006).

Wertham, Fredric. *Seduction of the Innocent.* London: Museum Press, 1955.

Westfahl, Gary and George Slusser (eds). *Science Fiction, Canonization, Marginalization, and the Academy.* Westport, CT: Greenwood Press, 2002.

Westfeldt, Wallace and Tom Wicker. *Indictment: The News Media and the Criminal Justice System.* Nashville: First Amendment Center, 1998.

What a Way to Go: Life at the End of Empire. DVD. Directed by Timothy S. Bennett. 2007; Hancock, VT: Vision Quest Pictures, 2007.

White Zombie. DVD. Directed by Victor Halperin. 1932; Narberth, PA: Alpha Video, 2002.

Who's The Boss? Live television. Directed by Asaad Kelaga. ABC, 1984–92.

Wilkinson, Tracy. "Court Widens Net for 22 CIA Agents to EU; Italian Prosecutors Seek to Try the Operatives in the 2003 Abduction of an Imam on a Milan street. The Warrants Expand the Hunt to 25 Nations." *Los Angeles Times,* December 24, 2005, p. A3.

Williams, Raymond. "Base and Superstructure in Marxist Cultural Theory." In *Problems in Materialism and Culture.* London: Verso Editions/NLB, 1980.

Williamson, Hugh. "Germany Pressed to Arrest CIA Team." *Financial Times,* September 22, 2006, 11.

Wilson, Karina. "Zombie Walks." In *Horror Film History.* 2007. http://www.horrorfilmhistory.com/index.php?pageID=ZombieWalk (accessed September 3, 2008).

Wilson, Scott and Al Kamen, "'Global War on Terror' Is Given New Name." *Washington Post* March 25, 2009, A04. http://www.washingtonpost.com/wp-dyn/content/article/2009/03/24/AR2009032402818.html (accessed April 4, 2009).

Wolf, Jeanne "Blue Tights, No Green Card . . ." (June 22, 2006). http://movies.go.com/jeannewolf?columnid=837103 (accessed June 26, 2007).

Wood, Robin. *Hollywood From Vietnam to Reagan.* New York: Columbia University Press, 2003.

Worth, Robert F. "Al Jazeera No Longer Nips at Saudis." *New York Times,* January 4, 2008, A1. http://www.nytimes.com/2008/01/04/world/middleeast/04jazeera.html?_r=1&th&emc=th&oref=slogin (accessed October 20, 2009).

WTC Living History Project. "Objective Evidence Shows There Were No Blue Jeans in the Firetruck and No Jeering Construction Workers." http://www.wtclivinghistory.org/introduction.htm (accessed October 20, 2009).

Yeats, W.B. "Easter, 1916." In *The Collected Poems of W.B. Yeats,* ed. Richard J. Finneran. Second edn. New York: Scribner, 1996.

Zangana, Haifa. "Songs of Resistance." In *War With No End,* authors John Berger, Naomi

Klein, Hanif Kureishi, China Mieville, Arundhati Roy, Ahdaf Soueif, Joe Sacco, and Haifa Zangana, 61–75. New York: Verso, 2007.

Zarazua, Jeorge. "Pastor Accused of Dragging Girl Behind His Van," *Religionnewsblog.com*, August 11, 2007. http://www.religionnewsblog.com/18991/charles-flowers (accessed March 10, 2008).

Zimbardo, Philip. *The Lucifer Effect*. New York: Random House, 2007.

Zircher, Patrick, with Derek Fridolfs and Hi-Fi, and text by Fabian Nicieza. Untitled entry. In *Heroes: The World's Greatest Superhero Creators Honor the World's Greatest Heroes, 9.11.2001*, ed. Rob Haynes, with Tim Townsend, Tim and David Self, second edn (New York: Marvel Comics, December 2001).

Žižek! DVD. Directed by Astra Taylor. 2005; New York: Zeitgeist Films, 2006.

Žižek, Slavoj. "On 9/11, New Yorkers Faced the Fire in the Minds of Men: Hollywood's Attempts to Mark the 2001 Attacks Ignore Their Political Context and the Return to History They Symbolise." *Guardian*, September 11, 2006, 30.

"The Zombie as Critic." *Unemployed Negativity*, June 11, 2007. http://unemployednegativity. blogspot.com/2007/06/zombie-as-critic.html (accessed June 8, 2009).

Index

Entries beginning with numbers are alphabetized as if spelled out. For example, 9/11 is alphabetized as if it were nine/eleven. Page numbers in **bold** refer to illustrations.